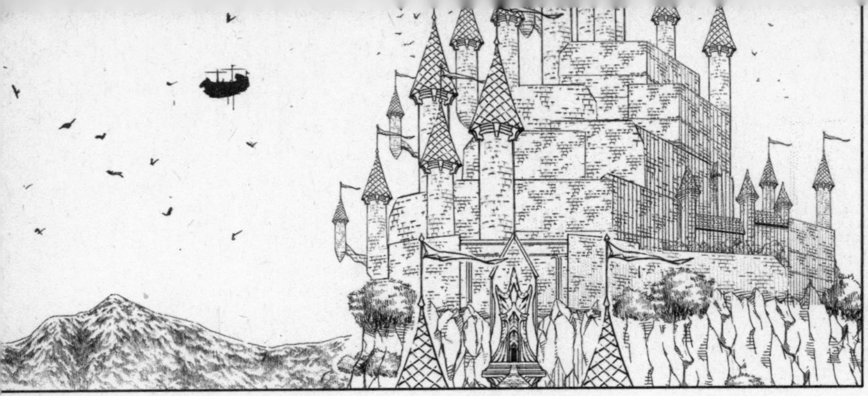

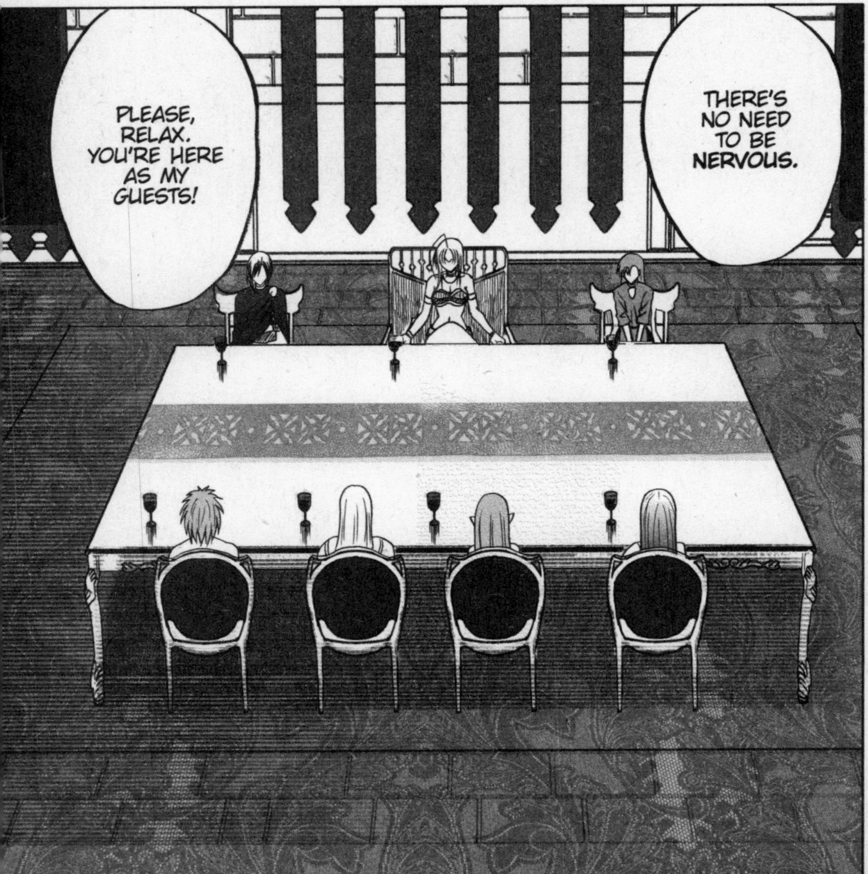
THERE'S NO NEED TO BE NERVOUS.
PLEASE, RELAX. YOU'RE HERE AS MY GUESTS!

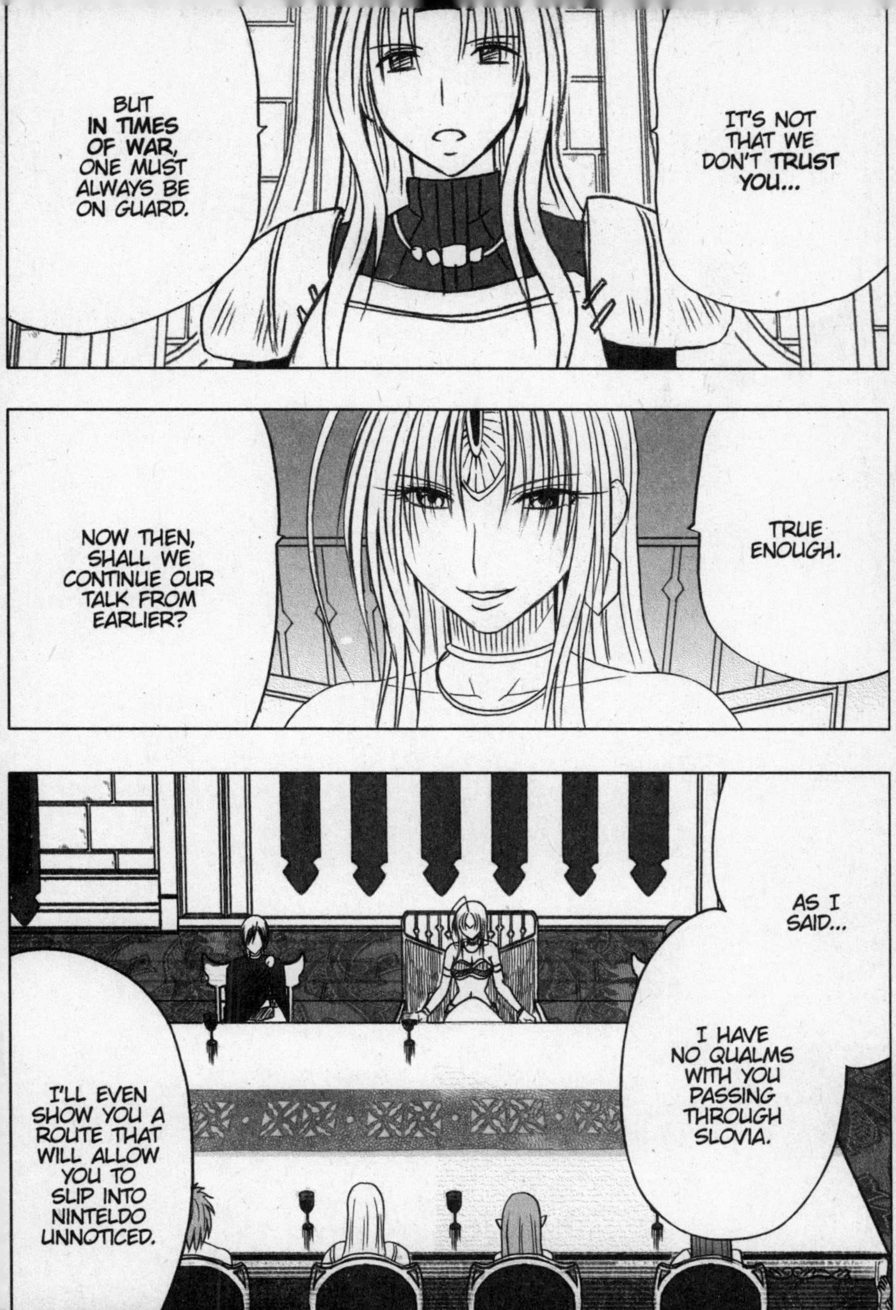
IT'S NOT THAT WE DON'T TRUST YOU...
BUT IN TIMES OF WAR, ONE MUST ALWAYS BE ON GUARD.
TRUE ENOUGH.
NOW THEN, SHALL WE CONTINUE OUR TALK FROM EARLIER?
AS I SAID...
I HAVE NO QUALMS WITH YOU PASSING THROUGH SLOVIA.
I'LL EVEN SHOW YOU A ROUTE THAT WILL ALLOW YOU TO SLIP INTO NINTELDO UNNOTICED.

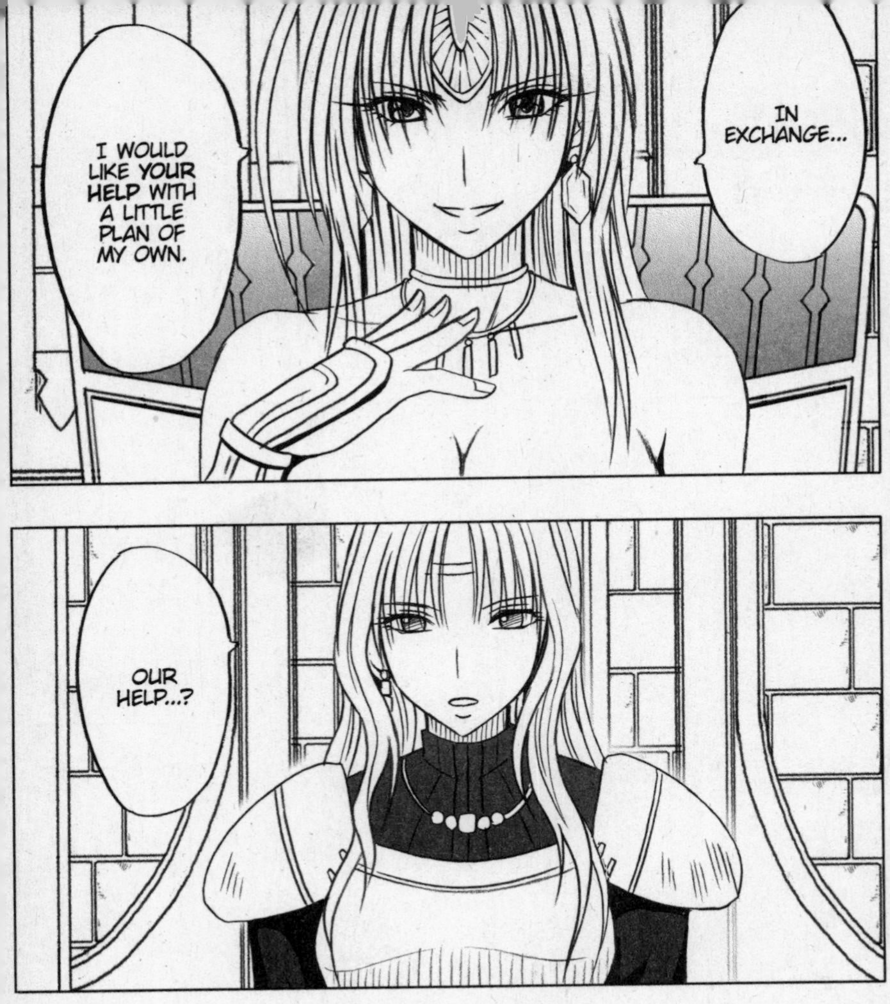
IN EXCHANGE...
I WOULD LIKE YOUR HELP WITH A LITTLE PLAN OF MY OWN.
OUR HELP...?

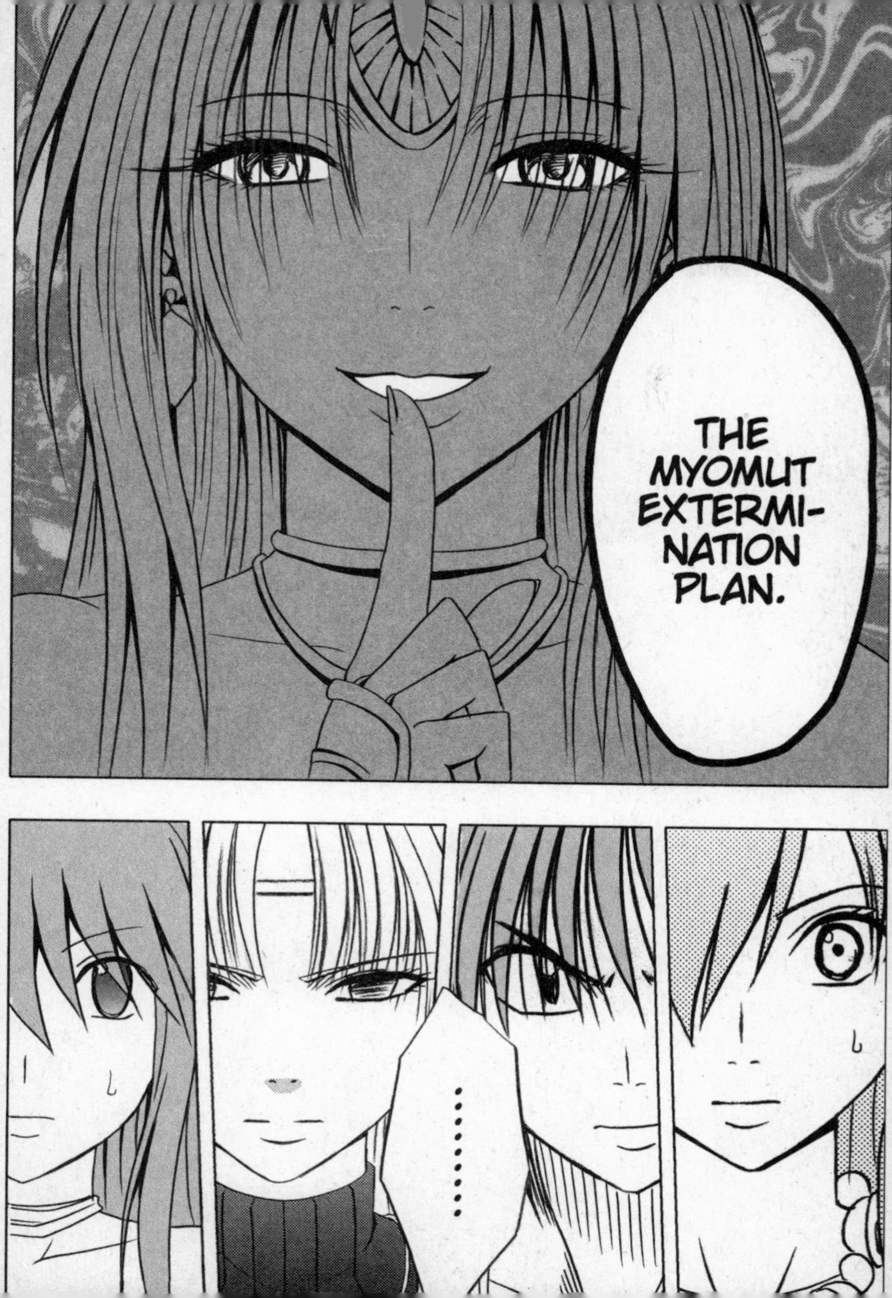
THE MYOMUT EXTERMINATION PLAN.
......

Part 2

CHAPTER 21

ONE-WINGED ANGEL

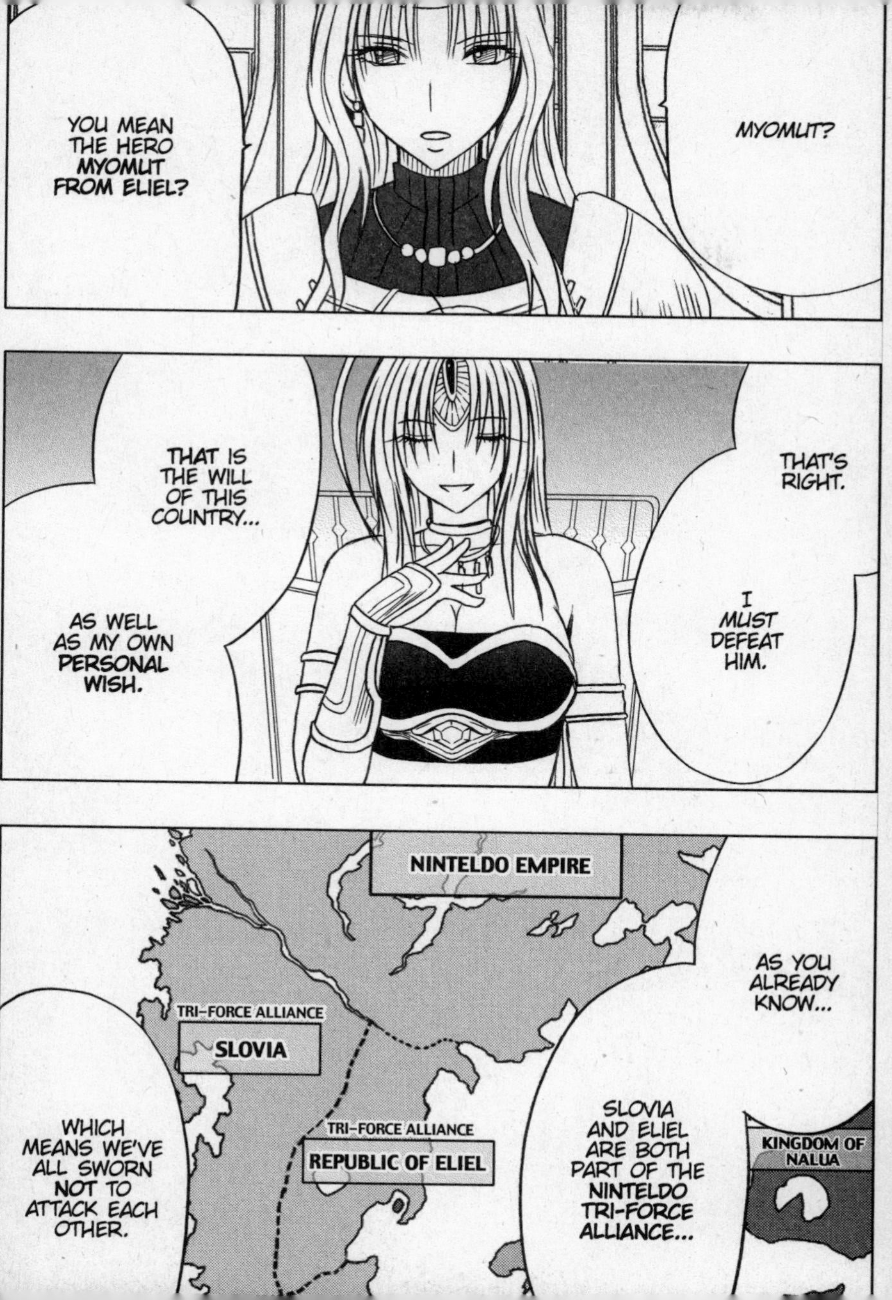
MYOMUT?
YOU MEAN THE HERO MYOMUT FROM ELIEL?
THAT'S RIGHT.
I MUST DEFEAT HIM.
THAT IS THE WILL OF THIS COUNTRY...
AS WELL AS MY OWN PERSONAL WISH.
NINTELDO EMPIRE
AS YOU ALREADY KNOW...
KINGDOM OF NALUA
SLOVIA AND ELIEL ARE BOTH PART OF THE NINTELDO TRI-FORCE ALLIANCE...
TRI-FORCE ALLIANCE SLOVIA
TRI-FORCE ALLIANCE REPUBLIC OF ELIEL
WHICH MEANS WE'VE ALL SWORN NOT TO ATTACK EACH OTHER.

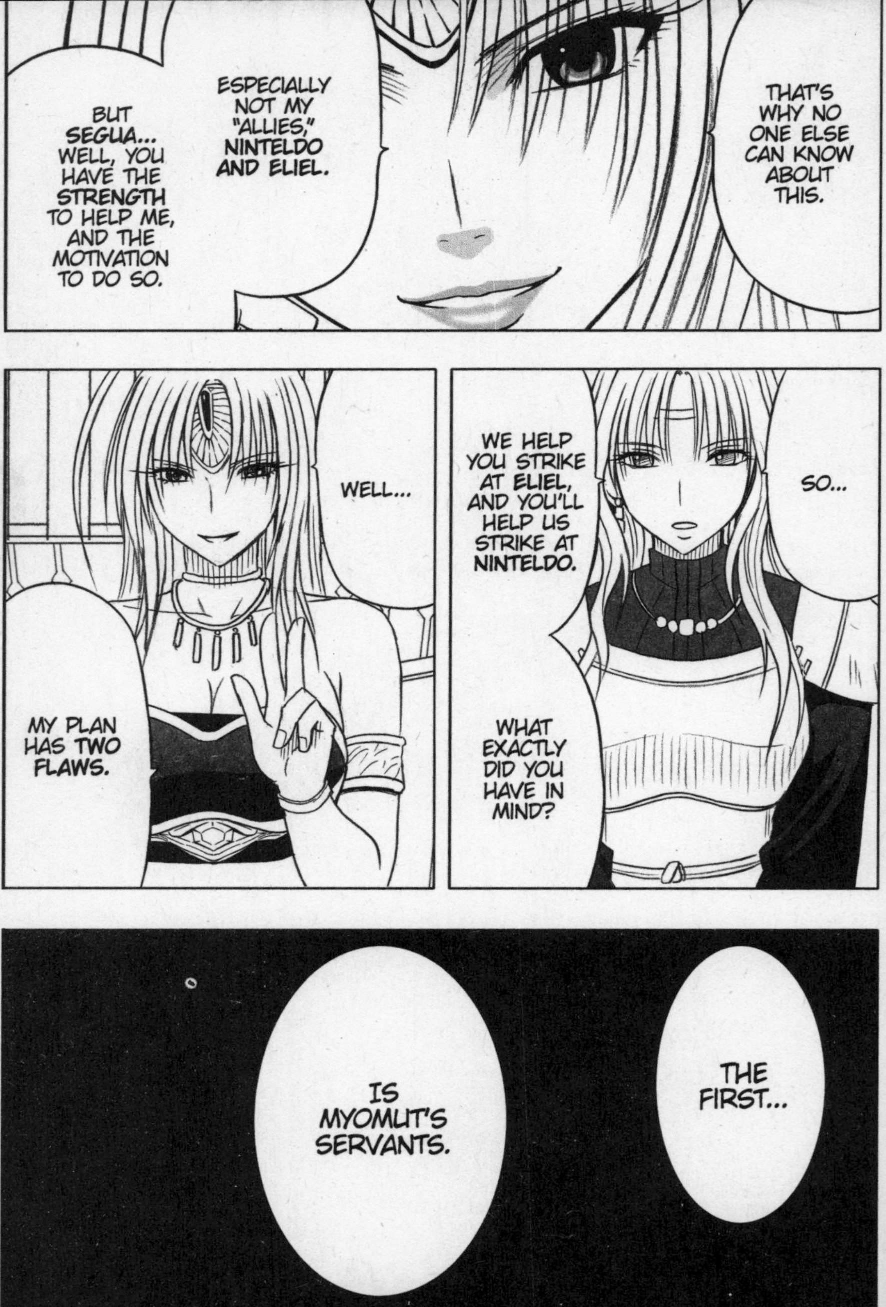
THAT'S WHY NO ONE ELSE CAN KNOW ABOUT THIS.
ESPECIALLY NOT MY "ALLIES," NINTELDO AND ELIEL.
BUT SEGUA... WELL, YOU HAVE THE STRENGTH TO HELP ME, AND THE MOTIVATION TO DO SO.
SO...
WE HELP YOU STRIKE AT ELIEL, AND YOU'LL HELP US STRIKE AT NINTELDO.
WHAT EXACTLY DID YOU HAVE IN MIND?
WELL...
MY PLAN HAS TWO FLAWS.
THE FIRST...
IS MYOMUT'S SERVANTS.

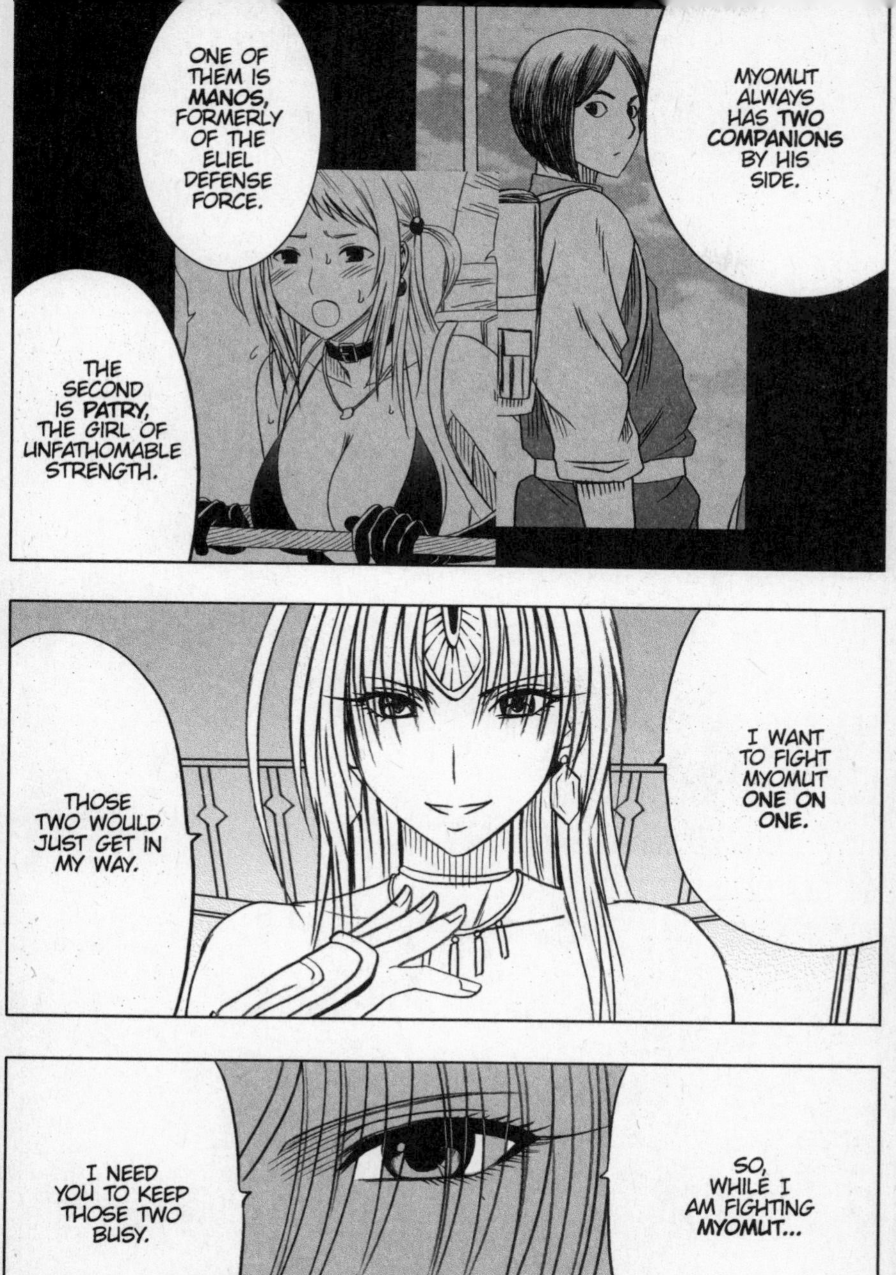
MYOMUT ALWAYS HAS TWO COMPANIONS BY HIS SIDE.
ONE OF THEM IS MANOS, FORMERLY OF THE ELIEL DEFENSE FORCE.
THE SECOND IS PATRY, THE GIRL OF UNFATHOMABLE STRENGTH.
I WANT TO FIGHT MYOMUT ONE ON ONE.
THOSE TWO WOULD JUST GET IN MY WAY.
SO, WHILE I AM FIGHTING MYOMUT...
I NEED YOU TO KEEP THOSE TWO BUSY.

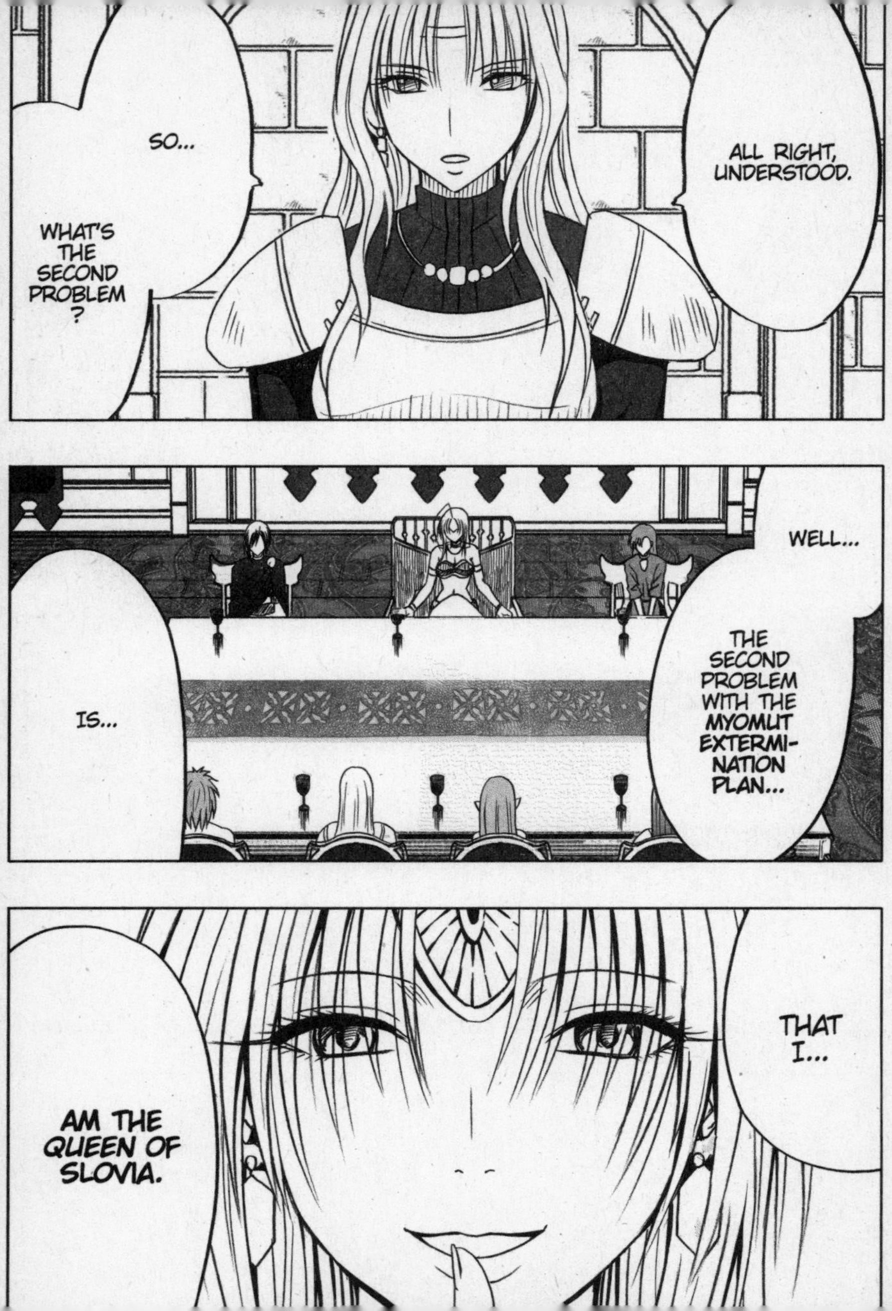
ALL RIGHT, UNDERSTOOD.
SO...
WHAT'S THE SECOND PROBLEM?
WELL...
THE SECOND PROBLEM WITH THE MYOMUT EXTERMI-NATION PLAN...
IS...
THAT I...
AM THE QUEEN OF SLOVIA.

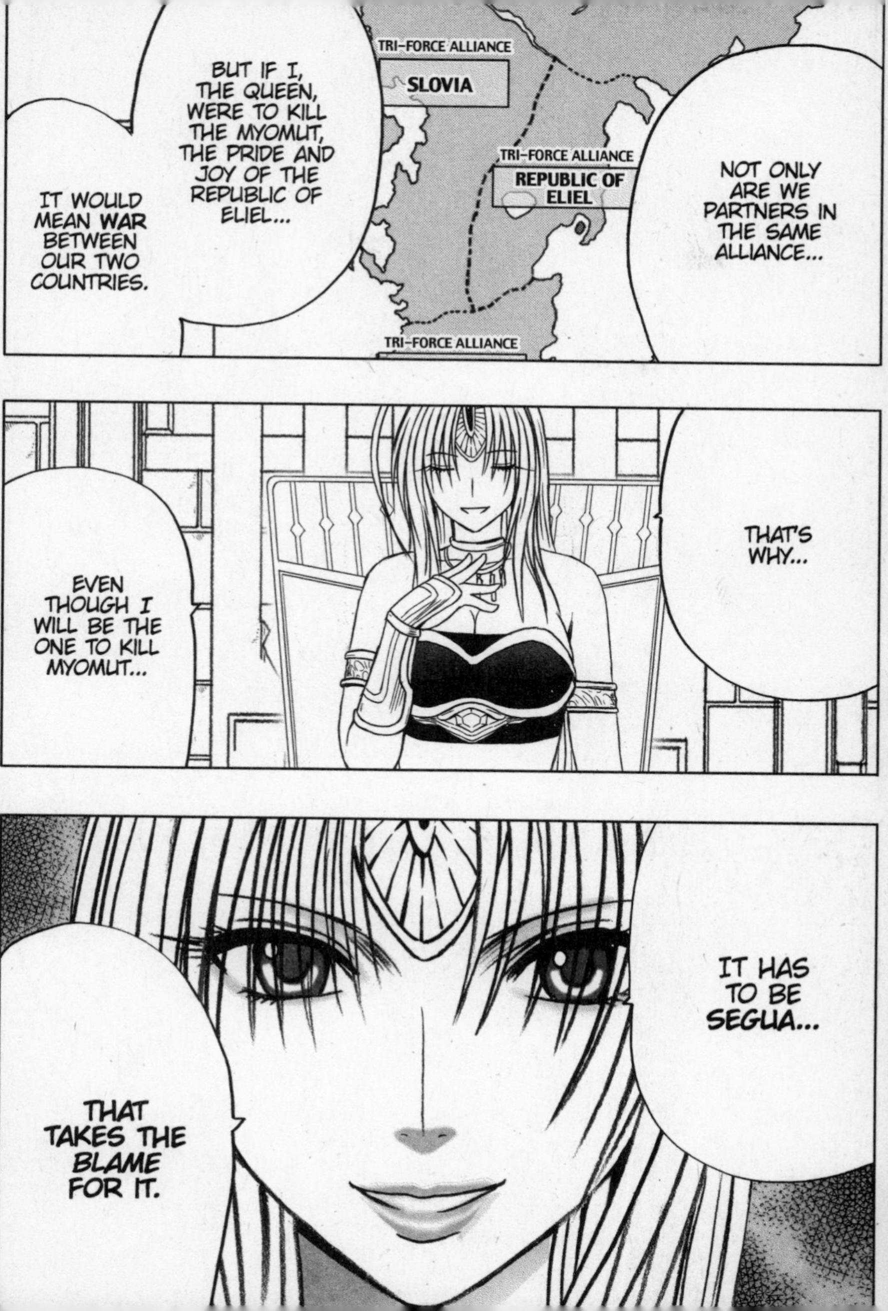
NOT ONLY ARE WE PARTNERS IN THE SAME ALLIANCE...
TRI-FORCE ALLIANCE
REPUBLIC OF ELIEL
TRI-FORCE ALLIANCE
SLOVIA
BUT IF I, THE QUEEN, WERE TO KILL THE MYOMUT, THE PRIDE AND JOY OF THE REPUBLIC OF ELIEL...
IT WOULD MEAN WAR BETWEEN OUR TWO COUNTRIES.
TRI-FORCE ALLIANCE
THAT'S WHY...
EVEN THOUGH I WILL BE THE ONE TO KILL MYOMUT...
IT HAS TO BE SEGUA...
THAT TAKES THE BLAME FOR IT.

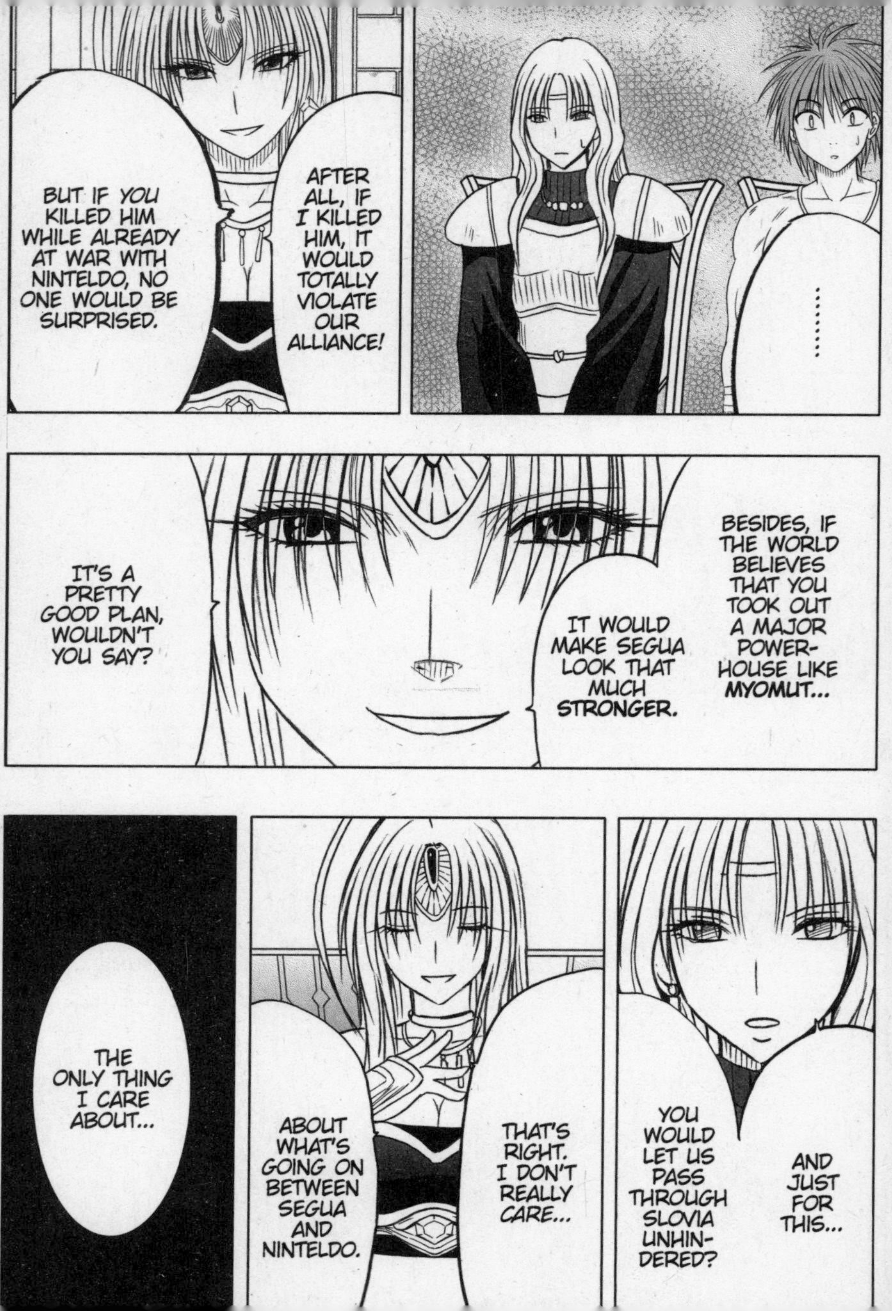

......
AFTER ALL, IF I KILLED HIM, IT WOULD TOTALLY VIOLATE OUR ALLIANCE!
BUT IF YOU KILLED HIM WHILE ALREADY AT WAR WITH NINTELDO, NO ONE WOULD BE SURPRISED.
BESIDES, IF THE WORLD BELIEVES THAT YOU TOOK OUT A MAJOR POWER-HOUSE LIKE MYOMUT...
IT WOULD MAKE SEGUA LOOK THAT MUCH STRONGER.
IT'S A PRETTY GOOD PLAN, WOULDN'T YOU SAY?
AND JUST FOR THIS...
YOU WOULD LET US PASS THROUGH SLOVIA UNHIN-DERED?
THAT'S RIGHT. I DON'T REALLY CARE...
ABOUT WHAT'S GOING ON BETWEEN SEGUA AND NINTELDO.
THE ONLY THING I CARE ABOUT...

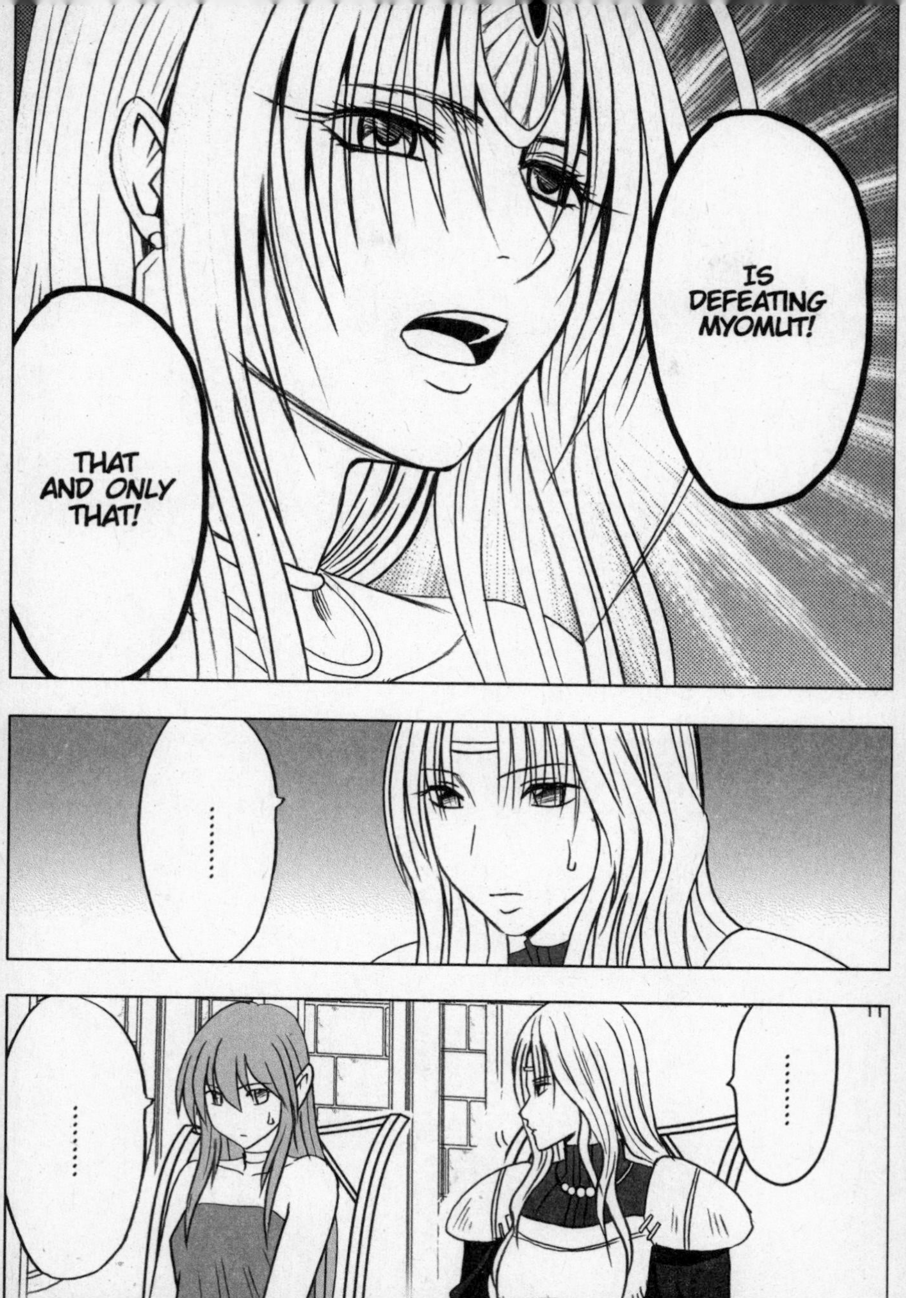
IS DEFEATING MYOMLIT!
THAT AND ONLY THAT!
......
......
......

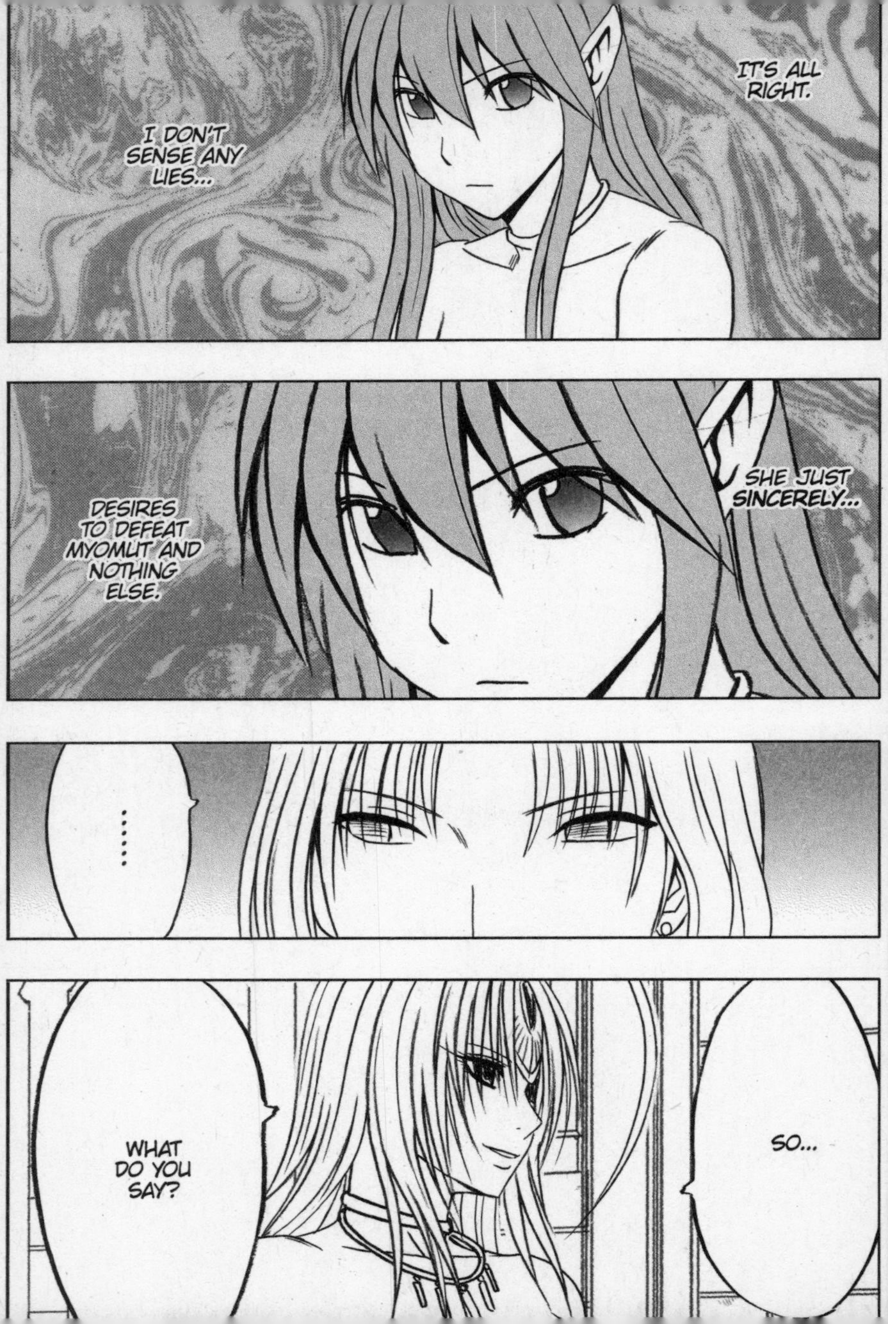
IT'S ALL RIGHT.
I DON'T SENSE ANY LIES...
SHE JUST SINCERELY...
DESIRES TO DEFEAT MYOMUT AND NOTHING ELSE.
......
SO...
WHAT DO YOU SAY?

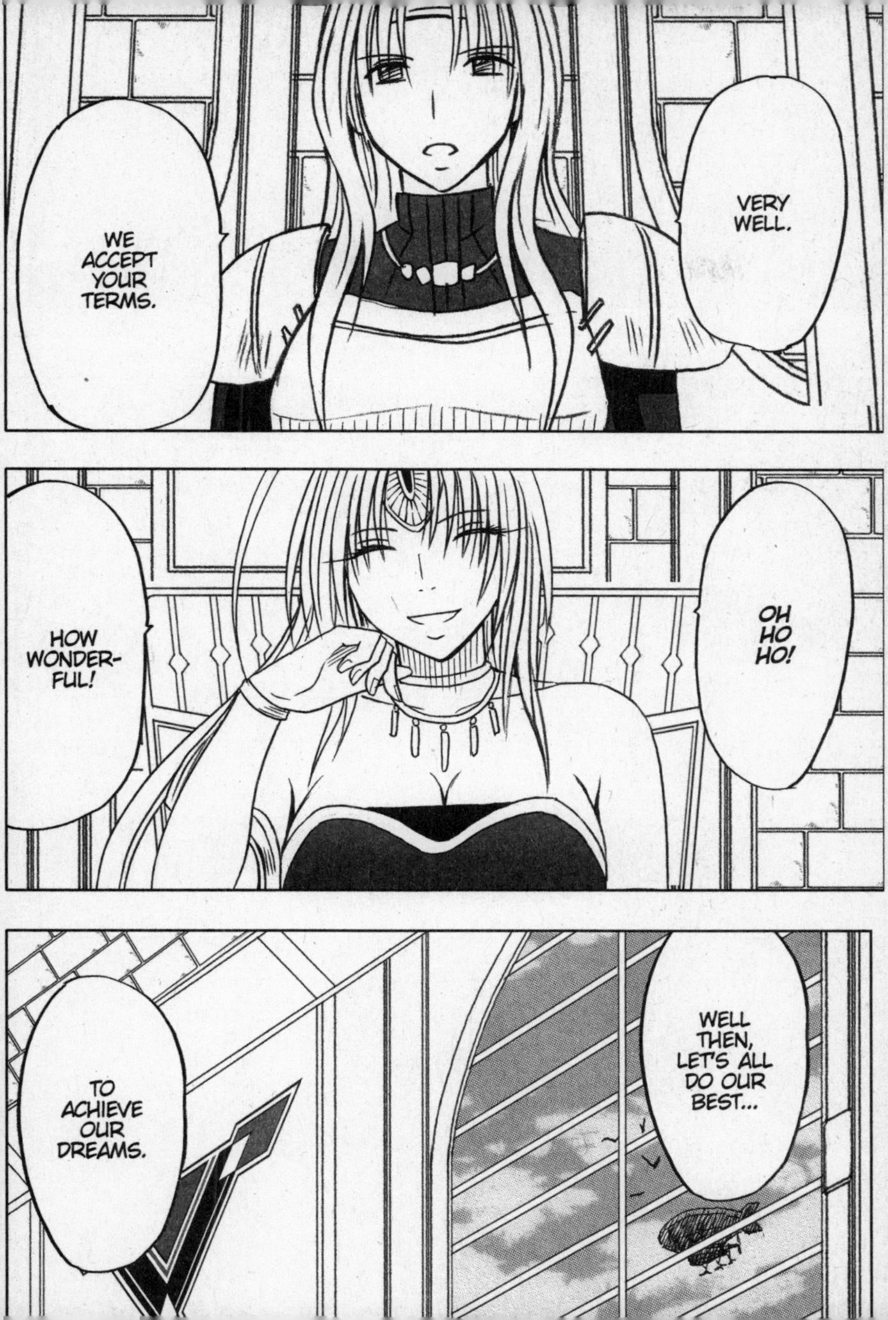
VERY WELL.
WE ACCEPT YOUR TERMS.
OH HO HO!
HOW WONDERFUL!
WELL THEN, LET'S ALL DO OUR BEST...
TO ACHIEVE OUR DREAMS.

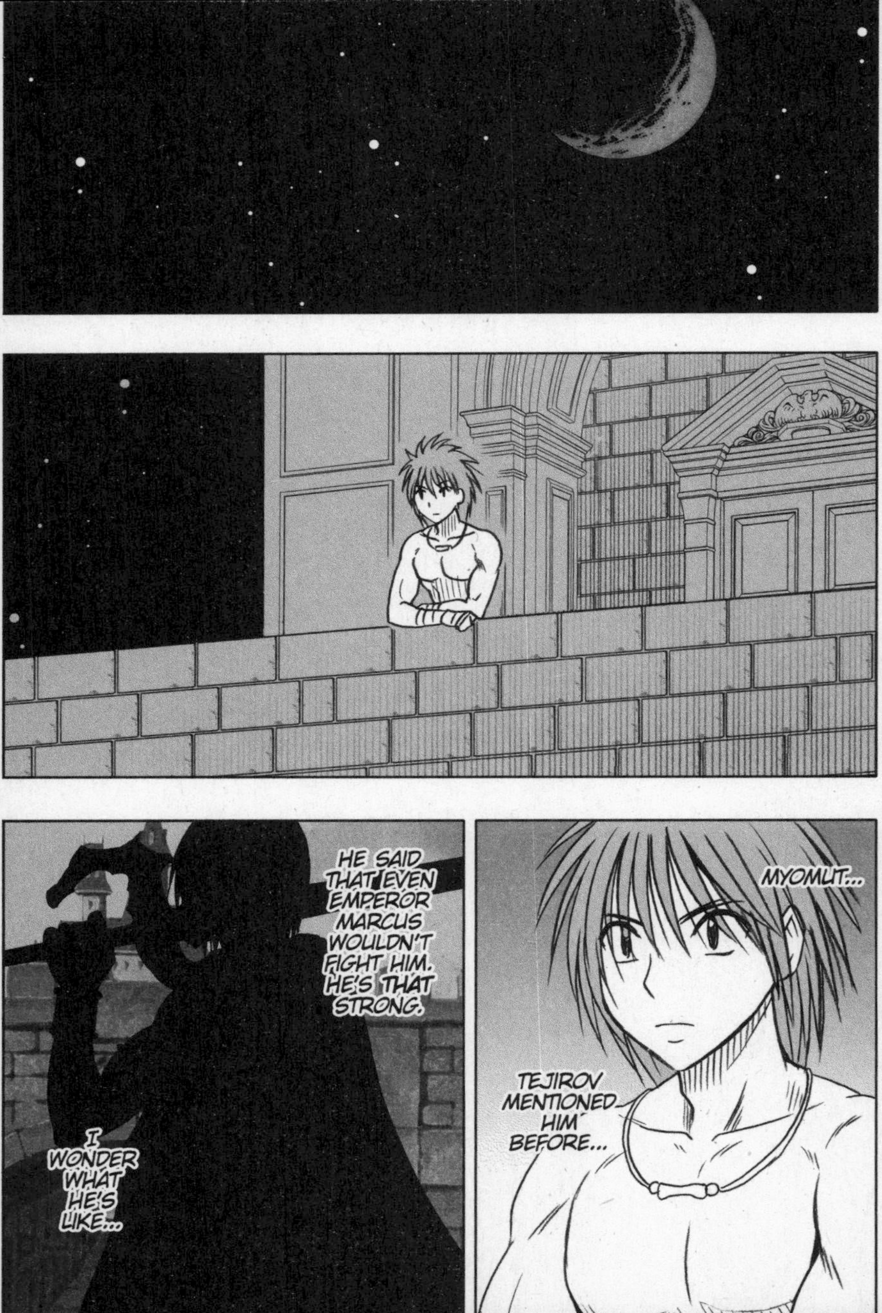
MYOMUT...
TEJIROV MENTIONED HIM BEFORE...
HE SAID THAT EVEN EMPEROR MARCUS WOULDN'T FIGHT HIM. HE'S THAT STRONG.
I WONDER WHAT HE'S LIKE...

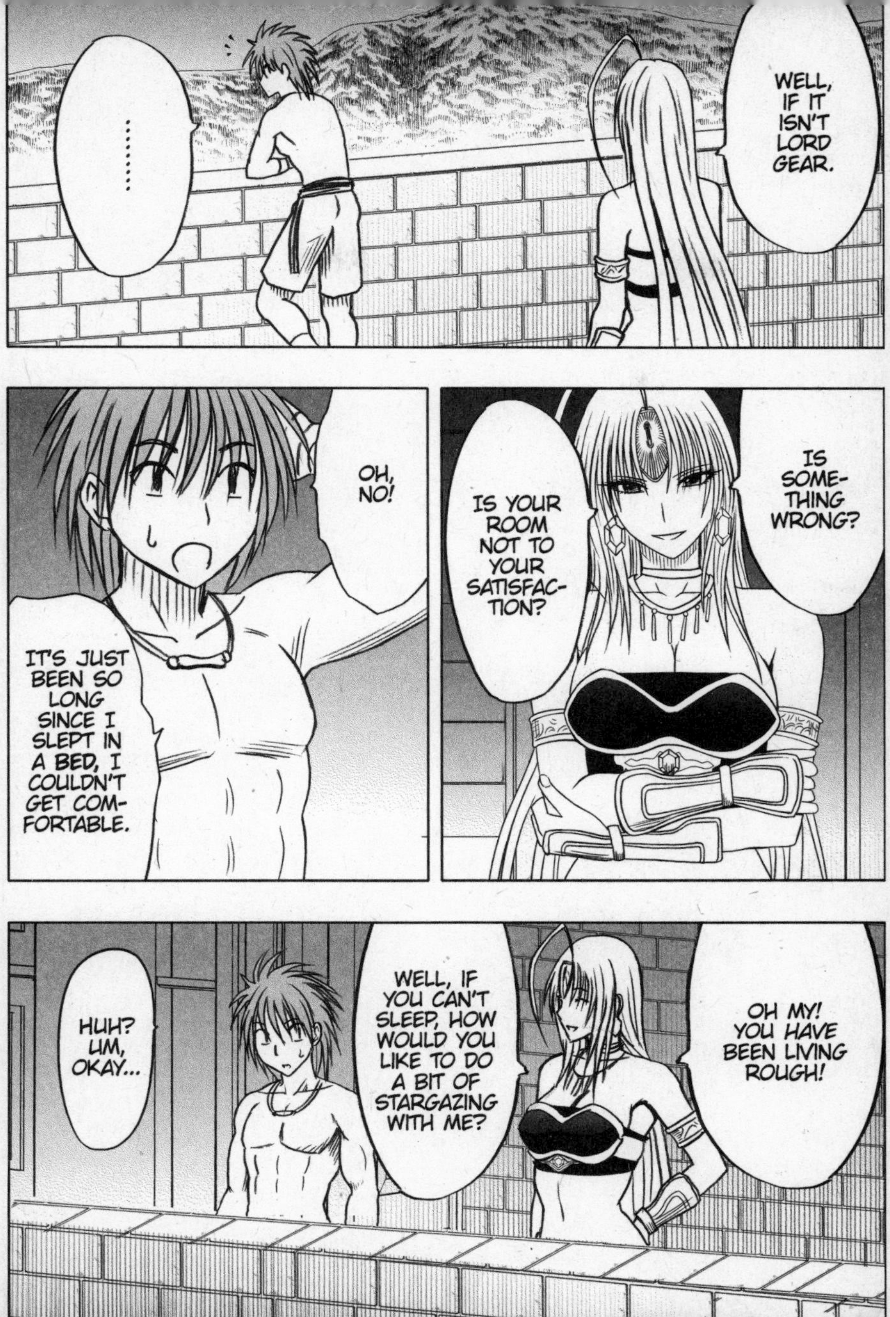
WELL, IF IT ISN'T LORD GEAR.
......
IS SOME-THING WRONG?
IS YOUR ROOM NOT TO YOUR SATISFAC-TION?
OH, NO!
IT'S JUST BEEN SO LONG SINCE I SLEPT IN A BED, I COULDN'T GET COM-FORTABLE.
OH MY! YOU HAVE BEEN LIVING ROUGH!
WELL, IF YOU CAN'T SLEEP, HOW WOULD YOU LIKE TO DO A BIT OF STARGAZING WITH ME?
HUH? UM, OKAY...

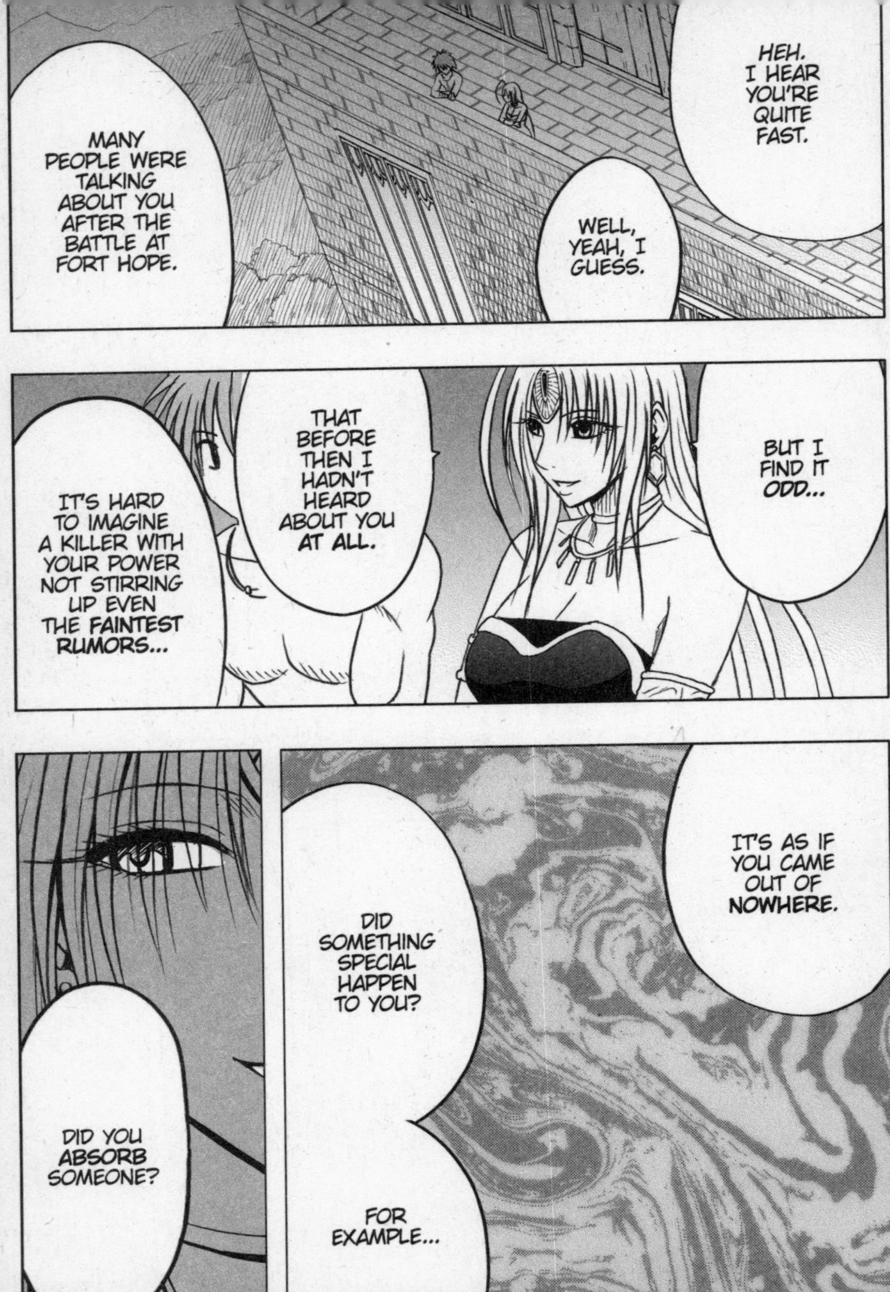
HEH. I HEAR YOU'RE QUITE FAST.
WELL, YEAH, I GUESS.
MANY PEOPLE WERE TALKING ABOUT YOU AFTER THE BATTLE AT FORT HOPE.
BUT I FIND IT ODD...
THAT BEFORE THEN I HADN'T HEARD ABOUT YOU AT ALL.
IT'S HARD TO IMAGINE A KILLER WITH YOUR POWER NOT STIRRING UP EVEN THE FAINTEST RUMORS...
IT'S AS IF YOU CAME OUT OF NOWHERE.
DID SOMETHING SPECIAL HAPPEN TO YOU?
FOR EXAMPLE...
DID YOU ABSORB SOMEONE?

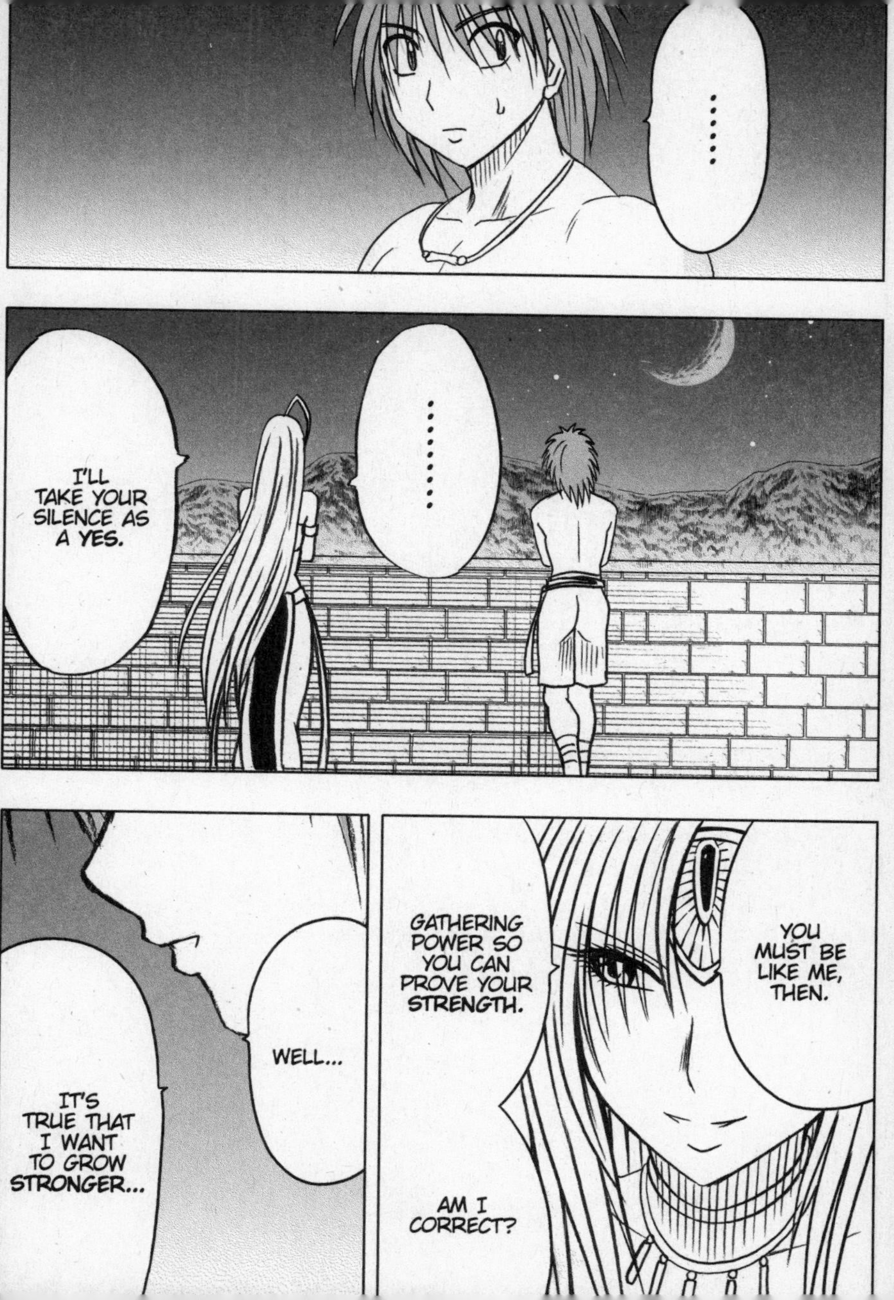
......
......
I'LL TAKE YOUR SILENCE AS A YES.
YOU MUST BE LIKE ME, THEN.
GATHERING POWER SO YOU CAN PROVE YOUR STRENGTH.
AM I CORRECT?
WELL...
IT'S TRUE THAT I WANT TO GROW STRONGER...

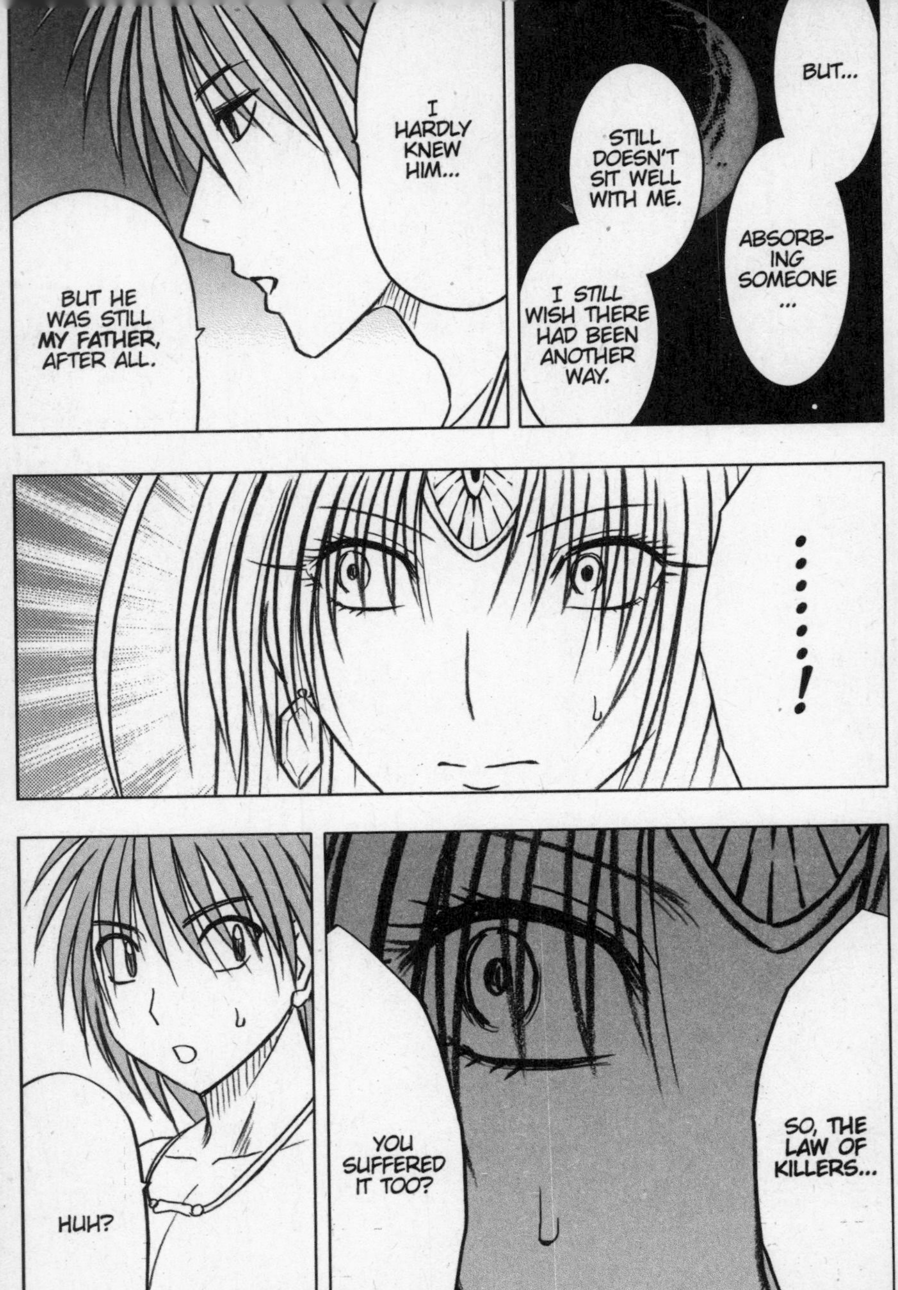
BUT...
ABSORB-
ING
SOMEONE
...
STILL
DOESN'T
SIT WELL
WITH ME.
I STILL
WISH THERE
HAD BEEN
ANOTHER
WAY.
I
HARDLY
KNEW
HIM...
BUT HE
WAS STILL
MY FATHER,
AFTER ALL.
......!
SO, THE
LAW OF
KILLERS...
YOU
SUFFERED
IT TOO?
HUH?

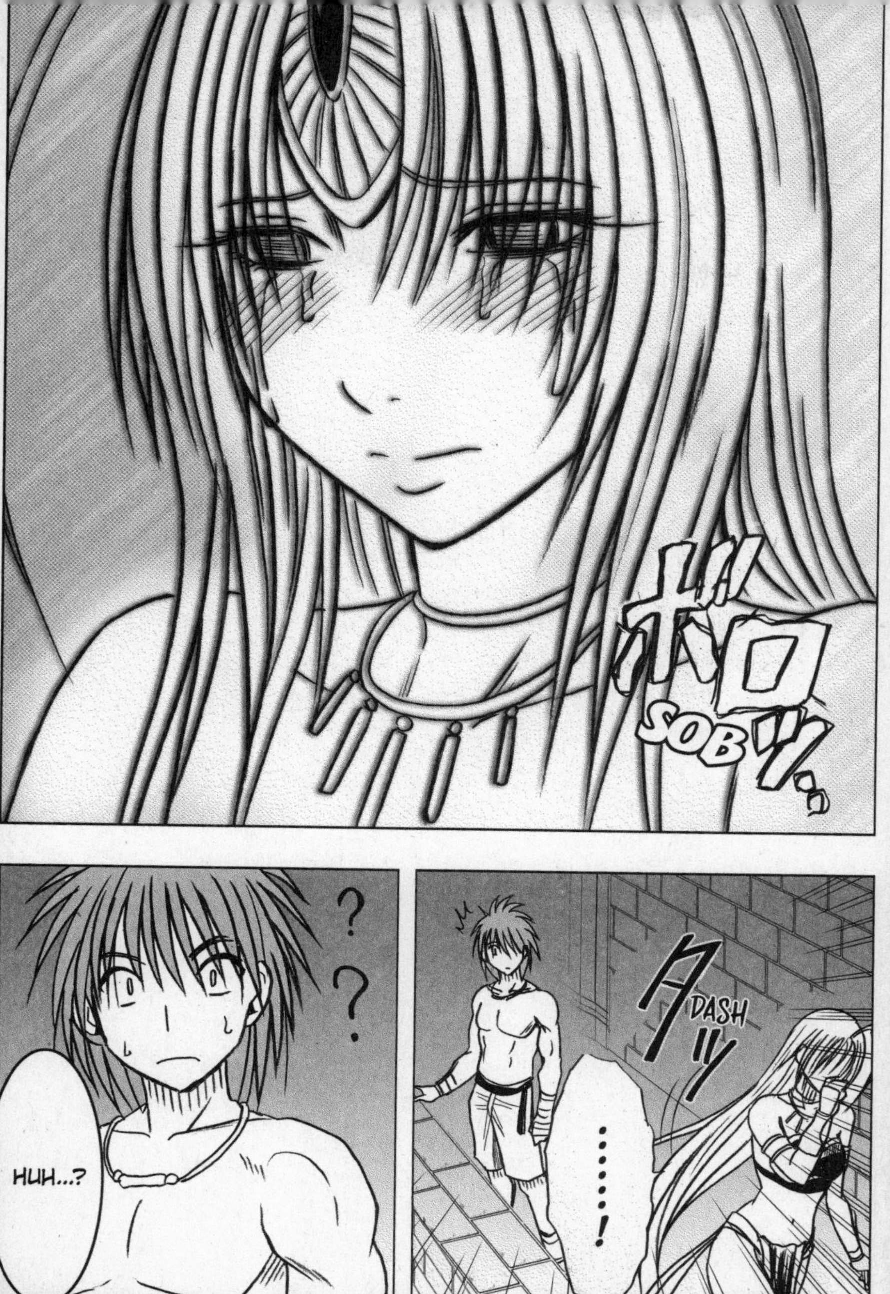
ボロ
SOB
ッ
タ
DASH
ッ
......!
??
HUH...?

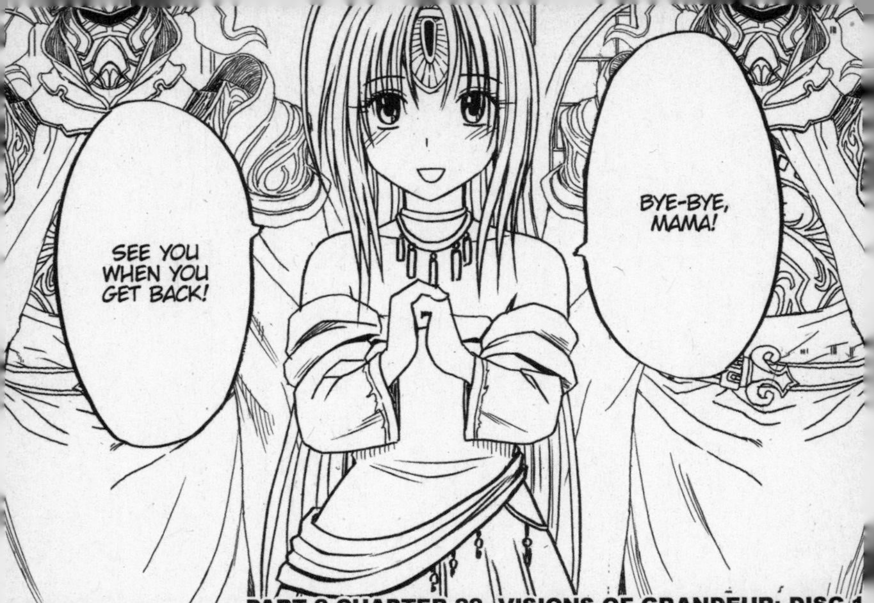
BYE-BYE, MAMA!
SEE YOU WHEN YOU GET BACK!

PART 2 CHAPTER 22 VISIONS OF GRANDEUR: DISC 1

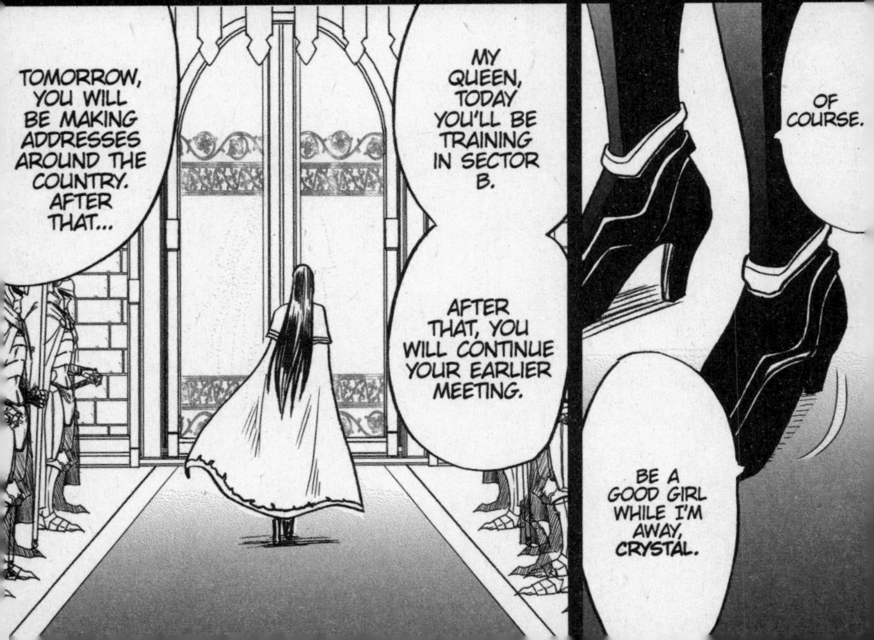
OF COURSE.
BE A GOOD GIRL WHILE I'M AWAY, CRYSTAL.
MY QUEEN, TODAY YOU'LL BE TRAINING IN SECTOR B.
AFTER THAT, YOU WILL CONTINUE YOUR EARLIER MEETING.
TOMORROW, YOU WILL BE MAKING ADDRESSES AROUND THE COUNTRY. AFTER THAT...

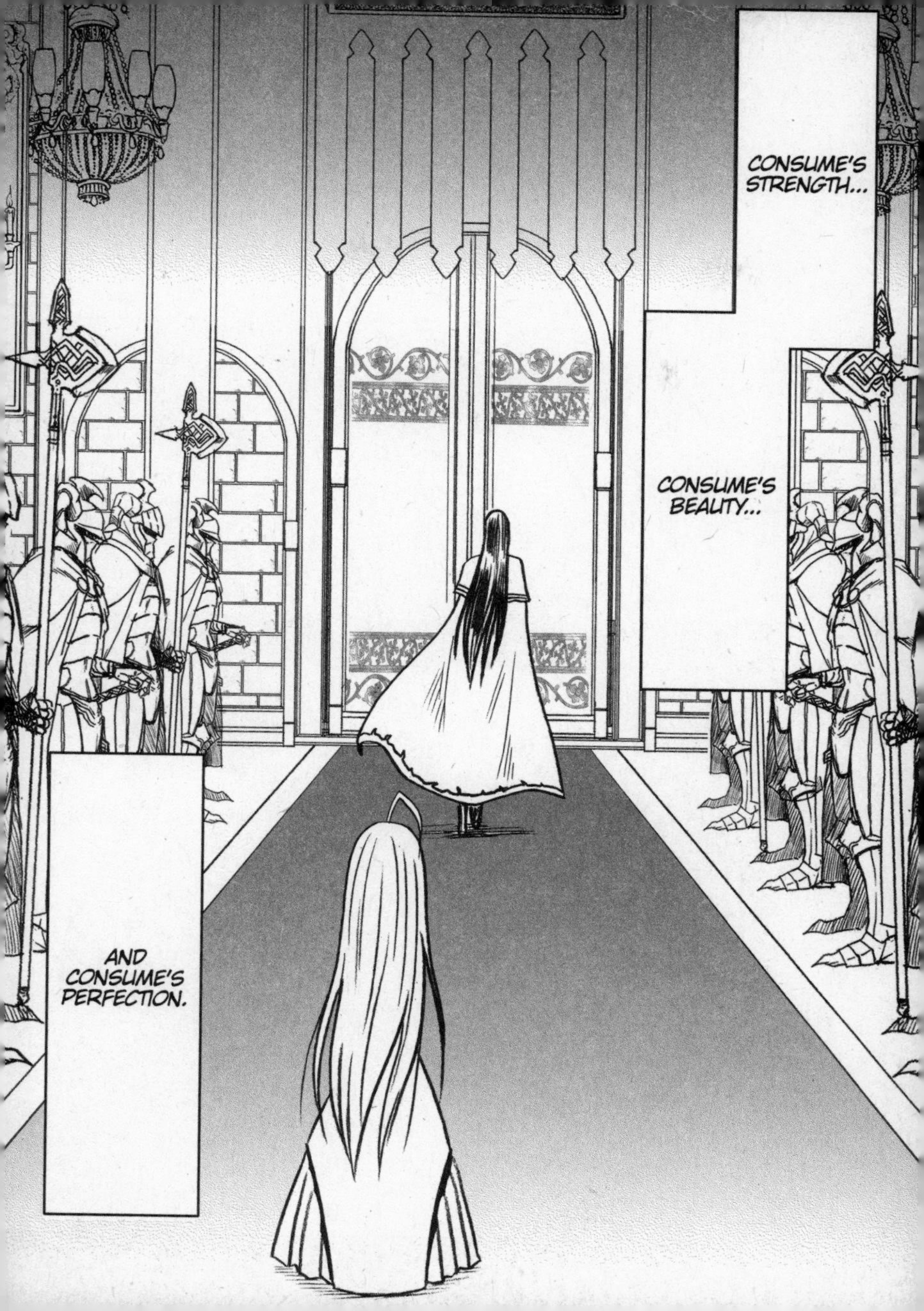
CONSUME'S STRENGTH...
CONSUME'S BEAUTY...
AND CONSUME'S PERFECTION.

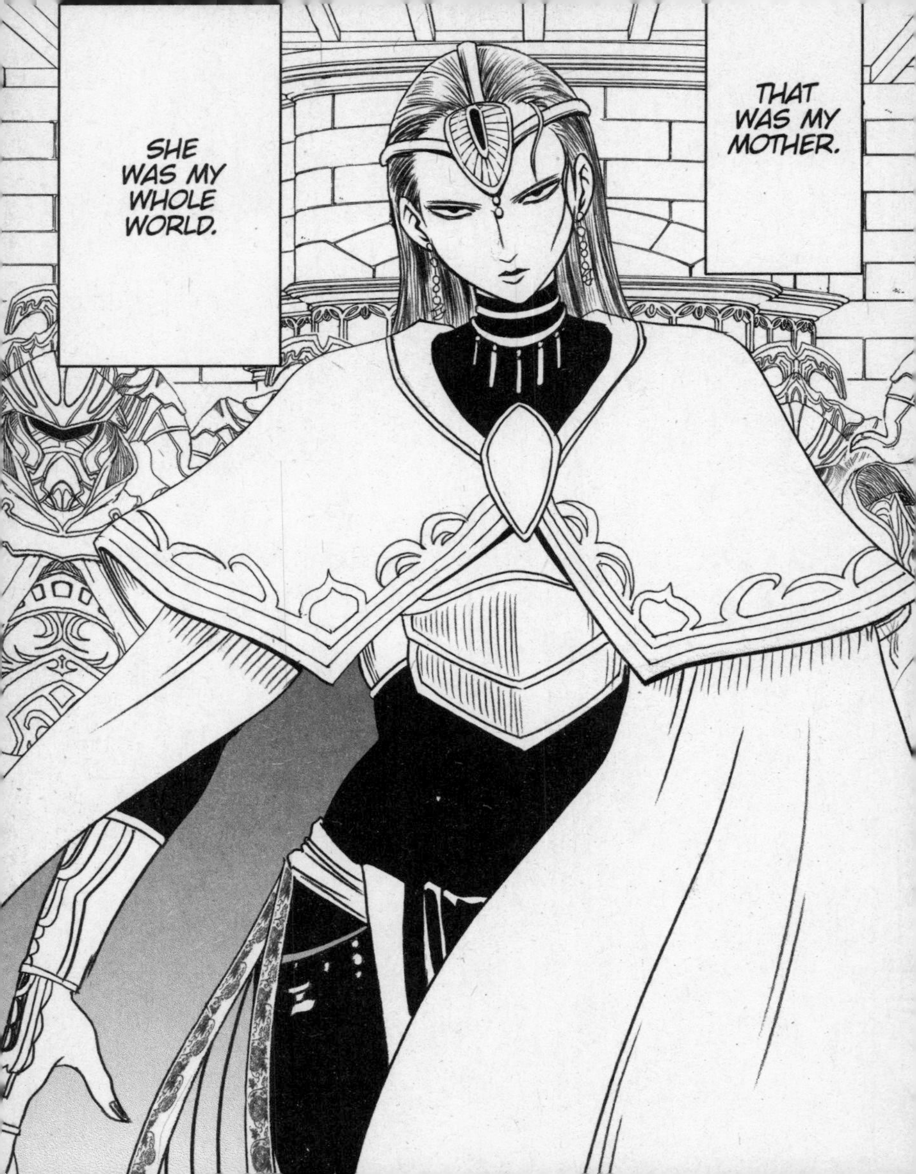
THAT WAS MY MOTHER.
SHE WAS MY WHOLE WORLD.

VISIONS OF GRANDEUR:

DISC 1

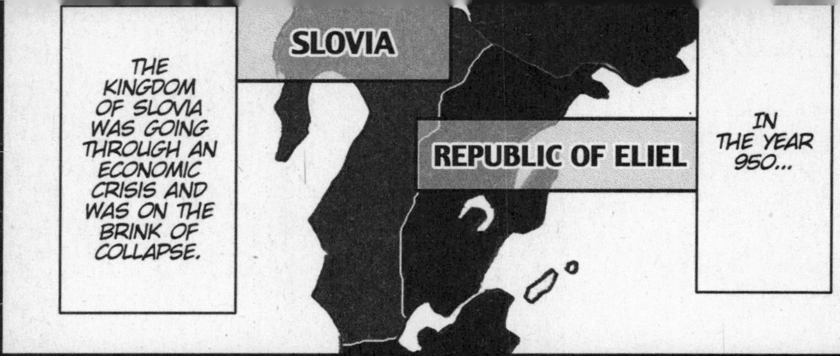
IN THE YEAR 950...
SLOVIA
REPUBLIC OF ELIEL
THE KINGDOM OF SLOVIA WAS GOING THROUGH AN ECONOMIC CRISIS AND WAS ON THE BRINK OF COLLAPSE.

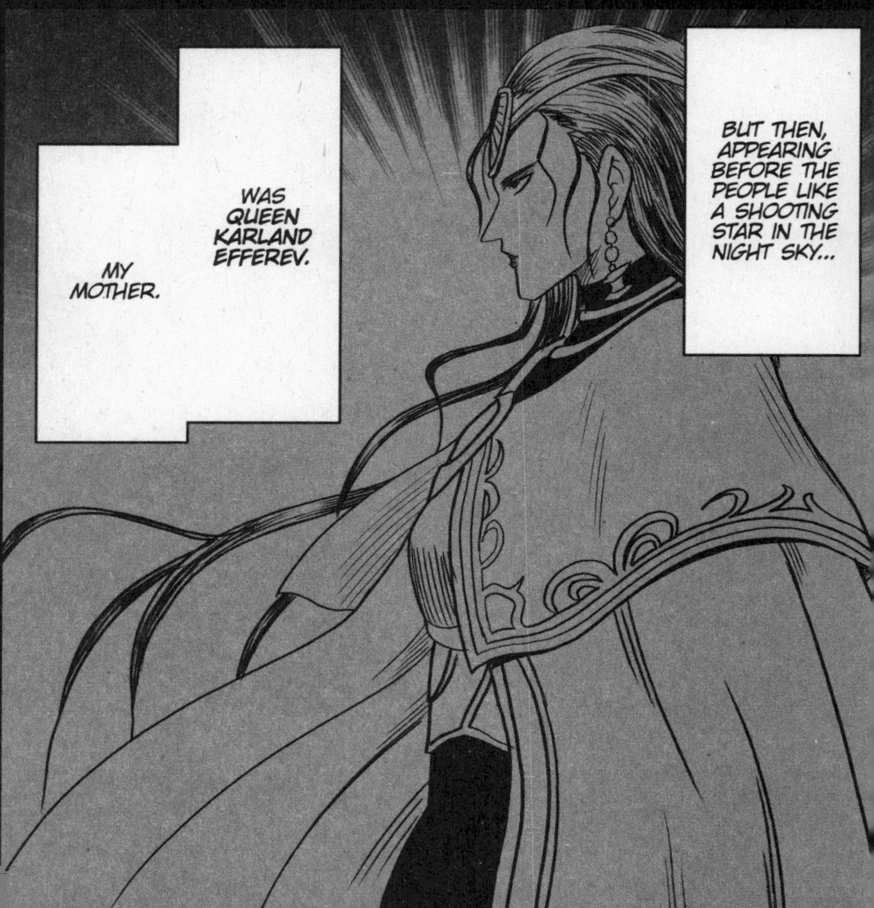
BUT THEN, APPEARING BEFORE THE PEOPLE LIKE A SHOOTING STAR IN THE NIGHT SKY...
WAS QUEEN KARLAND EFFEREV.
MY MOTHER.

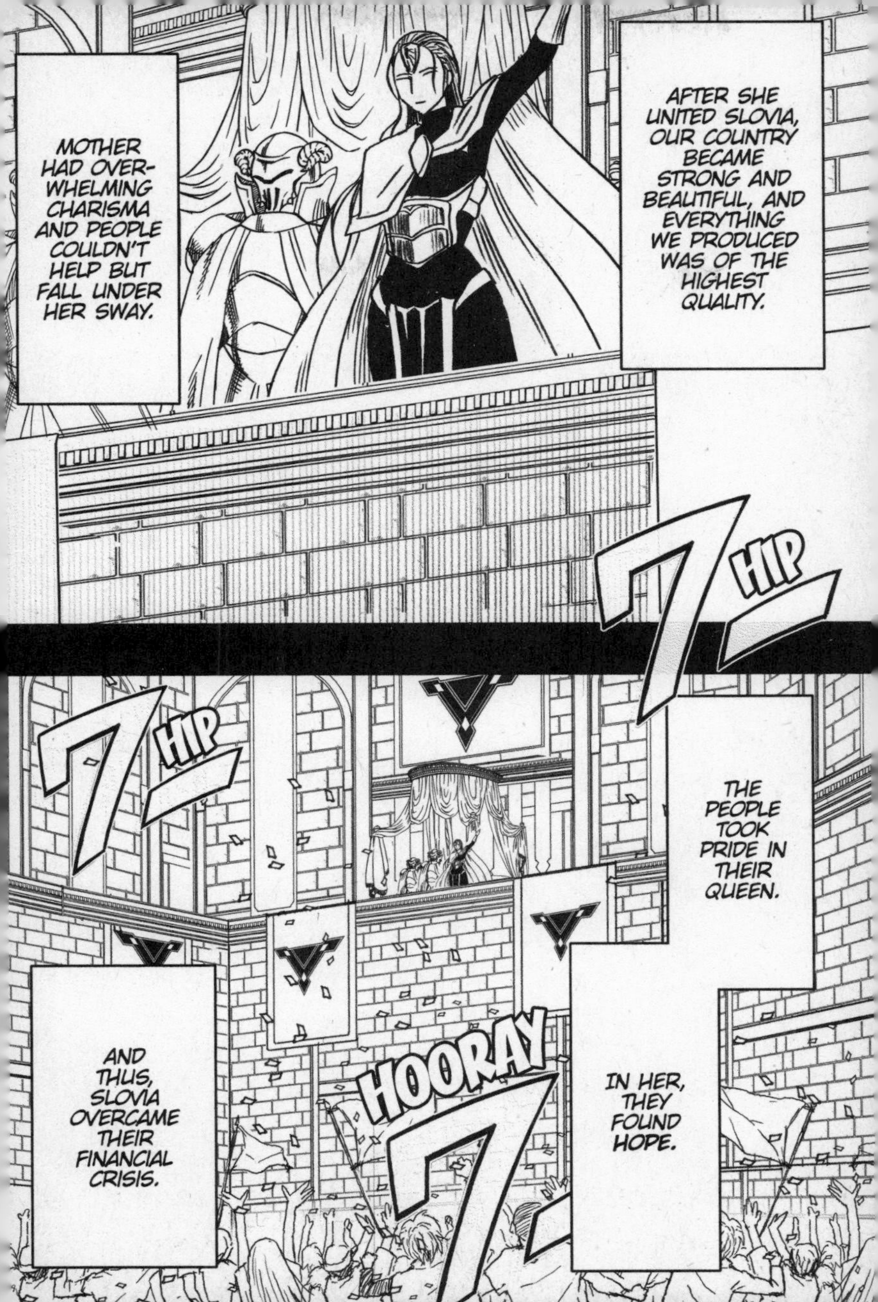
AFTER SHE UNITED SLOVIA, OUR COUNTRY BECAME STRONG AND BEAUTIFUL, AND EVERYTHING WE PRODUCED WAS OF THE HIGHEST QUALITY.
MOTHER HAD OVER-WHELMING CHARISMA AND PEOPLE COULDN'T HELP BUT FALL UNDER HER SWAY.
HIP
HIP
THE PEOPLE TOOK PRIDE IN THEIR QUEEN.
IN HER, THEY FOUND HOPE.
HOORAY
AND THUS, SLOVIA OVERCAME THEIR FINANCIAL CRISIS.

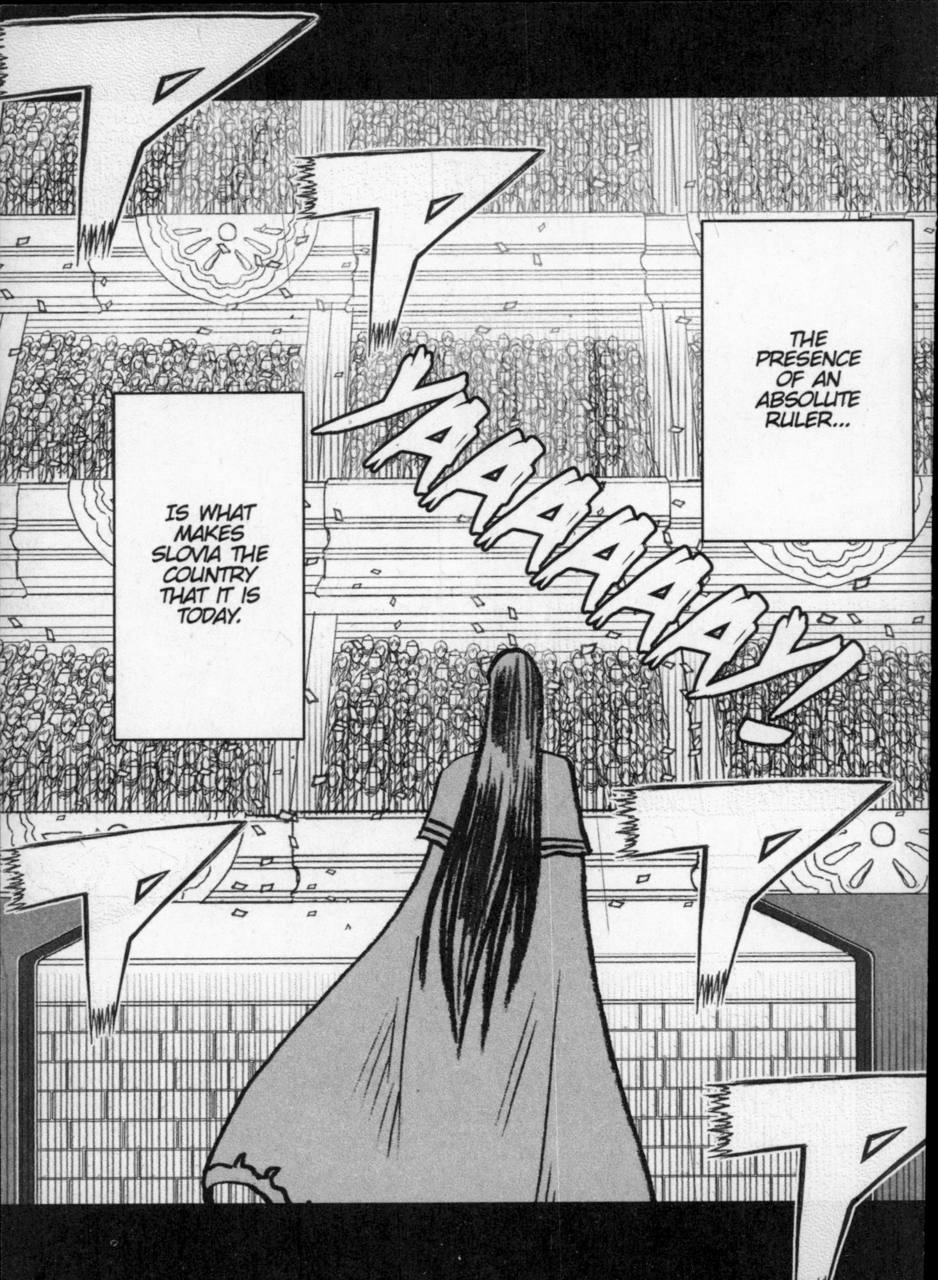
THE PRESENCE OF AN ABSOLUTE RULER...
YAAAAAAY!
IS WHAT MAKES SLOVIA THE COUNTRY THAT IT IS TODAY.

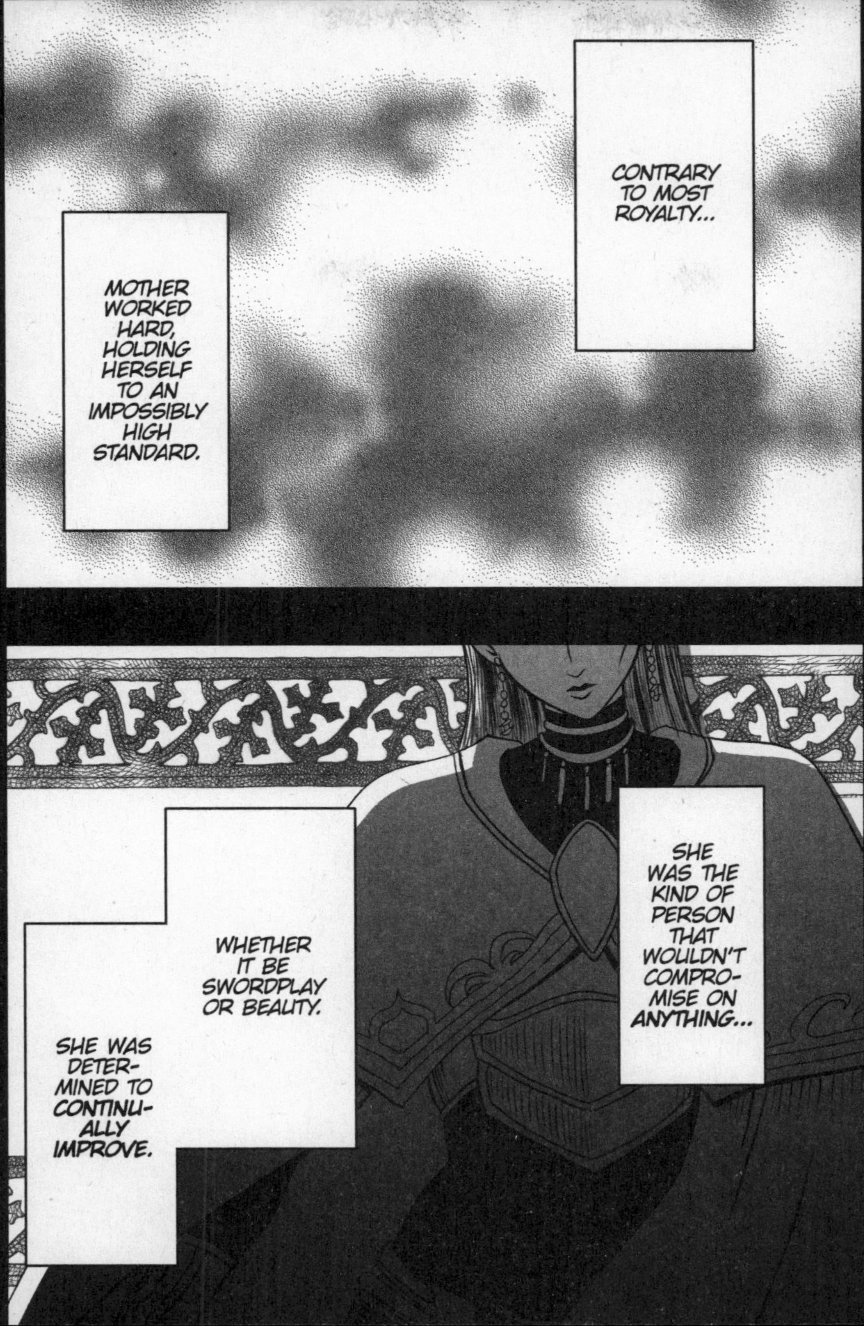
CONTRARY TO MOST ROYALTY...
MOTHER WORKED HARD, HOLDING HERSELF TO AN IMPOSSIBLY HIGH STANDARD.
SHE WAS THE KIND OF PERSON THAT WOULDN'T COMPROMISE ON ANYTHING...
WHETHER IT BE SWORDPLAY OR BEAUTY.
SHE WAS DETERMINED TO CONTINUALLY IMPROVE.

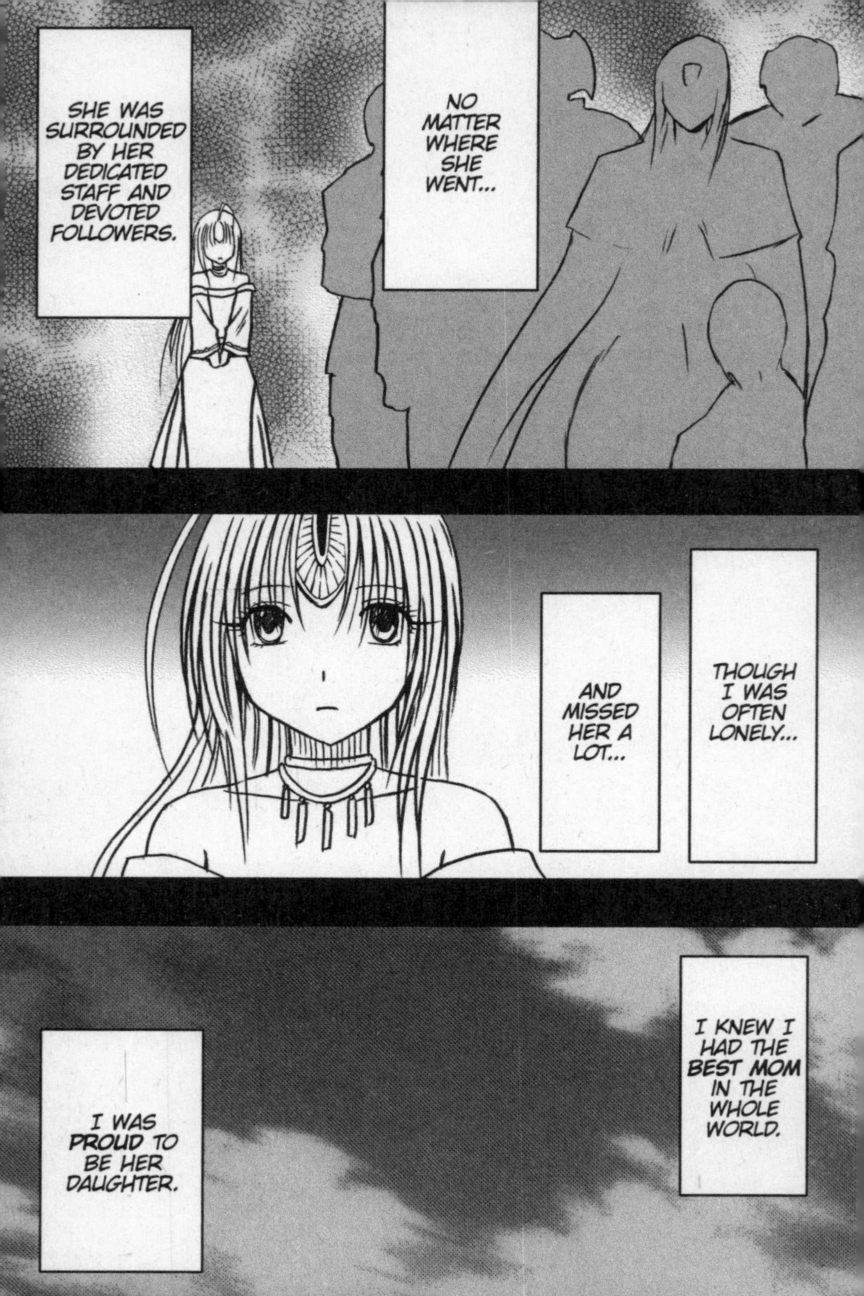
NO MATTER WHERE SHE WENT...
SHE WAS SURROUNDED BY HER DEDICATED STAFF AND DEVOTED FOLLOWERS.
THOUGH I WAS OFTEN LONELY...
AND MISSED HER A LOT...
I KNEW I HAD THE BEST MOM IN THE WHOLE WORLD.
I WAS PROUD TO BE HER DAUGHTER.

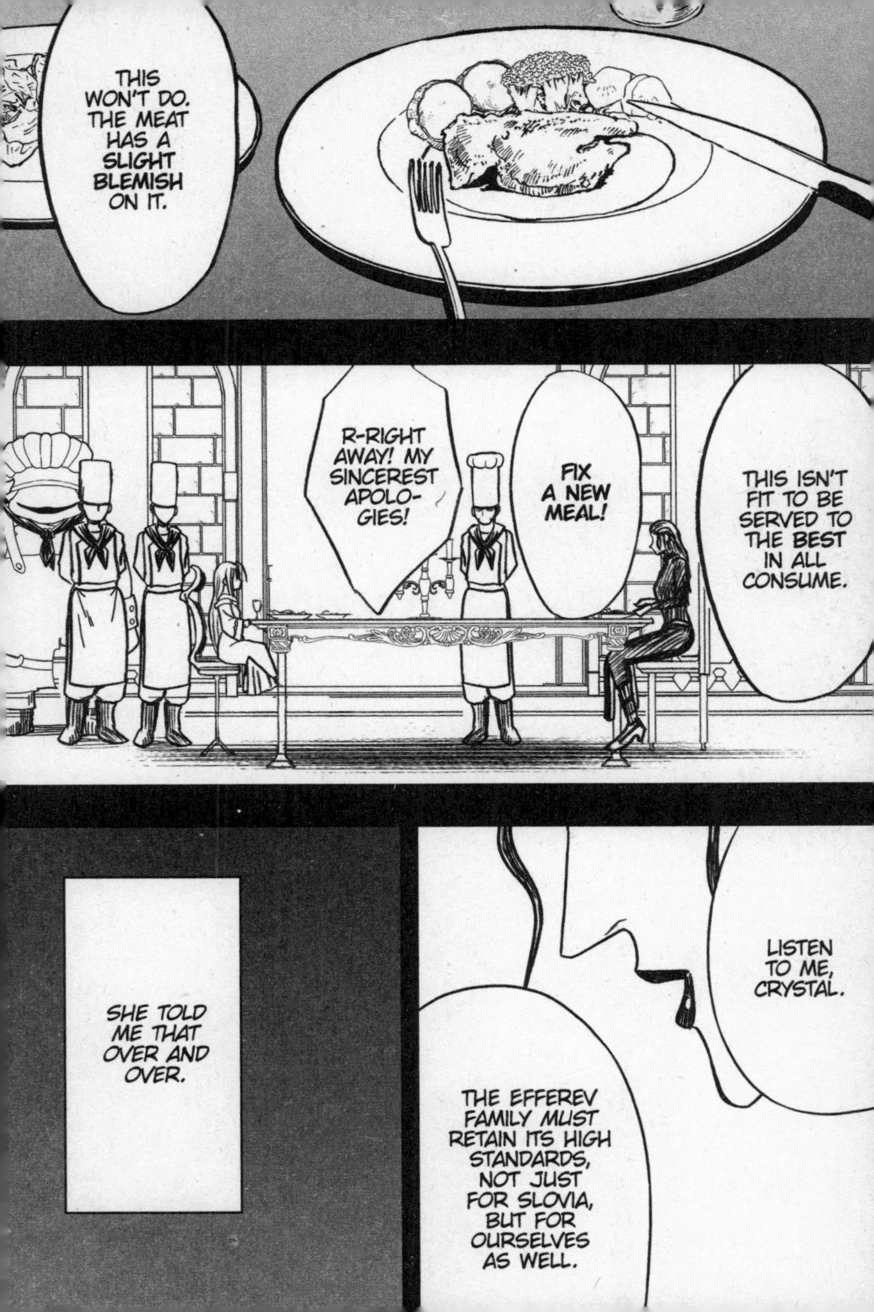
THIS WON'T DO. THE MEAT HAS A SLIGHT BLEMISH ON IT.
THIS ISN'T FIT TO BE SERVED TO THE BEST IN ALL CONSUME.
FIX A NEW MEAL!
R-RIGHT AWAY! MY SINCEREST APOLO-GIES!
LISTEN TO ME, CRYSTAL.
THE EFFEREV FAMILY MUST RETAIN ITS HIGH STANDARDS, NOT JUST FOR SLOVIA, BUT FOR OURSELVES AS WELL.
SHE TOLD ME THAT OVER AND OVER.

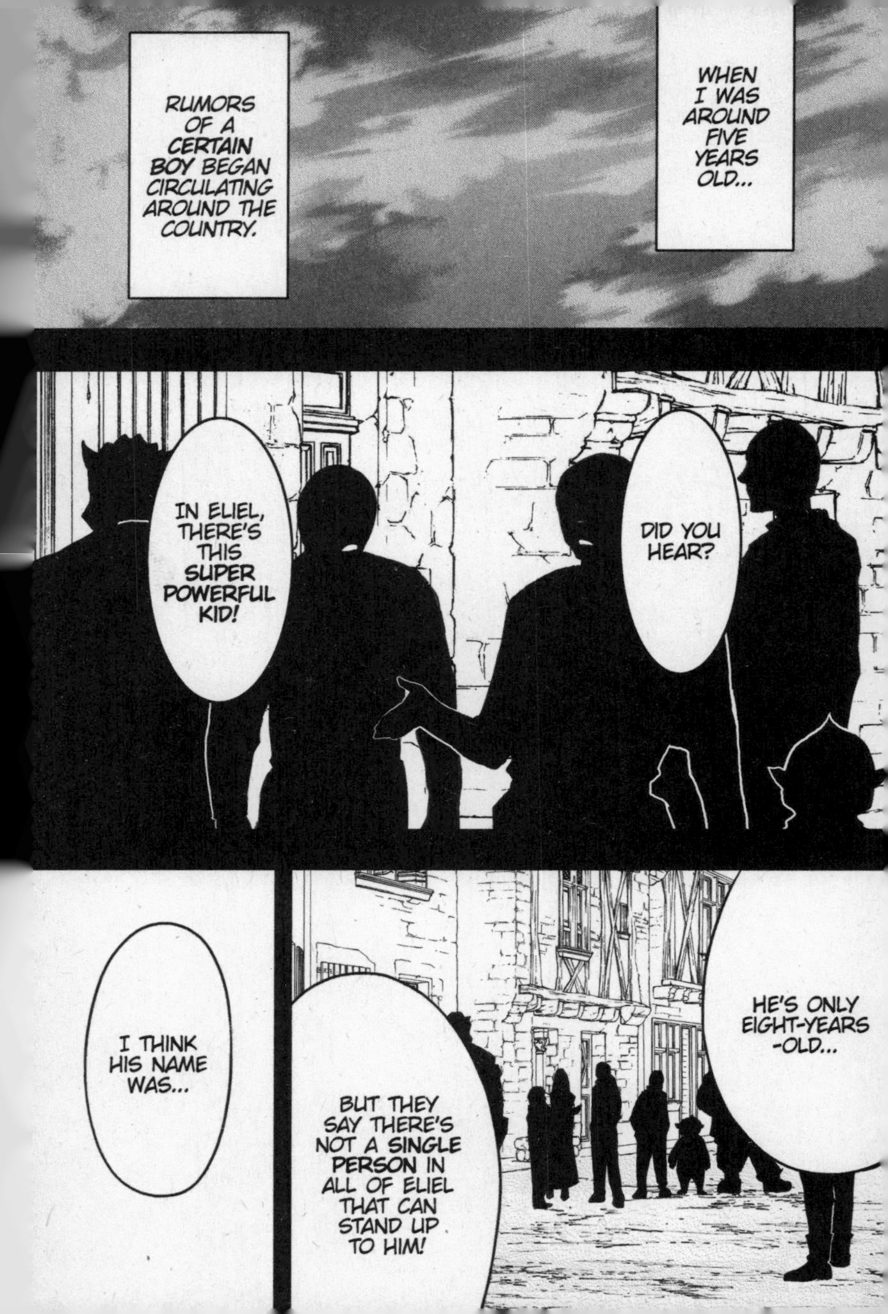
WHEN I WAS AROUND FIVE YEARS OLD...
RUMORS OF A CERTAIN BOY BEGAN CIRCULATING AROUND THE COUNTRY.
DID YOU HEAR?
IN ELIEL, THERE'S THIS SUPER POWERFUL KID!
HE'S ONLY EIGHT-YEARS -OLD...
BUT THEY SAY THERE'S NOT A SINGLE PERSON IN ALL OF ELIEL THAT CAN STAND UP TO HIM!
I THINK HIS NAME WAS...

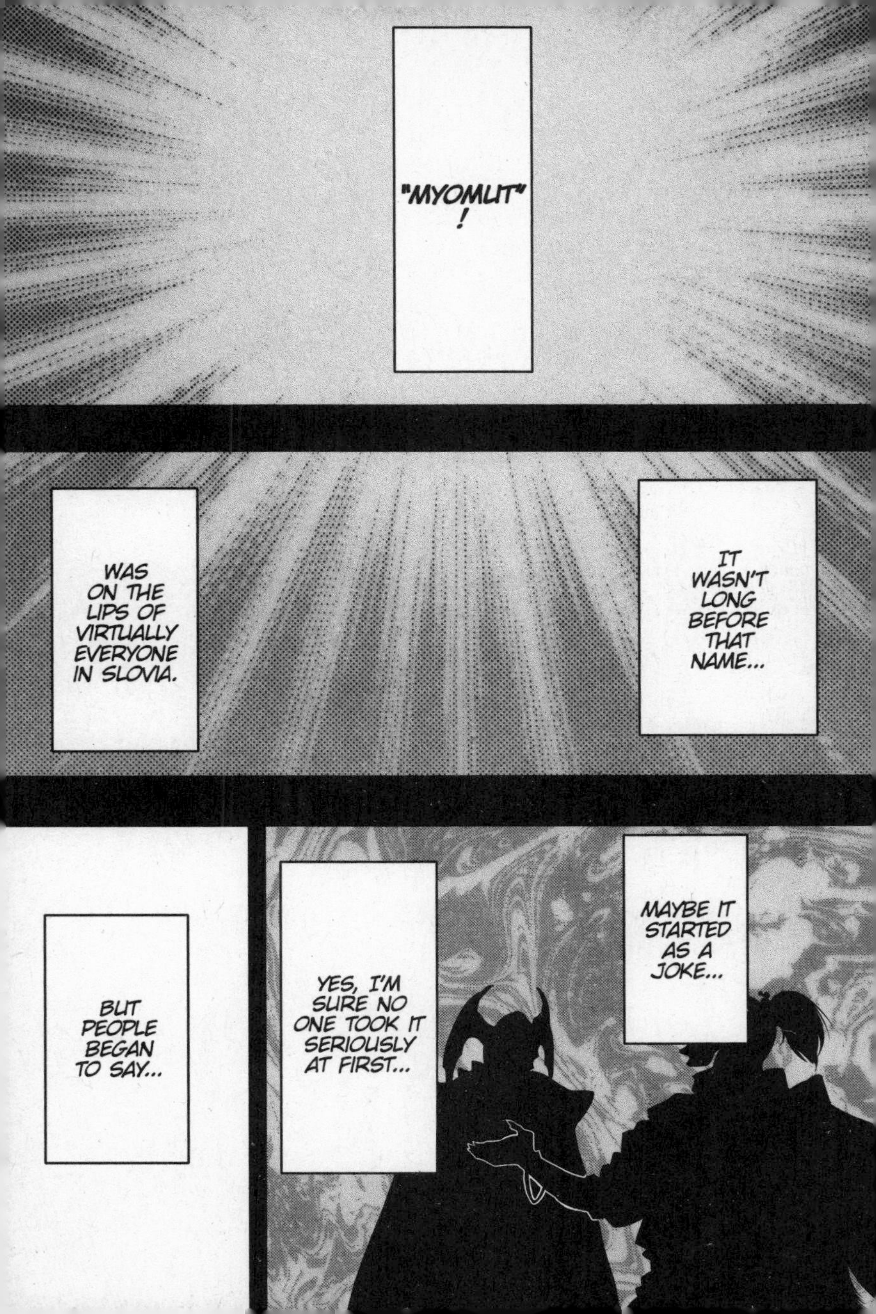
"MYOMUT" !
IT WASN'T LONG BEFORE THAT NAME...
WAS ON THE LIPS OF VIRTUALLY EVERYONE IN SLOVIA.
MAYBE IT STARTED AS A JOKE...
YES, I'M SURE NO ONE TOOK IT SERIOUSLY AT FIRST...
BUT PEOPLE BEGAN TO SAY...

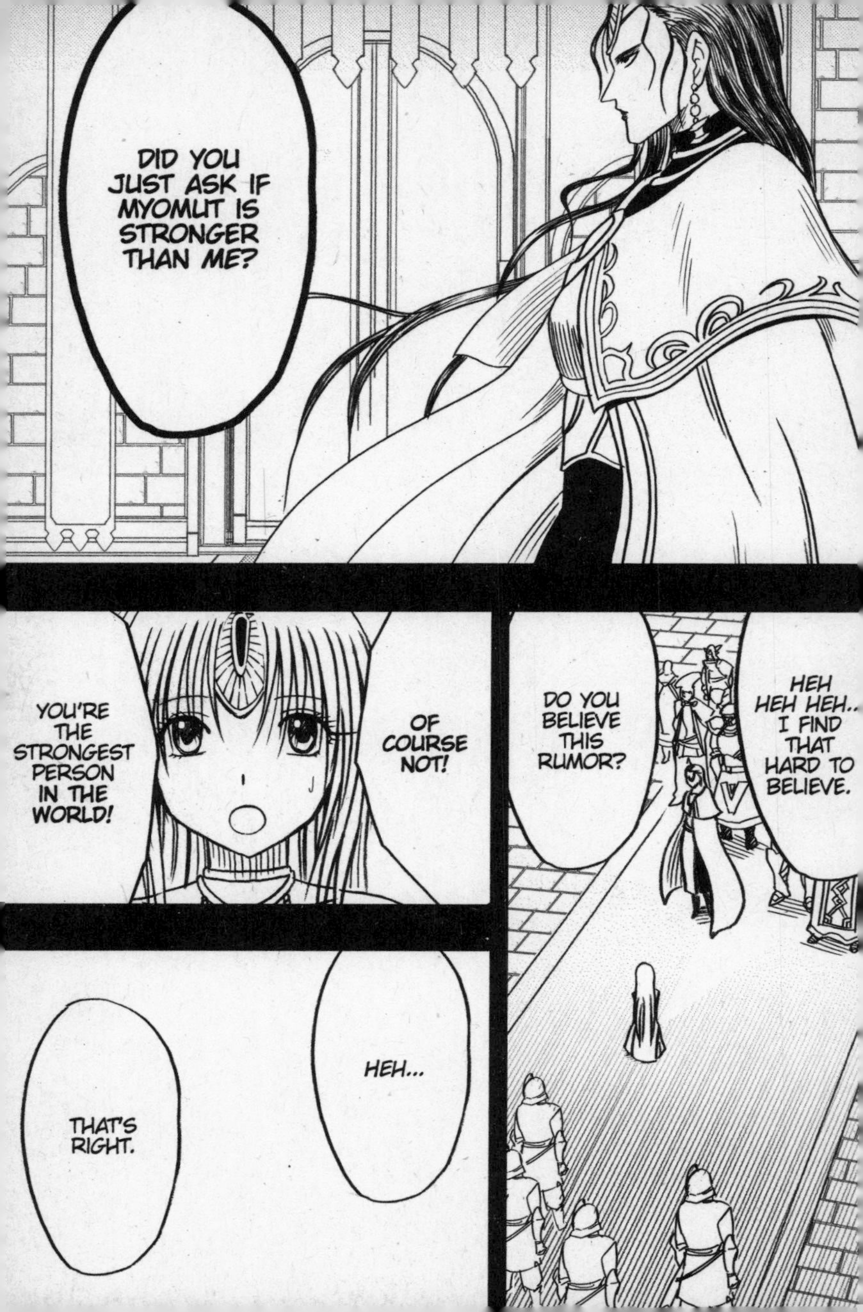
DID YOU JUST ASK IF MYOMUT IS STRONGER THAN ME?
HEH HEH HEH.. I FIND THAT HARD TO BELIEVE.
DO YOU BELIEVE THIS RUMOR?
OF COURSE NOT!
YOU'RE THE STRONGEST PERSON IN THE WORLD!
HEH...
THAT'S RIGHT.

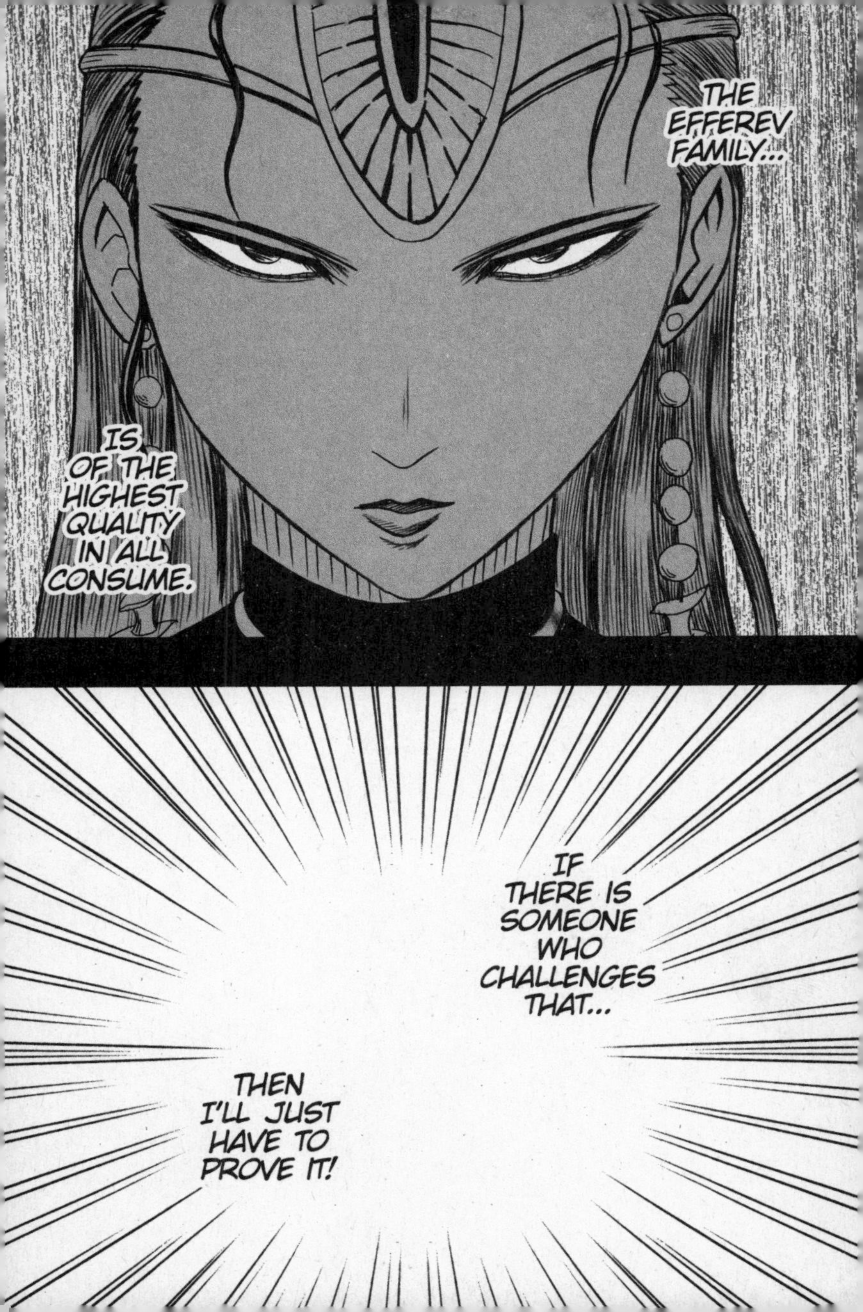
THE EFFEREV FAMILY...
IS OF THE HIGHEST QUALITY IN ALL CONSUME.
IF THERE IS SOMEONE WHO CHALLENGES THAT...
THEN I'LL JUST HAVE TO PROVE IT!

THUS, MOM
WENT OFF TO
CHALLENGE
MYOMUT TO
A DUEL.

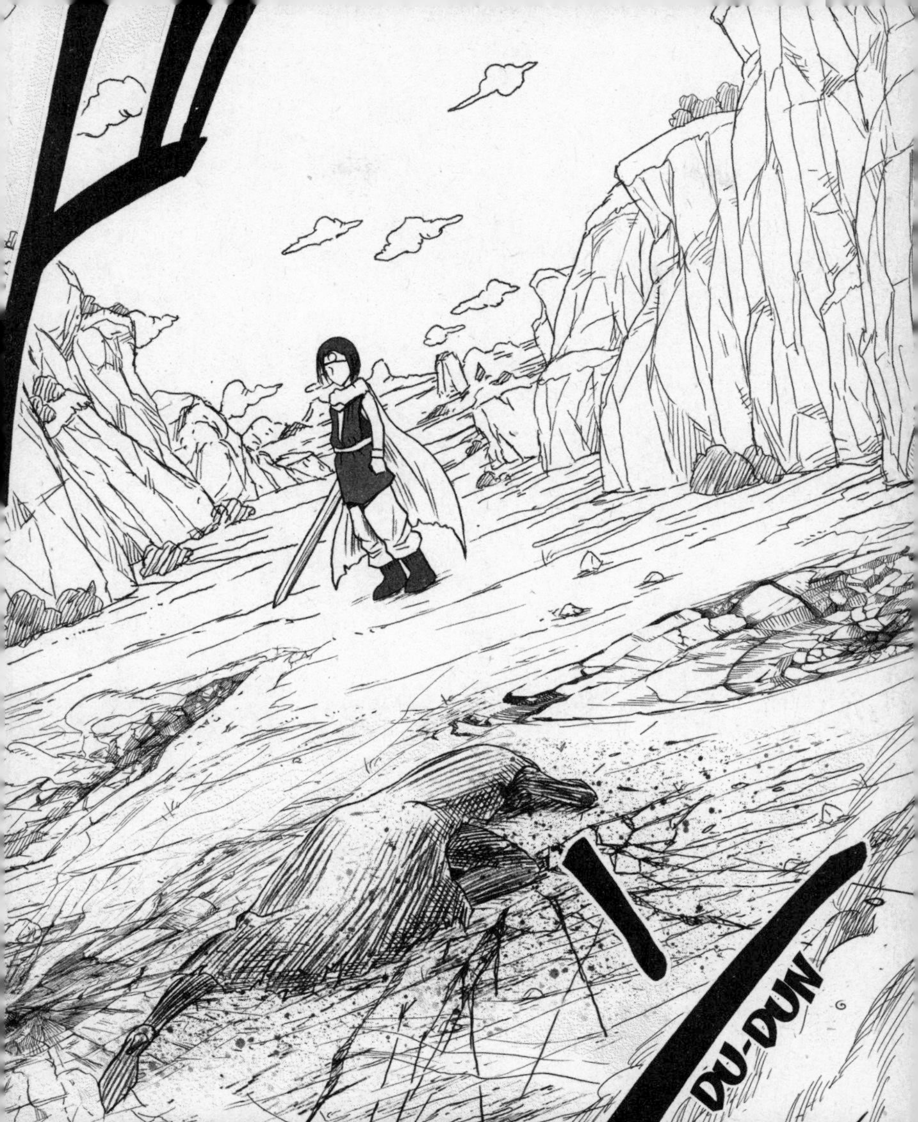
DU-DUN

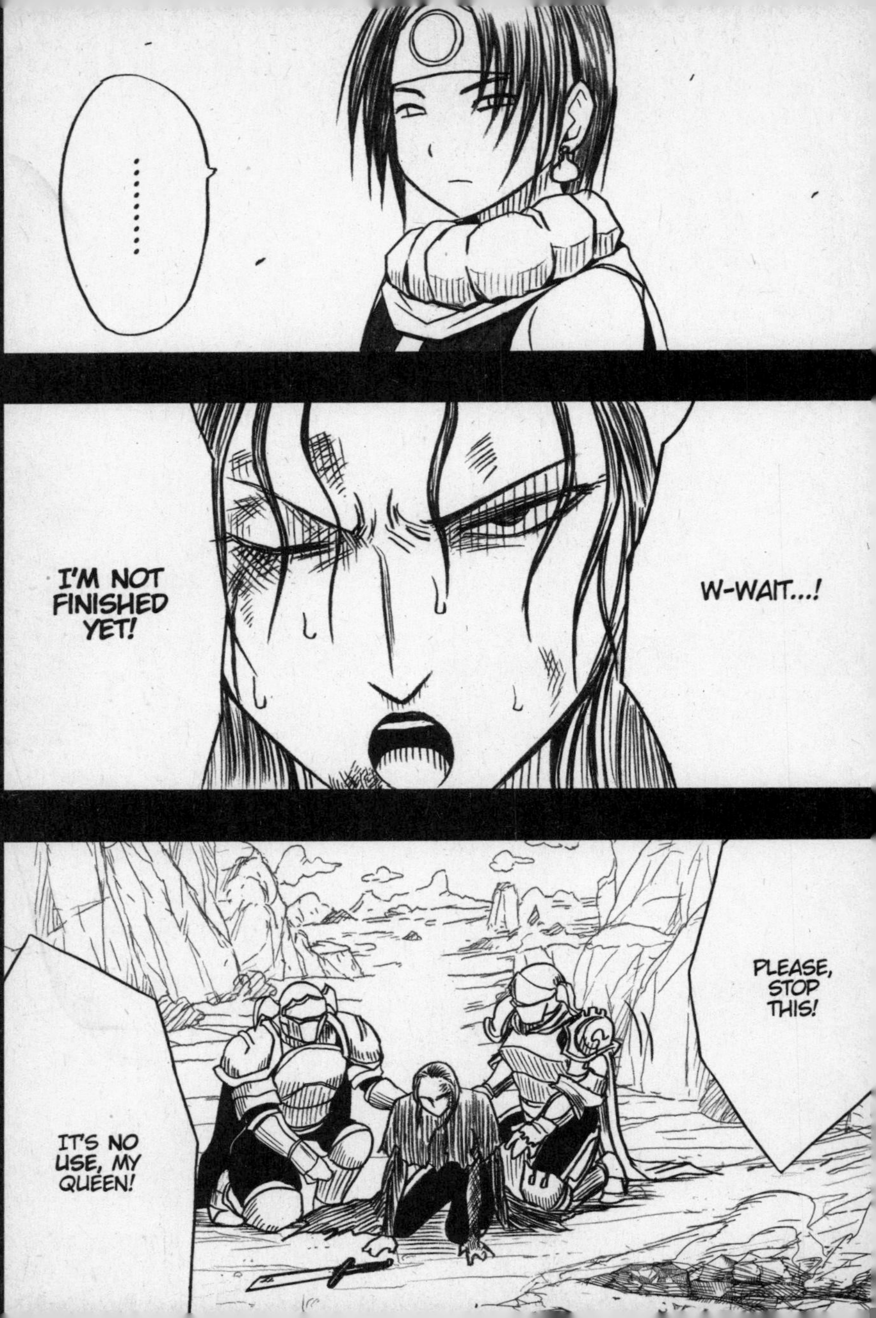
……
W-WAIT...!
I'M NOT FINISHED YET!
PLEASE, STOP THIS!
IT'S NO USE, MY QUEEN!

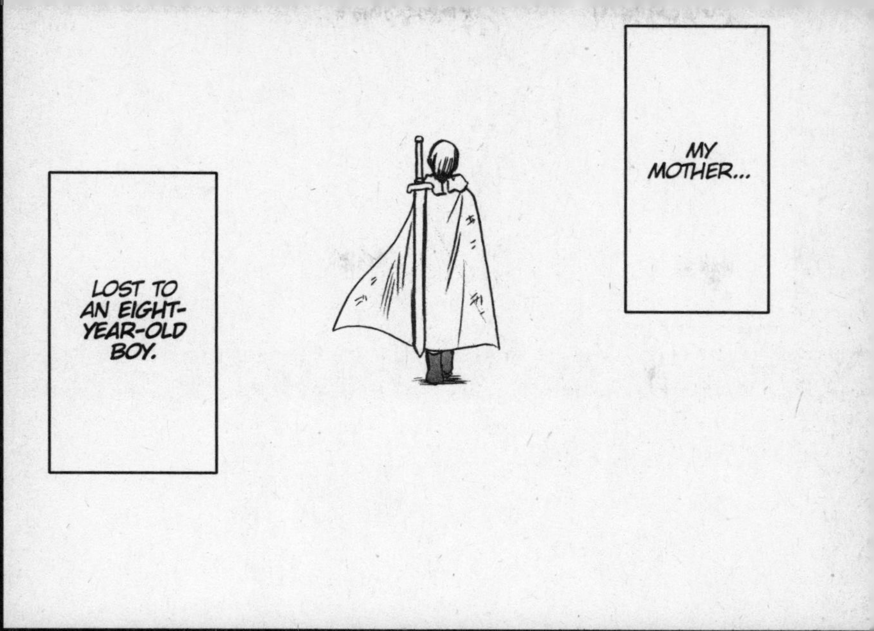
MY MOTHER...
LOST TO AN EIGHT-YEAR-OLD BOY.

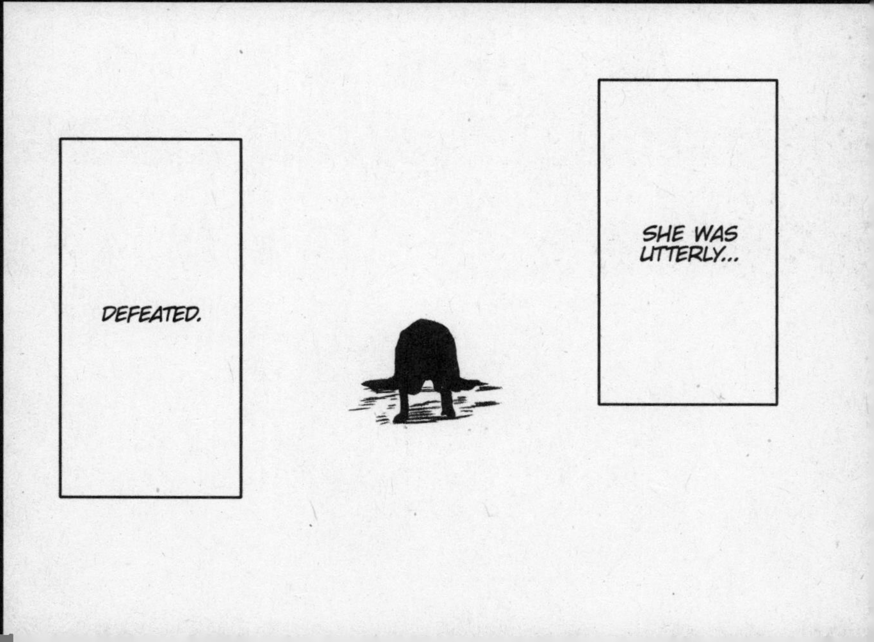
SHE WAS UTTERLY...
DEFEATED.

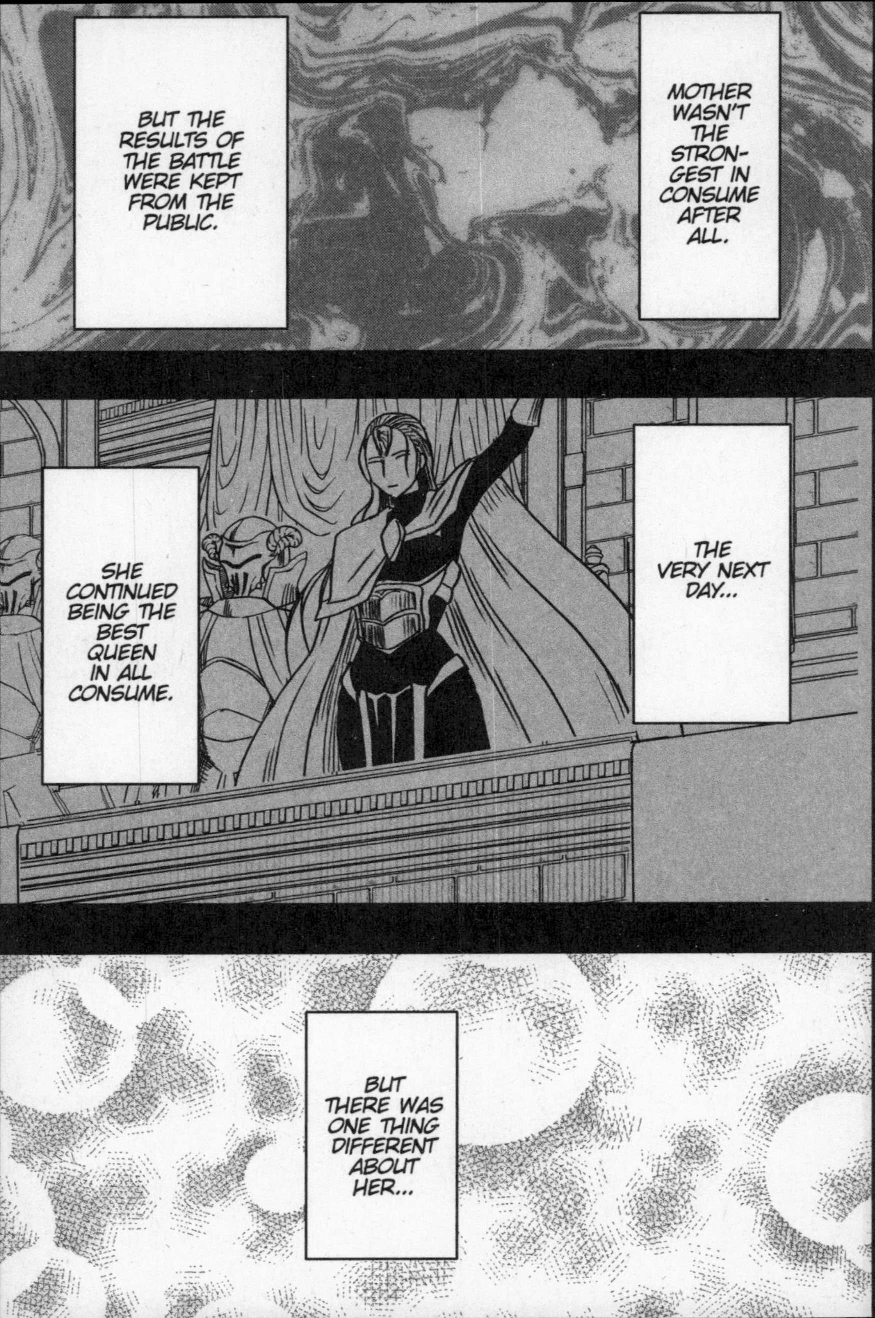
MOTHER WASN'T THE STRONGEST IN CONSUME AFTER ALL.
BUT THE RESULTS OF THE BATTLE WERE KEPT FROM THE PUBLIC.
THE VERY NEXT DAY...
SHE CONTINUED BEING THE BEST QUEEN IN ALL CONSUME.
BUT THERE WAS ONE THING DIFFERENT ABOUT HER...

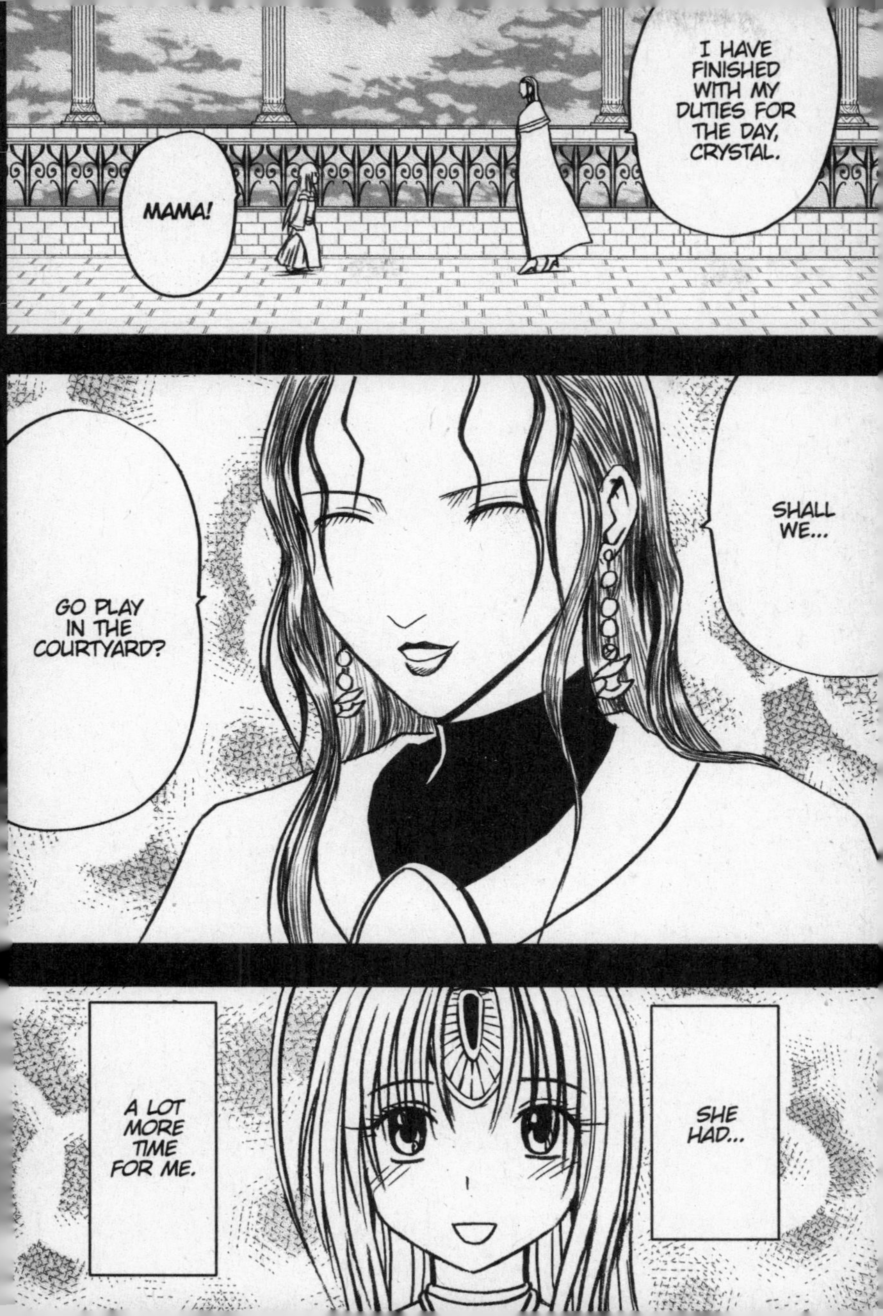
I HAVE FINISHED WITH MY DUTIES FOR THE DAY, CRYSTAL.
MAMA!
SHALL WE...
GO PLAY IN THE COURTYARD?
SHE HAD...
A LOT MORE TIME FOR ME.

VISIONS OF GRANDEUR:

DISC 2

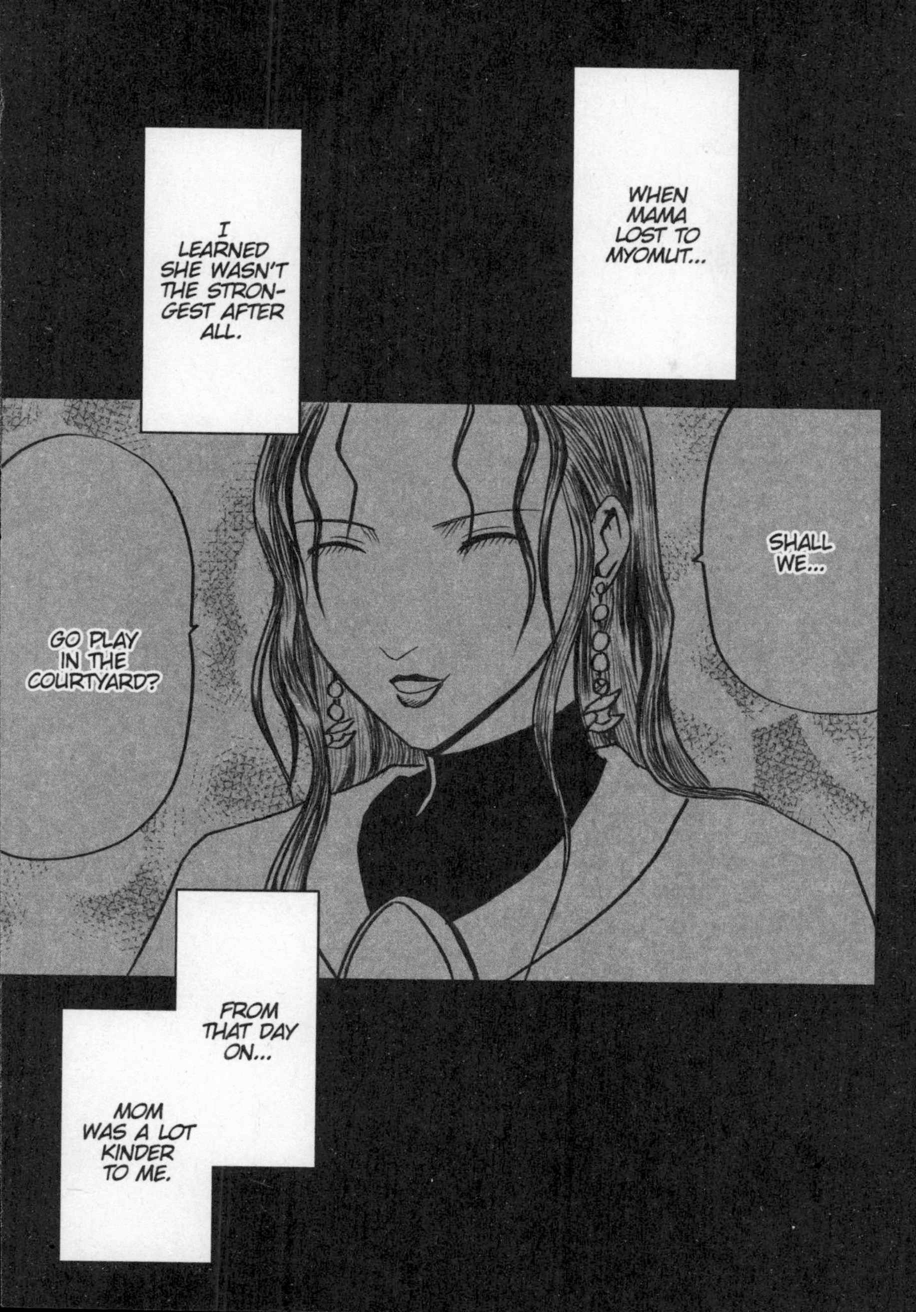
WHEN MAMA LOST TO MYOMUT...
I LEARNED SHE WASN'T THE STRON-GEST AFTER ALL.
SHALL WE...
GO PLAY IN THE COURTYARD?
FROM THAT DAY ON...
MOM WAS A LOT KINDER TO ME.

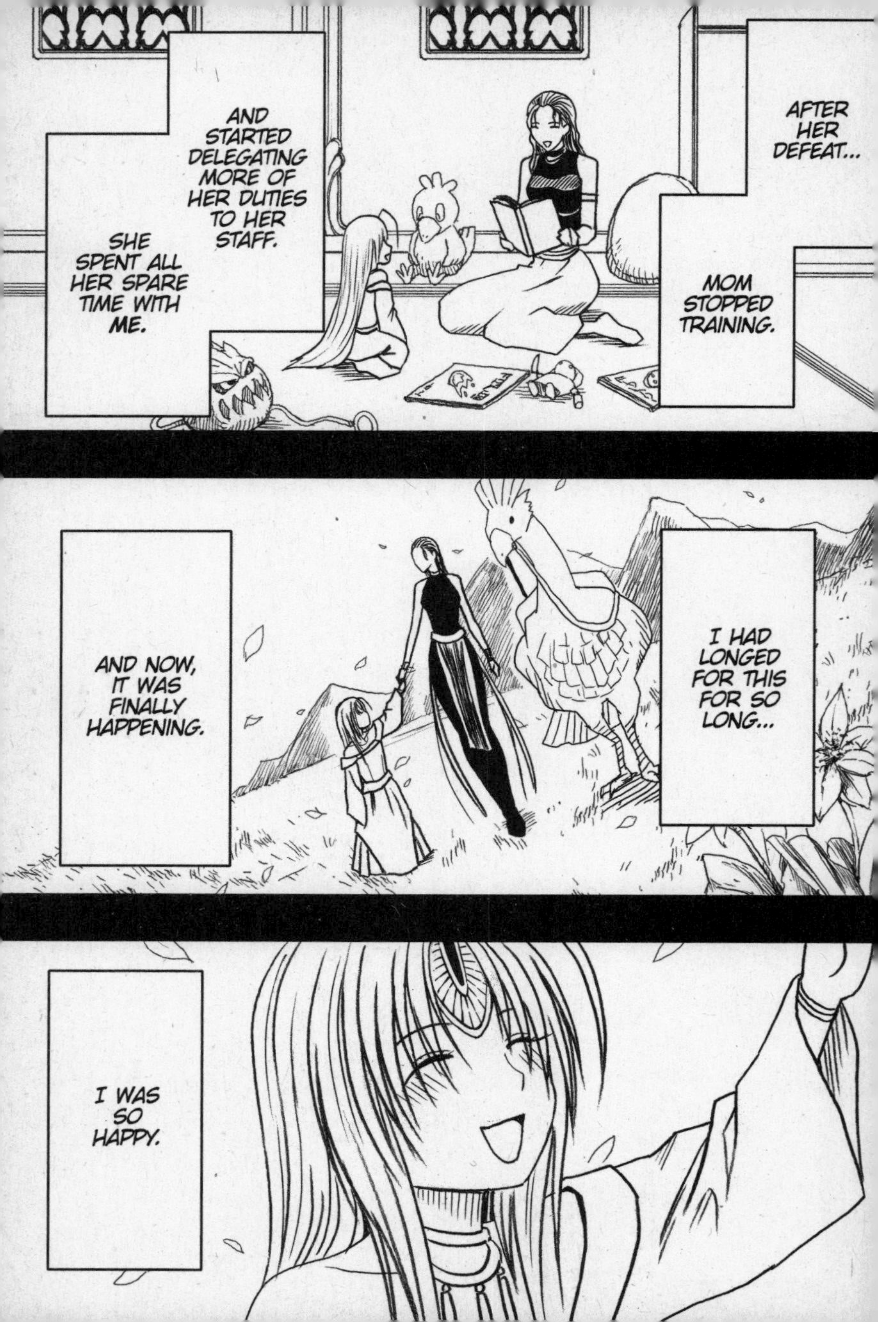
AFTER HER DEFEAT...
MOM STOPPED TRAINING.
AND STARTED DELEGATING MORE OF HER DUTIES TO HER STAFF.
SHE SPENT ALL HER SPARE TIME WITH ME.
I HAD LONGED FOR THIS FOR SO LONG...
AND NOW, IT WAS FINALLY HAPPENING.
I WAS SO HAPPY.

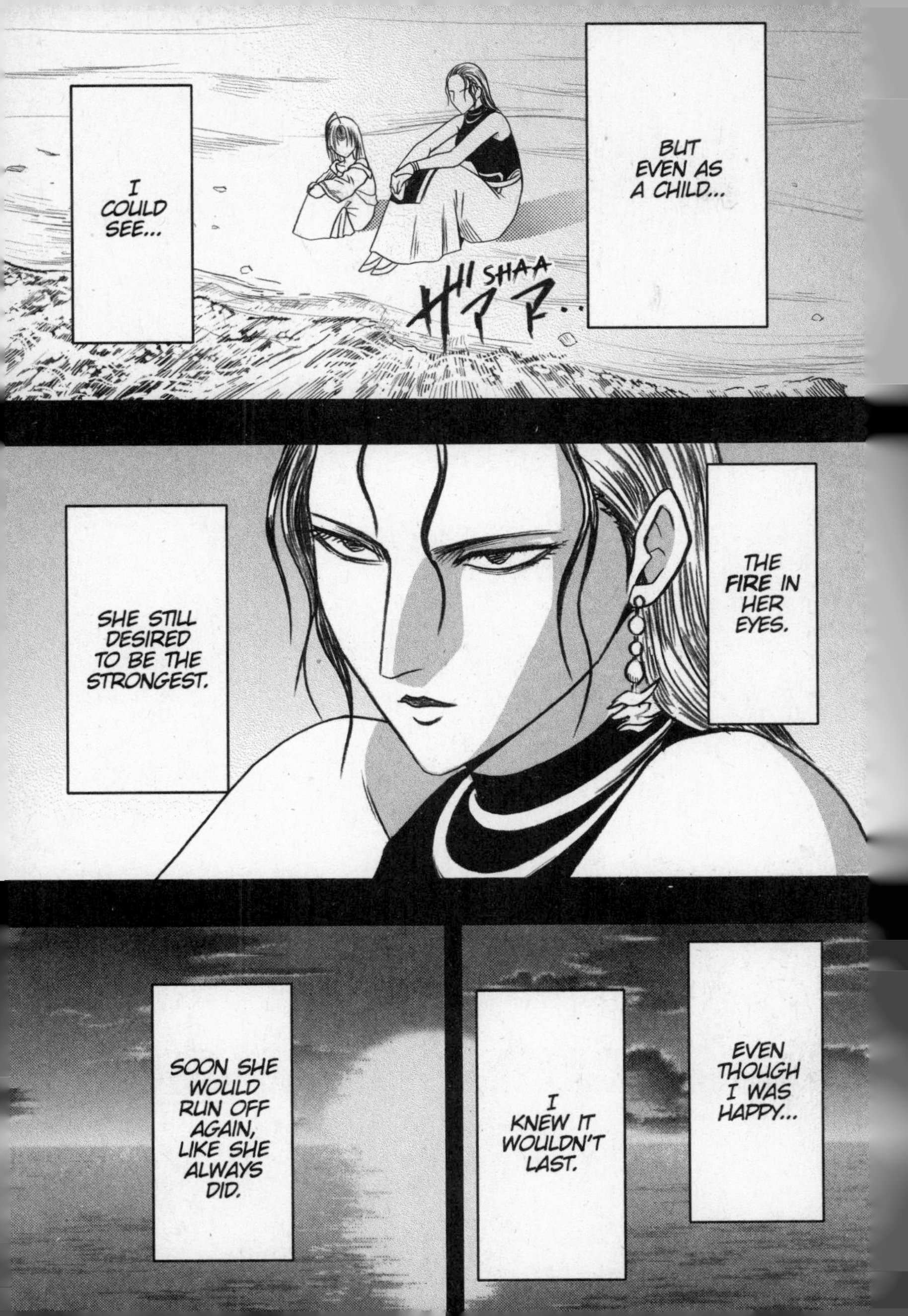

BUT EVEN AS A CHILD...
I COULD SEE...
SHAA
ザアア...
THE FIRE IN HER EYES.
SHE STILL DESIRED TO BE THE STRONGEST.
EVEN THOUGH I WAS HAPPY...
I KNEW IT WOULDN'T LAST.
SOON SHE WOULD RUN OFF AGAIN, LIKE SHE ALWAYS DID.

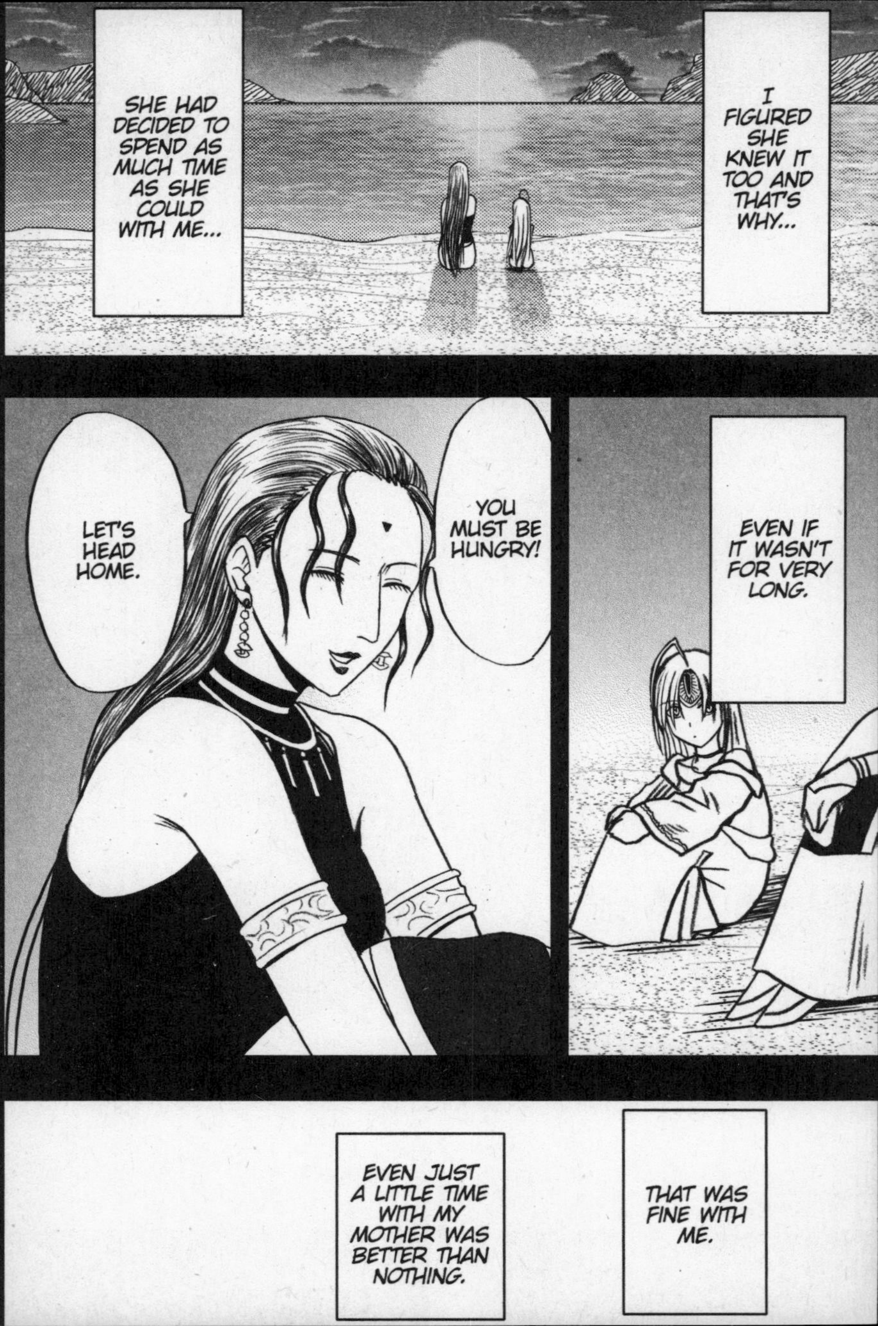
I FIGURED SHE KNEW IT TOO AND THAT'S WHY...
SHE HAD DECIDED TO SPEND AS MUCH TIME AS SHE COULD WITH ME...
EVEN IF IT WASN'T FOR VERY LONG.
YOU MUST BE HUNGRY!
LET'S HEAD HOME.
THAT WAS FINE WITH ME.
EVEN JUST A LITTLE TIME WITH MY MOTHER WAS BETTER THAN NOTHING.

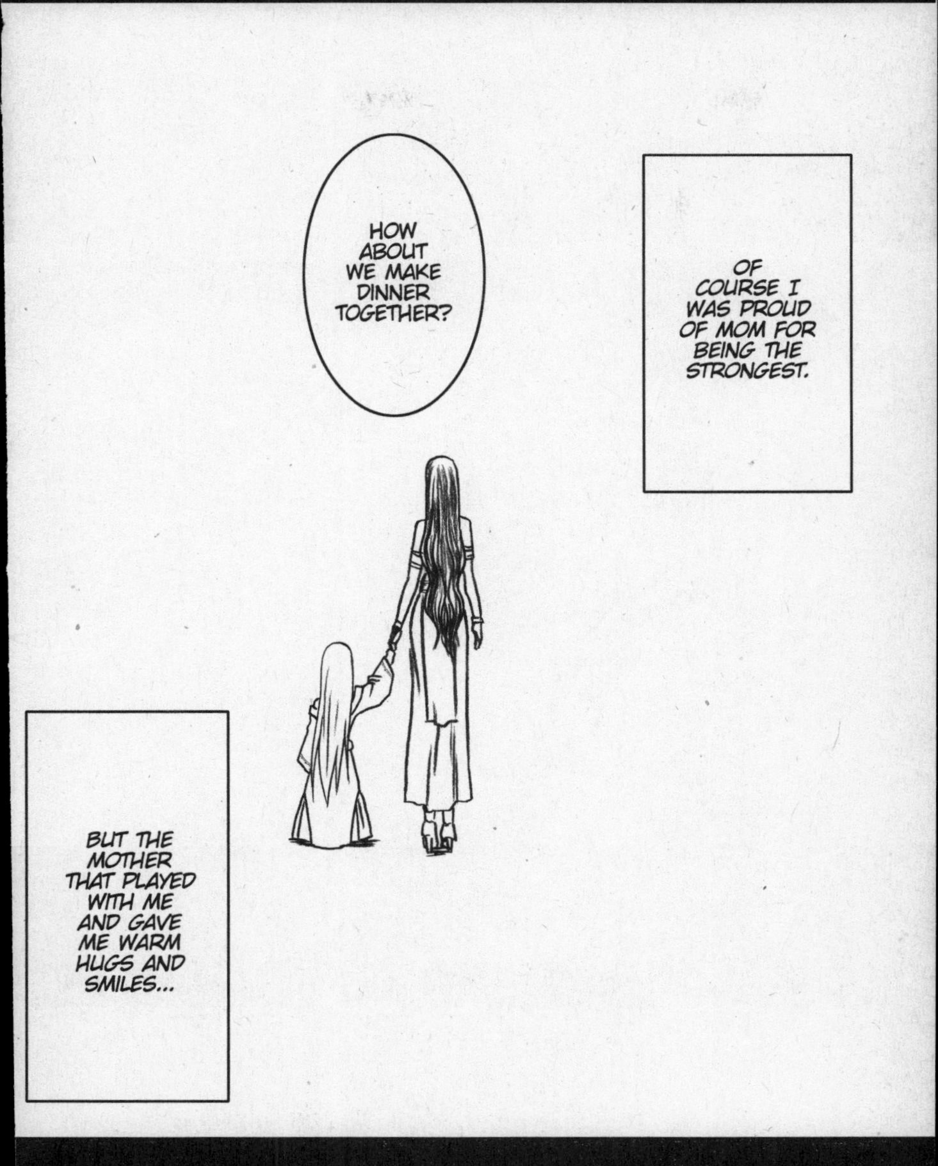
OF COURSE I WAS PROUD OF MOM FOR BEING THE STRONGEST.
HOW ABOUT WE MAKE DINNER TOGETHER?
BUT THE MOTHER THAT PLAYED WITH ME AND GAVE ME WARM HUGS AND SMILES...

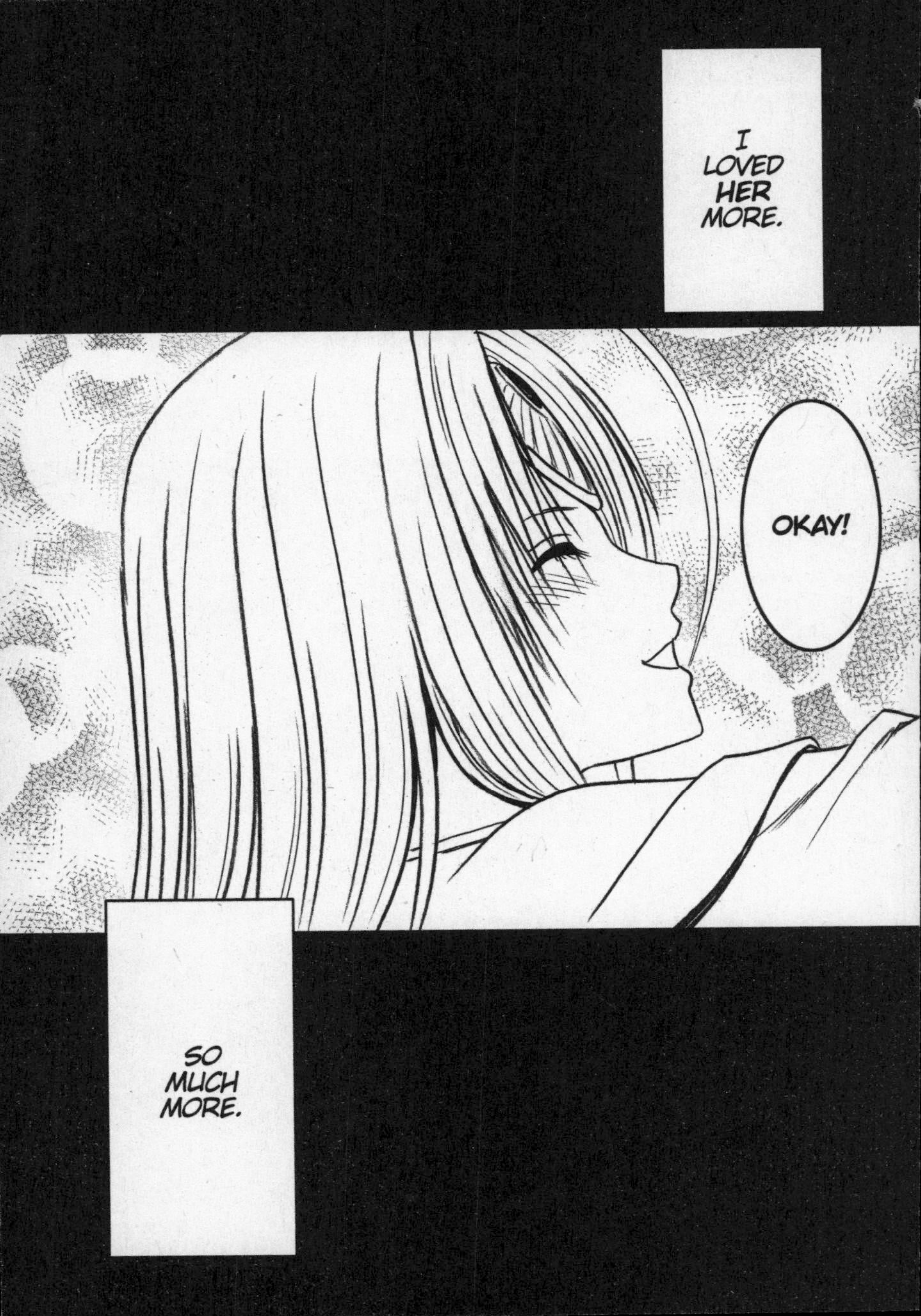
I LOVED HER MORE.
OKAY!
SO MUCH MORE.

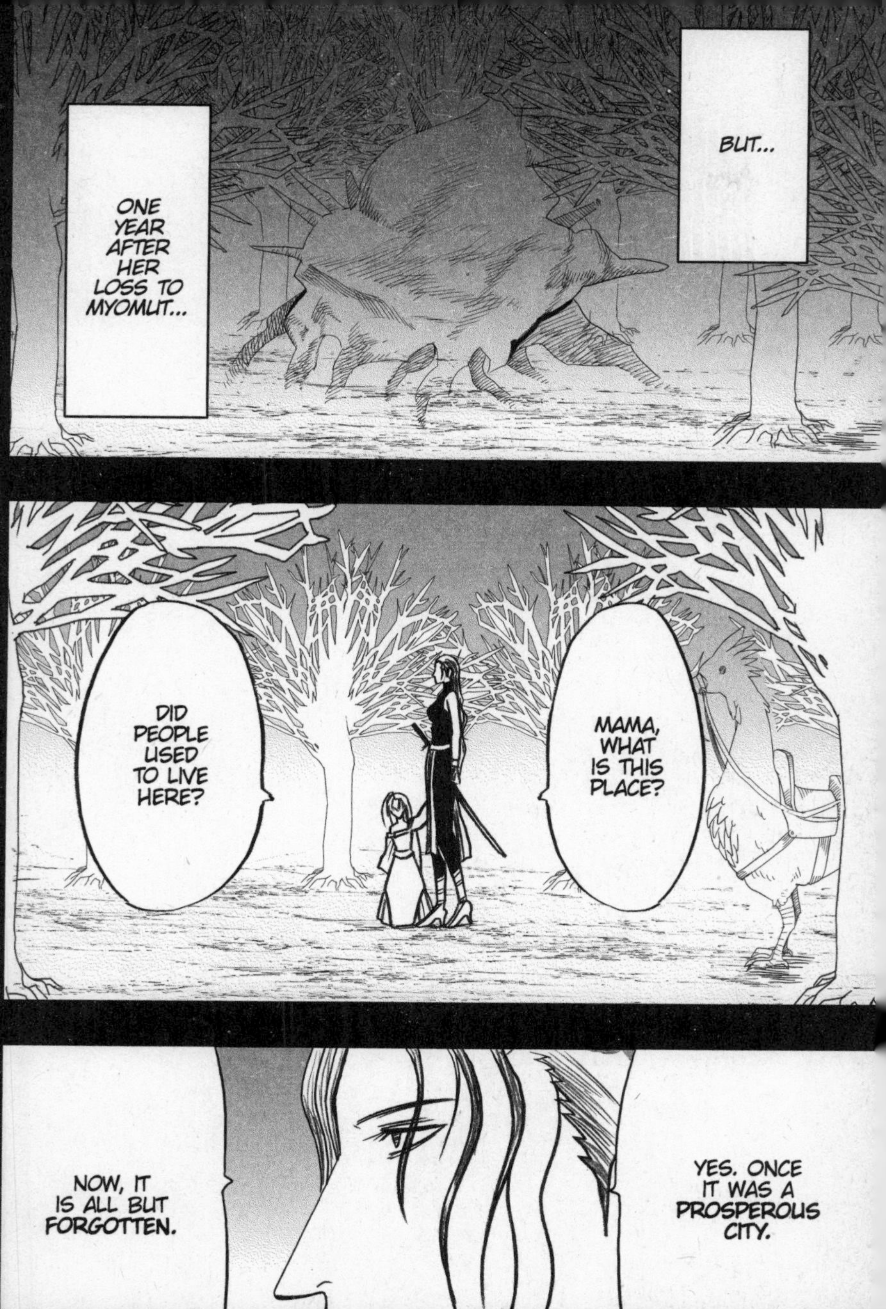
BUT...
ONE YEAR AFTER HER LOSS TO MYOMUT...
MAMA, WHAT IS THIS PLACE?
DID PEOPLE USED TO LIVE HERE?
YES. ONCE IT WAS A PROSPEROUS CITY.
NOW, IT IS ALL BUT FORGOTTEN.

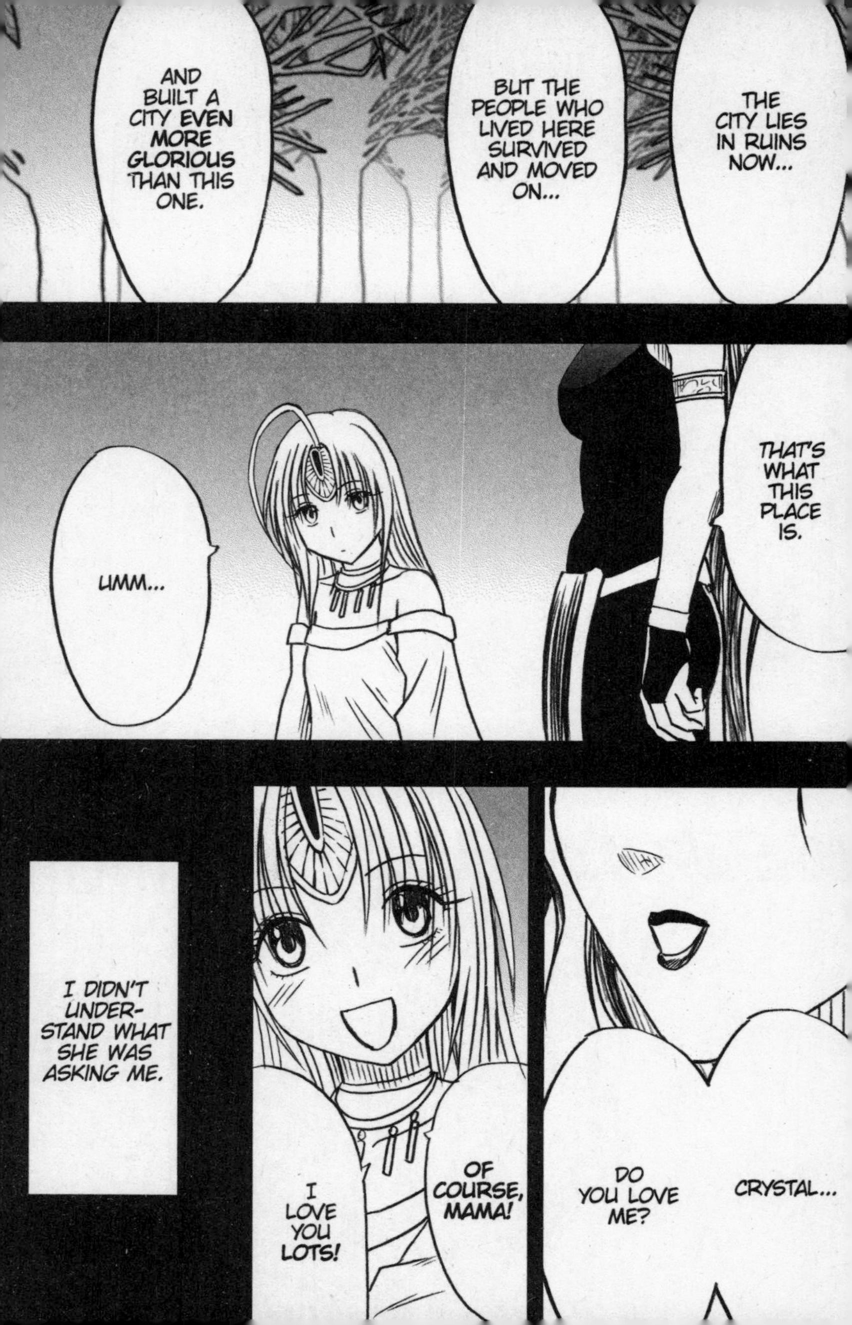
THE CITY LIES IN RUINS NOW...
BUT THE PEOPLE WHO LIVED HERE SURVIVED AND MOVED ON...
AND BUILT A CITY EVEN MORE GLORIOUS THAN THIS ONE.
THAT'S WHAT THIS PLACE IS.
UMM...
CRYSTAL...
DO YOU LOVE ME?
OF COURSE, MAMA!
I LOVE YOU LOTS!
I DIDN'T UNDER-STAND WHAT SHE WAS ASKING ME.

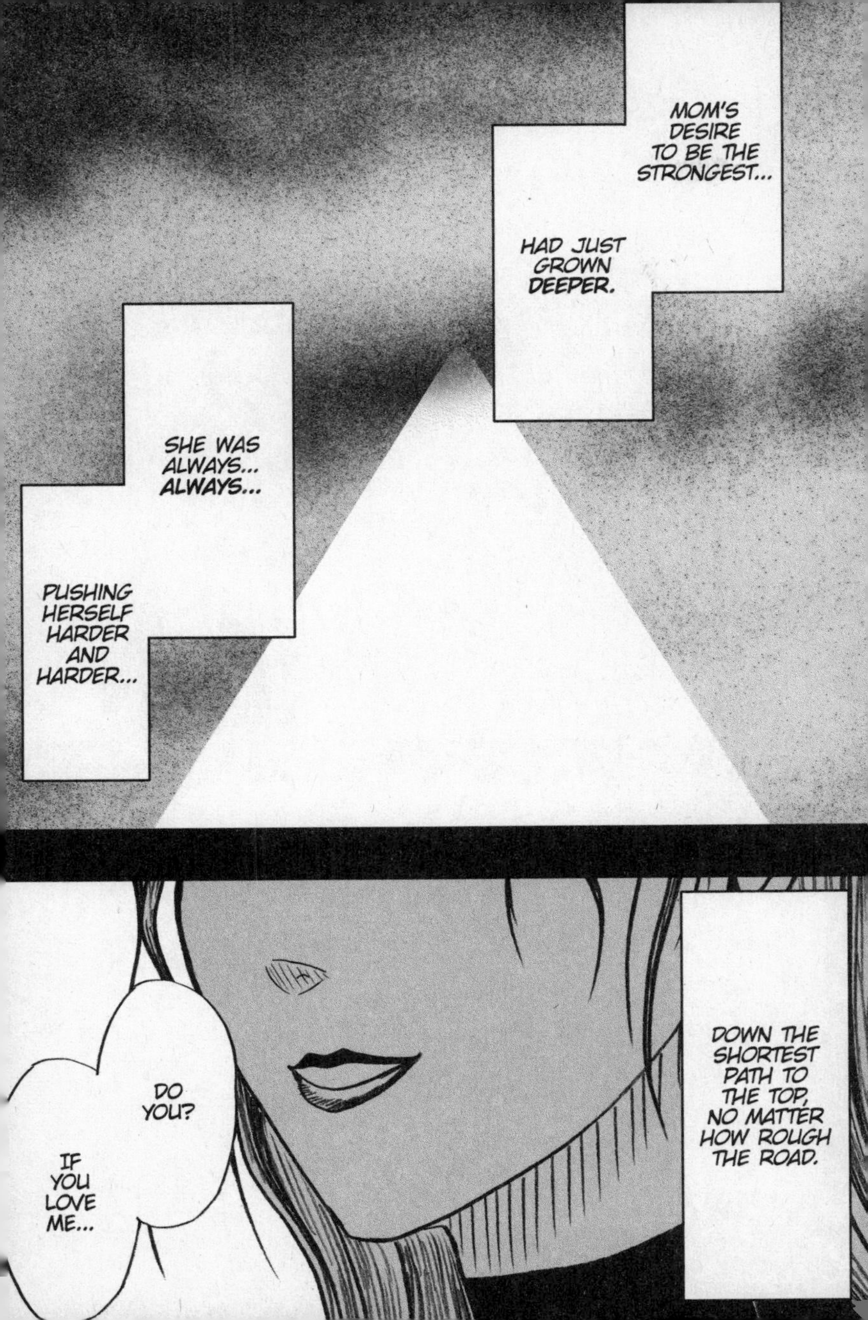
MOM'S DESIRE TO BE THE STRONGEST...
HAD JUST GROWN DEEPER.
SHE WAS ALWAYS... ALWAYS...
PUSHING HERSELF HARDER AND HARDER...
DOWN THE SHORTEST PATH TO THE TOP, NO MATTER HOW ROUGH THE ROAD.
DO YOU?
IF YOU LOVE ME...

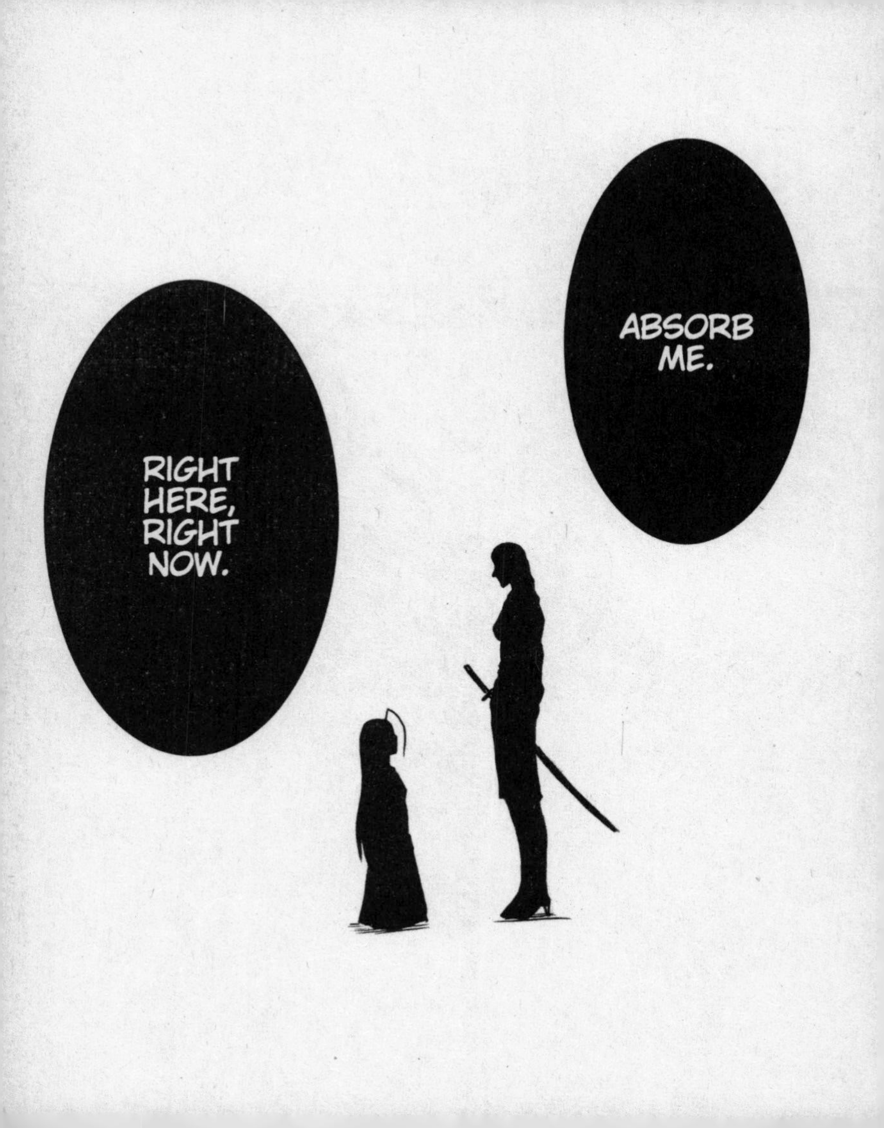
ABSORB ME.
RIGHT HERE, RIGHT NOW.

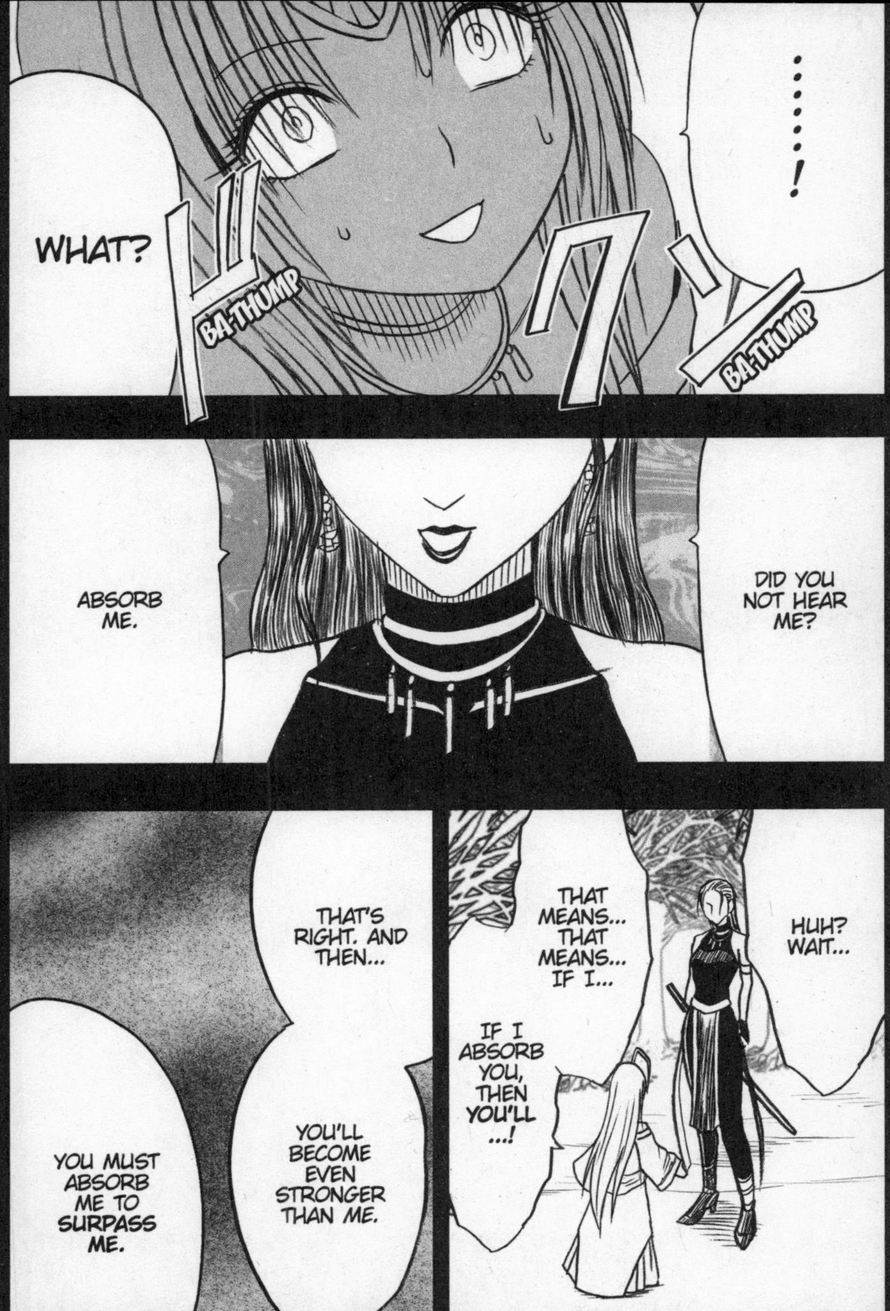
....!
BA-THUMP
WHAT?
BA-THUMP
DID YOU NOT HEAR ME?
ABSORB ME.
HUH? WAIT...
THAT MEANS... THAT MEANS... IF I...
IF I ABSORB YOU, THEN YOU'LL ...!
THAT'S RIGHT. AND THEN...
YOU'LL BECOME EVEN STRONGER THAN ME.
YOU MUST ABSORB ME TO SURPASS ME.

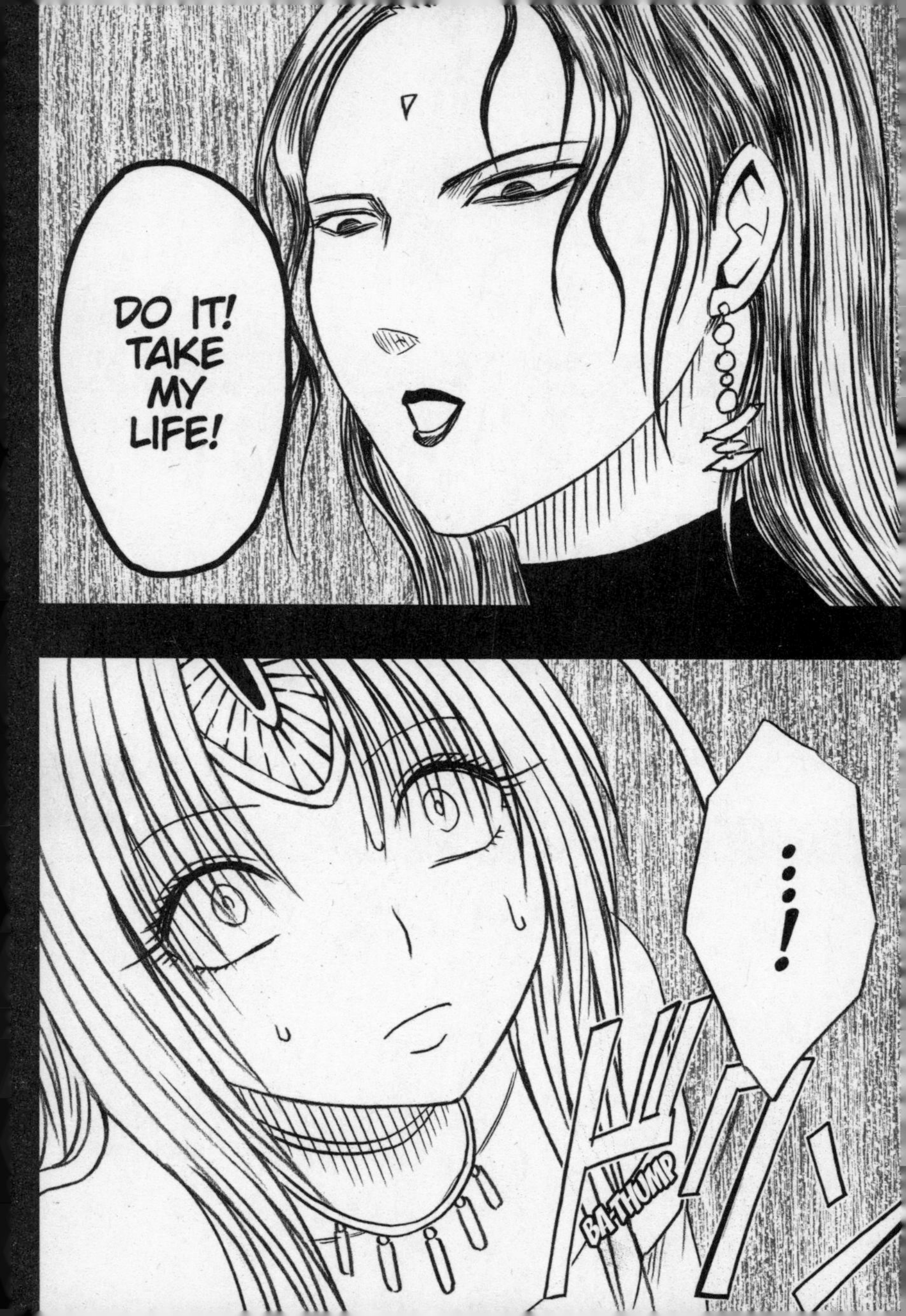
DO IT! TAKE MY LIFE!
...!
BA-THUMP

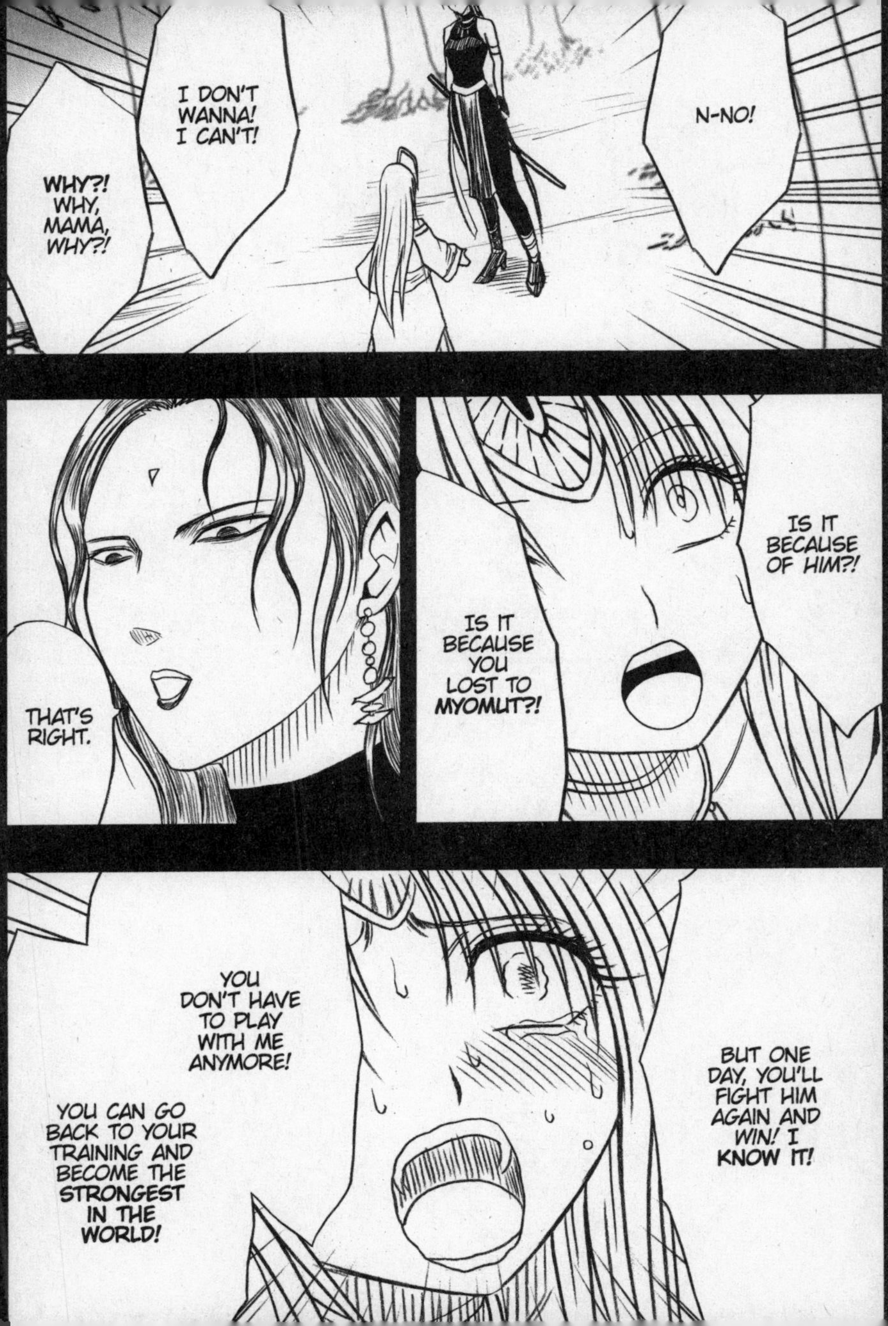
N-NO!
I DON'T WANNA! I CAN'T!
WHY?! WHY, MAMA, WHY?!
IS IT BECAUSE OF HIM?!
IS IT BECAUSE YOU LOST TO MYOMUT?!
THAT'S RIGHT.
BUT ONE DAY, YOU'LL FIGHT HIM AGAIN AND WIN! I KNOW IT!
YOU DON'T HAVE TO PLAY WITH ME ANYMORE!
YOU CAN GO BACK TO YOUR TRAINING AND BECOME THE STRONGEST IN THE WORLD!

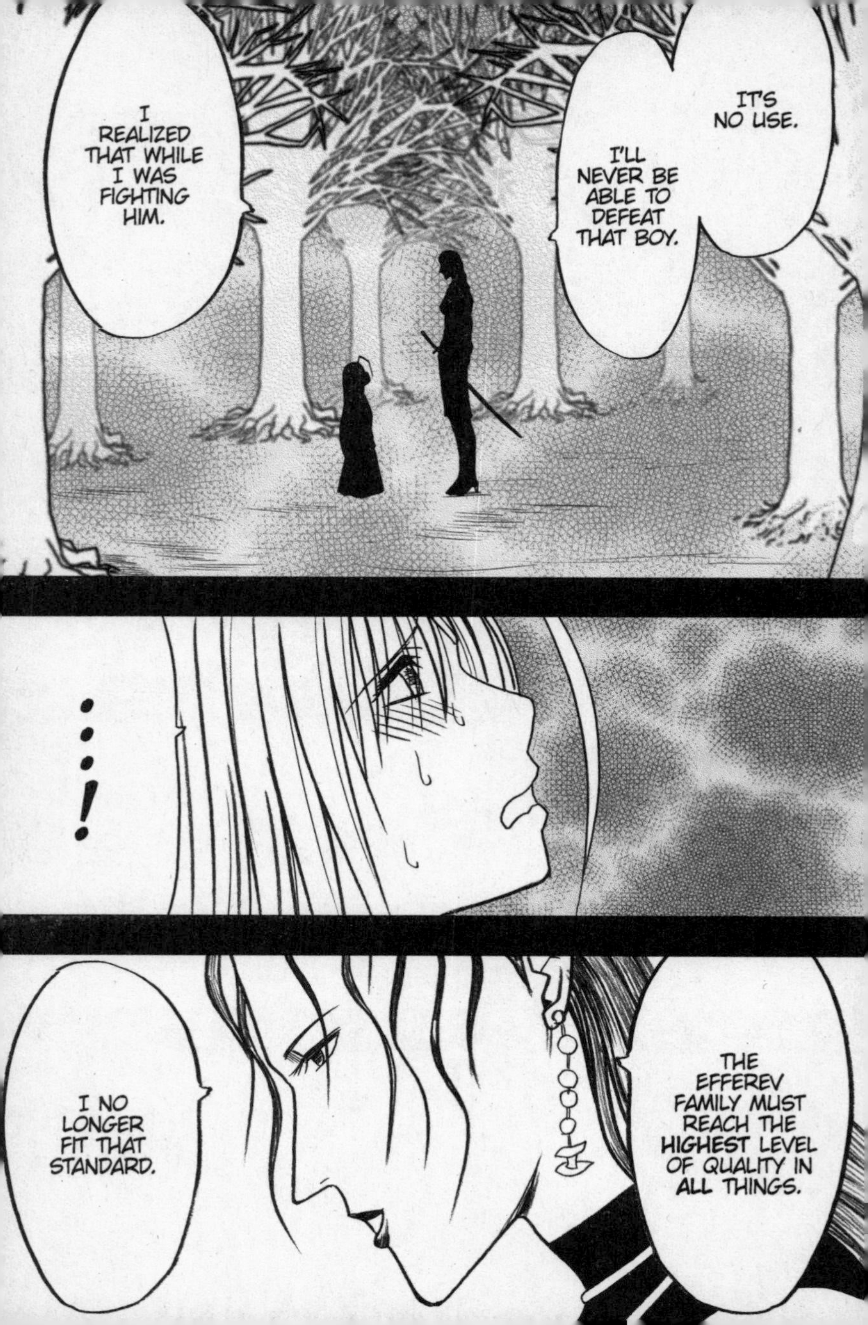
IT'S NO USE.
I'LL NEVER BE ABLE TO DEFEAT THAT BOY.
I REALIZED THAT WHILE I WAS FIGHTING HIM.
...!
THE EFFEREV FAMILY MUST REACH THE HIGHEST LEVEL OF QUALITY IN ALL THINGS.
I NO LONGER FIT THAT STANDARD.

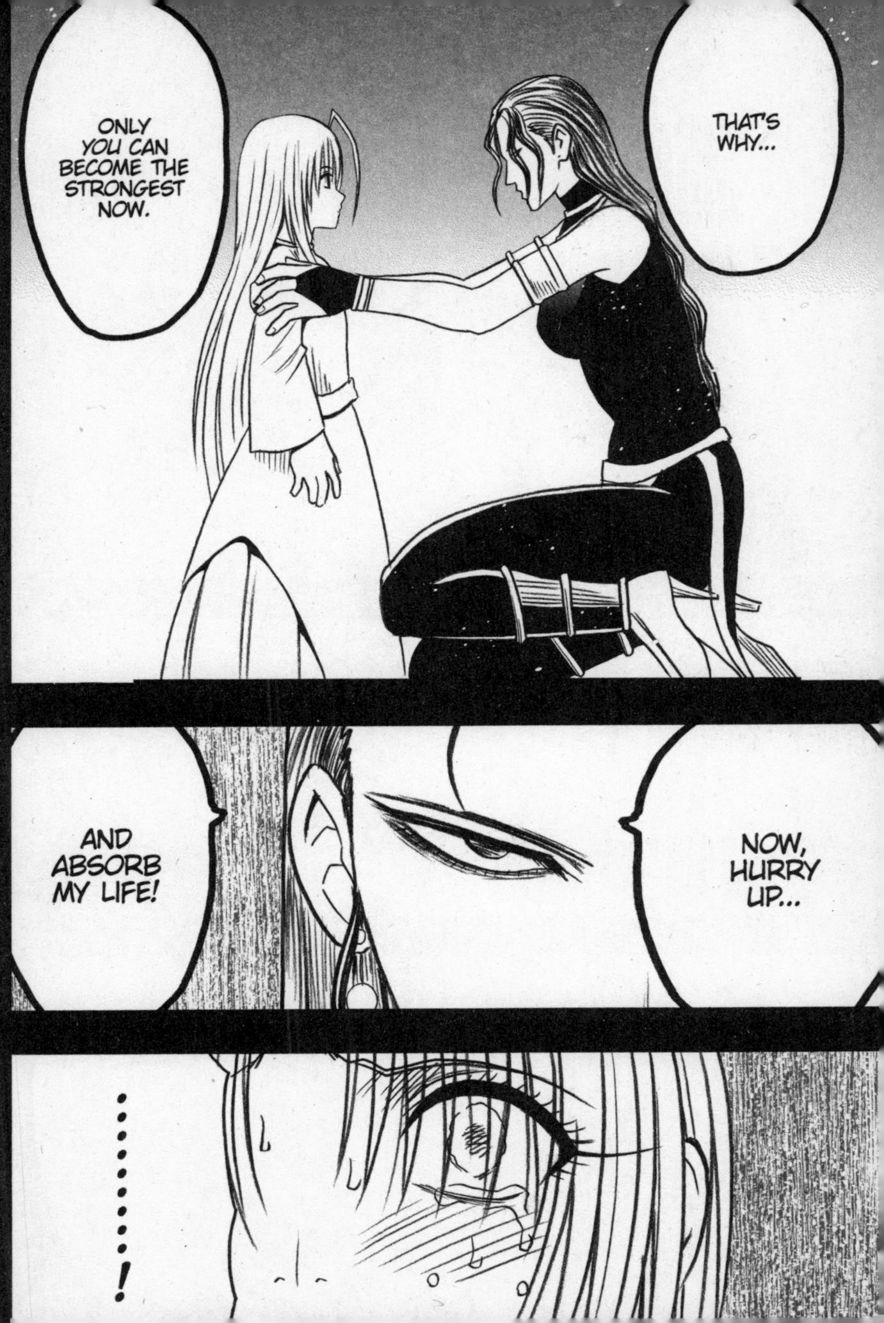
THAT'S WHY...
ONLY YOU CAN BECOME THE STRONGEST NOW.
NOW, HURRY UP...
AND ABSORB MY LIFE!
...........!

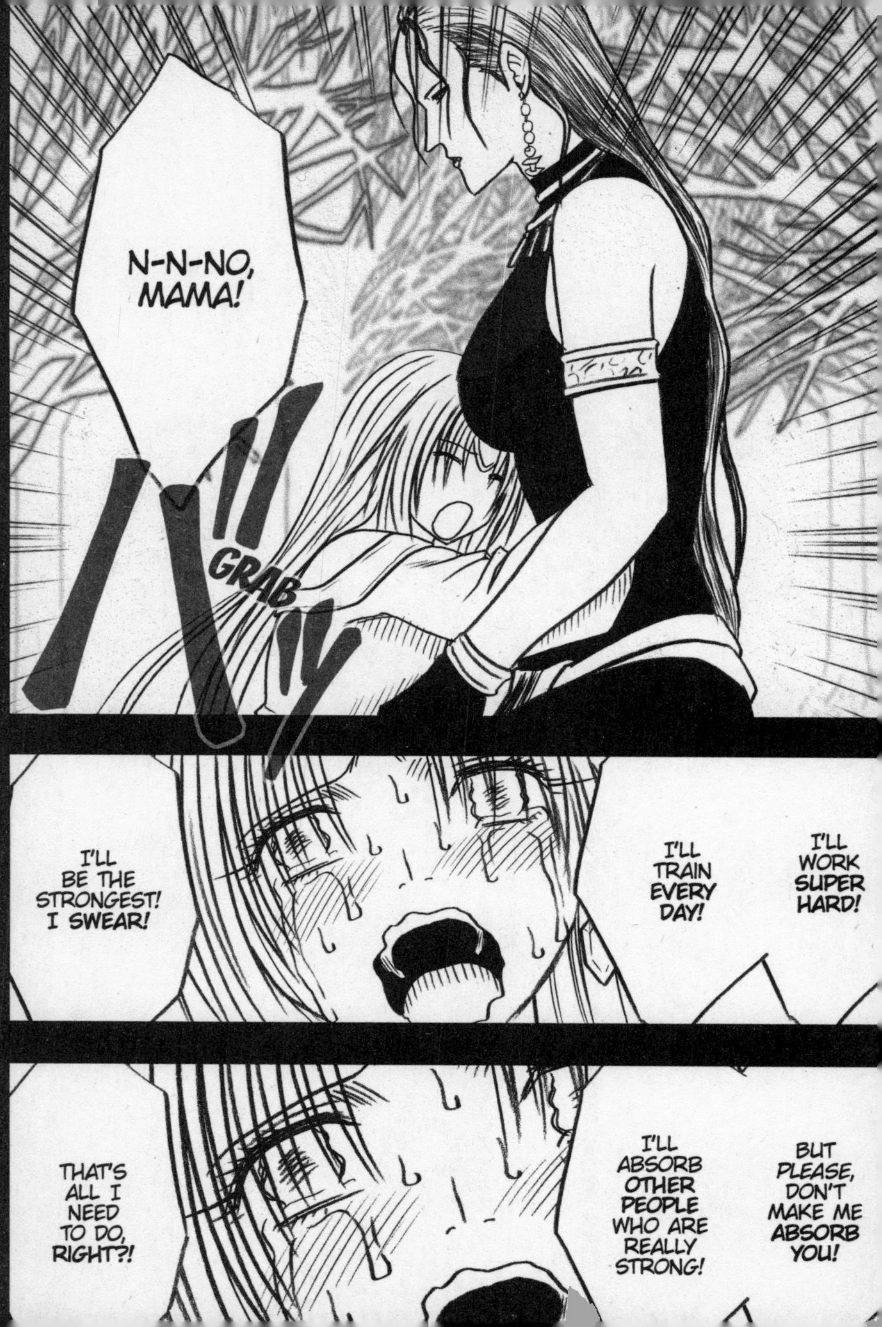
N-N-NO, MAMA!
GRAB
I'LL WORK SUPER HARD!
I'LL TRAIN EVERY DAY!
I'LL BE THE STRONGEST! I SWEAR!
BUT PLEASE, DON'T MAKE ME ABSORB YOU!
I'LL ABSORB OTHER PEOPLE WHO ARE REALLY STRONG!
THAT'S ALL I NEED TO DO, RIGHT?!

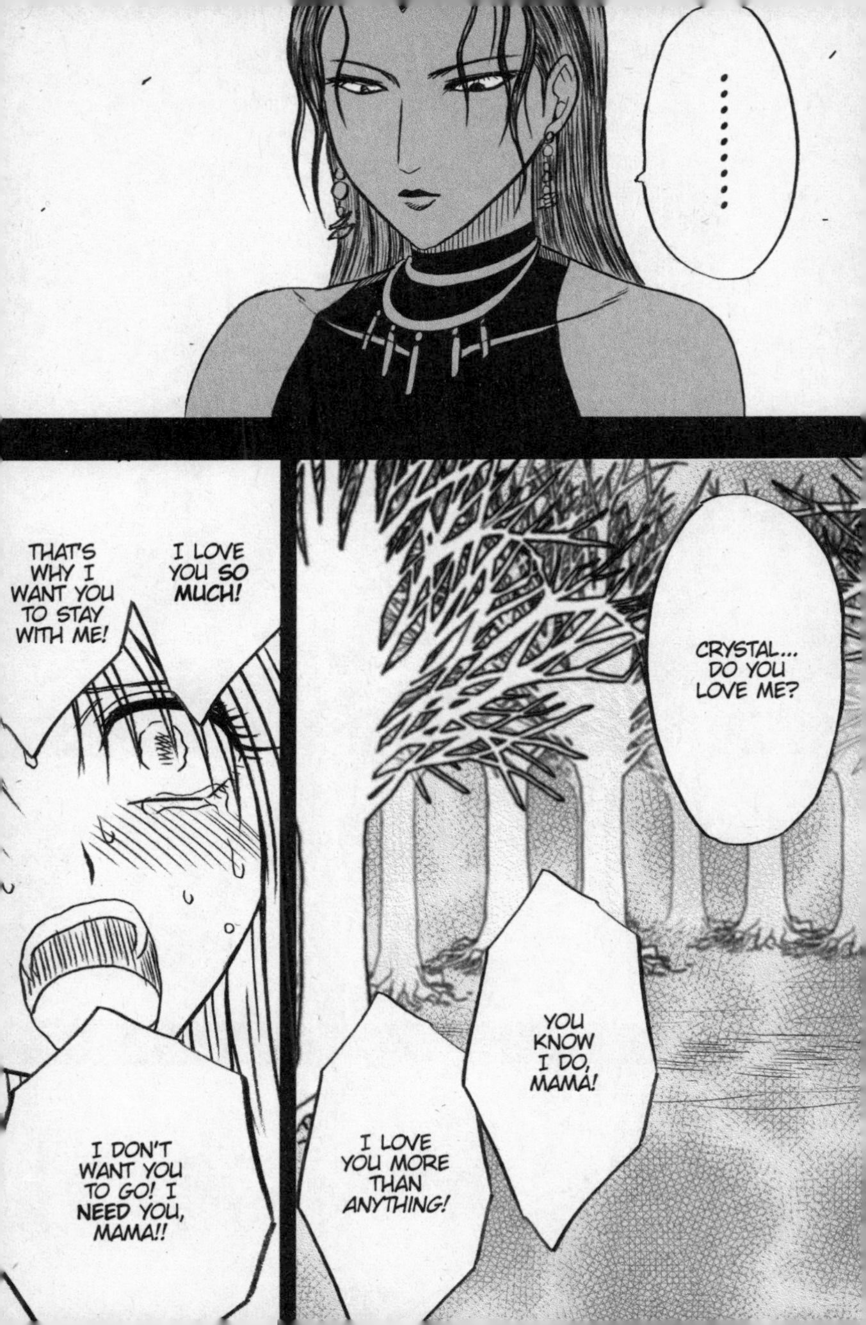
....
CRYSTAL... DO YOU LOVE ME?
YOU KNOW I DO, MAMA!
I LOVE YOU MORE THAN ANYTHING!
I LOVE YOU SO MUCH!
THAT'S WHY I WANT YOU TO STAY WITH ME!
I DON'T WANT YOU TO GO! I NEED YOU, MAMA!!

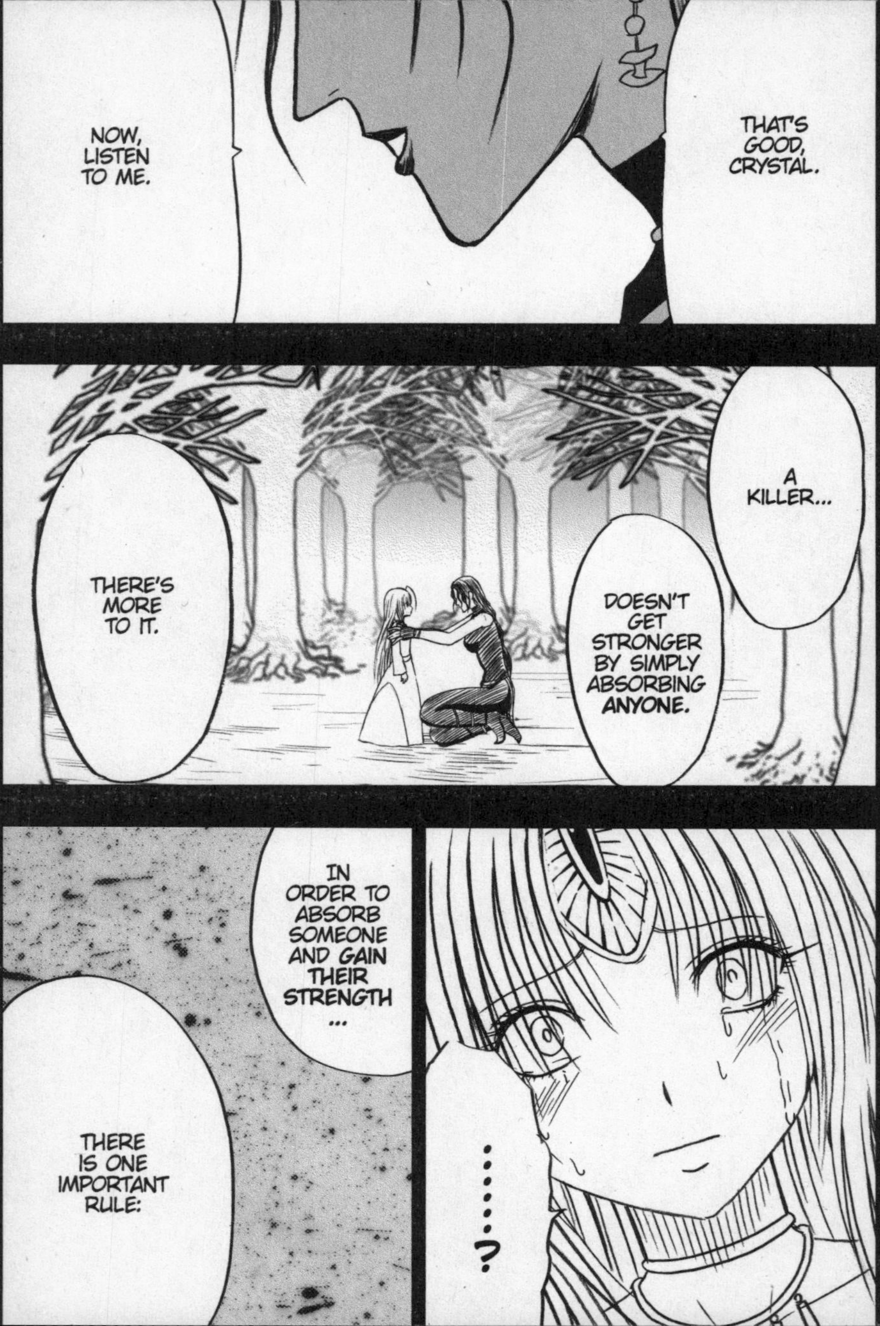
THAT'S GOOD, CRYSTAL.
NOW, LISTEN TO ME.
A KILLER...
DOESN'T GET STRONGER BY SIMPLY ABSORBING ANYONE.
THERE'S MORE TO IT.
......?
IN ORDER TO ABSORB SOMEONE AND GAIN THEIR STRENGTH...
THERE IS ONE IMPORTANT RULE:

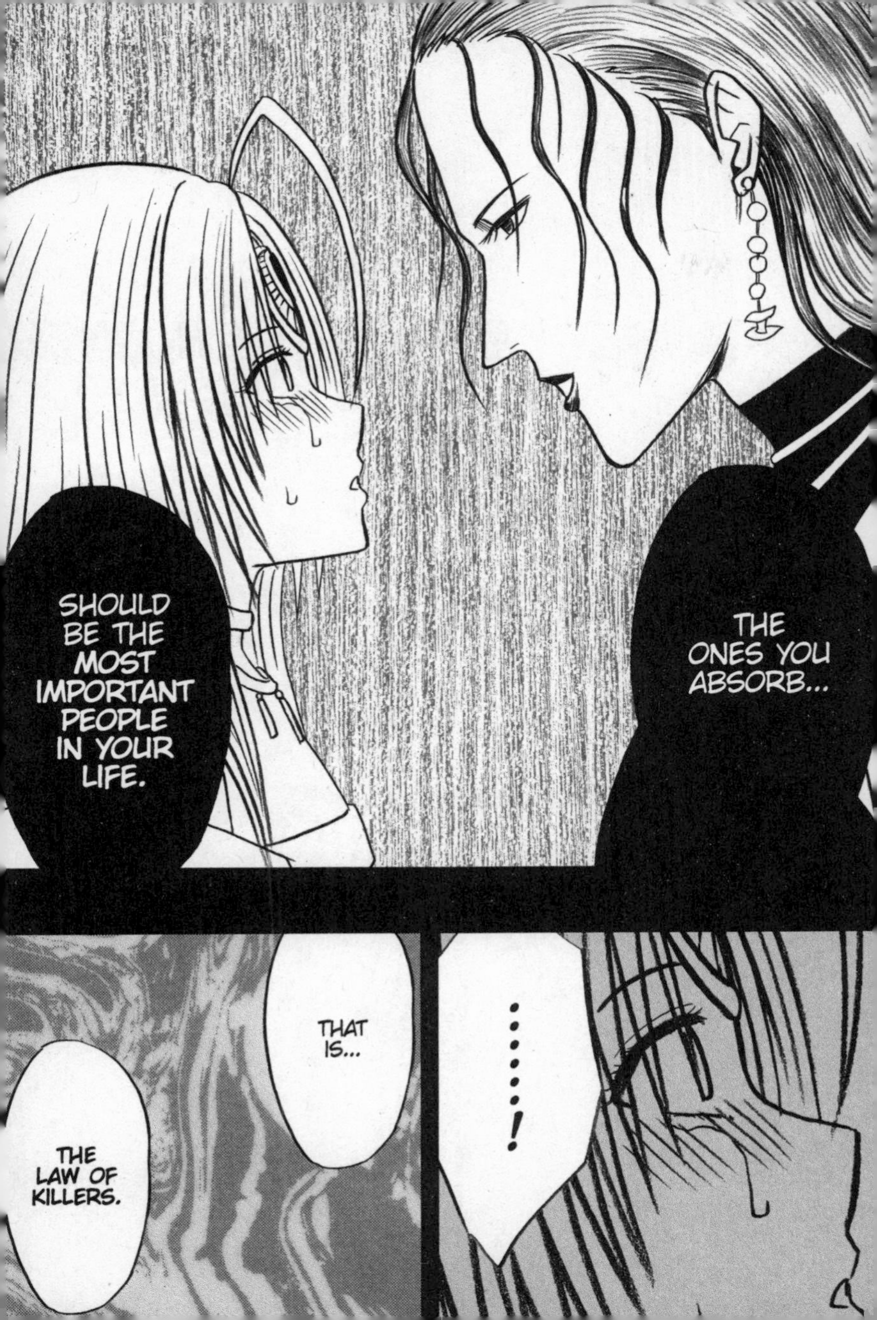
THE ONES YOU ABSORB...
SHOULD BE THE MOST IMPORTANT PEOPLE IN YOUR LIFE.
......!
THAT IS...
THE LAW OF KILLERS.

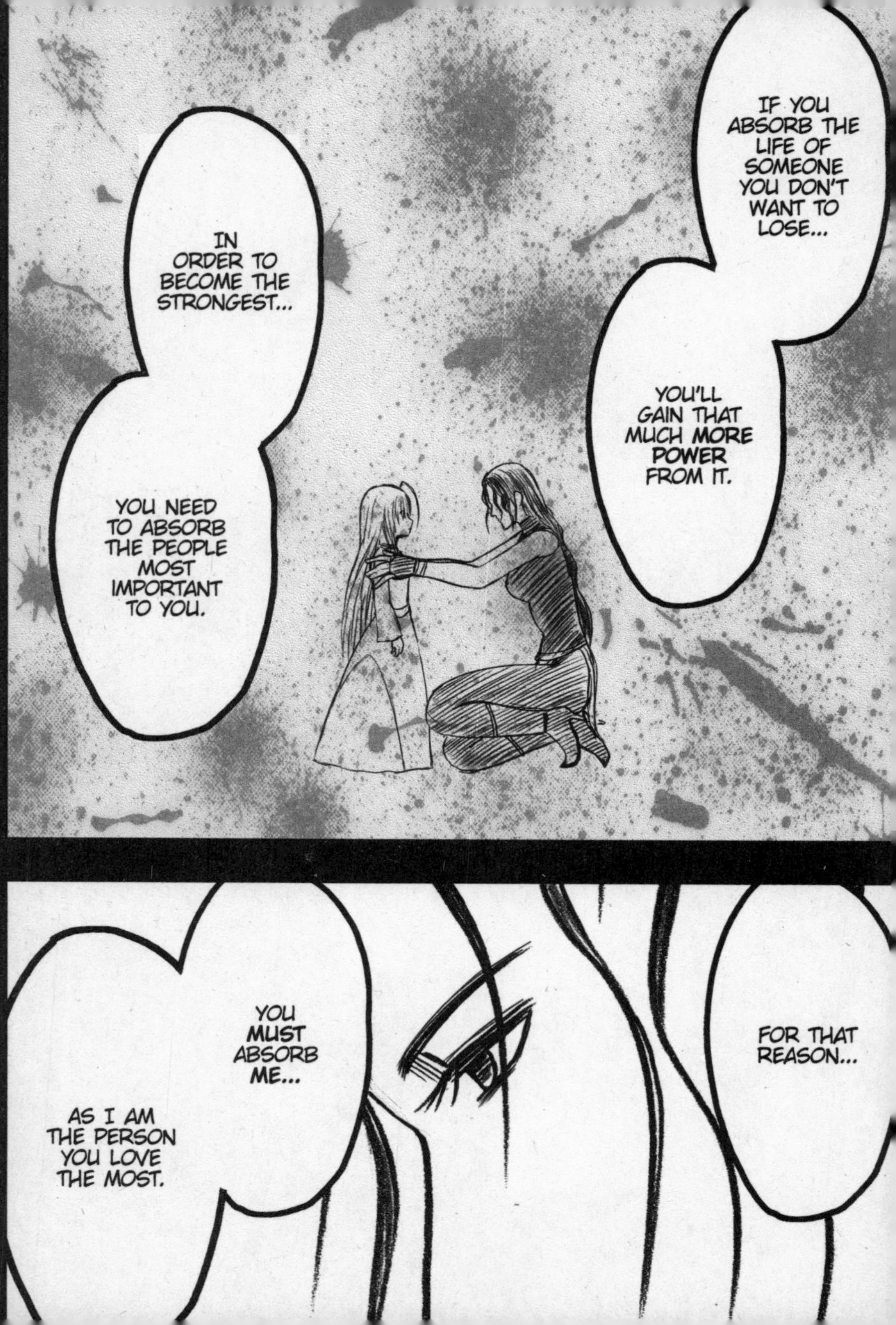
IF YOU ABSORB THE LIFE OF SOMEONE YOU DON'T WANT TO LOSE...
YOU'LL GAIN THAT MUCH MORE POWER FROM IT.
IN ORDER TO BECOME THE STRONGEST...
YOU NEED TO ABSORB THE PEOPLE MOST IMPORTANT TO YOU.
FOR THAT REASON...
YOU MUST ABSORB ME...
AS I AM THE PERSON YOU LOVE THE MOST.

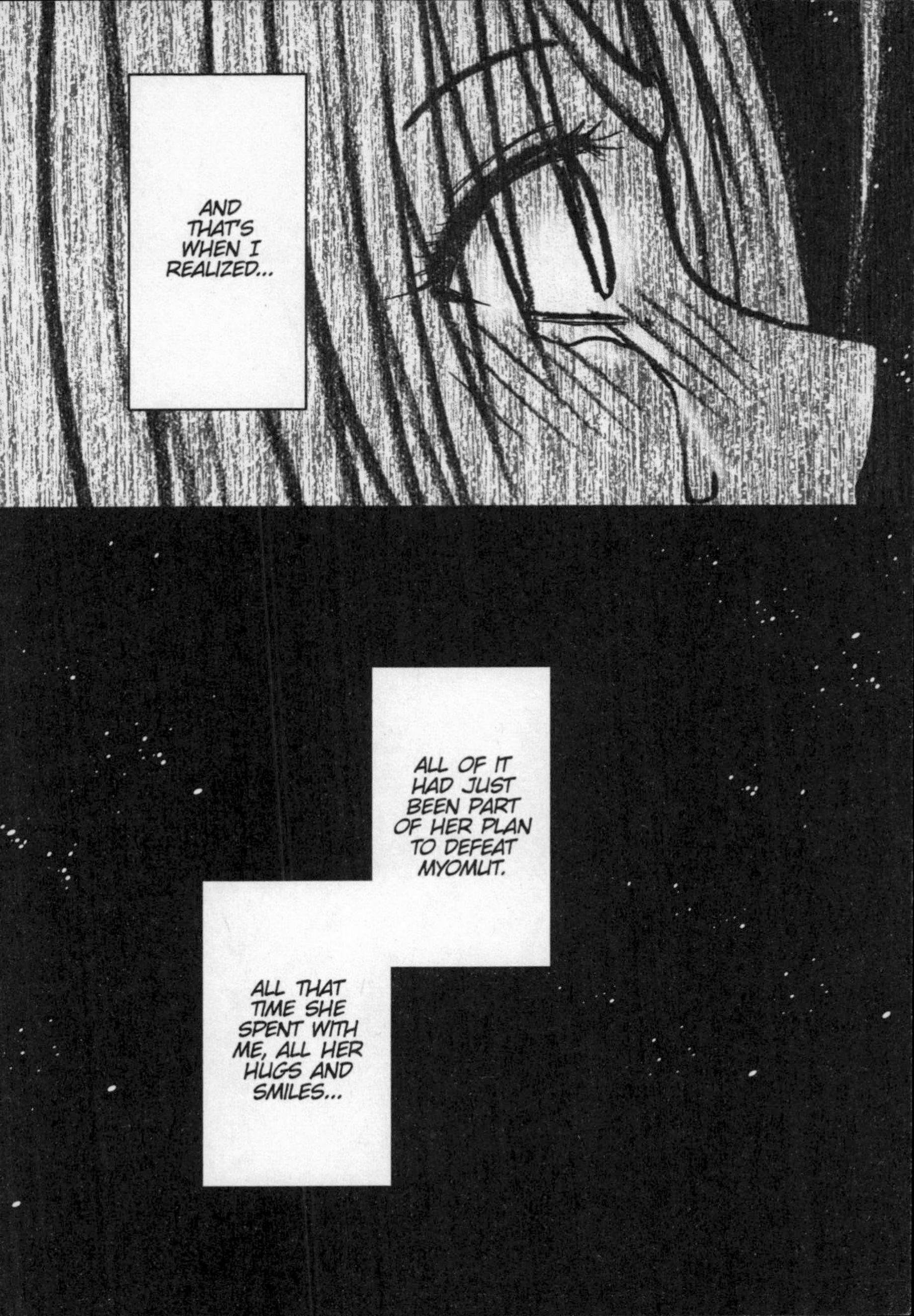
AND THAT'S WHEN I REALIZED...
ALL OF IT HAD JUST BEEN PART OF HER PLAN TO DEFEAT MYOMUT.
ALL THAT TIME SHE SPENT WITH ME, ALL HER HUGS AND SMILES...

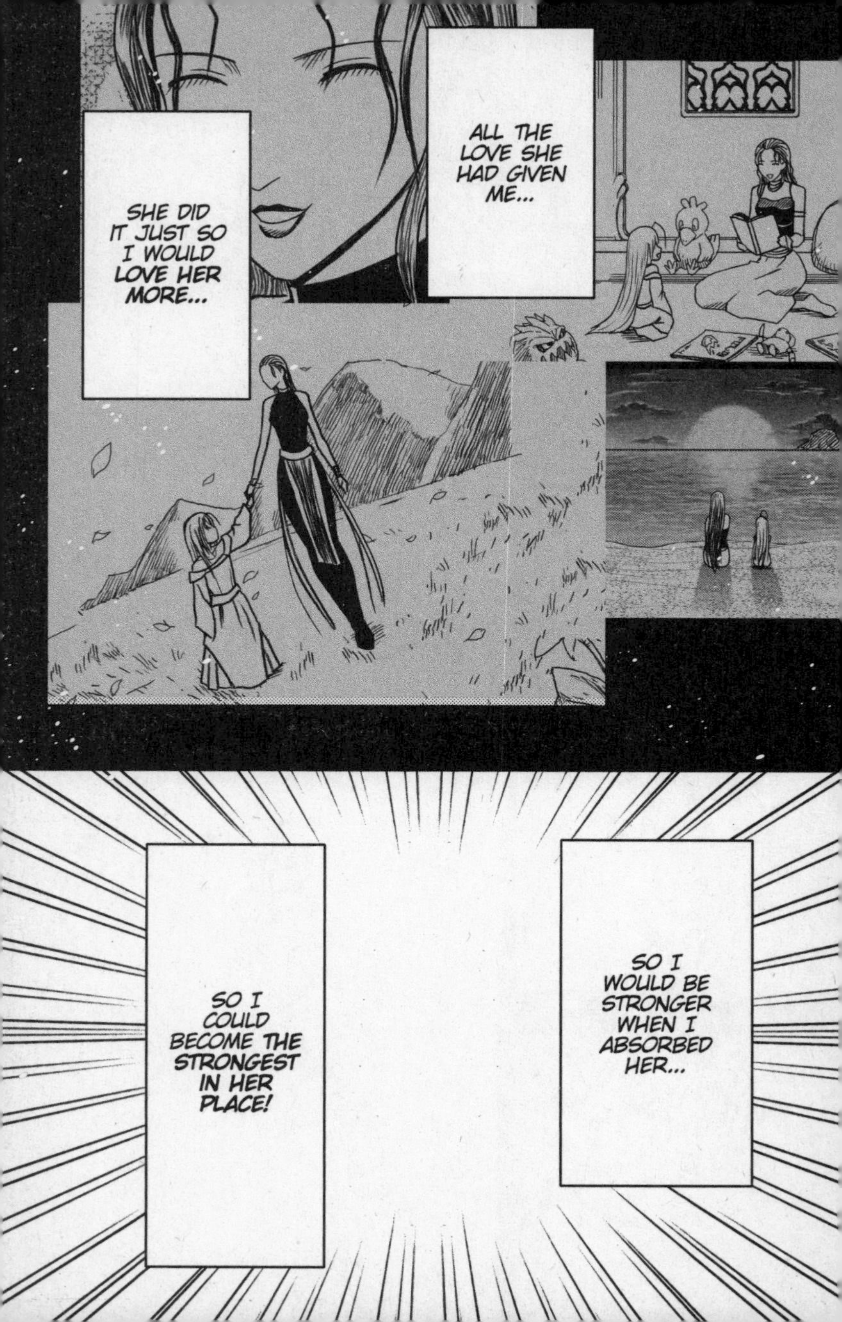
ALL THE LOVE SHE HAD GIVEN ME...
SHE DID IT JUST SO I WOULD LOVE HER MORE...
SO I WOULD BE STRONGER WHEN I ABSORBED HER...
SO I COULD BECOME THE STRONGEST IN HER PLACE!

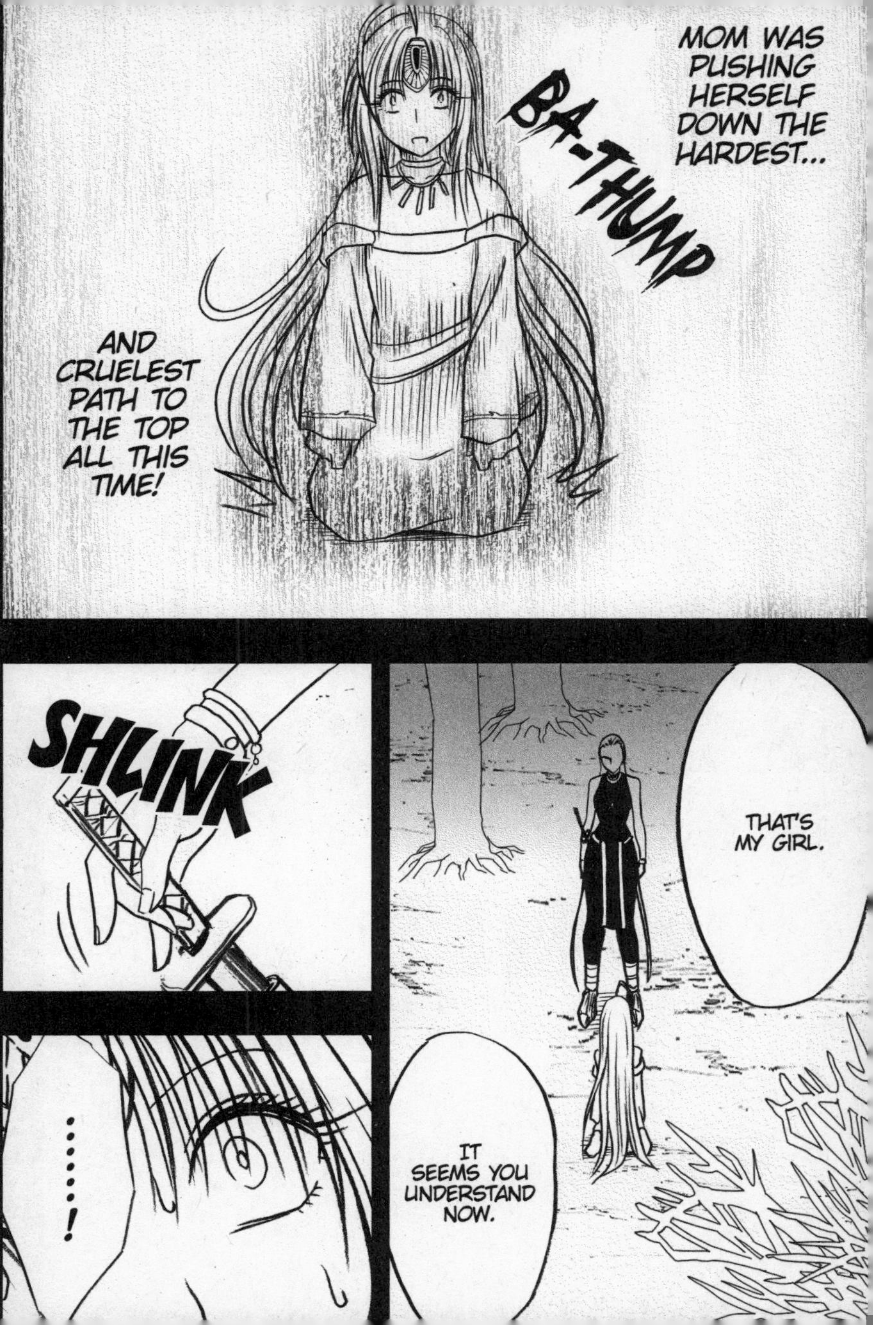
MOM WAS PUSHING HERSELF DOWN THE HARDEST...
BA-THUMP
AND CRUELEST PATH TO THE TOP ALL THIS TIME!
THAT'S MY GIRL.
IT SEEMS YOU UNDERSTAND NOW.
SHLINK
......!

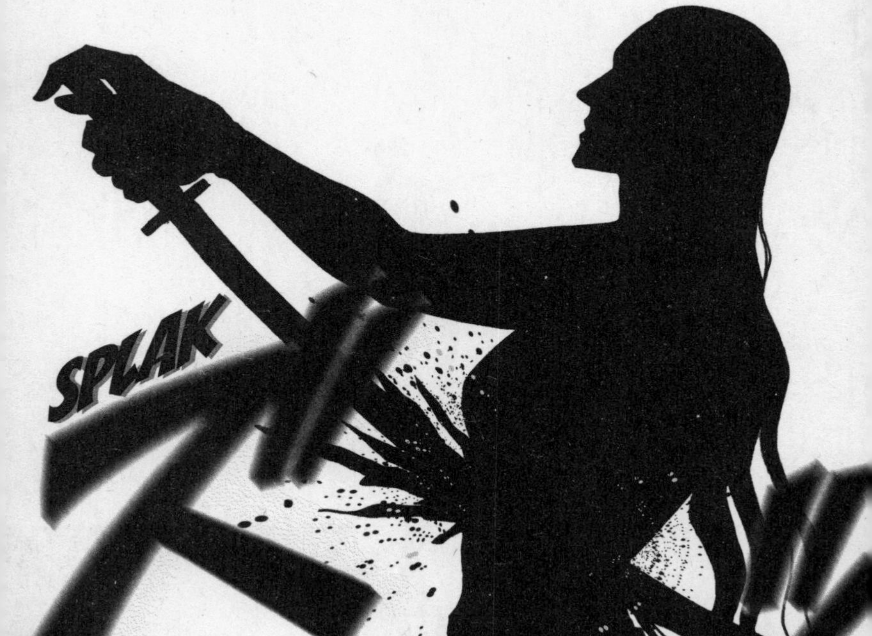
SPLAK
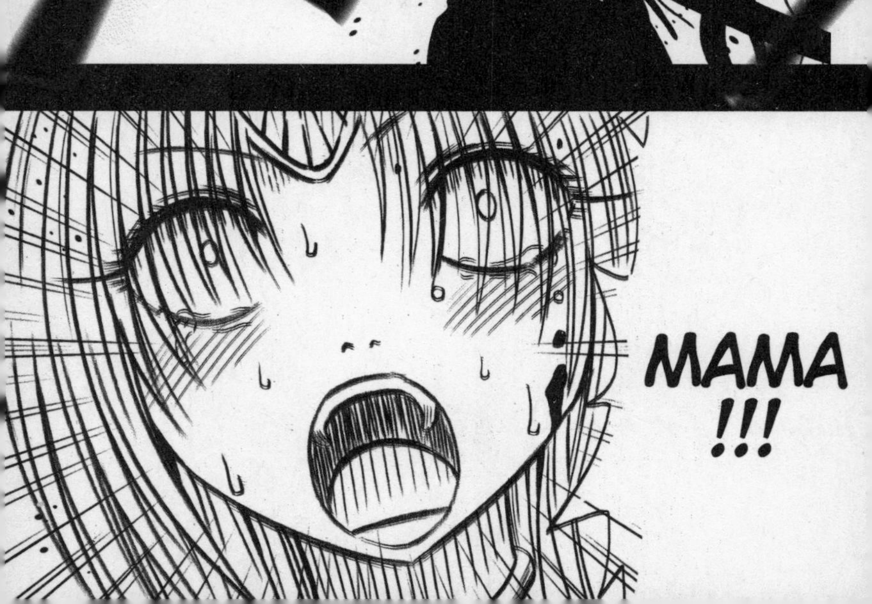
MAMA
!!!

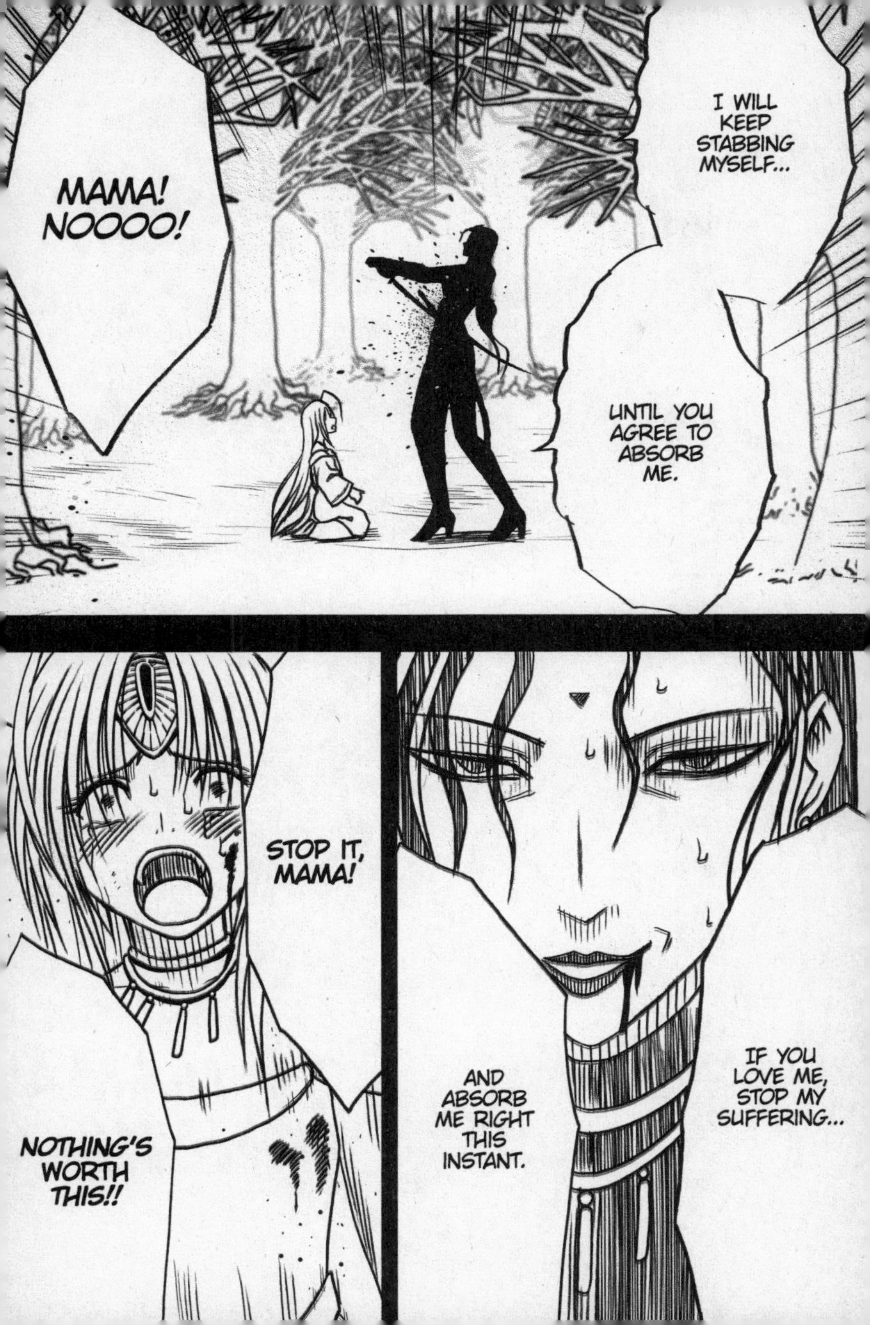
I WILL KEEP STABBING MYSELF...
UNTIL YOU AGREE TO ABSORB ME.
MAMA! NOOOO!
IF YOU LOVE ME, STOP MY SUFFERING...
AND ABSORB ME RIGHT THIS INSTANT.
STOP IT, MAMA!
NOTHING'S WORTH THIS!!

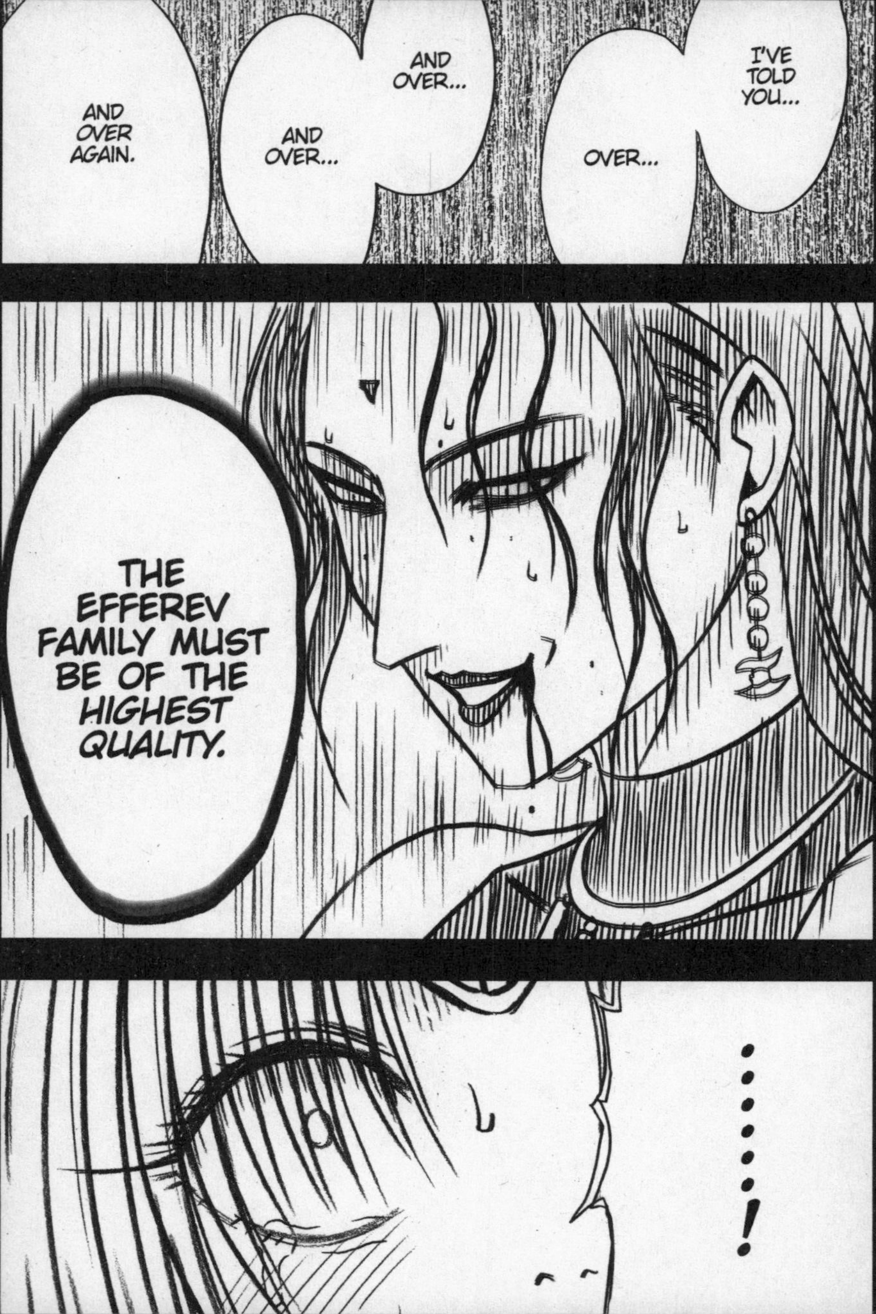
I'VE TOLD YOU...
OVER...
AND OVER...
AND OVER...
AND OVER AGAIN.
THE EFFEREV FAMILY MUST BE OF THE HIGHEST QUALITY.
......!

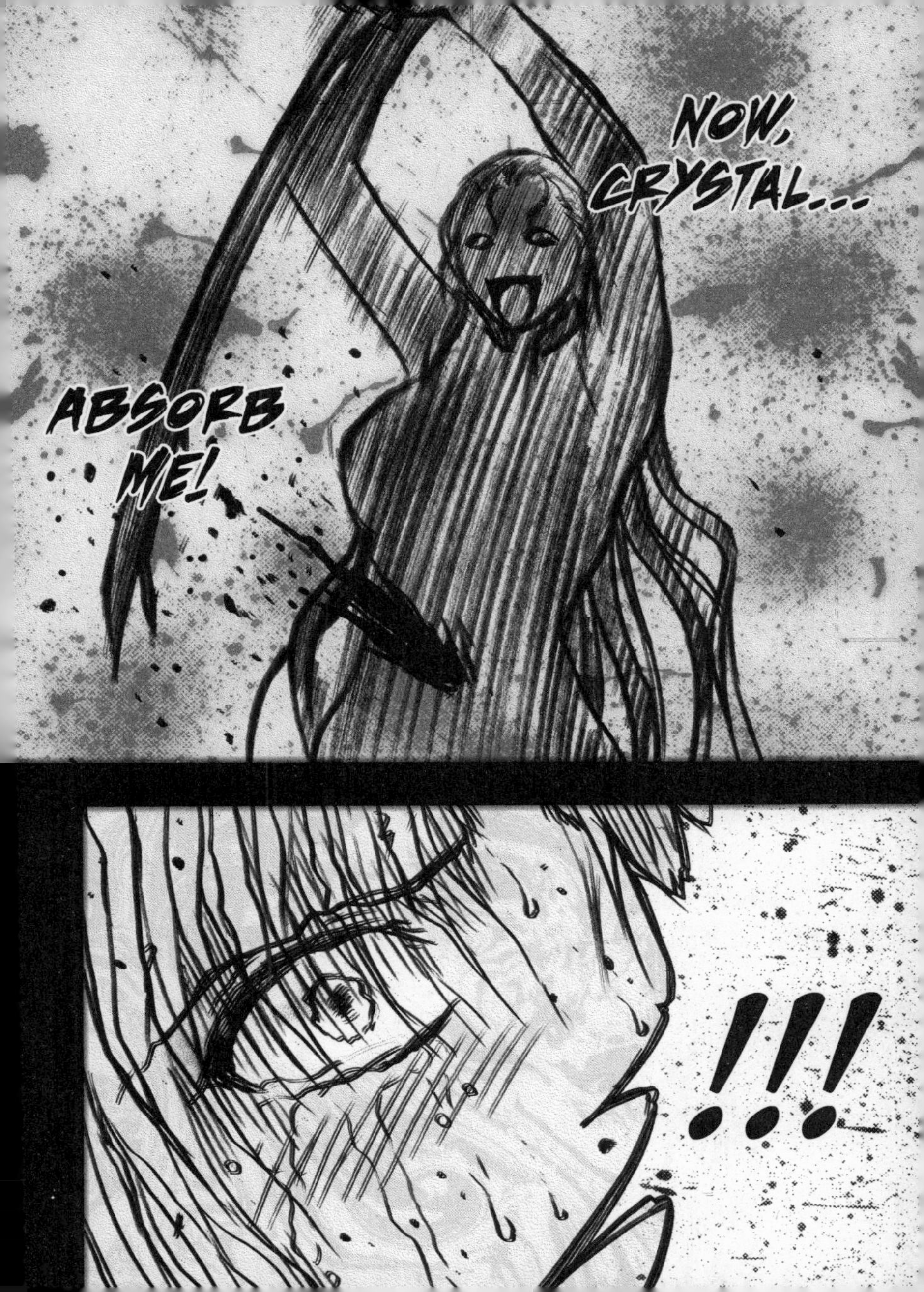
NOW, CRYSTAL...
ABSORB ME!
!!!

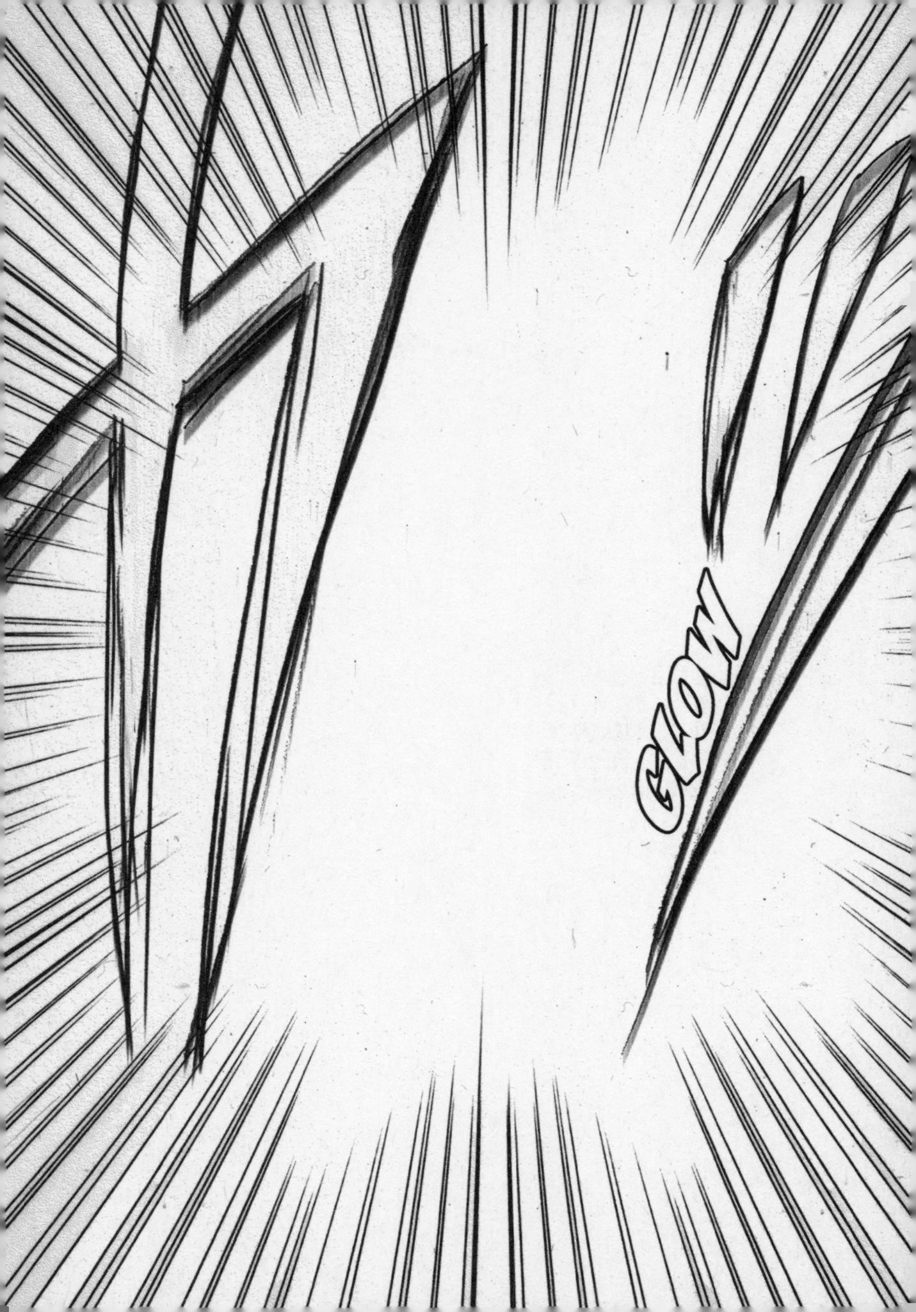
GLOW

FROM THAT
MOMENT
ON...

IT BECAME
MY DUTY TO
BECOME THE
STRONGEST IN
CONSUME...

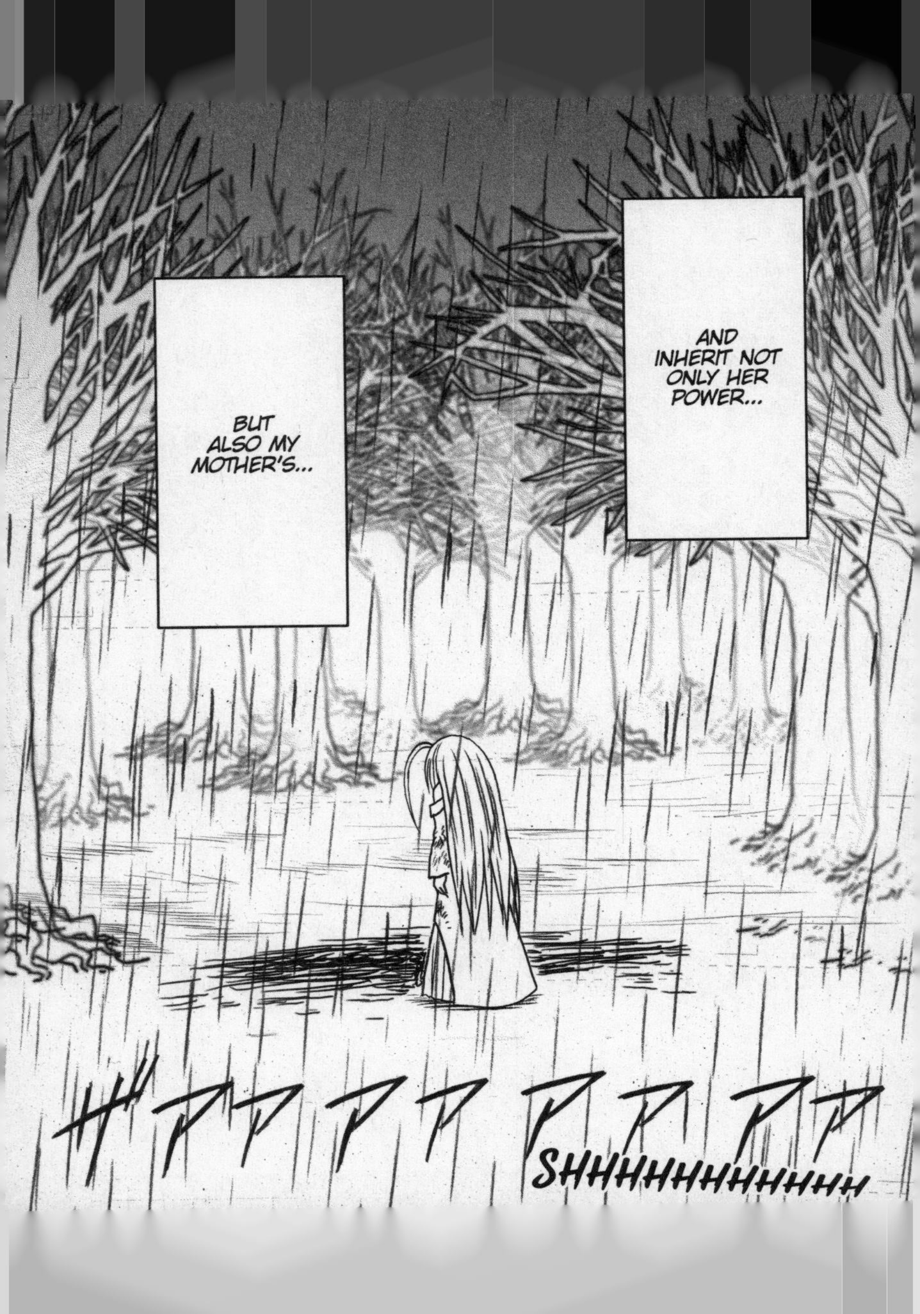
AND INHERIT NOT ONLY HER POWER...
BUT ALSO MY MOTHER'S...
SHHHHHHHHHHH

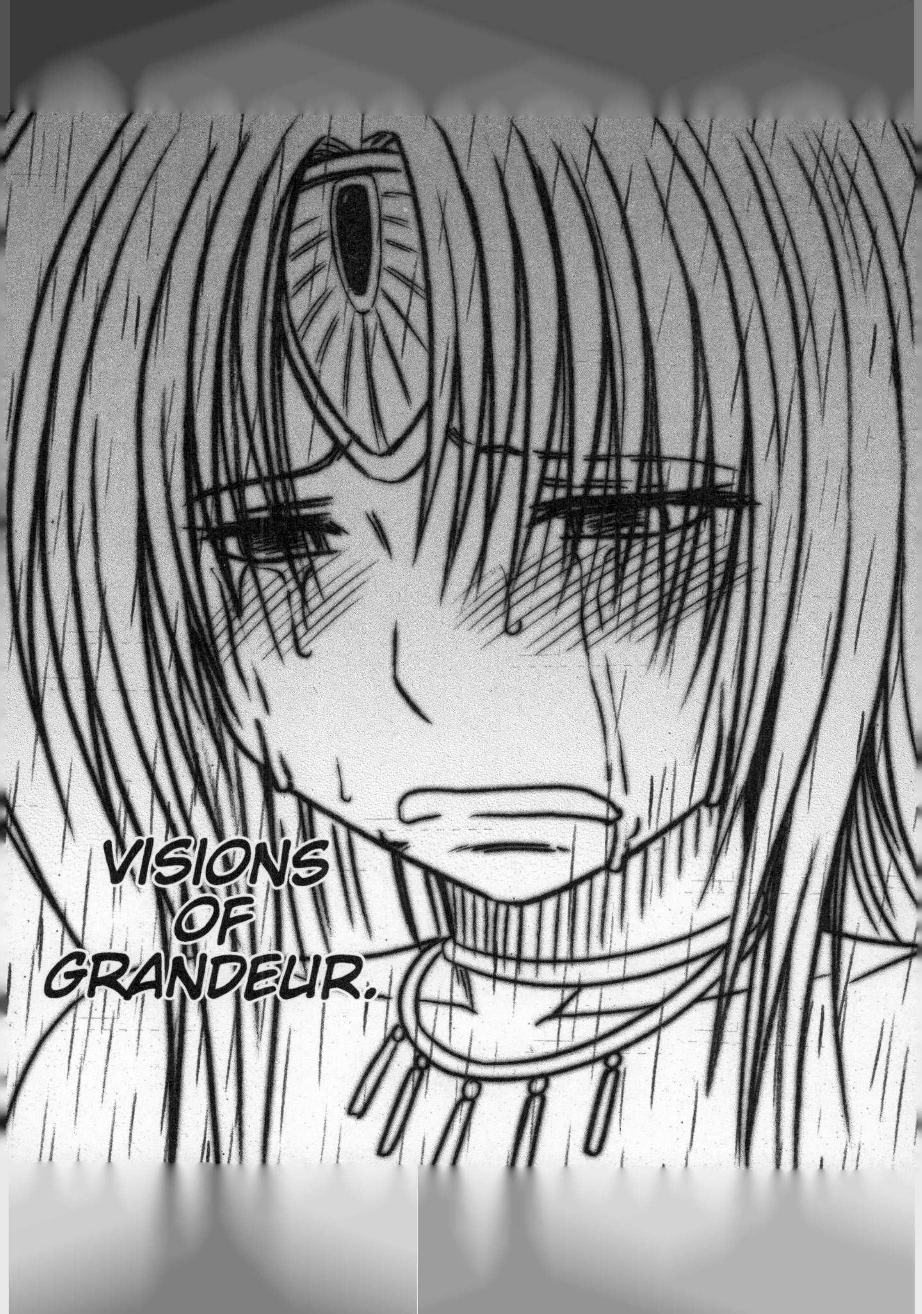
VISIONS OF GRANDEUR.

Perusing Video Game History

ON THE EDGE OF THE BLUE WORLD

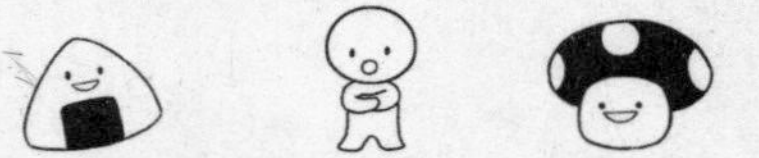

Dr. Onigiri   Mr. Why   Prof. Mushroom

Today's Topic

THE TWO BIG RPGS

Mr. Why: Hello, everyone! Just like in the previous volumes, the Doctor, the Professor, and I are going to chat a little bit about video games and their history. As always, please keep in mind that this has nothing to do with the main story of the manga in any way.

Prof. Mushroom: Thanks for joining us again. I'm Professor Mushroom. And Mr. Why's correct: this has nothing to do **what-so-ever** with the manga.

Dr. Onigiri: Dr. Onigiri here. It seems you guys are stressing that point awfully hard this time around.

Prof. Mushroom: Oh, don't worry about it. It's nothing to be concerned about.

Mr. Why: With that settled, today we're going to talk about the two big role-playing games.

Prof. Mushroom: That would be *Final Fantasy* from SquareSoft and *Dragon Quest* from Enix. These two games are very mature-feeling RPGs that are often called the two giants of console role-playing games.

Dr. Onigiri: Fans often argue over which series is better. I remember hearing "*FF* is really awesome!" followed by "No, *DQ* is the best!"

Mr. Why: They were big rivals, weren't they?

Prof. Mushroom: The truth is, SquareSoft was in a real financial pinch before *Final Fantasy* was released.

Dr. Onigiri: "Final" means "Last," after all--it was their last hope...

Mr. Why: *Final Fantasy* ended up being SquareSoft's savior, though! What made it sell so well?

Prof. Mushroom: Well, it had an interesting story, for starters. But the technical aspects of it were also top notch. For its time, the graphics were polished and the interface was elegant.

Mr. Why: Oh, tell me more!

To be continued...

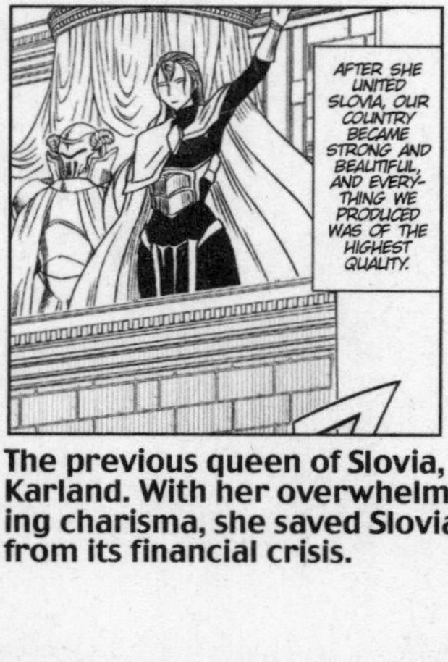
AFTER SHE UNITED SLOVIA, OUR COUNTRY BECAME STRONG AND BEAUTIFUL, AND EVERY-THING WE PRODUCED WAS OF THE HIGHEST QUALITY.

The previous queen of Slovia, Karland. With her overwhelming charisma, she saved Slovia from its financial crisis.

WORLD WAR BLUE

CHARACTER INTRODUCTION

The Queen of Slovia
KARLAND

Hails from Slovia.

Like a shooting star in the night, she came to Slovia during a time of financial turmoil and, with her excellent leadership skills, saved the country from ruin.

She prided herself on being a member of the Efferev family. She polished herself in every way, shape, and form, from combat prowess to beauty, in order to live up to her high standards.

After losing to Myomut in a duel, she tasked her daughter, Crystal, with absorbing her life and becoming the strongest in her stead.

Author Comment

Her face says it all, really. She's cold and proud, thinking herself above all other people. I wouldn't usually draw a character with facial features like hers, but here it gives her a kind of fresh and different feel.

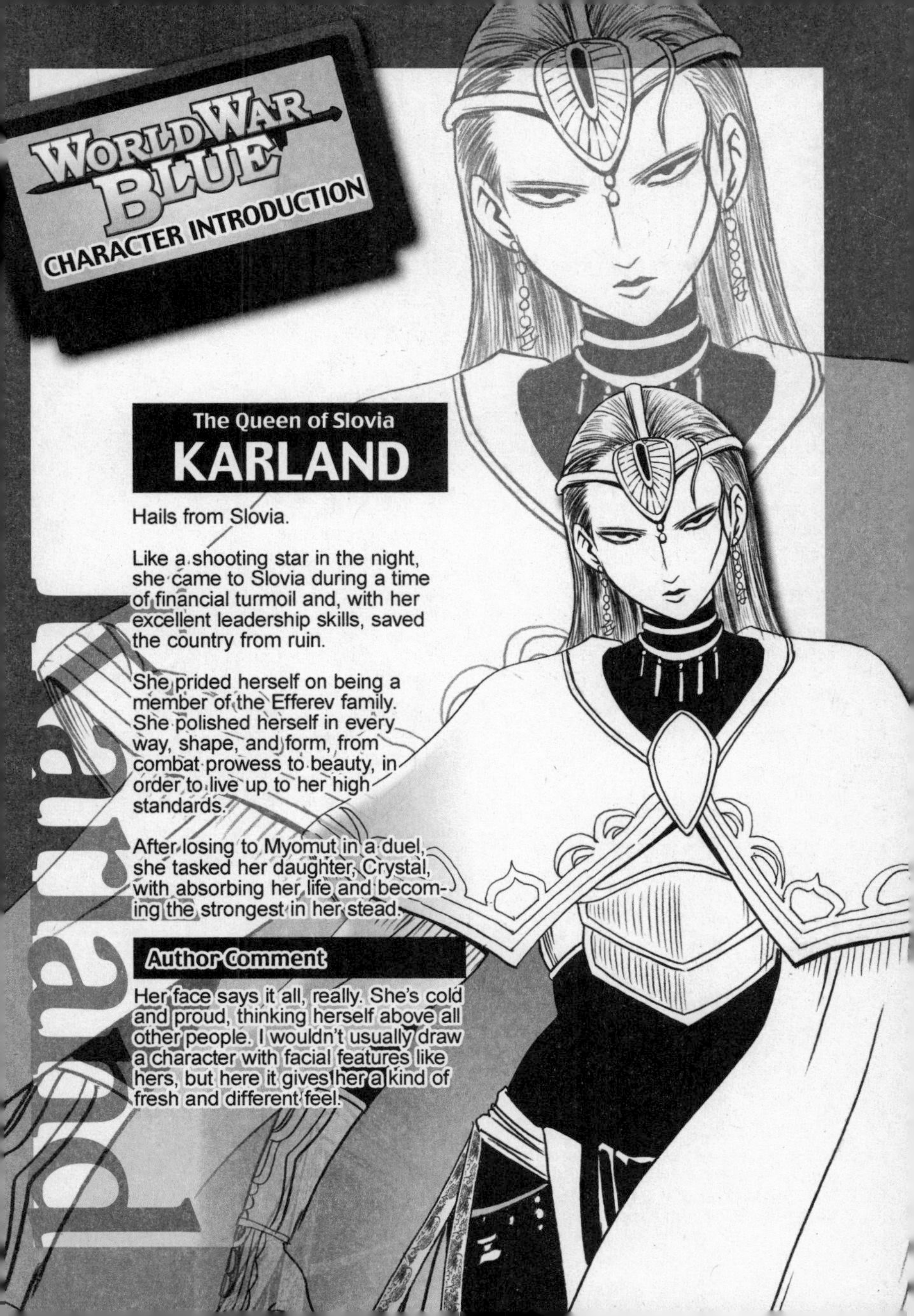

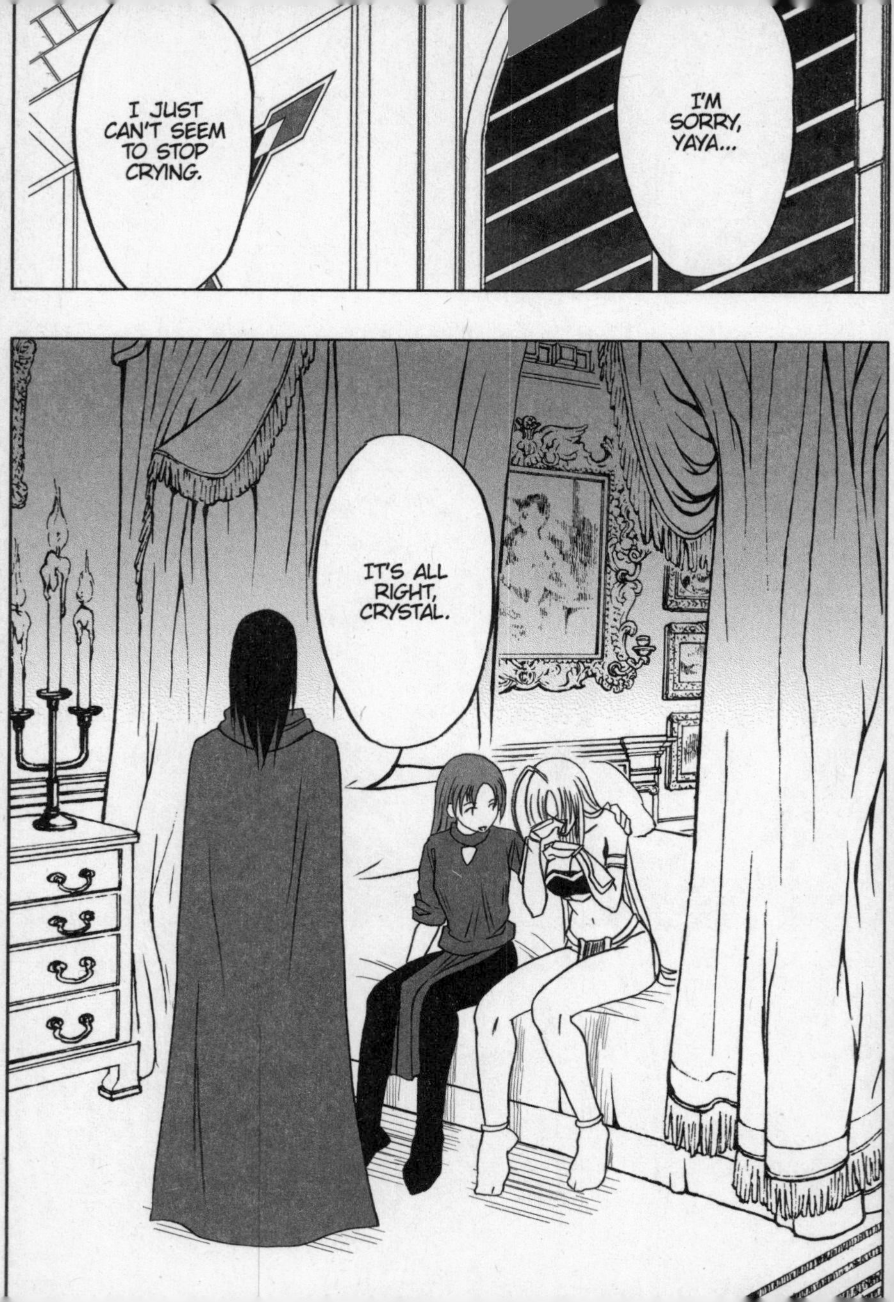
I'M SORRY, YAYA...
I JUST CAN'T SEEM TO STOP CRYING.
IT'S ALL RIGHT, CRYSTAL.

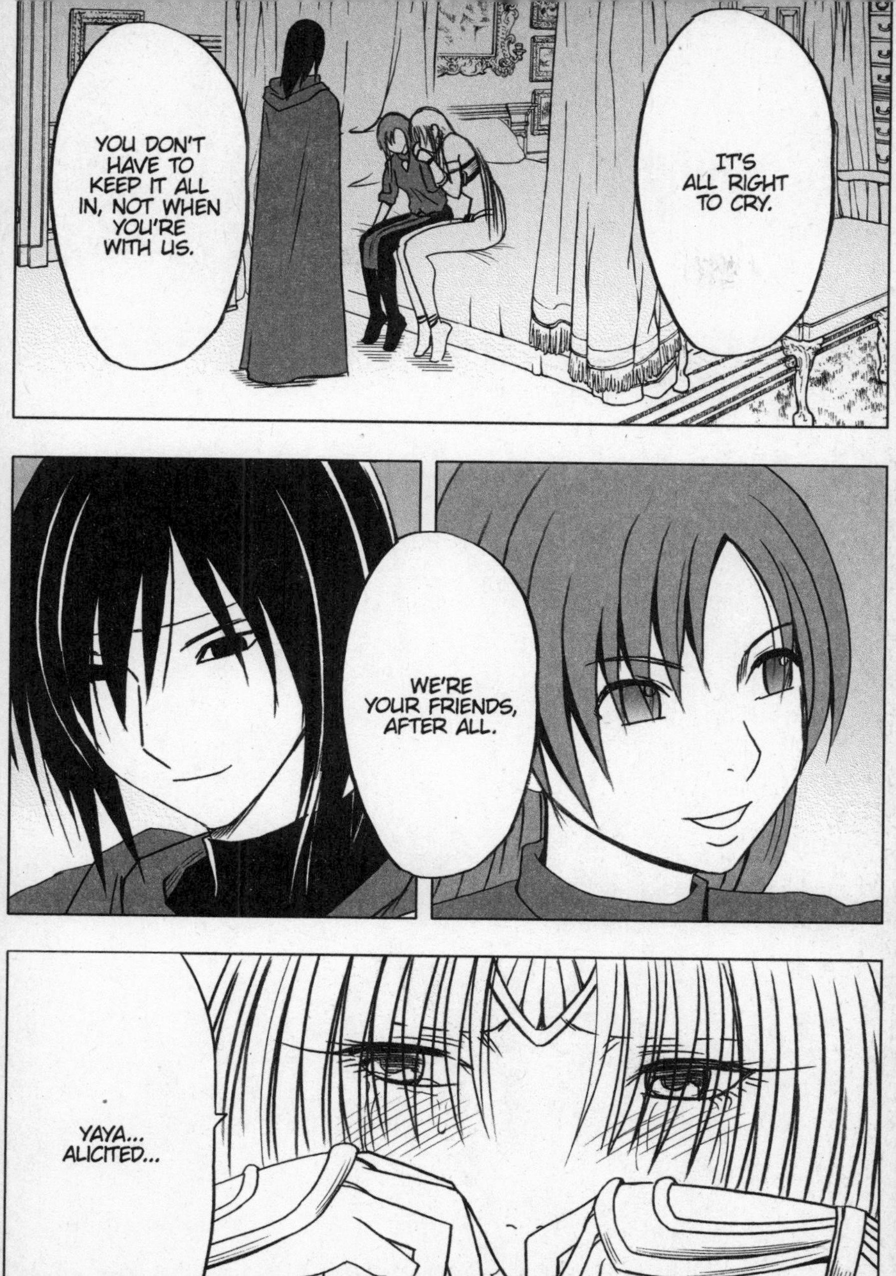
IT'S ALL RIGHT TO CRY.
YOU DON'T HAVE TO KEEP IT ALL IN, NOT WHEN YOU'RE WITH US.
WE'RE YOUR FRIENDS, AFTER ALL.
YAYA... ALICITED...

Part 2

CHAPTER 24

EYES ON ME

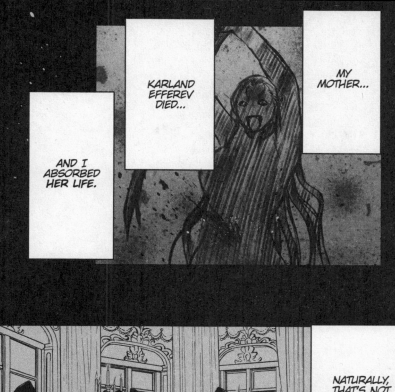

KARLAND EFFEREV DIED...

MY MOTHER...

AND I ABSORBED HER LIFE.

NATURALLY, THAT'S NOT SOMETHING YOU CAN JUST TELL THE PUBLIC.

THUS, IT BECAME TOP SECRET INFORMATION KNOWN ONLY TO ME, THE SENATE, AND A SELECT FEW PEOPLE.

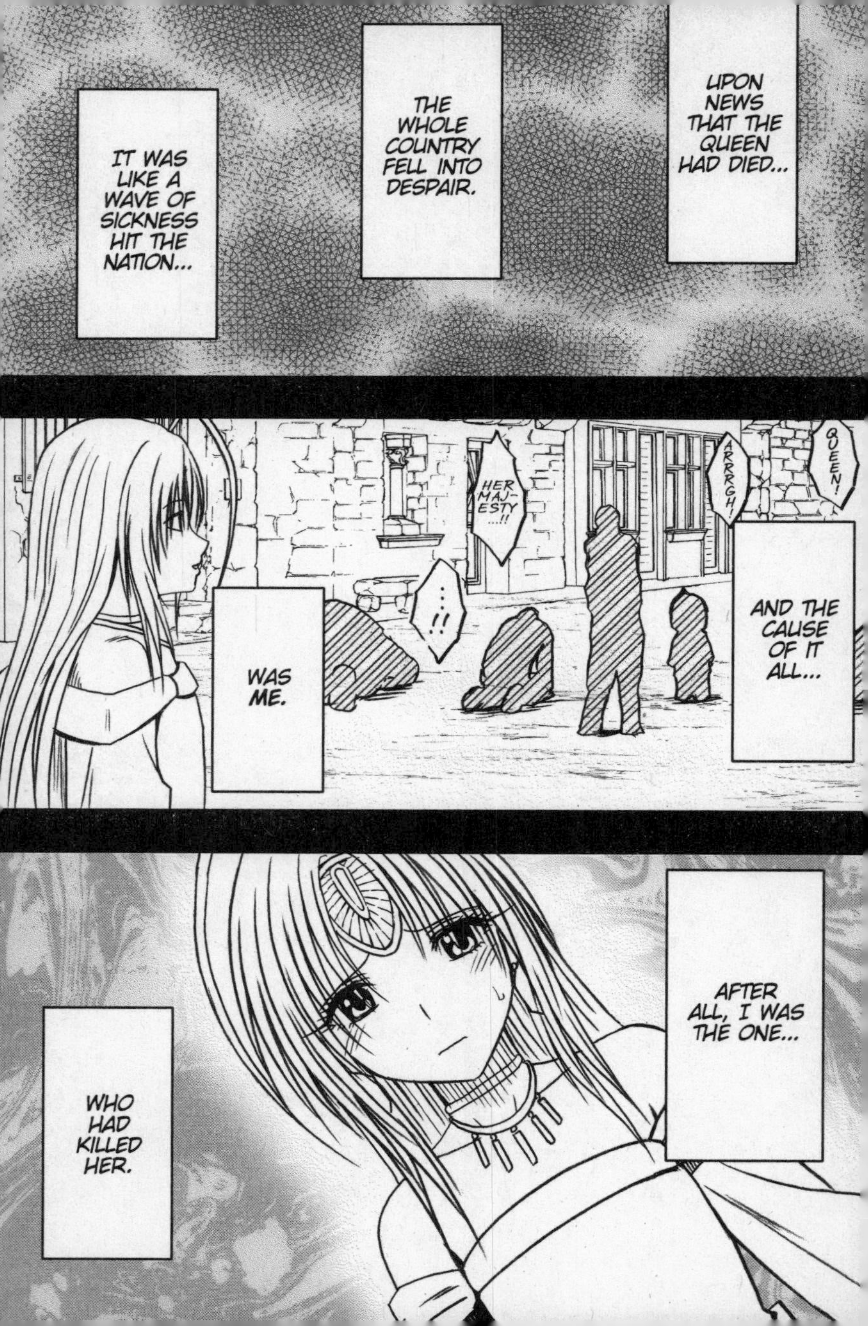
UPON NEWS THAT THE QUEEN HAD DIED...
THE WHOLE COUNTRY FELL INTO DESPAIR.
IT WAS LIKE A WAVE OF SICKNESS HIT THE NATION...
QUEEN!
ARRRGH!
HER MAJESTY ...!!
AND THE CAUSE OF IT ALL...
...!!
WAS ME.
AFTER ALL, I WAS THE ONE...
WHO HAD KILLED HER.

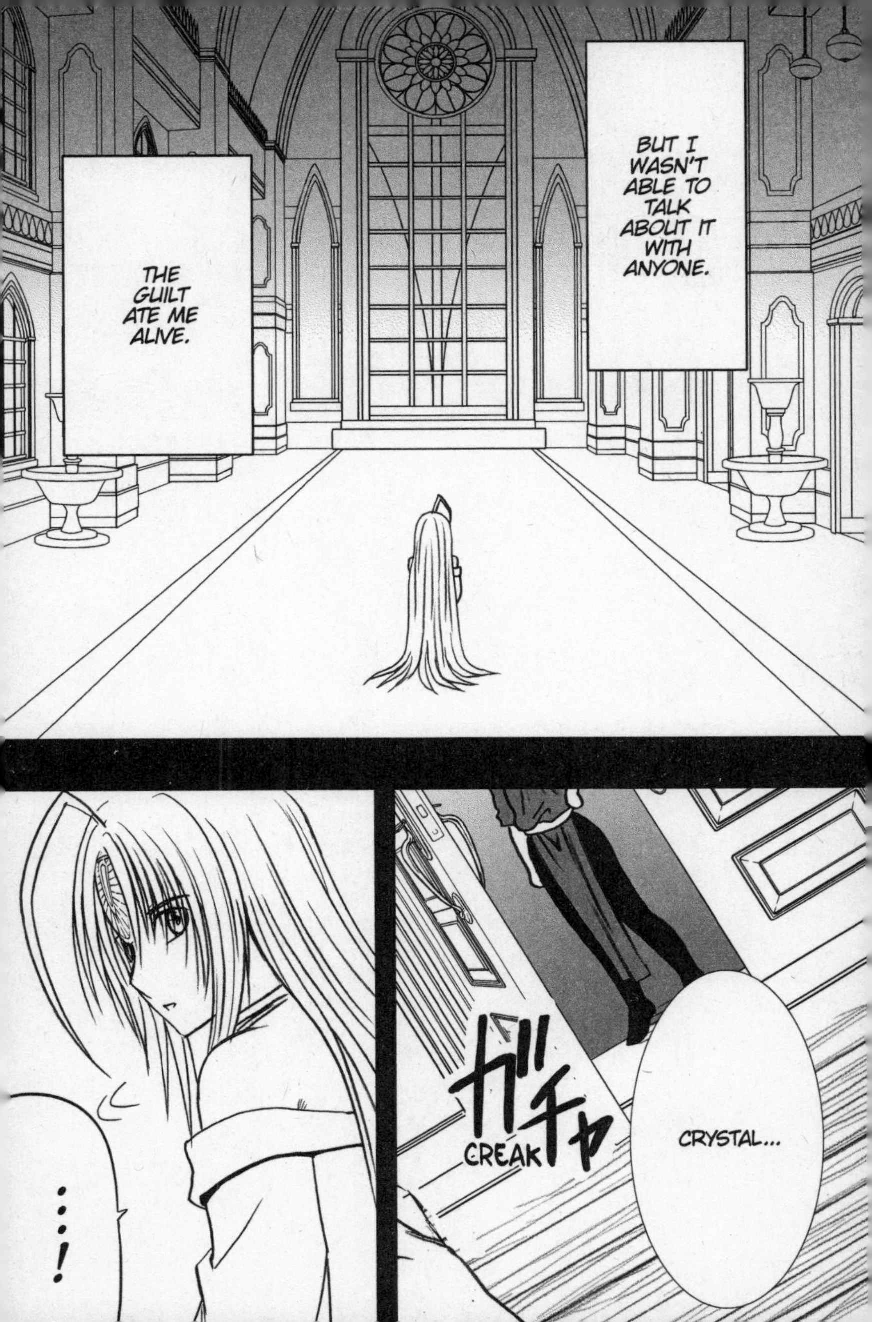
BUT I WASN'T ABLE TO TALK ABOUT IT WITH ANYONE.
THE GUILT ATE ME ALIVE.
ガチャ
CREAK
CRYSTAL...
...!

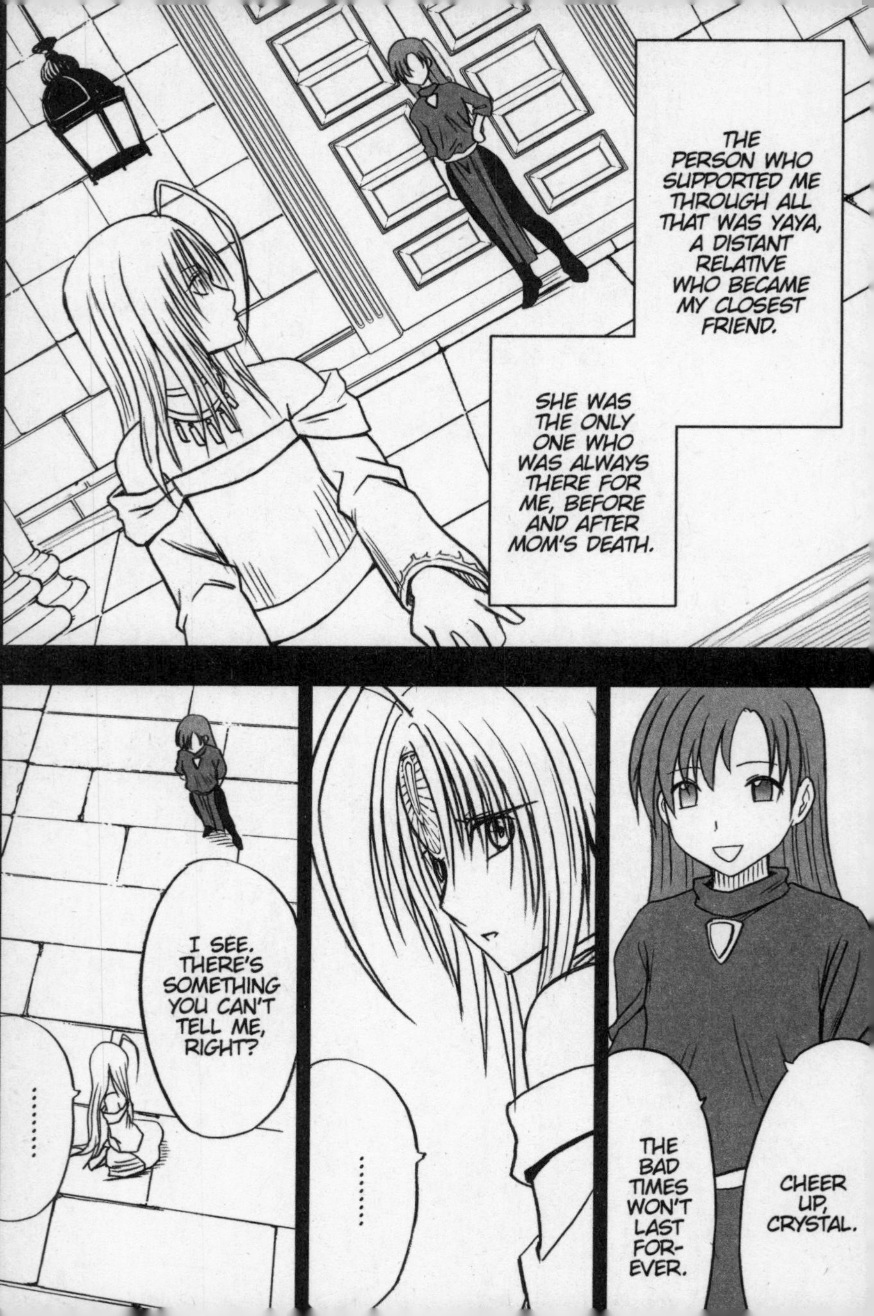
THE PERSON WHO SUPPORTED ME THROUGH ALL THAT WAS YAYA, A DISTANT RELATIVE WHO BECAME MY CLOSEST FRIEND.
SHE WAS THE ONLY ONE WHO WAS ALWAYS THERE FOR ME, BEFORE AND AFTER MOM'S DEATH.
CHEER UP, CRYSTAL.
THE BAD TIMES WON'T LAST FOR-EVER.
......
I SEE. THERE'S SOMETHING YOU CAN'T TELL ME, RIGHT?
......

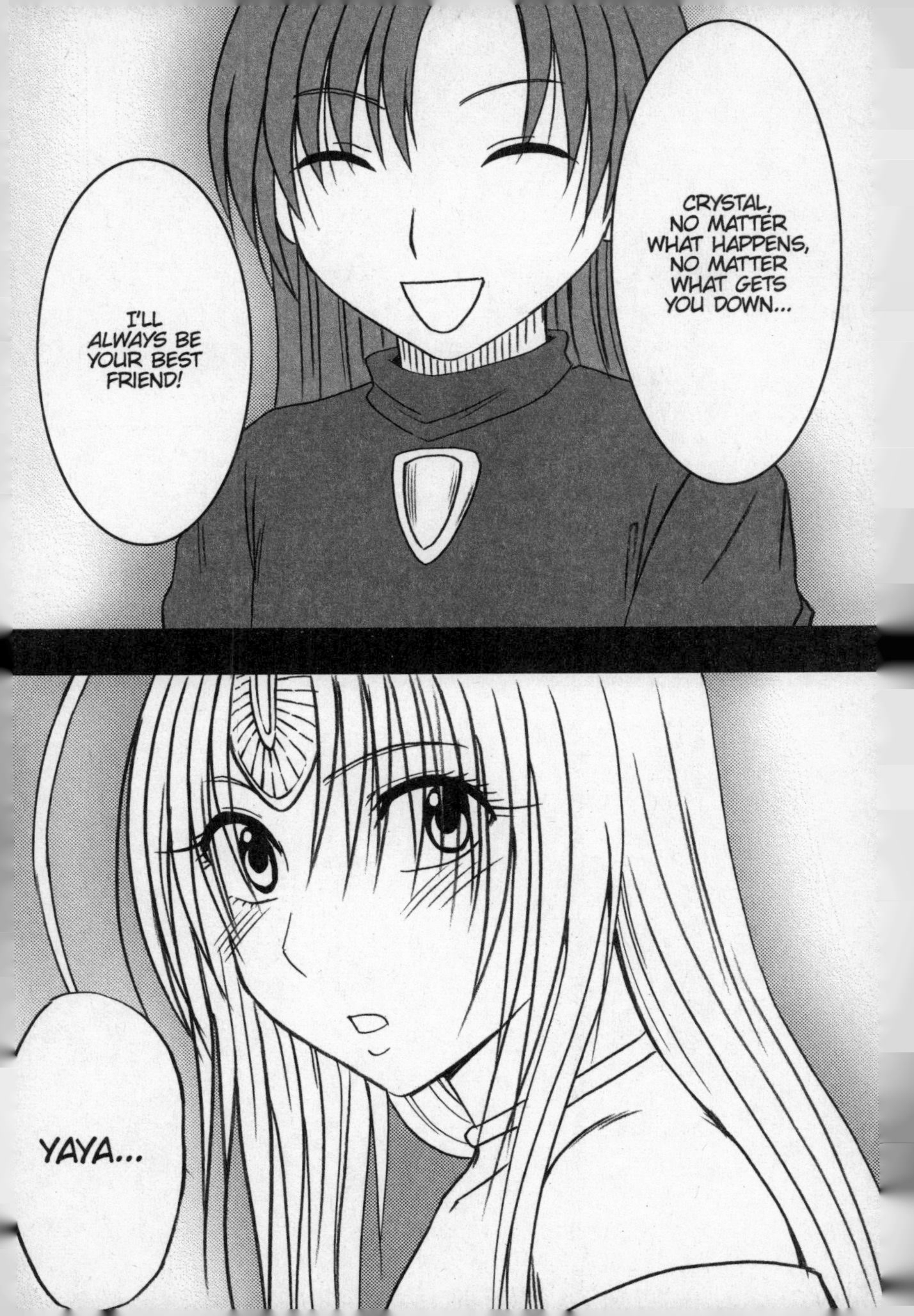
CRYSTAL, NO MATTER WHAT HAPPENS, NO MATTER WHAT GETS YOU DOWN...
I'LL ALWAYS BE YOUR BEST FRIEND!
YAYA...

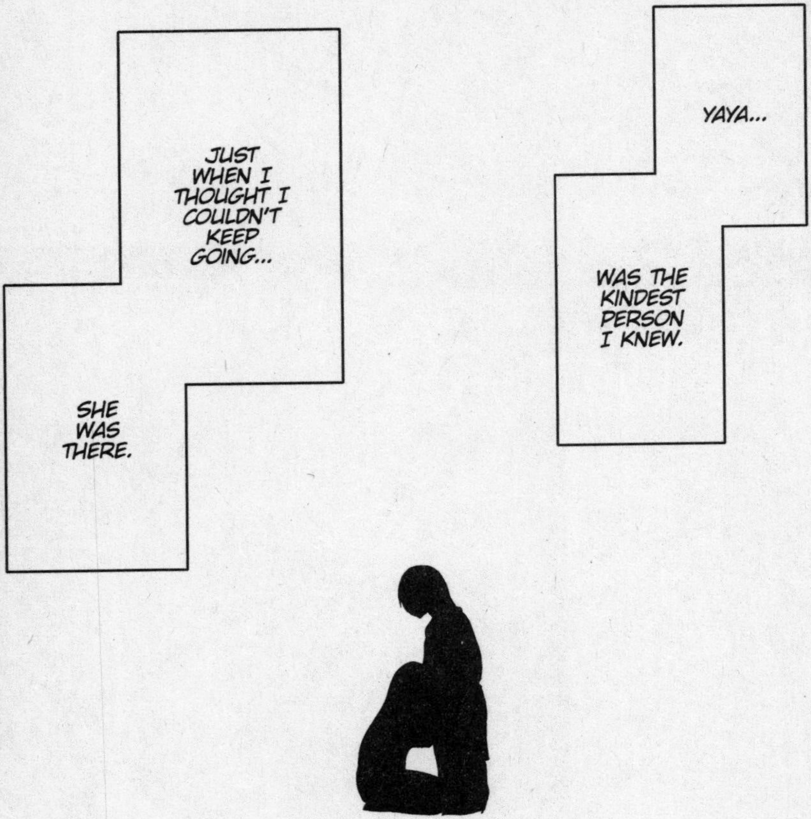
YAYA...
WAS THE KINDEST PERSON I KNEW.
JUST WHEN I THOUGHT I COULDN'T KEEP GOING...
SHE WAS THERE.

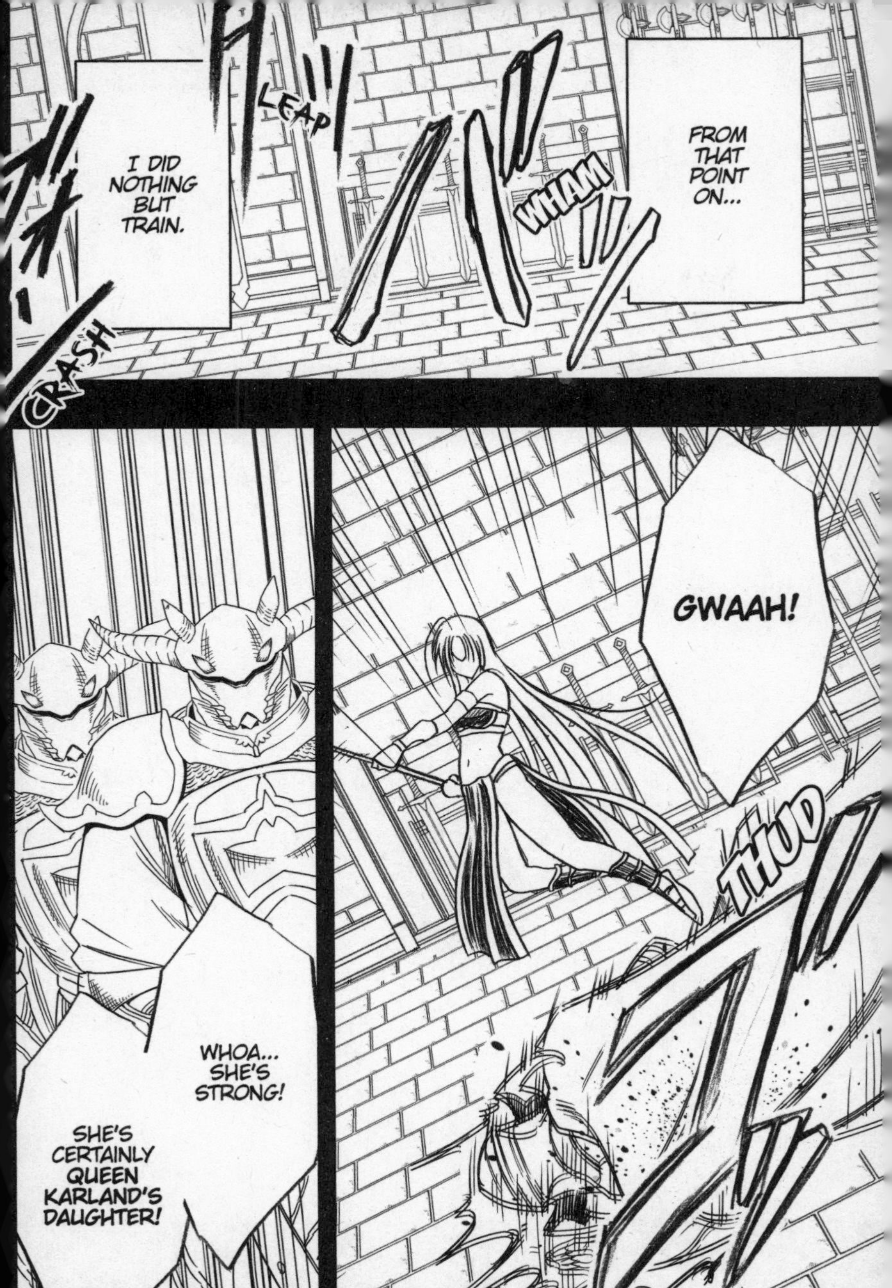
FROM THAT POINT ON...
WHAM
LEAP
I DID NOTHING BUT TRAIN.
CRASH
GWAAH!
THUD
WHOA... SHE'S STRONG!
SHE'S CERTAINLY QUEEN KARLAND'S DAUGHTER!

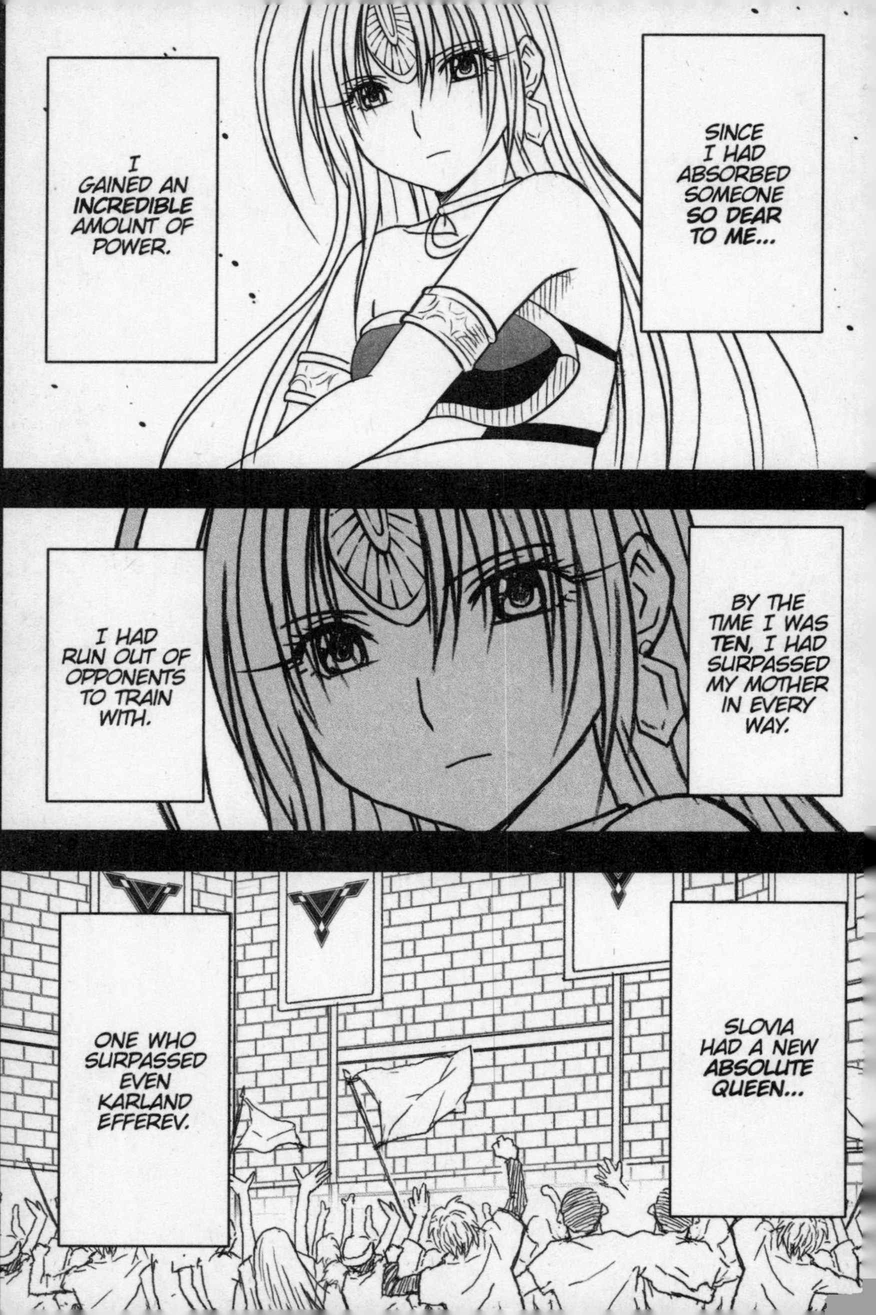
SINCE I HAD ABSORBED SOMEONE SO DEAR TO ME...
I GAINED AN INCREDIBLE AMOUNT OF POWER.
BY THE TIME I WAS TEN, I HAD SURPASSED MY MOTHER IN EVERY WAY.
I HAD RUN OUT OF OPPONENTS TO TRAIN WITH.
SLOVIA HAD A NEW ABSOLUTE QUEEN...
ONE WHO SURPASSED EVEN KARLAND EFFEREV.

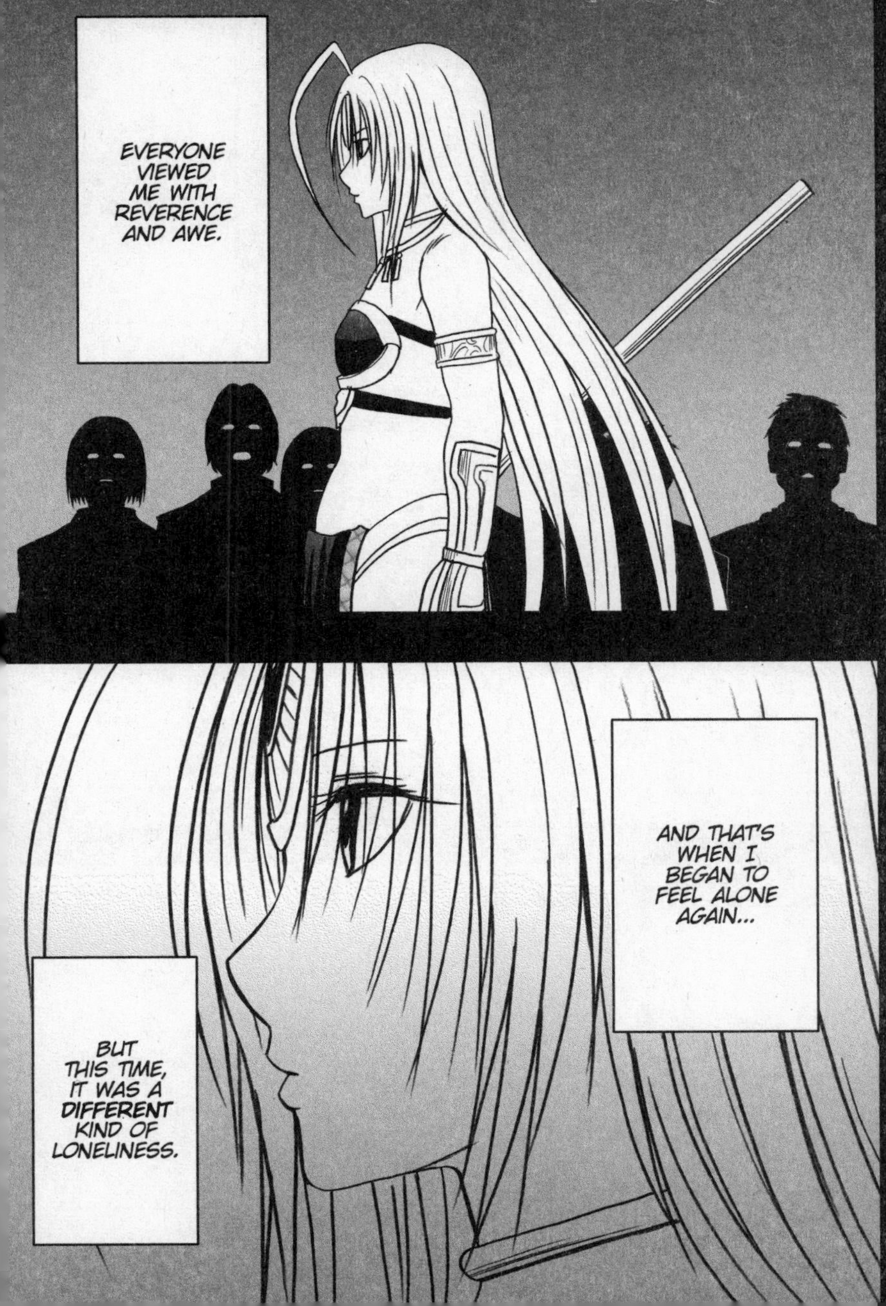
EVERYONE VIEWED ME WITH REVERENCE AND AWE.
AND THAT'S WHEN I BEGAN TO FEEL ALONE AGAIN...
BUT THIS TIME, IT WAS A DIFFERENT KIND OF LONELINESS.

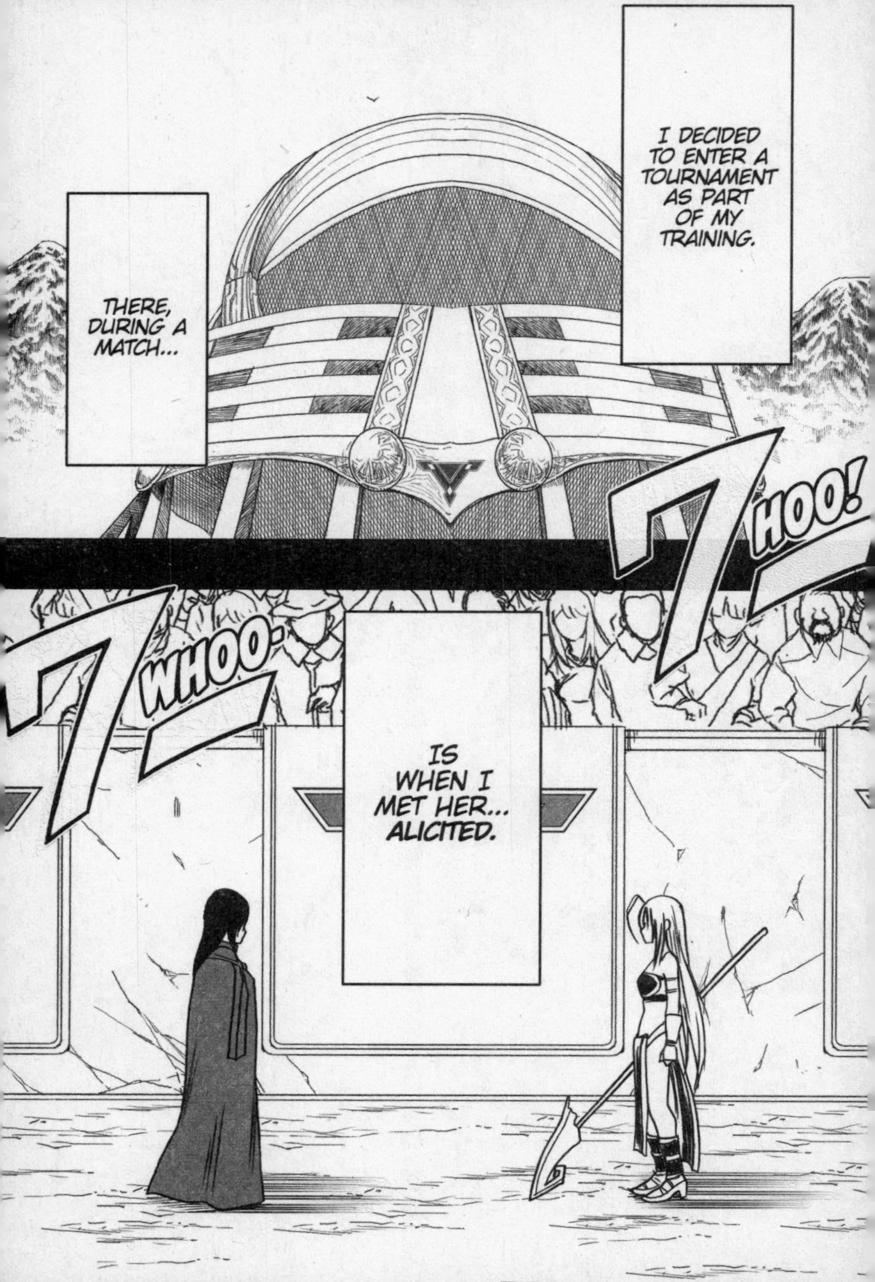
I DECIDED TO ENTER A TOURNAMENT AS PART OF MY TRAINING.
THERE, DURING A MATCH...
WHOO-
HOO!
IS WHEN I MET HER... ALICITED.

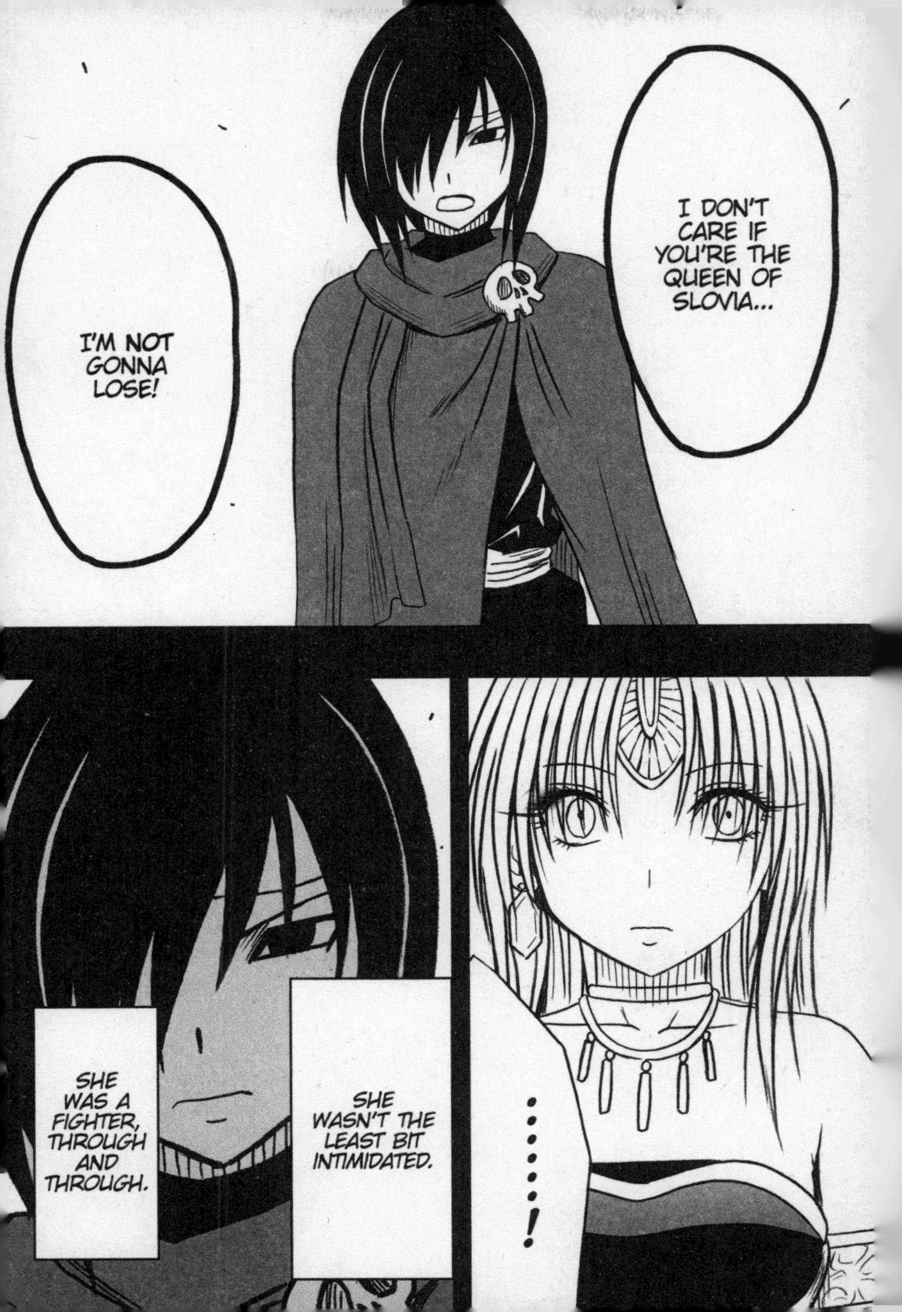
I DON'T CARE IF YOU'RE THE QUEEN OF SLOVIA...
I'M NOT GONNA LOSE!
......!
SHE WASN'T THE LEAST BIT INTIMIDATED.
SHE WAS A FIGHTER, THROUGH AND THROUGH.

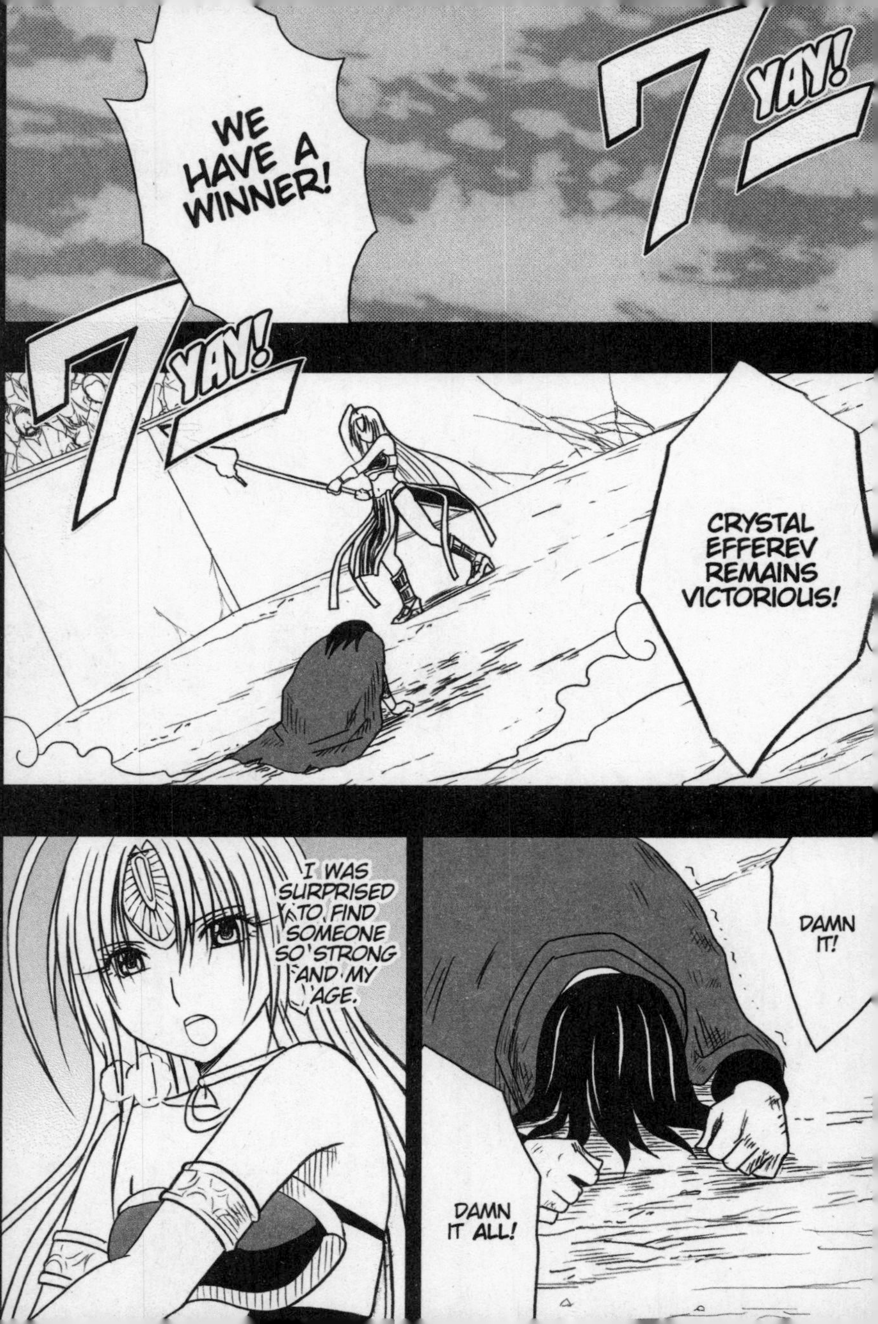
YAY!
WE HAVE A WINNER!
YAY!
CRYSTAL EFFEREV REMAINS VICTORIOUS!
DAMN IT!
DAMN IT ALL!
I WAS SURPRISED TO FIND SOMEONE SO STRONG AND MY AGE.

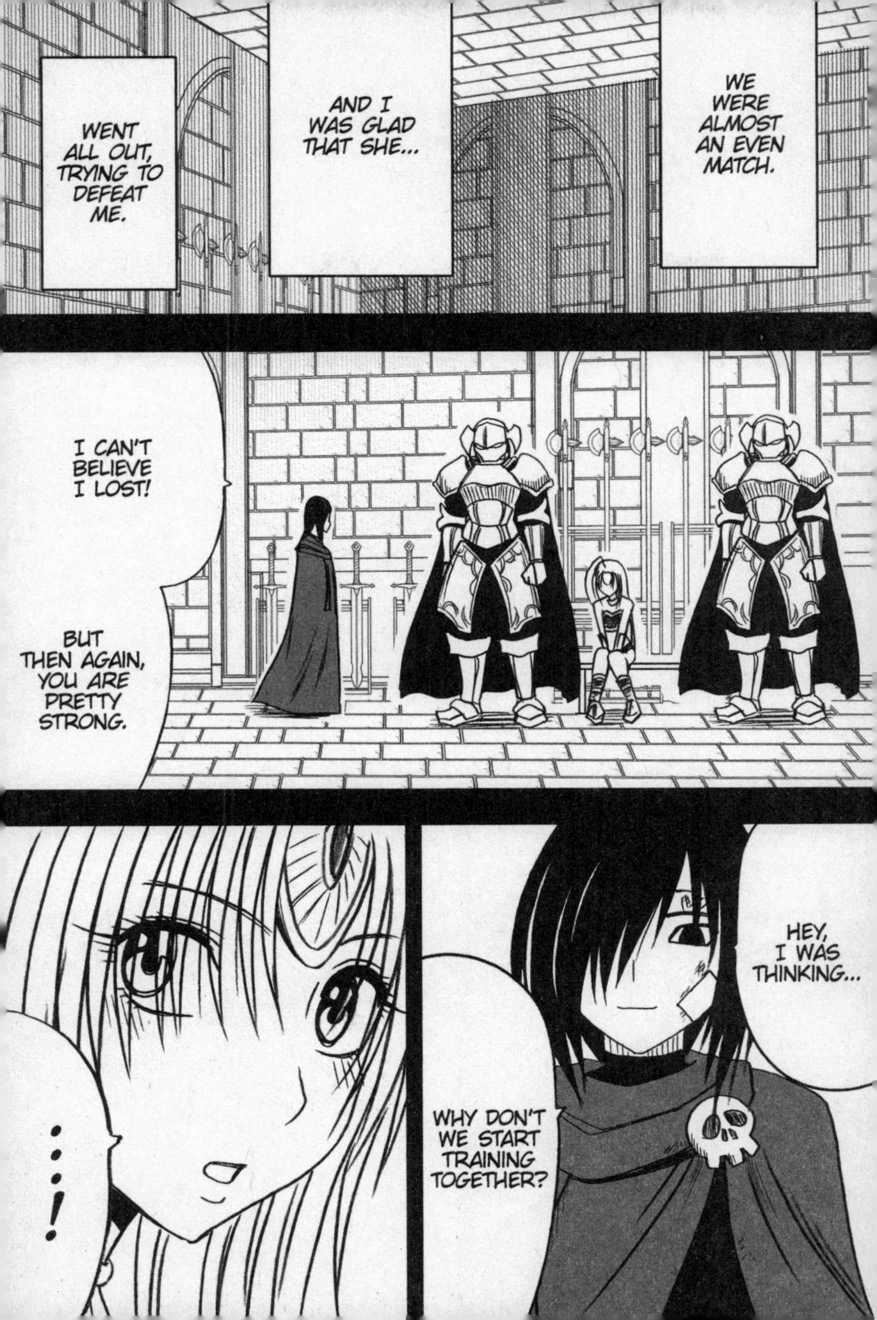
WE WERE ALMOST AN EVEN MATCH.
AND I WAS GLAD THAT SHE...
WENT ALL OUT, TRYING TO DEFEAT ME.
I CAN'T BELIEVE I LOST!
BUT THEN AGAIN, YOU ARE PRETTY STRONG.
HEY, I WAS THINKING...
WHY DON'T WE START TRAINING TOGETHER?
...!

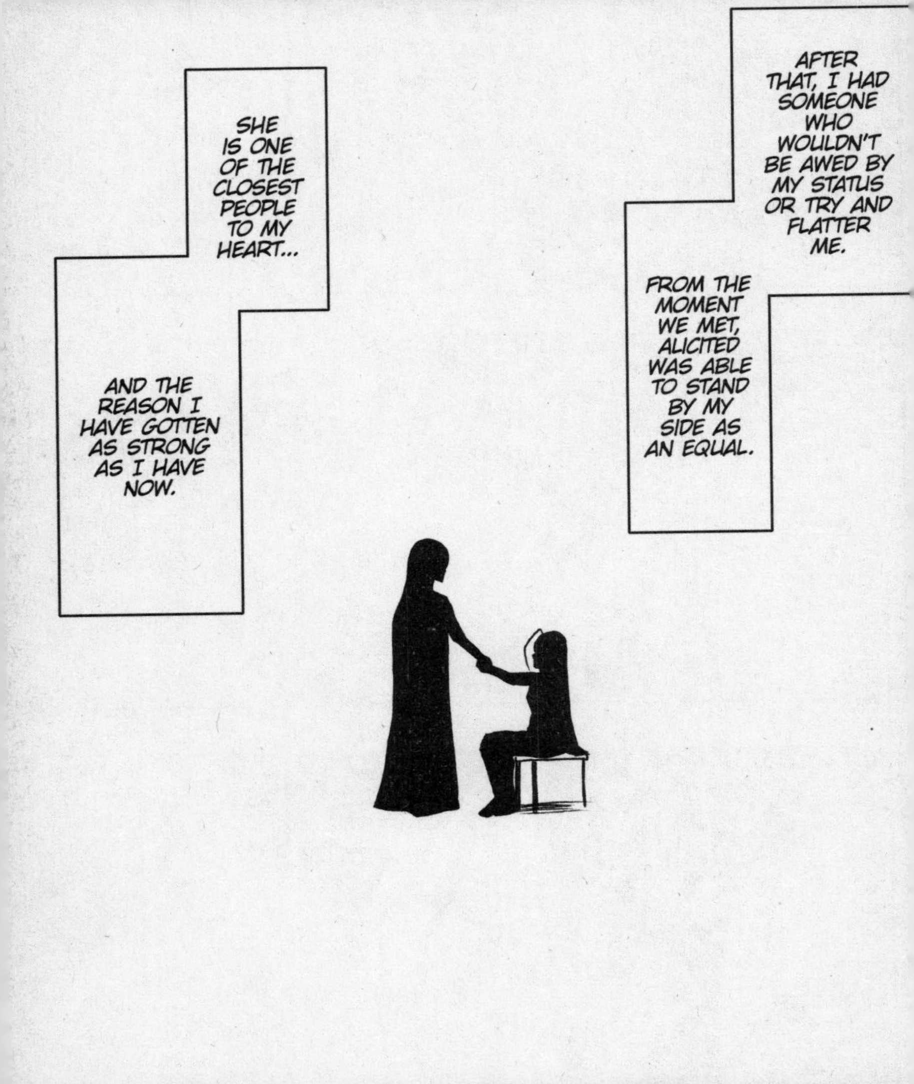
AFTER THAT, I HAD SOMEONE WHO WOULDN'T BE AWED BY MY STATUS OR TRY AND FLATTER ME.
FROM THE MOMENT WE MET, ALICITED WAS ABLE TO STAND BY MY SIDE AS AN EQUAL.
SHE IS ONE OF THE CLOSEST PEOPLE TO MY HEART...
AND THE REASON I HAVE GOTTEN AS STRONG AS I HAVE NOW.

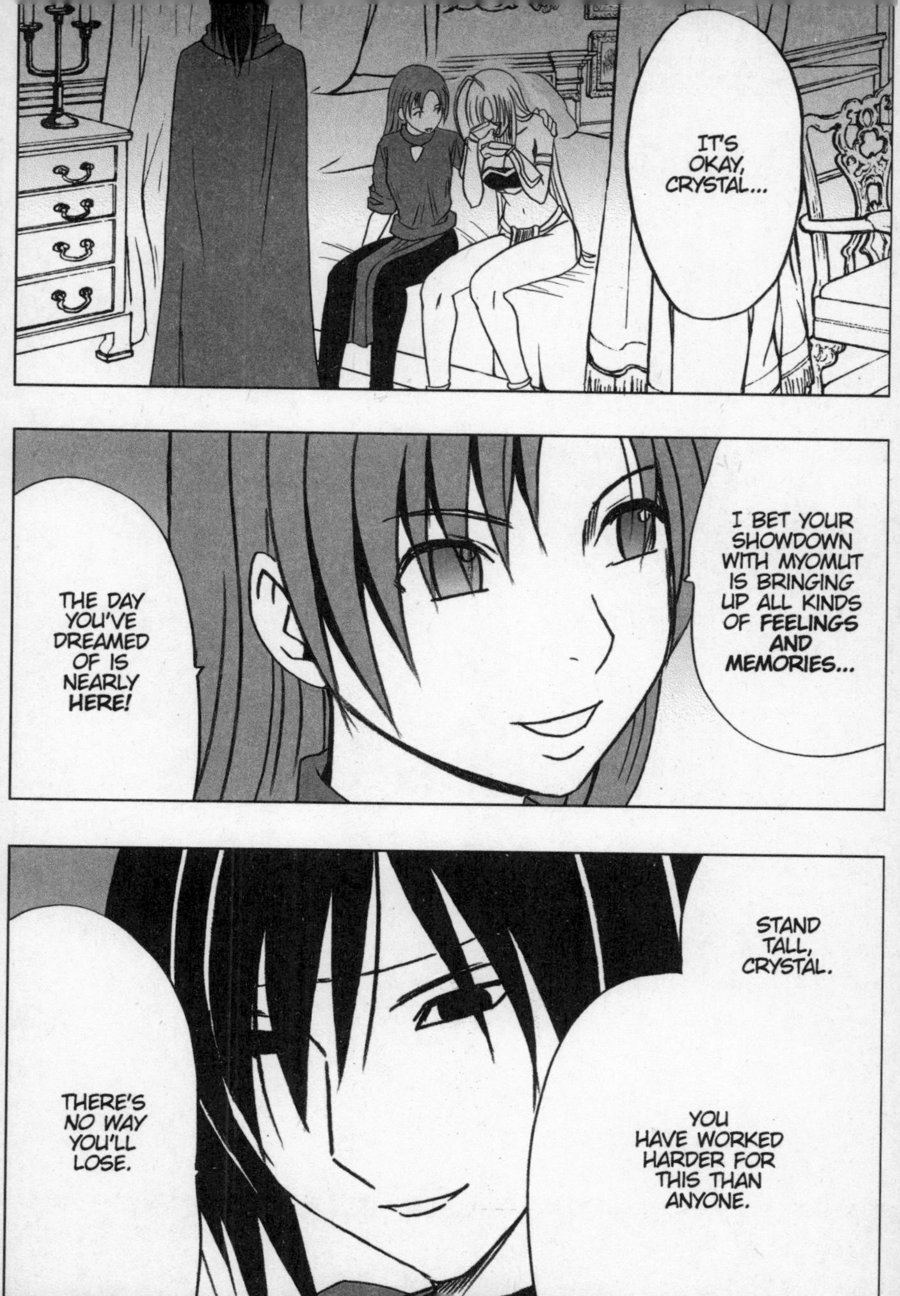
IT'S OKAY, CRYSTAL...
I BET YOUR SHOWDOWN WITH MYOMUT IS BRINGING UP ALL KINDS OF FEELINGS AND MEMORIES...
THE DAY YOU'VE DREAMED OF IS NEARLY HERE!
STAND TALL, CRYSTAL.
YOU HAVE WORKED HARDER FOR THIS THAN ANYONE.
THERE'S NO WAY YOU'LL LOSE.

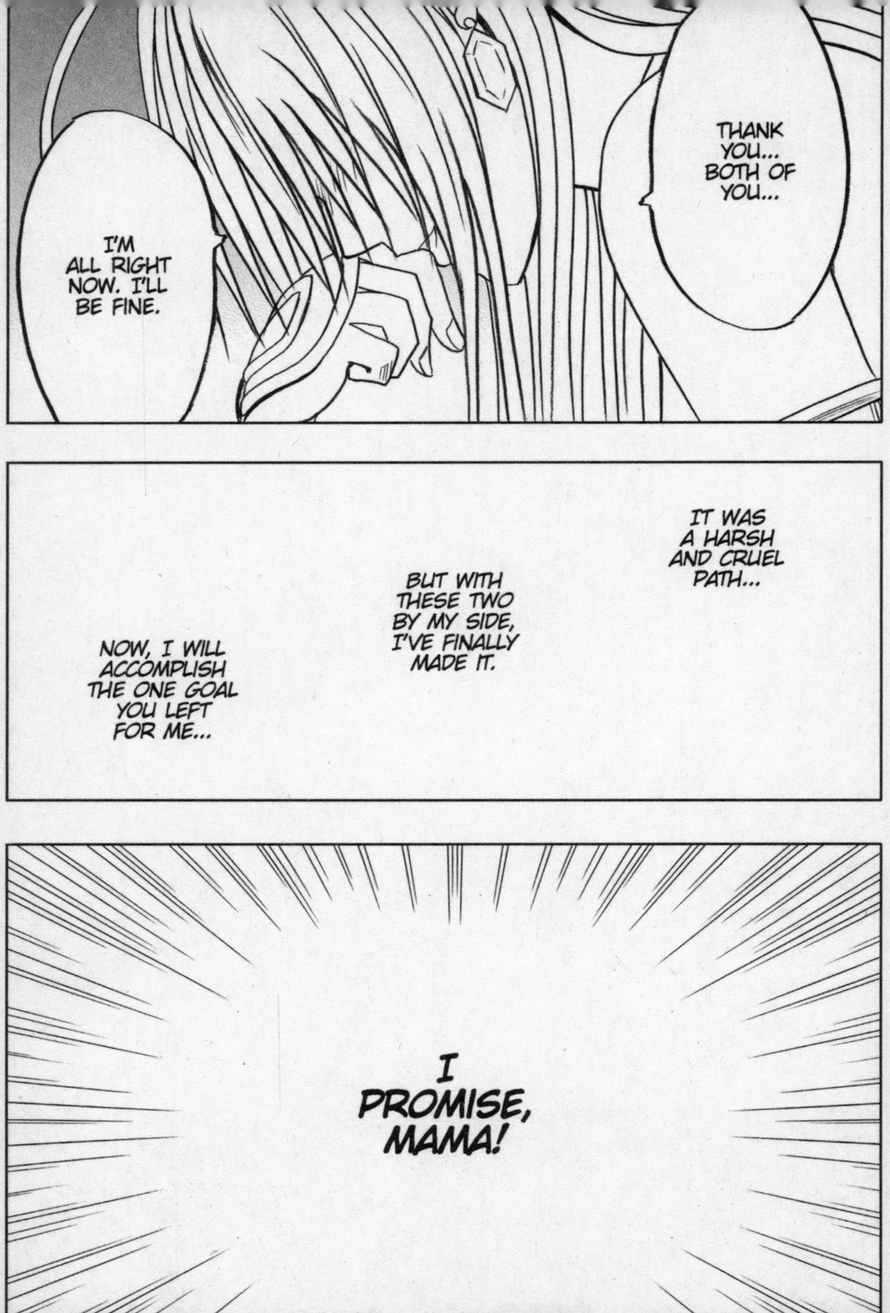
THANK YOU... BOTH OF YOU...
I'M ALL RIGHT NOW. I'LL BE FINE.
IT WAS A HARSH AND CRUEL PATH...
BUT WITH THESE TWO BY MY SIDE, I'VE FINALLY MADE IT.
NOW, I WILL ACCOMPLISH THE ONE GOAL YOU LEFT FOR ME...
I PROMISE, MAMA!

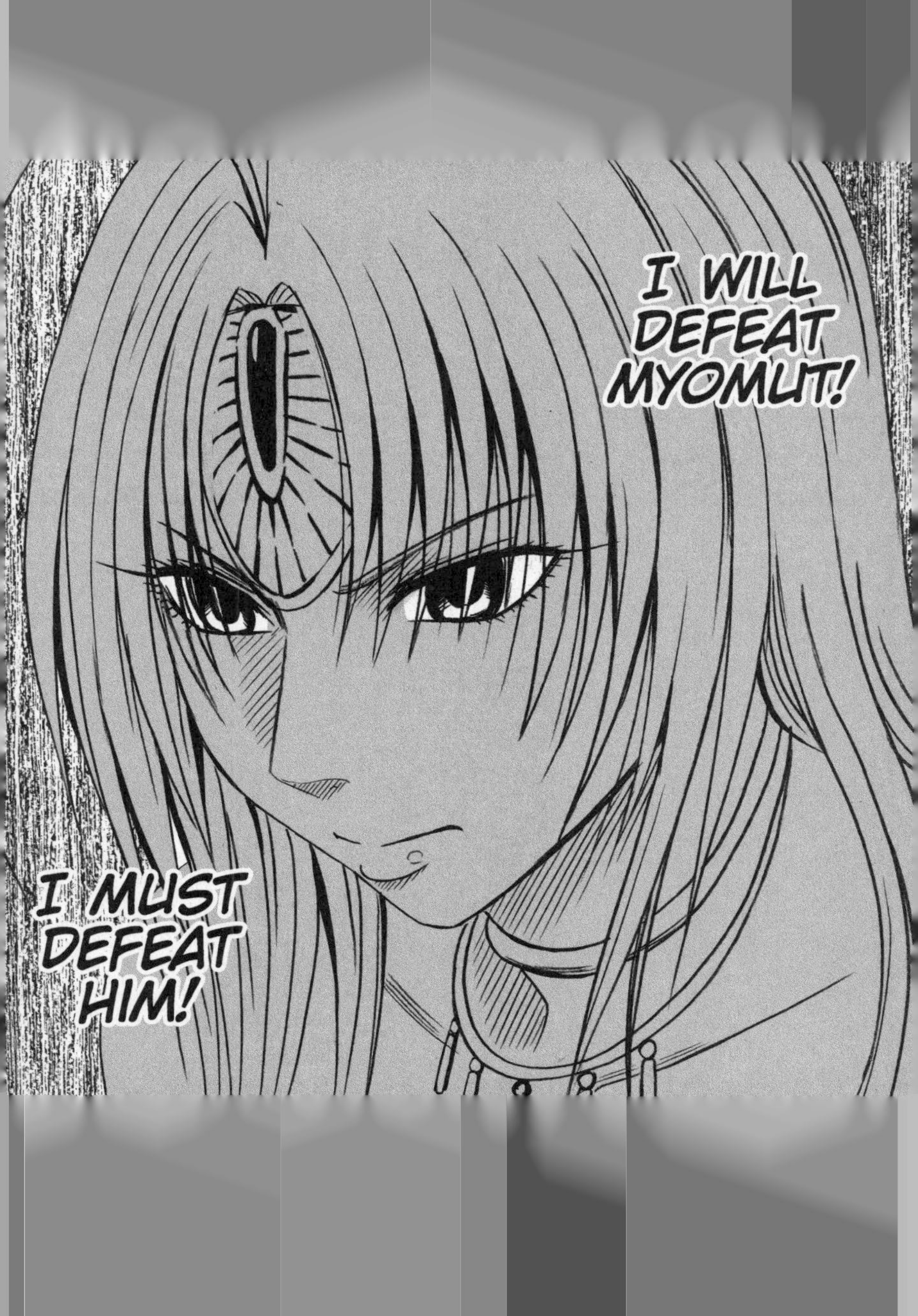
I WILL DEFEAT MYOMUT!
I MUST DEFEAT HIM!

Perusing Video Game History

ON THE EDGE OF THE BLUE WORLD

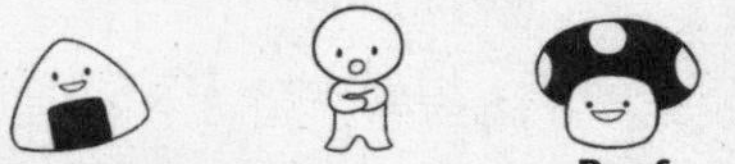

Dr. Onigiri Mr. Why Prof. Mushroom

Today's Topic

THE TWO BIG RPGS (Part 2)

Mr. Why: Last time, we were talking about SquareSoft's *Final Fantasy* series. Just what was so awesome about it anyway?

Dr. Onigiri: Well, *Final Fantasy* certainly had a well-told story and amazingly beautiful graphics (for its time), but that's not all.

Prof. Mushroom: That's right! There was also the music. The musical tracks, such as "Four Emperors (Dreadful Fight)," " HYPERLINK "http://www.you-tube.com/watch?v=6CMTXyEx-kel&feature=kp" Battle with Gilgamesh (Clash on the Big Bridge)," "Aria di Mezzo Carat-tere," and the unforgettable "One Winged Angel," really elevated the series.

Dr. Onigiri: When *Final Fantasy VIII* was released on the PlayStation in 1999, it had a pop ballad called "Eyes on Me" in it. The song was so popular that the CD single sold over 500,000 copies.

Prof. Mushroom: Of course, it wasn't just the music either. The story and the worlds were immersive and well-made. Some lines had a real impact and became catch phrases, such as "I will defeat Sin. I must defeat *Sin.*" from *Final Fantasy X*. For many gamers, *Final Fantasy* became synonymous with "Ultimate Fantasy."

Mr. Why: That's really saying something.

Prof. Mushroom: It is, but even in the original *Final Fantasy* for the Famicom and NES, the story was mature and complicated, with the villain, Garland, sending our heroes into a time loop. The series always had a heavy feel to it.

Dr. Onigiri: But it's those deep and heavy plotlines that give the series its charm.

To be continued...

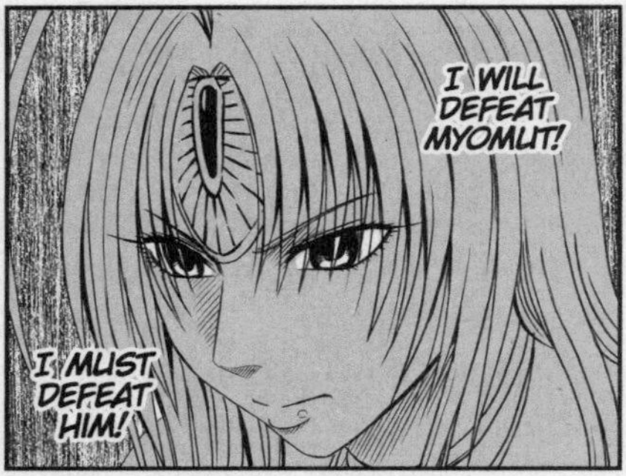
I WILL DEFEAT MYOMUT!
I MUST DEFEAT HIM!

Crystal vowing to defeat Myomut. The duty entrusted to her by her mother has been a heavy burden.

**Crystal,
Age 12**

Q: Why does Crystal wear such skimpy clothes?

A: After her mother died, Crystal wanted to say goodbye to her old self for good. Besides, since she's following in her mother's footsteps, she must not only look good but wear clothes she can train in. Yaya helped her pick it out.

Q: Where did Karland learn about the "Law of Killers"? Is it widely known?

A: There aren't a whole lot of people who know about it. Including Ramses in Segua, there are about ten people aware of it. Karland learned about it from the Slovia Senate.

Q: If a killer absorbs someone who is skilled in Action or Puzzle, will they gain the ability to use it as well?

A: Abilities and skills don't get passed along, just pure strength and power. It's like a boost in physical attributes, life energy, etc.

Q: The Law of Killers states: "The amount of power you can take from a target depends on the amount of affection you have for them." What does that mean exactly?

A: To give you an explanation, let me give you some examples:

If you have a Level 90 friend who is very dear to you, and a Level 5 friend who is equally dear, then you will get a lot more power from absorbing the Level 90 friend than from the Level 5 friend.

But if you have a hated enemy who is Level 90, absorbing him would net you less power than if you absorbed the Level 5 friend.

Basically: power gained = (target's power) × (your affection for them)

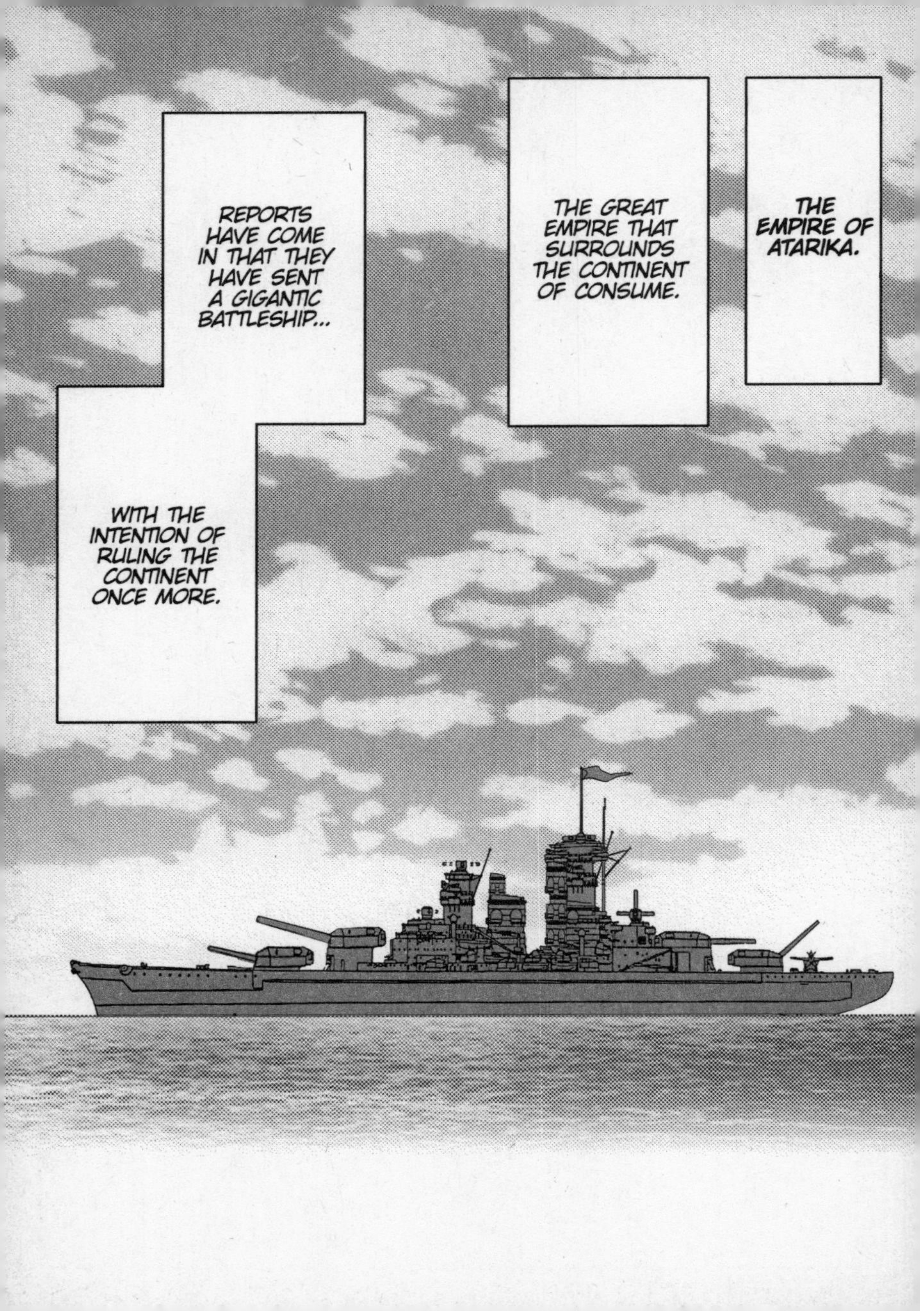
THE EMPIRE OF ATARIKA.
THE GREAT EMPIRE THAT SURROUNDS THE CONTINENT OF CONSUME.
REPORTS HAVE COME IN THAT THEY HAVE SENT A GIGANTIC BATTLESHIP...
WITH THE INTENTION OF RULING THE CONTINENT ONCE MORE.

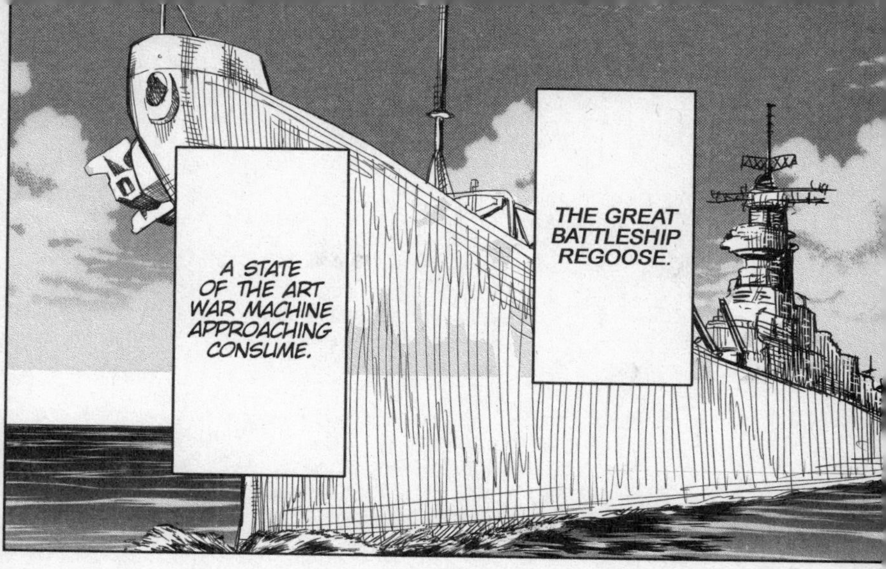
THE GREAT BATTLESHIP REGOOSE.
A STATE OF THE ART WAR MACHINE APPROACHING CONSUME.

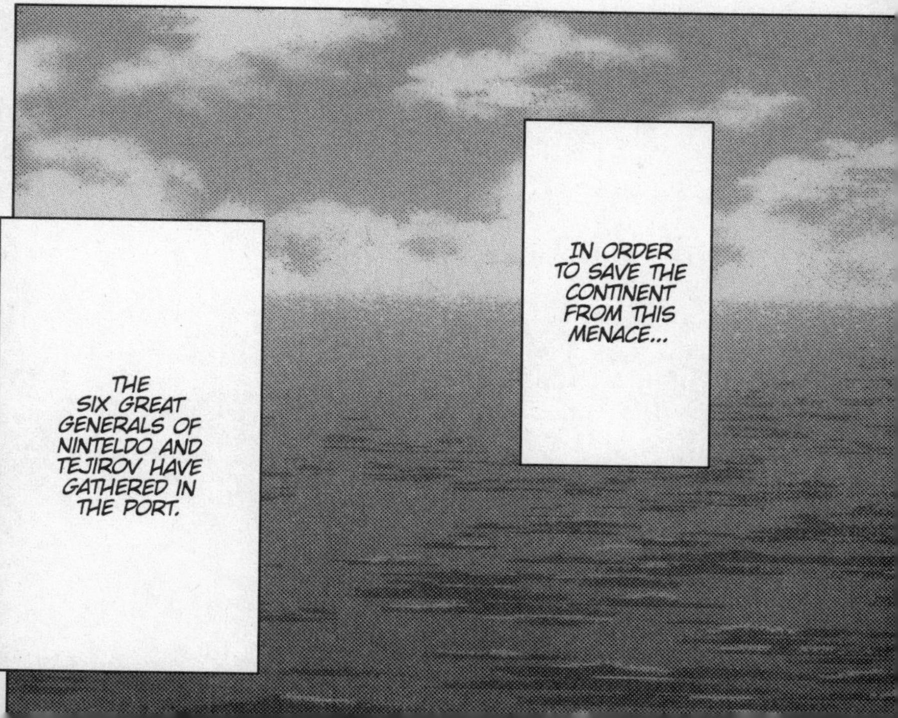
IN ORDER TO SAVE THE CONTINENT FROM THIS MENACE...
THE SIX GREAT GENERALS OF NINTELDO AND TEJIROV HAVE GATHERED IN THE PORT.

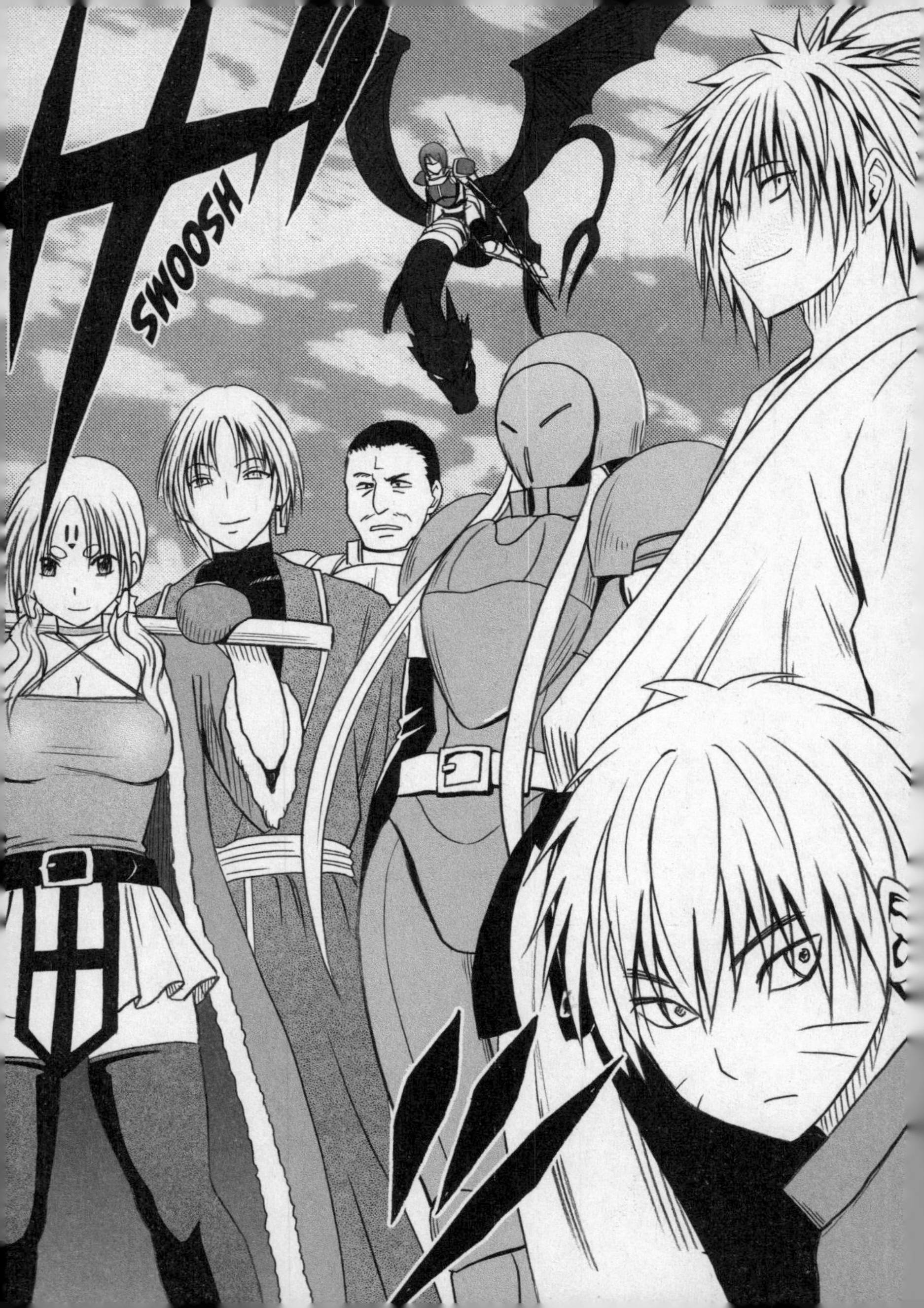
SWOOSH

World War Blue

SIDE STORY

BOY POWER

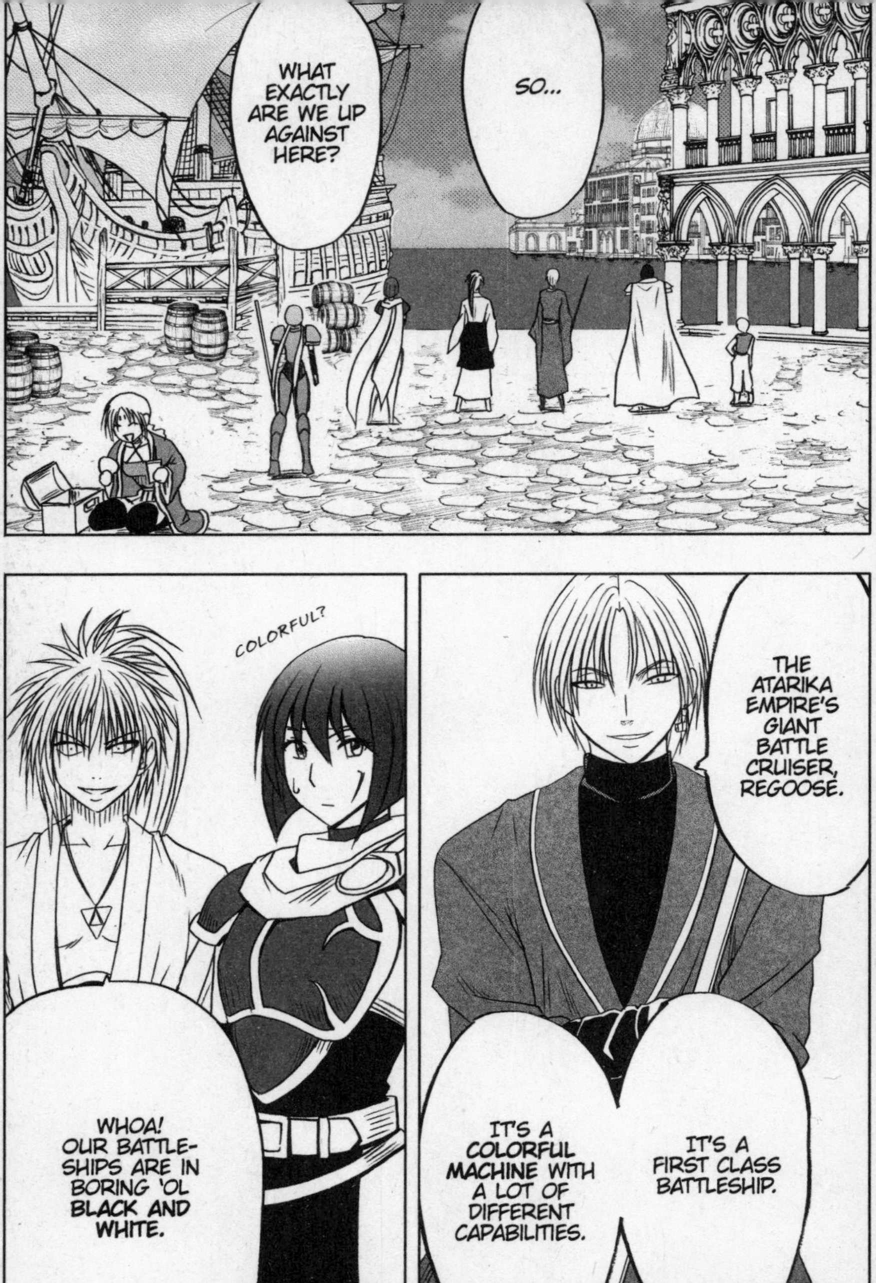
SO...
WHAT EXACTLY ARE WE UP AGAINST HERE?
THE ATARIKA EMPIRE'S GIANT BATTLE CRUISER, REGOOSE.
IT'S A FIRST CLASS BATTLESHIP.
IT'S A COLORFUL MACHINE WITH A LOT OF DIFFERENT CAPABILITIES.
COLORFUL?
WHOA! OUR BATTLE-SHIPS ARE IN BORING 'OL BLACK AND WHITE.

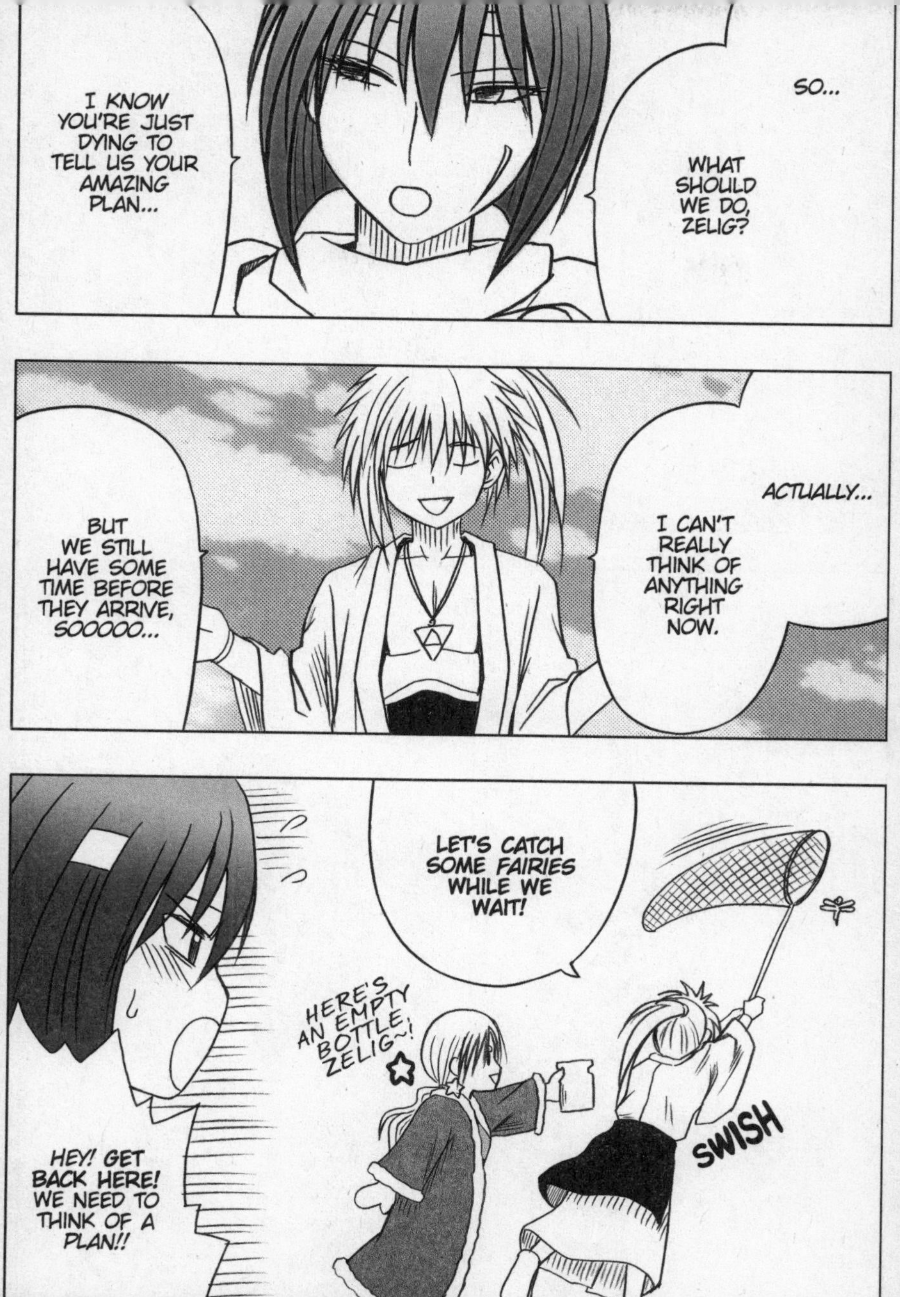
SO...
WHAT SHOULD WE DO, ZELIG?
I KNOW YOU'RE JUST DYING TO TELL US YOUR AMAZING PLAN...
ACTUALLY...
I CAN'T REALLY THINK OF ANYTHING RIGHT NOW.
BUT WE STILL HAVE SOME TIME BEFORE THEY ARRIVE, SOOOOO...
LET'S CATCH SOME FAIRIES WHILE WE WAIT!
SWISH
HERE'S AN EMPTY BOTTLE, ZELIG~!
HEY! GET BACK HERE! WE NEED TO THINK OF A PLAN!!

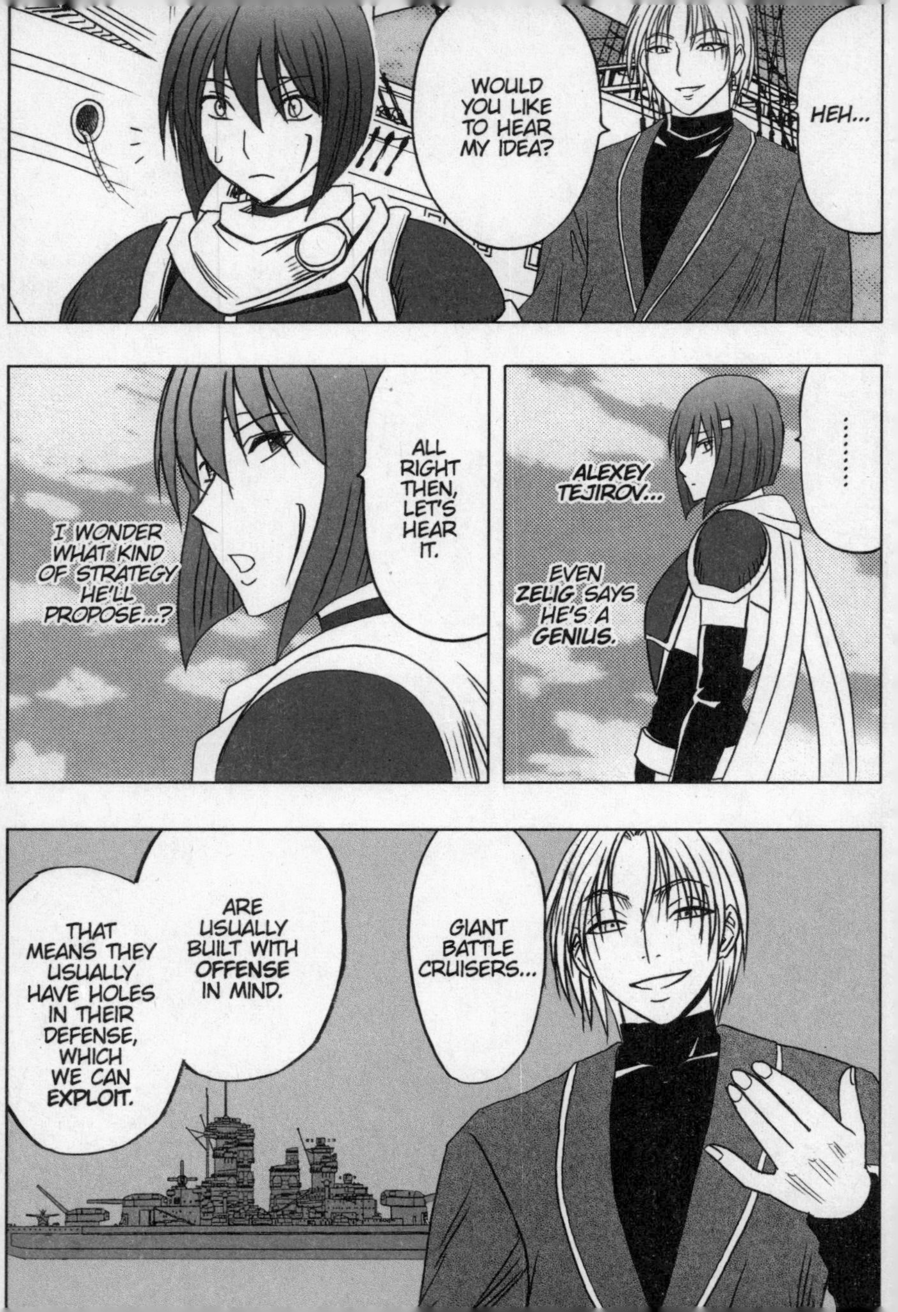
HEH...
WOULD YOU LIKE TO HEAR MY IDEA?
......
ALEXEY TEJIROV...
EVEN ZELIG SAYS HE'S A GENIUS.
ALL RIGHT THEN, LET'S HEAR IT.
I WONDER WHAT KIND OF STRATEGY HE'LL PROPOSE...?
GIANT BATTLE CRUISERS...
ARE USUALLY BUILT WITH OFFENSE IN MIND.
THAT MEANS THEY USUALLY HAVE HOLES IN THEIR DEFENSE, WHICH WE CAN EXPLOIT.

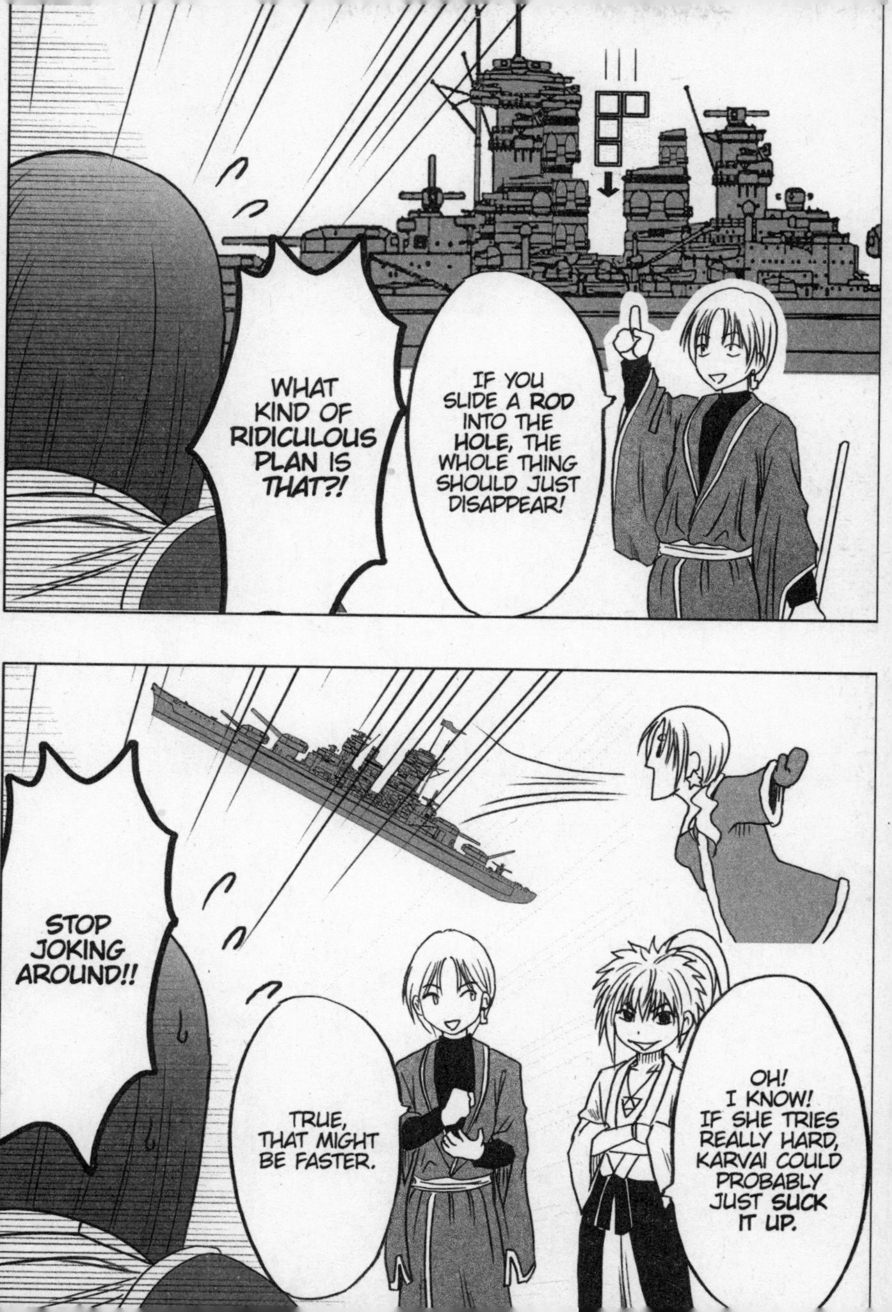
IF YOU SLIDE A ROD INTO THE HOLE, THE WHOLE THING SHOULD JUST DISAPPEAR!
WHAT KIND OF RIDICULOUS PLAN IS THAT?!
STOP JOKING AROUND!!
OH! I KNOW! IF SHE TRIES REALLY HARD, KARVAI COULD PROBABLY JUST SUCK IT UP.
TRUE, THAT MIGHT BE FASTER.

HOW WOULD SINGING HELP US?!

FIGHT	AUTO
PSI	GUARD
ITEMS	♪SING
CHECK	FORMATION

WHY DON'T WE ALL JUST SING TO KILL IT?

KARVAI'S GONNA SING TOO! ★

AM I THE ONLY SANE ONE HERE?

GOOD GOD...

HUH? ME?

BA-THUMP BA-THUMP

POINT

WELL, FAYE, DO YOU HAVE ANY IDEAS?

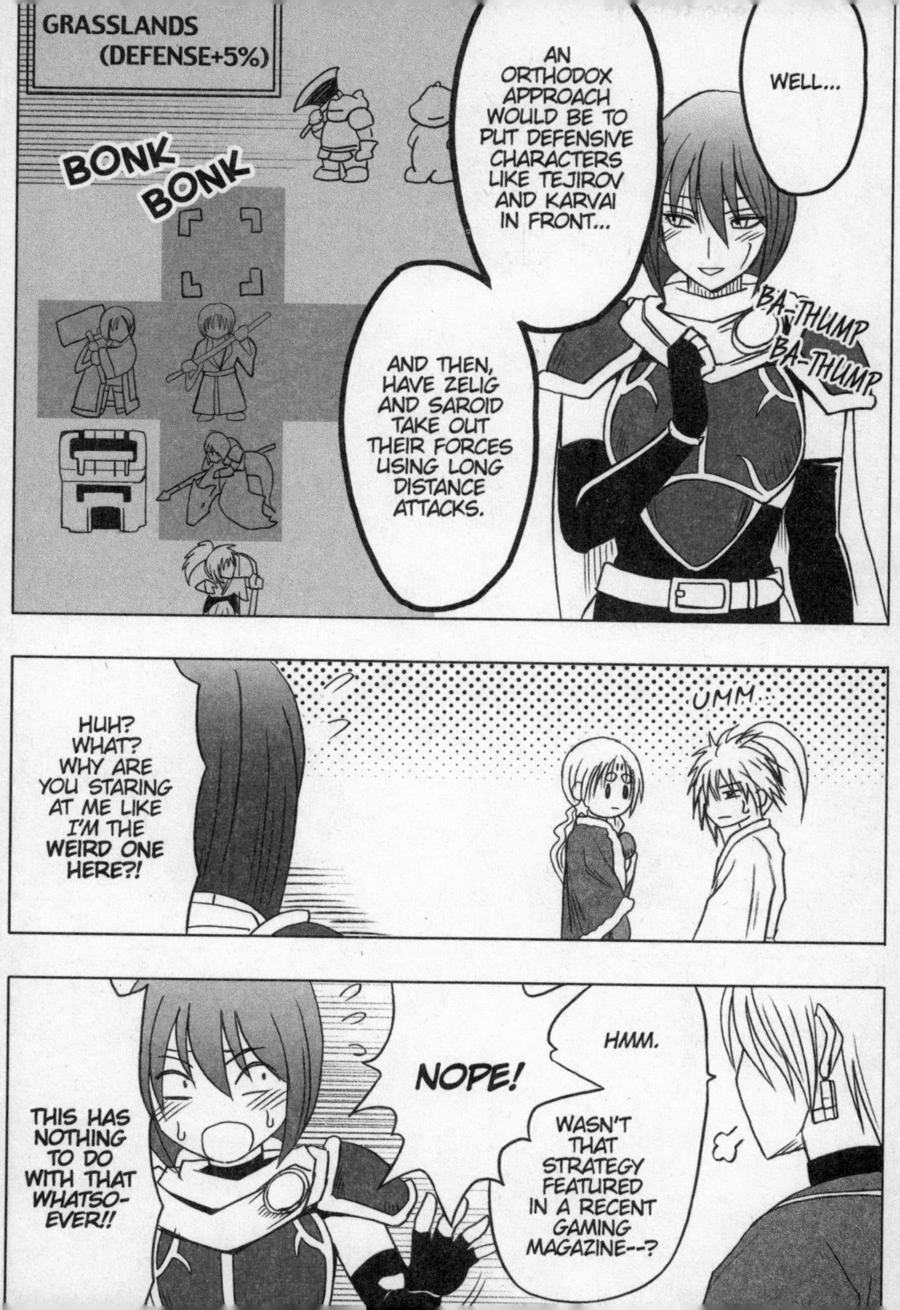
WELL...
AN ORTHODOX APPROACH WOULD BE TO PUT DEFENSIVE CHARACTERS LIKE TEJIROV AND KARVAI IN FRONT...
BA-THUMP BA-THUMP
AND THEN, HAVE ZELIG AND SAROID TAKE OUT THEIR FORCES USING LONG DISTANCE ATTACKS.
GRASSLANDS (DEFENSE+5%)
BONK BONK
UMM
HUH? WHAT? WHY ARE YOU STARING AT ME LIKE I'M THE WEIRD ONE HERE?!
HMM.
WASN'T THAT STRATEGY FEATURED IN A RECENT GAMING MAGAZINE--?
NOPE!
THIS HAS NOTHING TO DO WITH THAT WHATSO-EVER!!

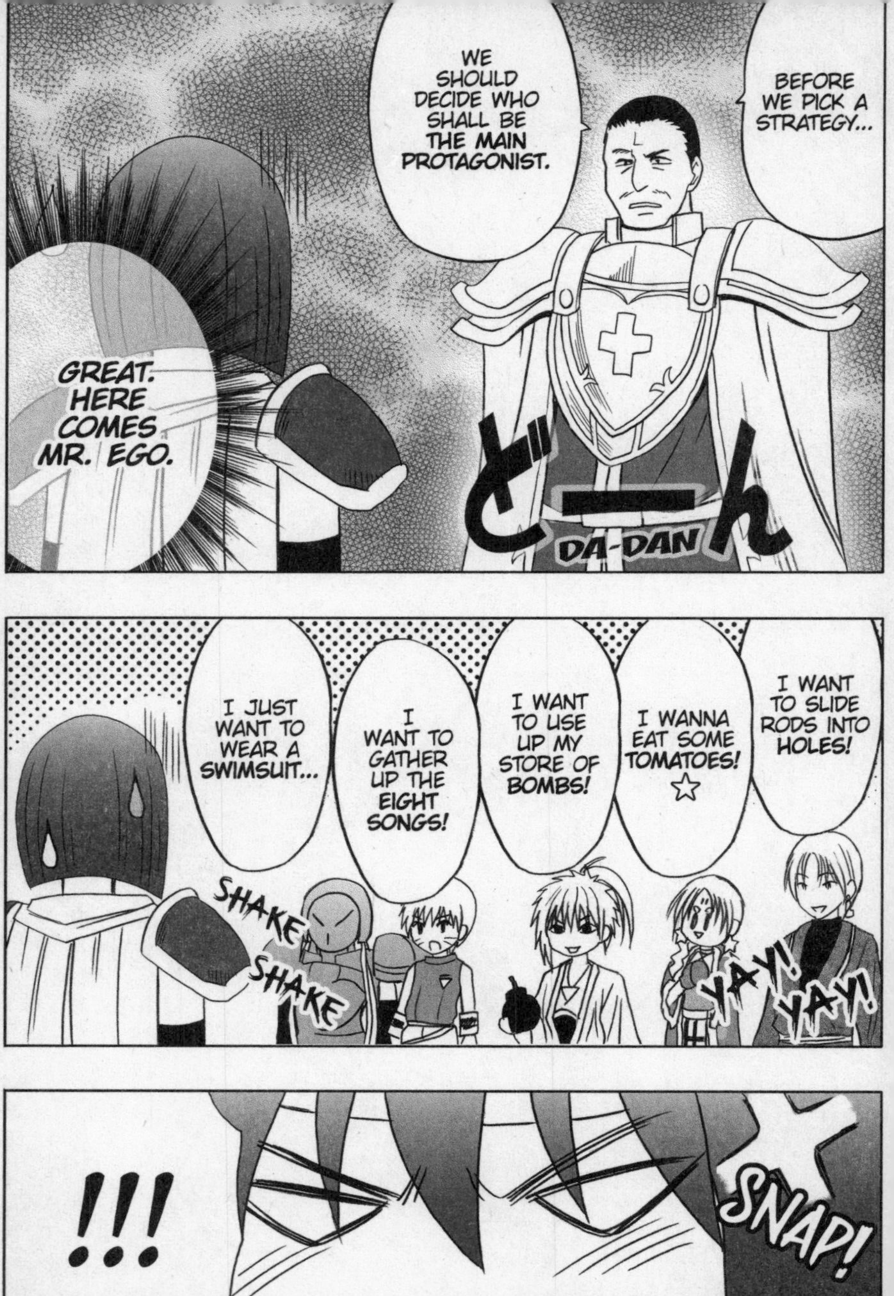
BEFORE WE PICK A STRATEGY...
WE SHOULD DECIDE WHO SHALL BE THE MAIN PROTAGONIST.
どーん
DA-DAN
GREAT. HERE COMES MR. EGO.
I WANT TO SLIDE RODS INTO HOLES!
I WANNA EAT SOME TOMATOES! ☆
YAY! YAY!
I WANT TO USE UP MY STORE OF BOMBS!
I WANT TO GATHER UP THE EIGHT SONGS!
I JUST WANT TO WEAR A SWIMSUIT...
SHAKE SHAKE
SNAP!
!!!

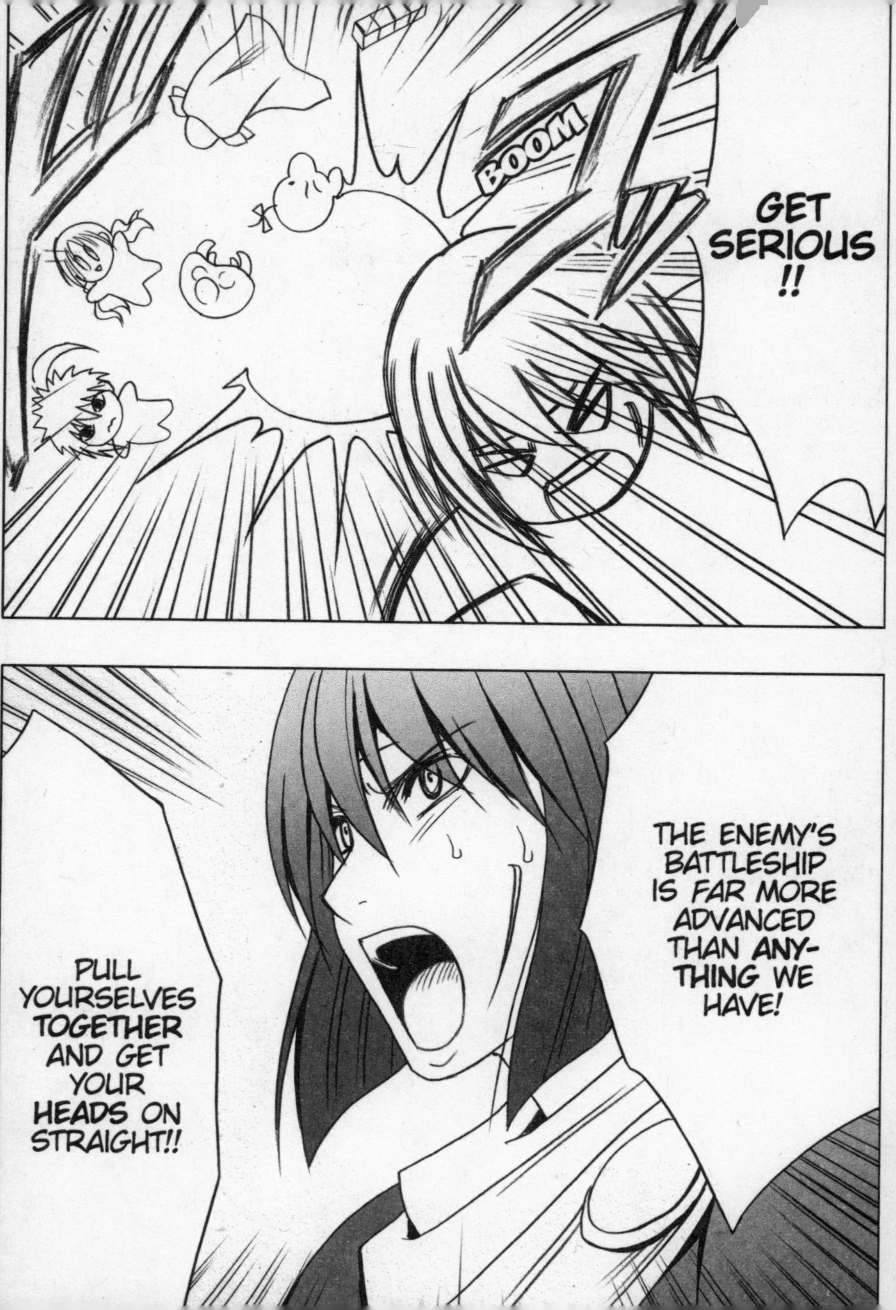
BOOM
GET SERIOUS!!
THE ENEMY'S BATTLESHIP IS FAR MORE ADVANCED THAN ANYTHING WE HAVE!
PULL YOURSELVES TOGETHER AND GET YOUR HEADS ON STRAIGHT!!

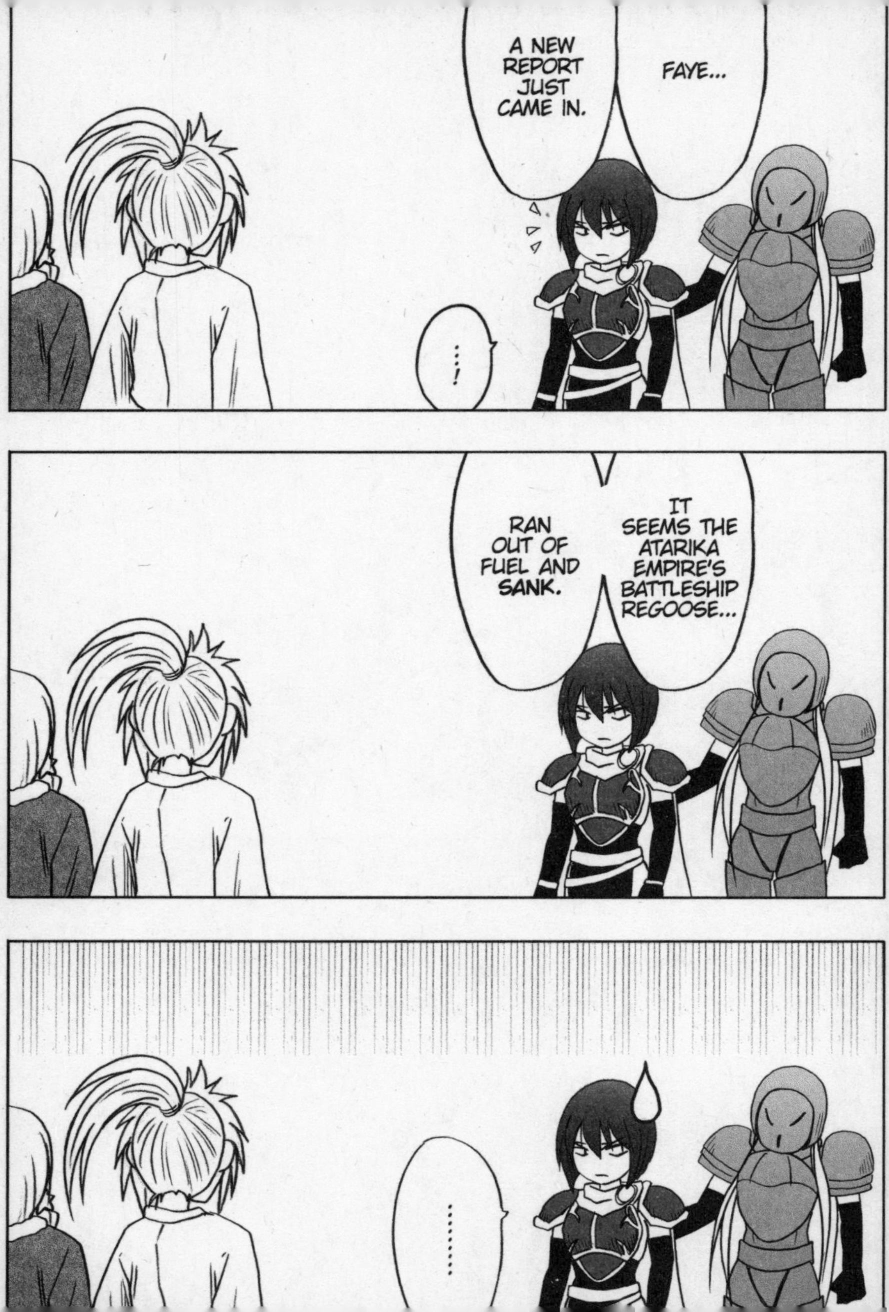
FAYE...
A NEW REPORT JUST CAME IN.
...!
IT SEEMS THE ATARIKA EMPIRE'S BATTLESHIP REGOOSE...
RAN OUT OF FUEL AND SANK.
......

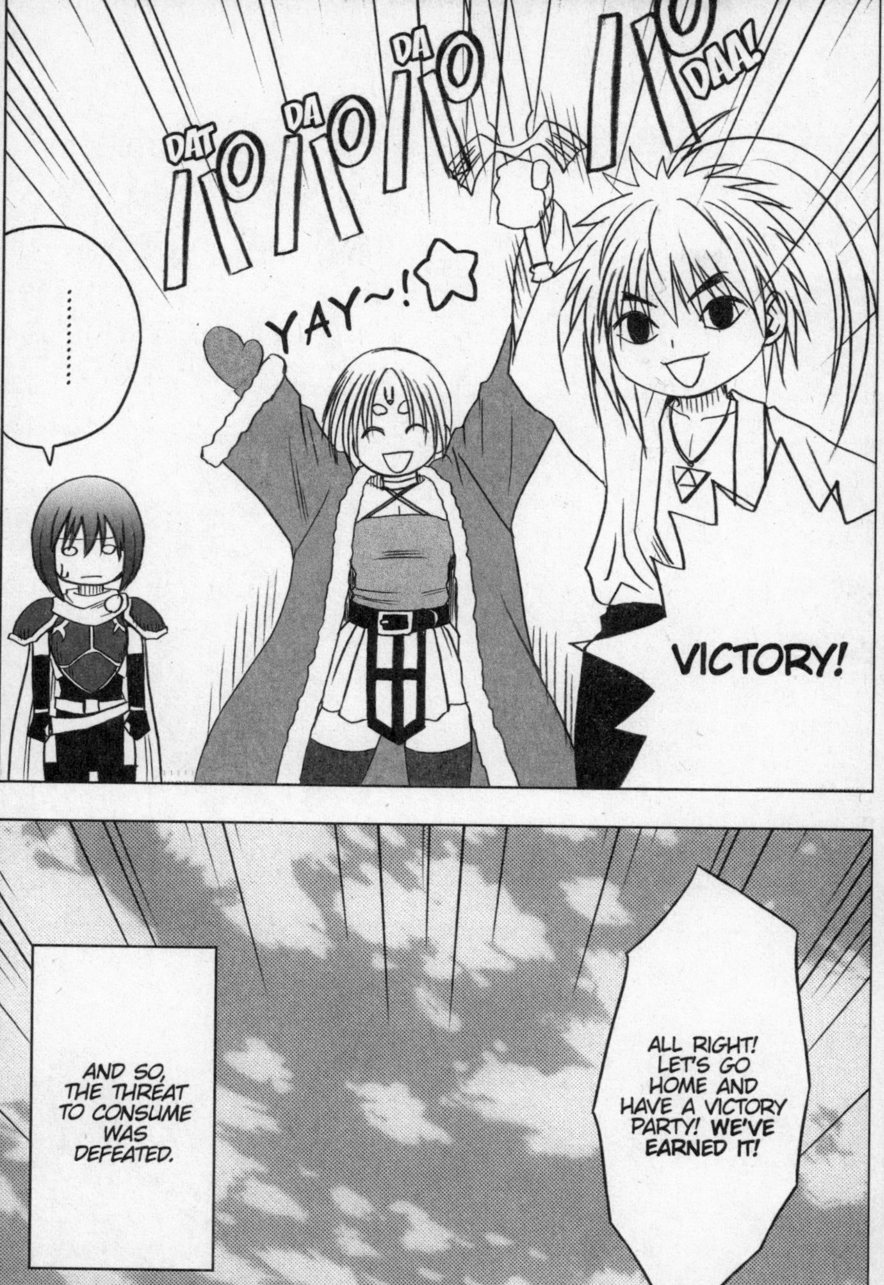
DAT DA DA DAA!
VICTORY!
YAY~!
......
ALL RIGHT! LET'S GO HOME AND HAVE A VICTORY PARTY! WE'VE EARNED IT!
AND SO, THE THREAT TO CONSUME WAS DEFEATED.

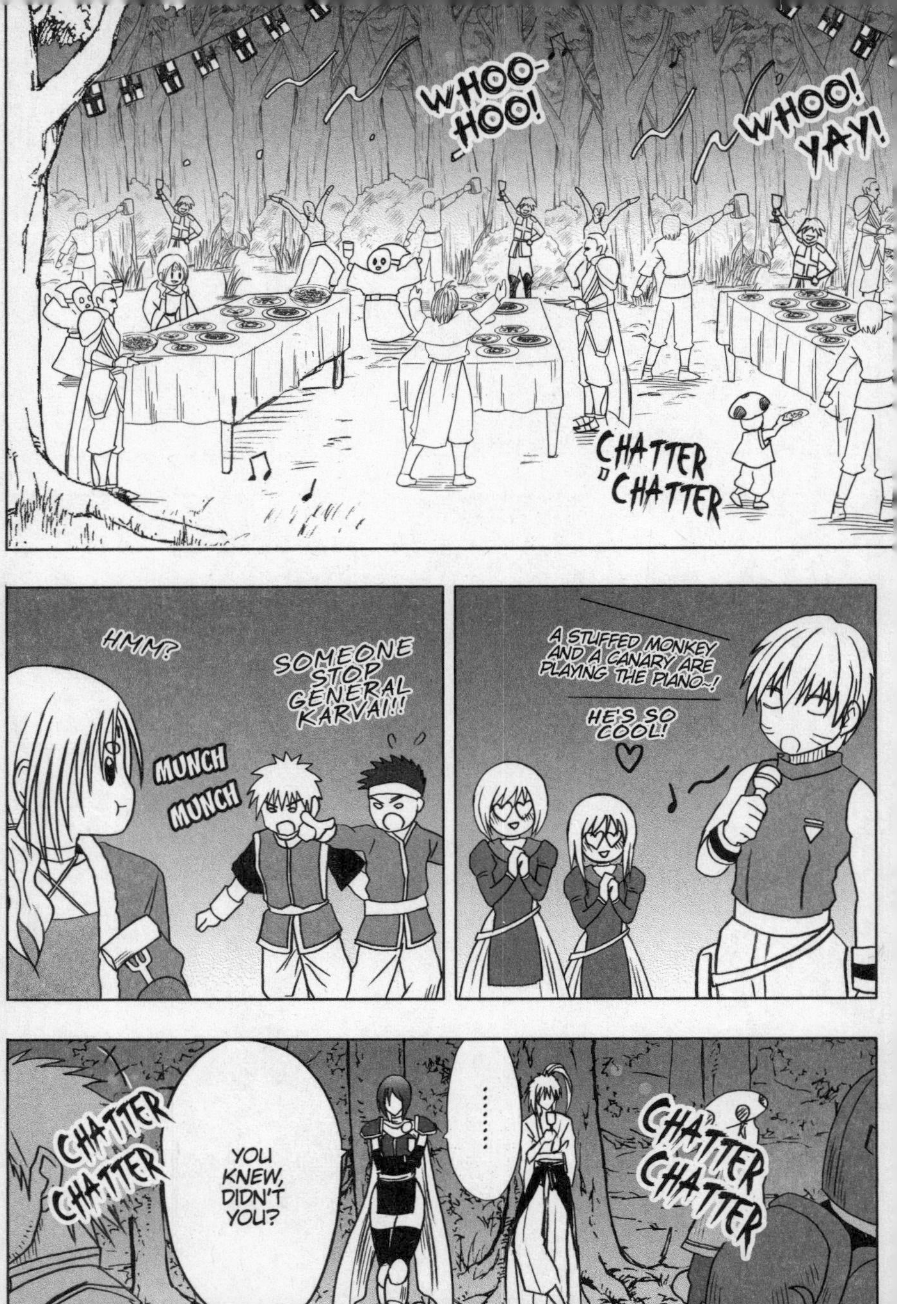
WHOO! YAY!
WHOO-HOO!
CHATTER CHATTER
A STUFFED MONKEY AND A CANARY ARE PLAYING THE PIANO~!
HE'S SO COOL!
SOMEONE STOP GENERAL KARVAI!!
HMM?
MUNCH MUNCH
CHATTER CHATTER
......
YOU KNEW, DIDN'T YOU?
CHATTER CHATTER

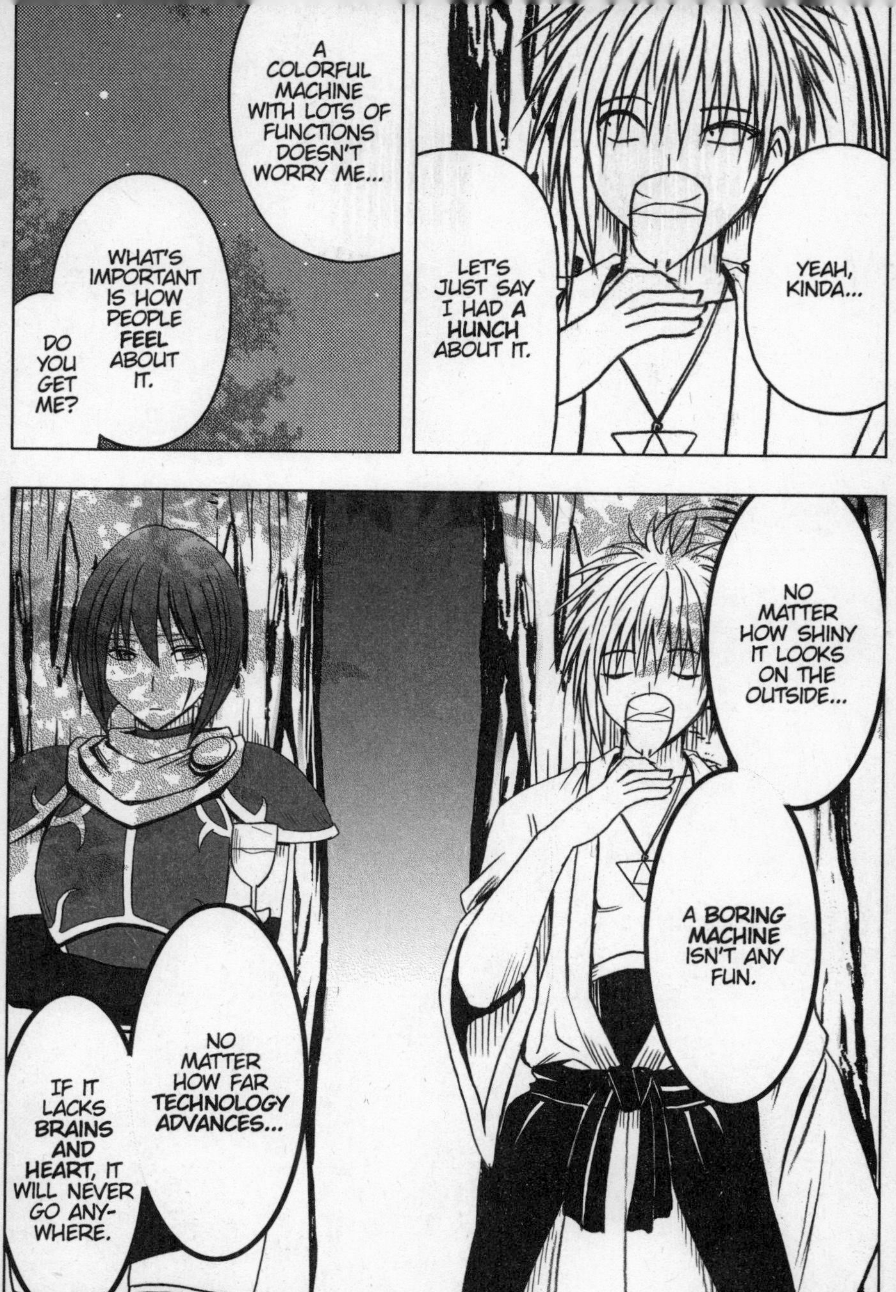
YEAH, KINDA...
LET'S JUST SAY I HAD A HUNCH ABOUT IT.
A COLORFUL MACHINE WITH LOTS OF FUNCTIONS DOESN'T WORRY ME...
WHAT'S IMPORTANT IS HOW PEOPLE FEEL ABOUT IT.
DO YOU GET ME?
NO MATTER HOW SHINY IT LOOKS ON THE OUTSIDE...
A BORING MACHINE ISN'T ANY FUN.
NO MATTER HOW FAR TECHNOLOGY ADVANCES...
IF IT LACKS BRAINS AND HEART, IT WILL NEVER GO ANY-WHERE.

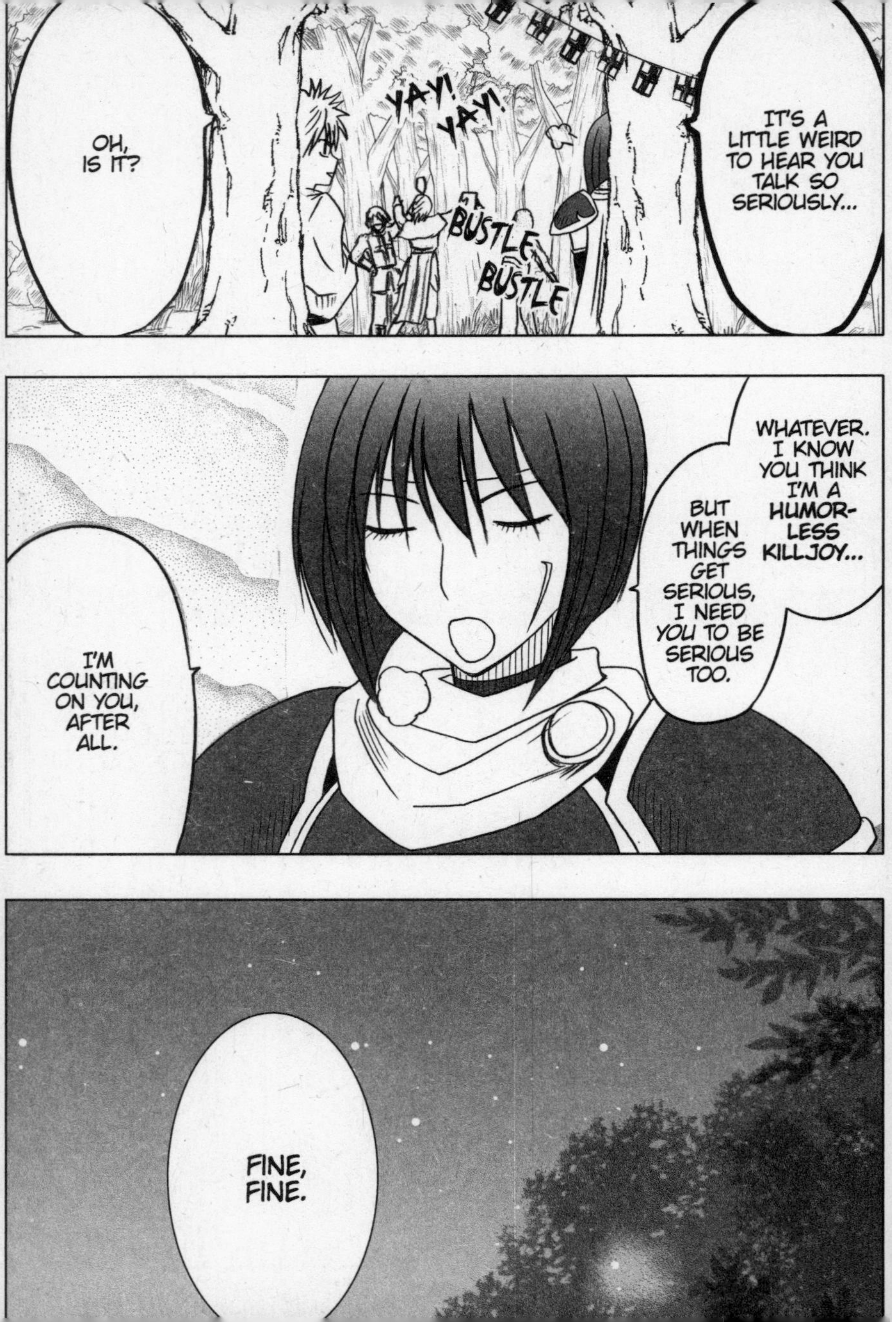
IT'S A LITTLE WEIRD TO HEAR YOU TALK SO SERIOUSLY...
YAY! YAY!
BUSTLE BUSTLE
OH, IS IT?
WHATEVER. I KNOW YOU THINK I'M A HUMORLESS KILLJOY...
BUT WHEN THINGS GET SERIOUS, I NEED YOU TO BE SERIOUS TOO.
I'M COUNTING ON YOU, AFTER ALL.
FINE, FINE.

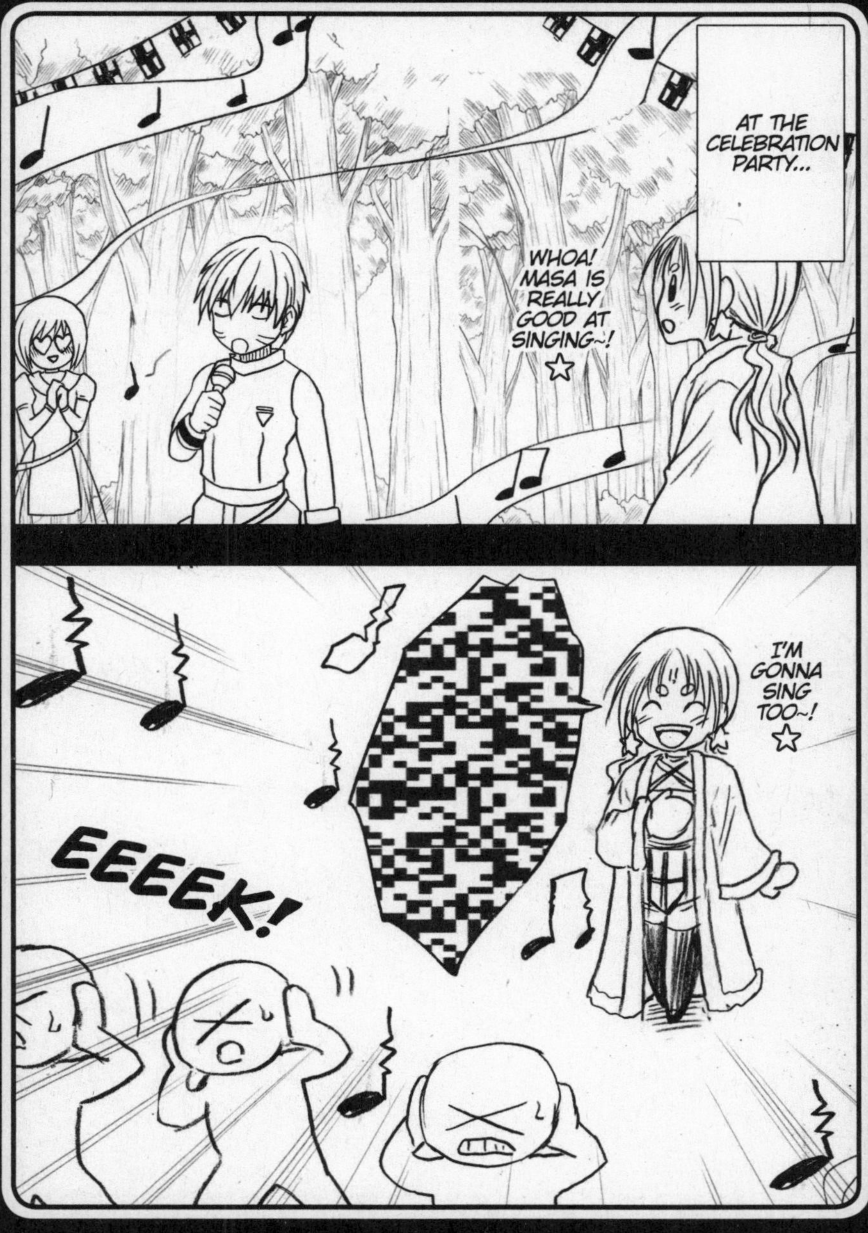
AT THE CELEBRATION PARTY...
WHOA! MASA IS REALLY GOOD AT SINGING~! ☆
I'M GONNA SING TOO~! ☆
EEEEK!

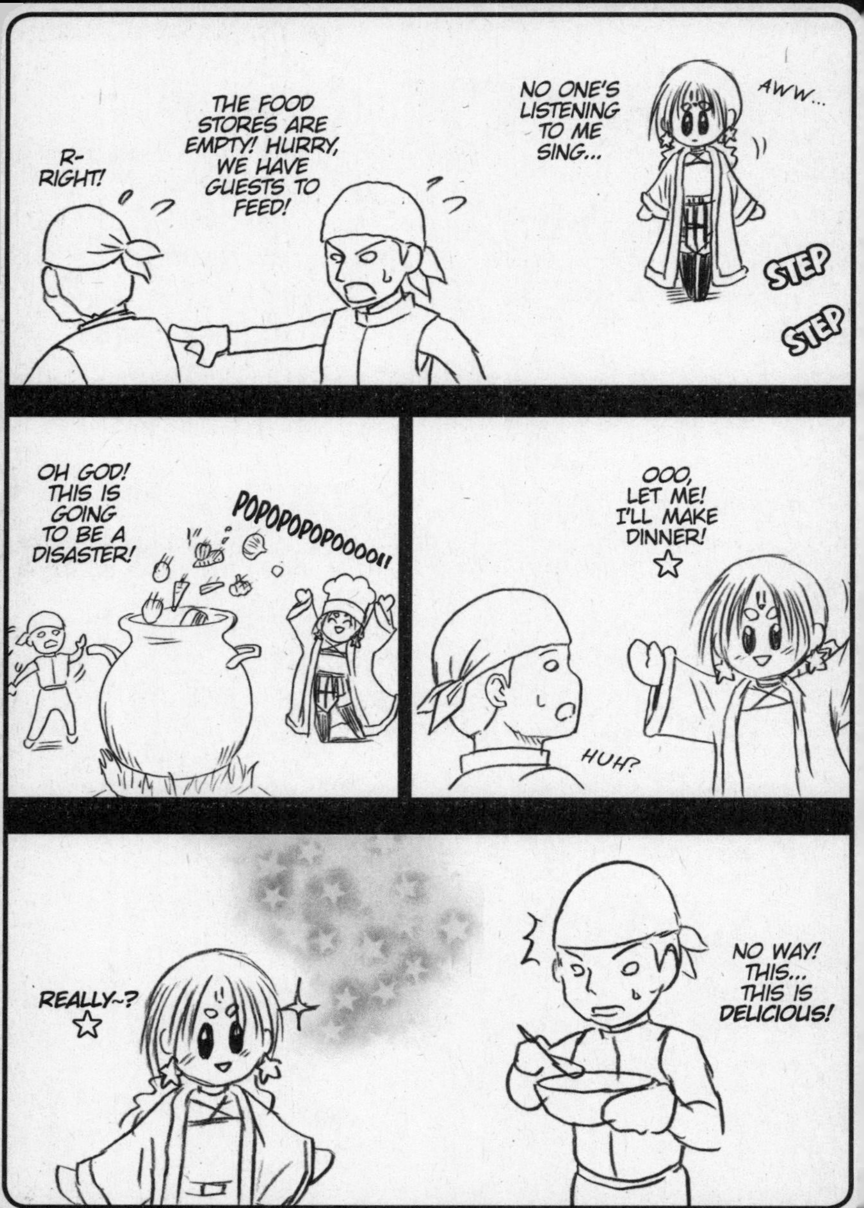
AWW...
NO ONE'S LISTENING TO ME SING...
STEP
STEP
THE FOOD STORES ARE EMPTY! HURRY, WE HAVE GUESTS TO FEED!
R-RIGHT!
OOO, LET ME! I'LL MAKE DINNER! ☆
HUH?
POPOPOPOPOOOOO!!
OH GOD! THIS IS GOING TO BE A DISASTER!
NO WAY! THIS... THIS IS DELICIOUS!
REALLY~? ☆

KARVAI'S TERRIBLE AT SINGING, BUT SHE'S AN EXCELLENT COOK!☆

Perusing Video Game History

ON THE EDGE OF THE BLUE WORLD

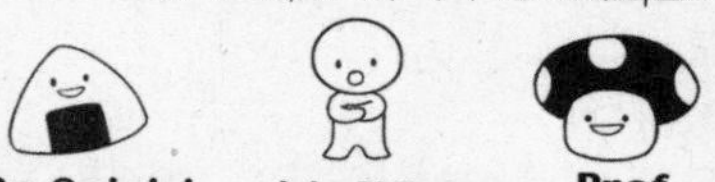

Dr. Onigiri Mr. Why Prof. Mushroom

Today's Topic

THE ATARI LYNX

Mr. Why: Now that I think about it, we've only really covered game consoles that were made in Japan. There must have been some consoles that were made overseas, right?

Dr. Onirigi: Well, let's see... How about we touch a little on Atari, the company Atarika is named for, and their 16-bit handheld gaming console, the Atari Lynx?

Mr. Why: Wow... That name sounds kind of menacing.

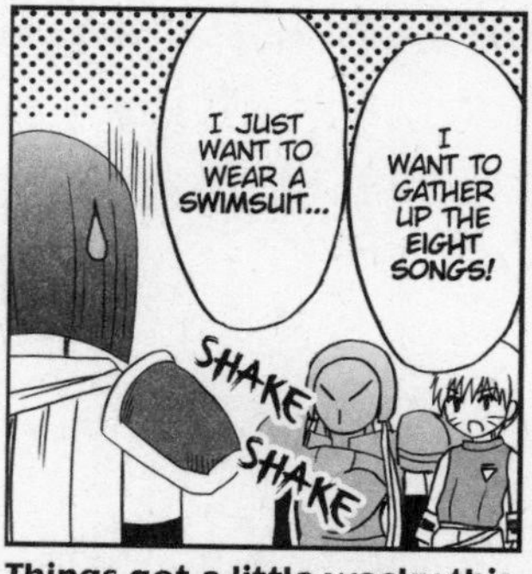
I WANT TO GATHER UP THE EIGHT SONGS!
I JUST WANT TO WEAR A SWIMSUIT...
SHAKE
SHAKE

Things got a little wacky this chapter and I don't really know why...

Prof. Mushroom: The Atari Lynx was released in September 1989, which was the same year that Nintendo Game Boy hit the market. (Note: The Game Boy was released in Japan on April 21, 1989 and in North America in August 1989.) The Atari Lynx was also the first handheld electronic game with a color LCD (liquid crystal display) screen and also featured backlighting.

Dr. Onigiri: And it was jam packed with features! The Game Boy could hardly stand up to it on a technical level.

Mr. Why: Wow, the Lynx sounds awesome! And LCD must have been pretty cutting edge. Did it sell well?

Prof. Mushroom: Nope. Not well at all.

Mr. Why: What?! Why?!

Dr. Onigiri: While it had really good specs, the whole unit was quite large and weighed around 700 grams (1.54 lbs), so it was quite heavy.

Prof. Mushroom: Not only that, but its power efficiency was terrible. The whole thing needed **six AA batteries** to run, and even then, it could only run for about two to three hours at a time. Compare that to the Nintendo Game Boy, which could run on four AA batteries for 20 hours. That's a huge difference.

Dr. Onigiri: And when it launched in North America, its initial retail price was $189.95, which made it too expensive for the average consumer--especially when compared to the Nintendo Game Boy's $89.95 price point. The Atari Lynx just didn't stand a chance.

Prof. Mushroom: And the games that came out for the Lynx just weren't that good. By trying to sell itself using only its high specs and color LCD screen, you could say the Atari Lynx just sank itself.

Mr. Why: I guess that shows that programming makes the games, not their appearance.

To Be Continued...

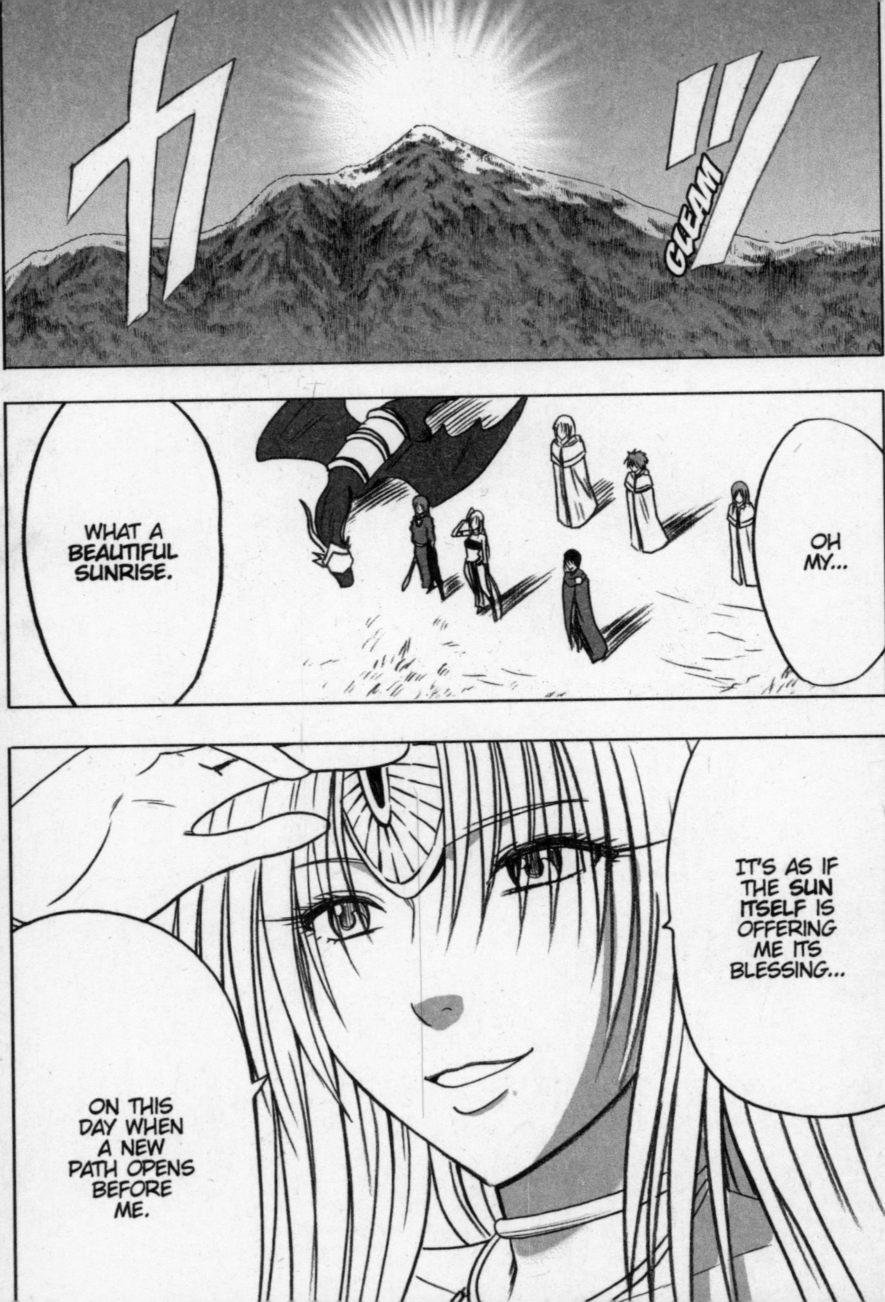
GLEAM
カッ
OH MY...
WHAT A BEAUTIFUL SUNRISE.
IT'S AS IF THE SUN ITSELF IS OFFERING ME ITS BLESSING...
ON THIS DAY WHEN A NEW PATH OPENS BEFORE ME.

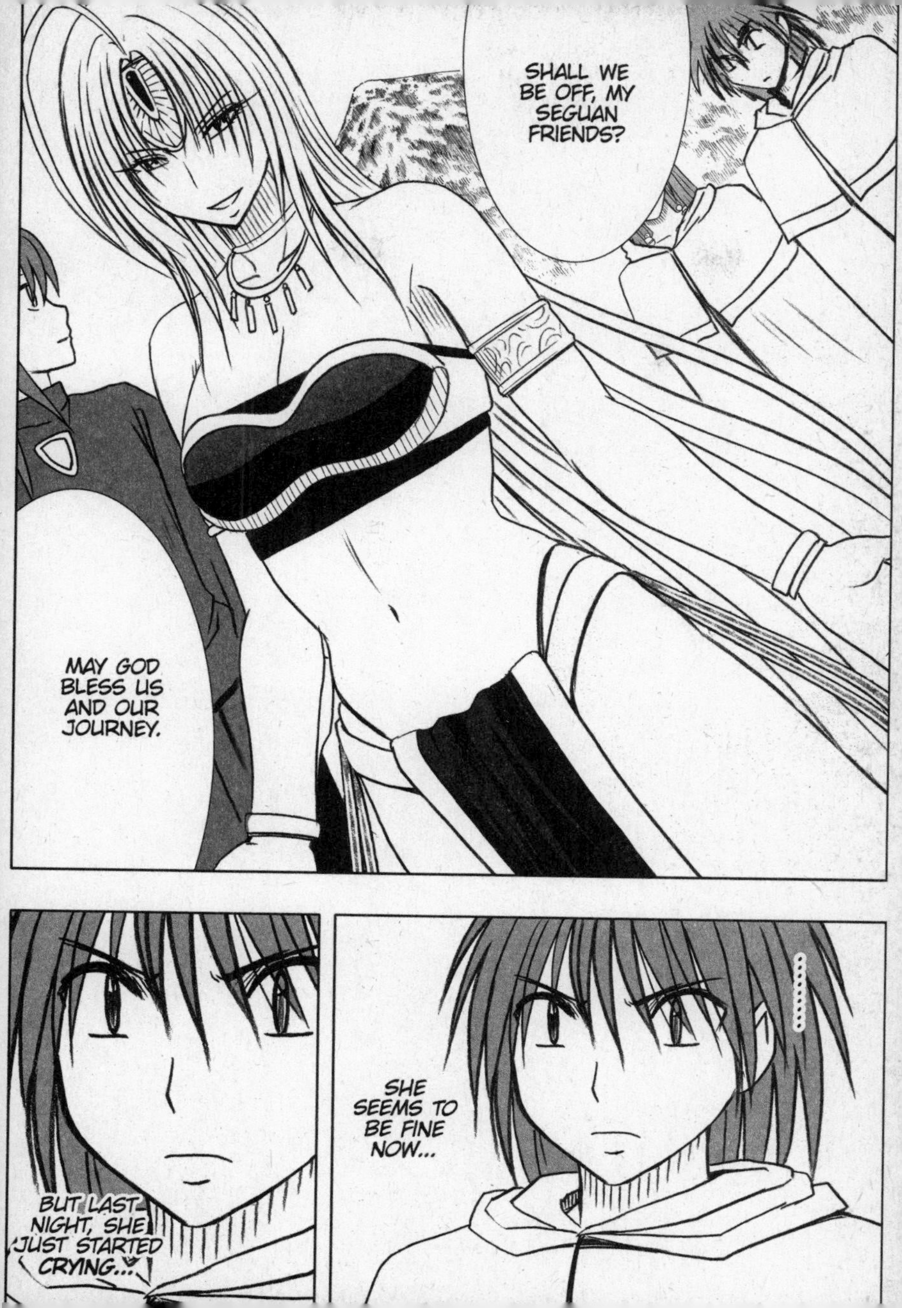
SHALL WE BE OFF, MY SEGUAN FRIENDS?
MAY GOD BLESS US AND OUR JOURNEY.
......
SHE SEEMS TO BE FINE NOW...
BUT LAST NIGHT, SHE JUST STARTED CRYING...

CHAPTER 25

CLASH UNDER THE
BIG BRIDGE

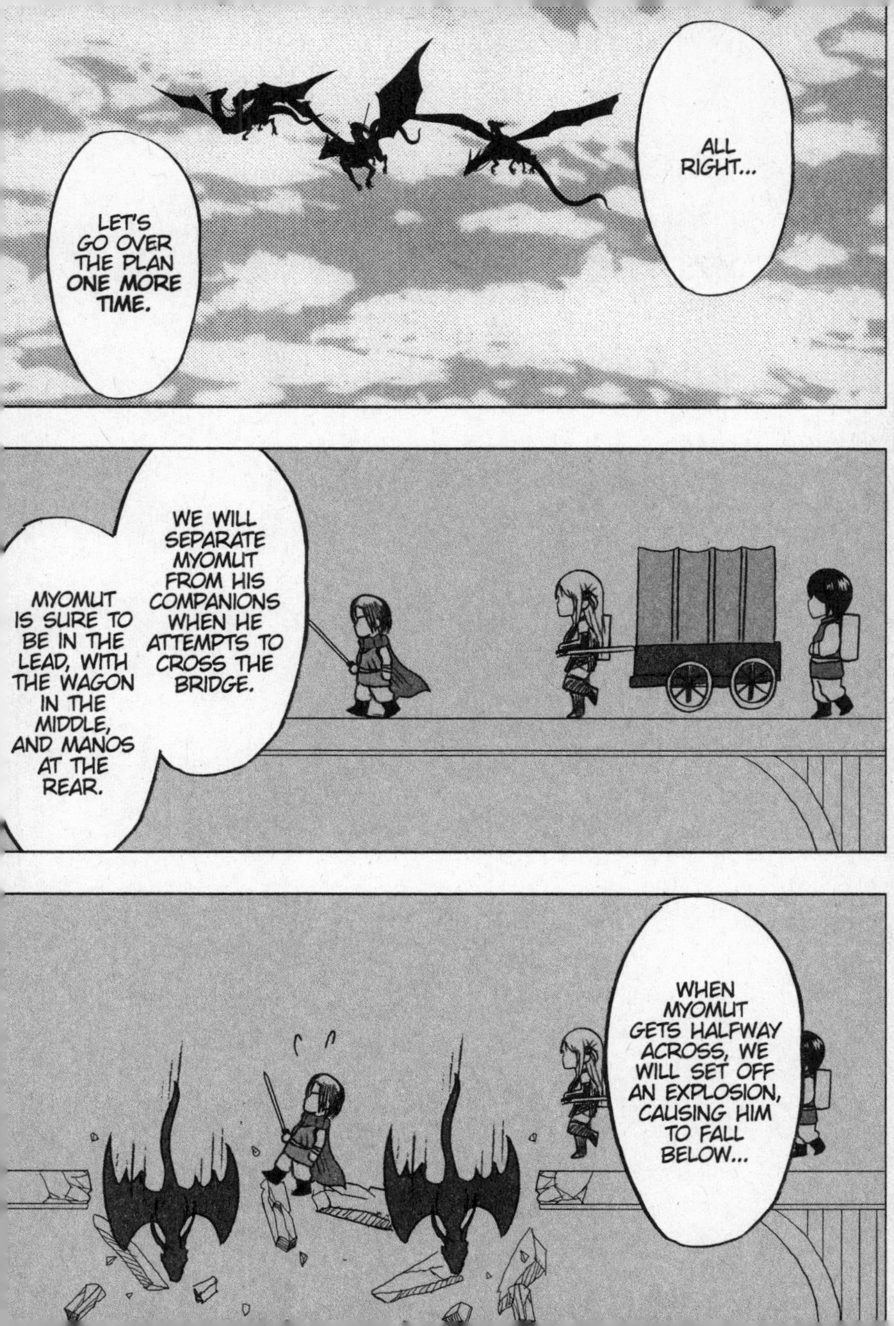
ALL RIGHT...
LET'S GO OVER THE PLAN ONE MORE TIME.
WE WILL SEPARATE MYOMUT FROM HIS COMPANIONS WHEN HE ATTEMPTS TO CROSS THE BRIDGE.
MYOMUT IS SURE TO BE IN THE LEAD, WITH THE WAGON IN THE MIDDLE, AND MANOS AT THE REAR.
WHEN MYOMUT GETS HALFWAY ACROSS, WE WILL SET OFF AN EXPLOSION, CAUSING HIM TO FALL BELOW...

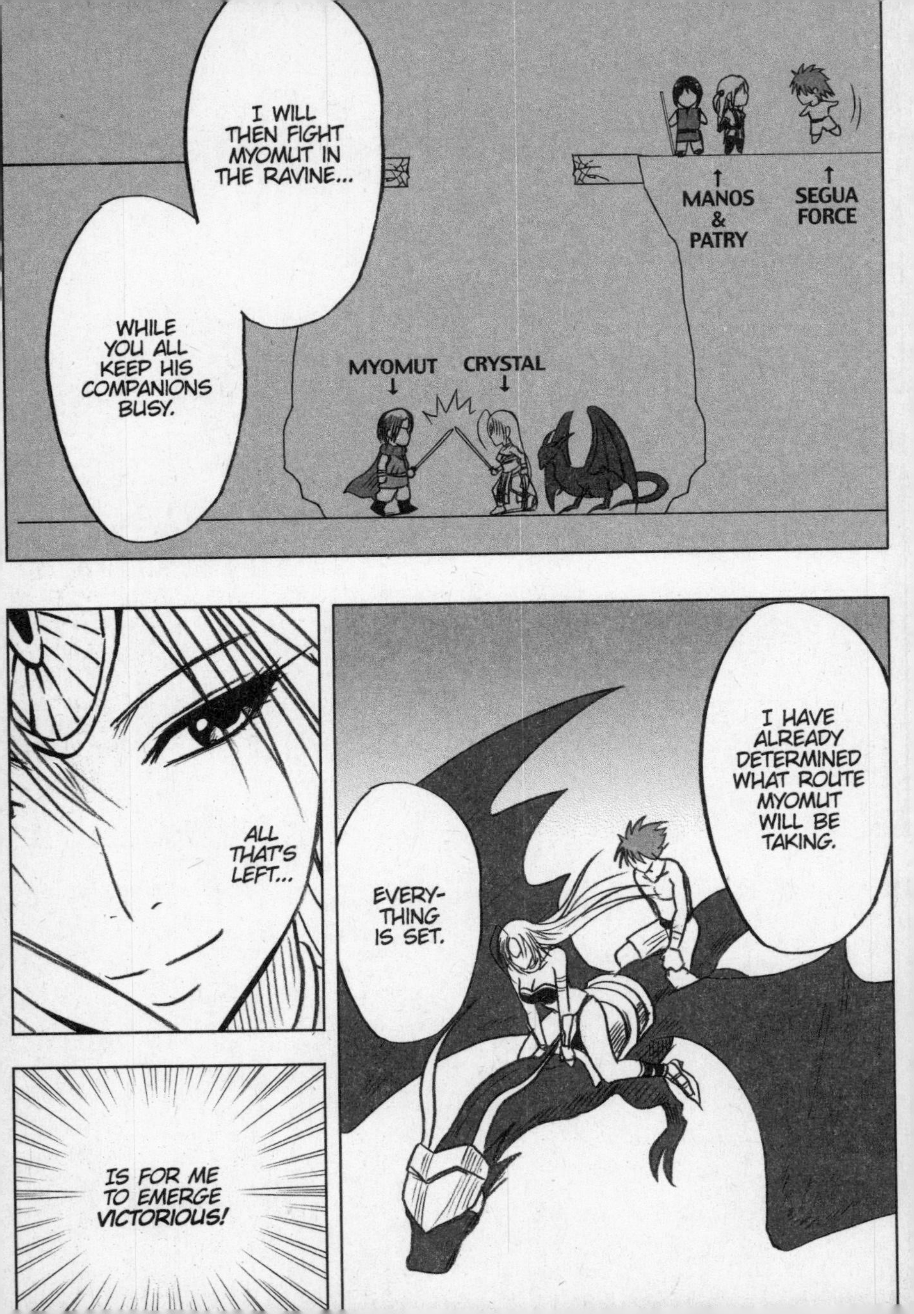
SEGUA FORCE
MANOS & PATRY
I WILL THEN FIGHT MYOMUT IN THE RAVINE...
WHILE YOU ALL KEEP HIS COMPANIONS BUSY.
CRYSTAL
MYOMUT
I HAVE ALREADY DETERMINED WHAT ROUTE MYOMUT WILL BE TAKING.
EVERY-THING IS SET.
ALL THAT'S LEFT...
IS FOR ME TO EMERGE VICTORIOUS!

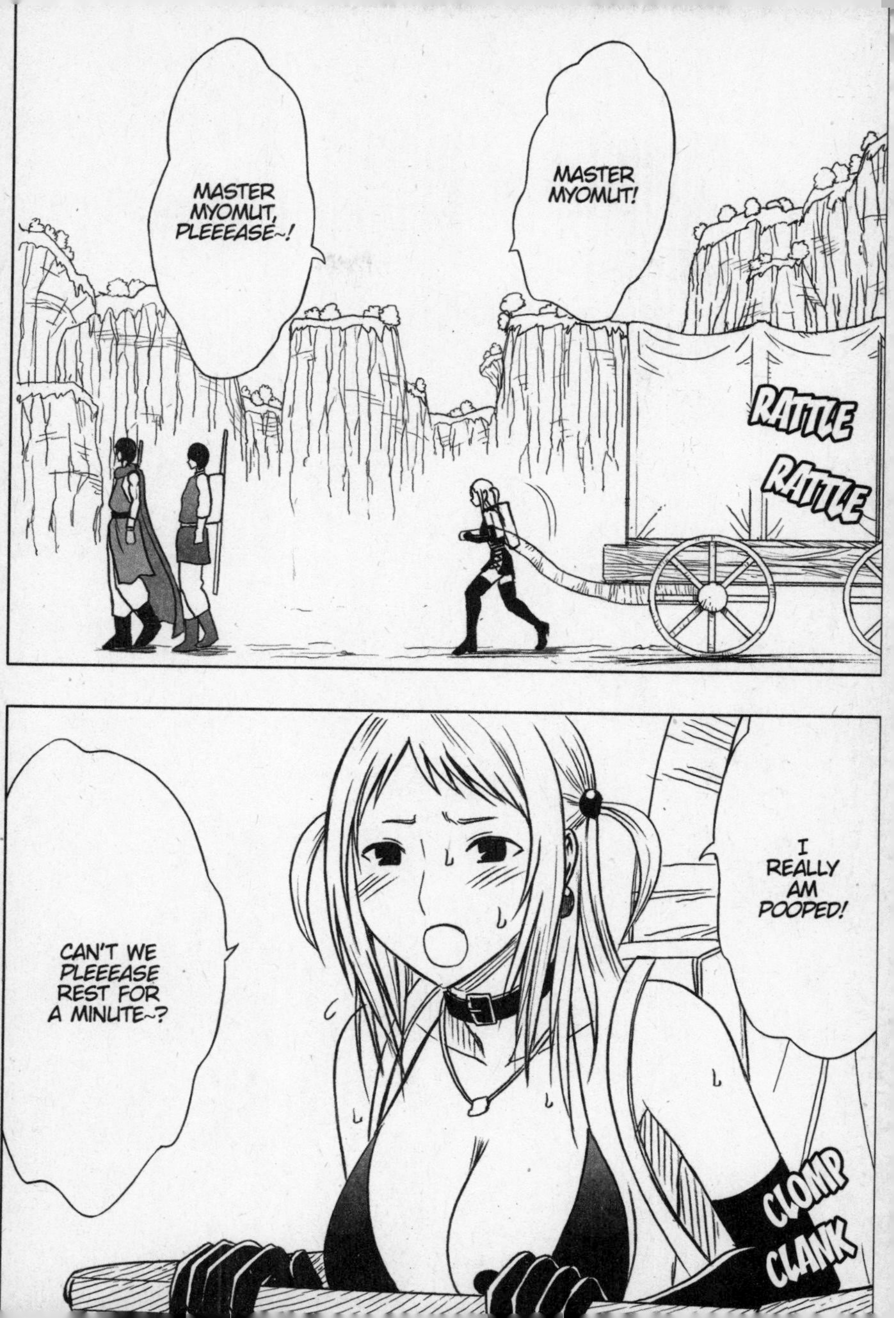
MASTER MYOMUT!
MASTER MYOMUT, PLEEEASE~!
RATTLE
RATTLE
I REALLY AM POOPED!
CAN'T WE PLEEEASE REST FOR A MINUTE~?
CLOMP
CLANK

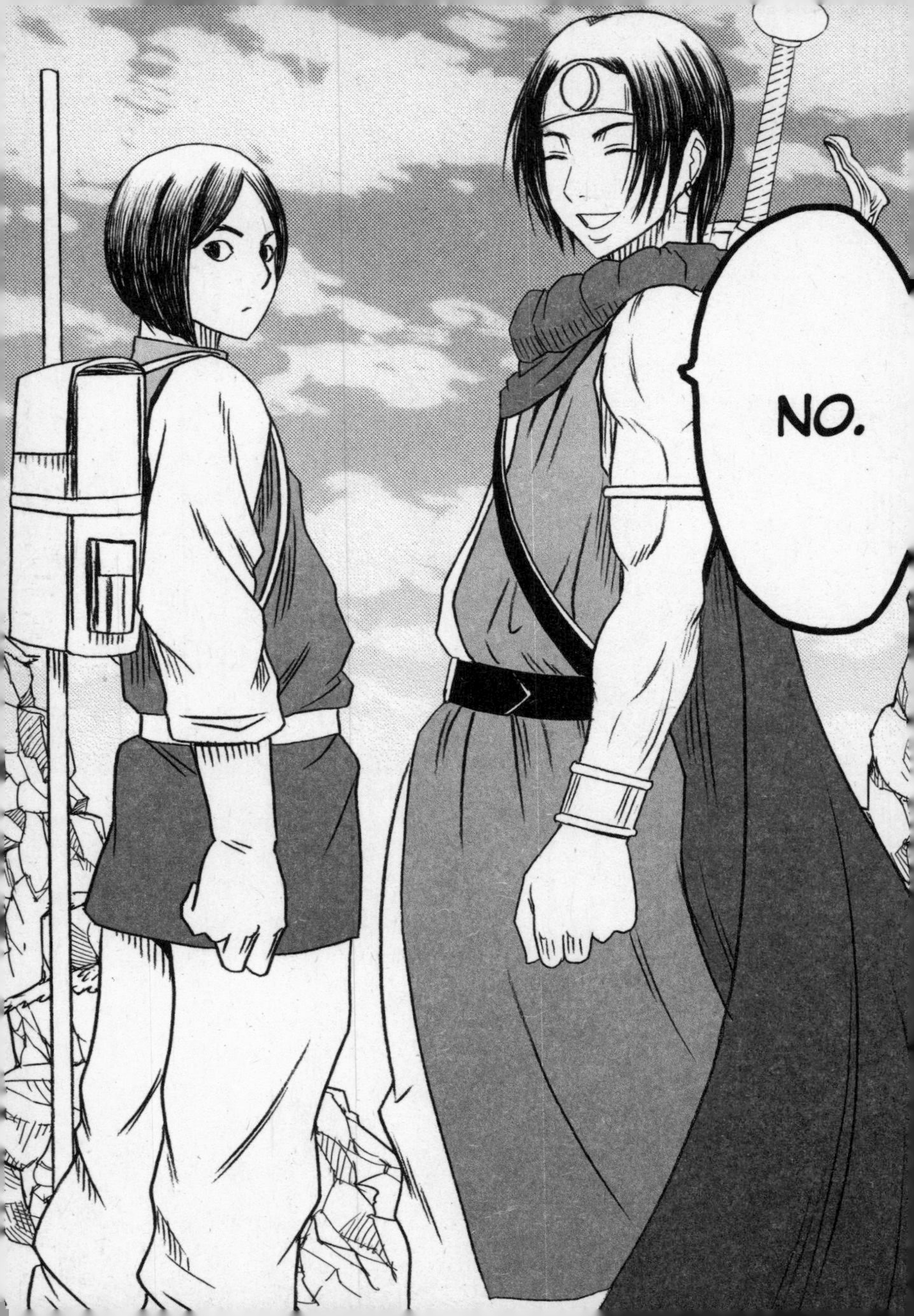
NO.

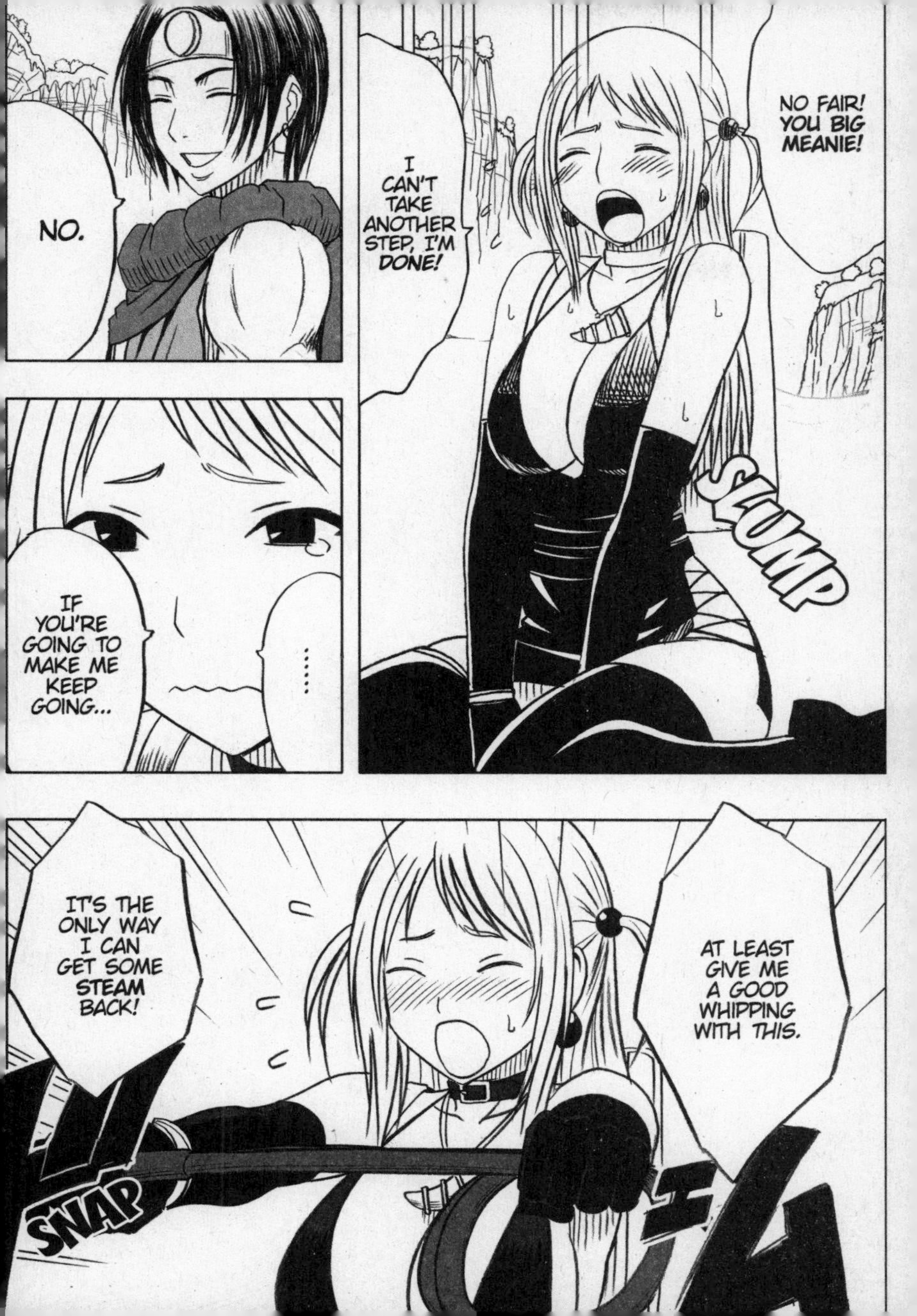
NO FAIR! YOU BIG MEANIE!
I CAN'T TAKE ANOTHER STEP, I'M DONE!
SLUMP
NO.
......
IF YOU'RE GOING TO MAKE ME KEEP GOING...
AT LEAST GIVE ME A GOOD WHIPPING WITH THIS.
IT'S THE ONLY WAY I CAN GET SOME STEAM BACK!
SNAP

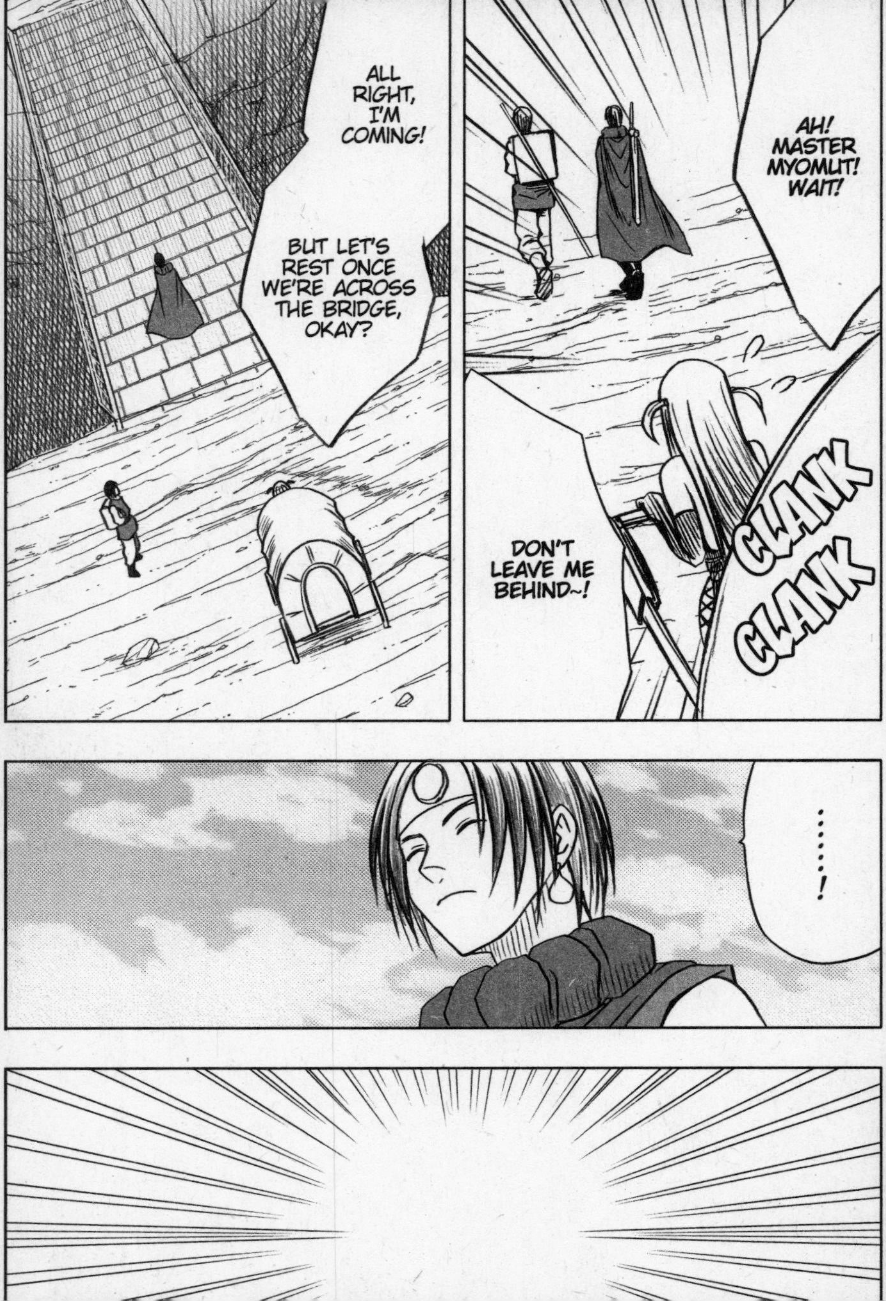
AH! MASTER MYOMUT! WAIT!
DON'T LEAVE ME BEHIND~!
CLANK CLANK
ALL RIGHT, I'M COMING!
BUT LET'S REST ONCE WE'RE ACROSS THE BRIDGE, OKAY?
......!

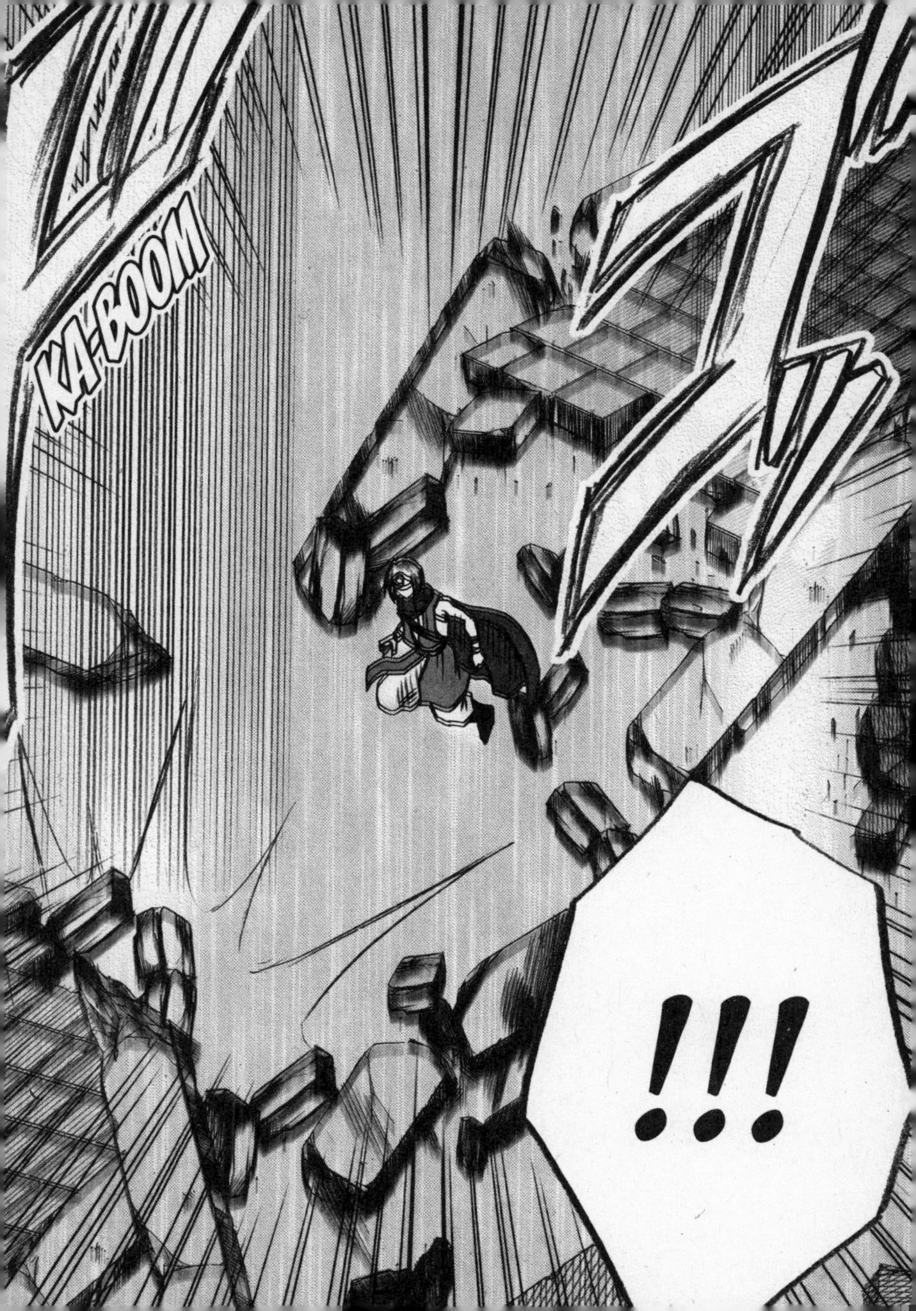
KA-BOOM
!!!

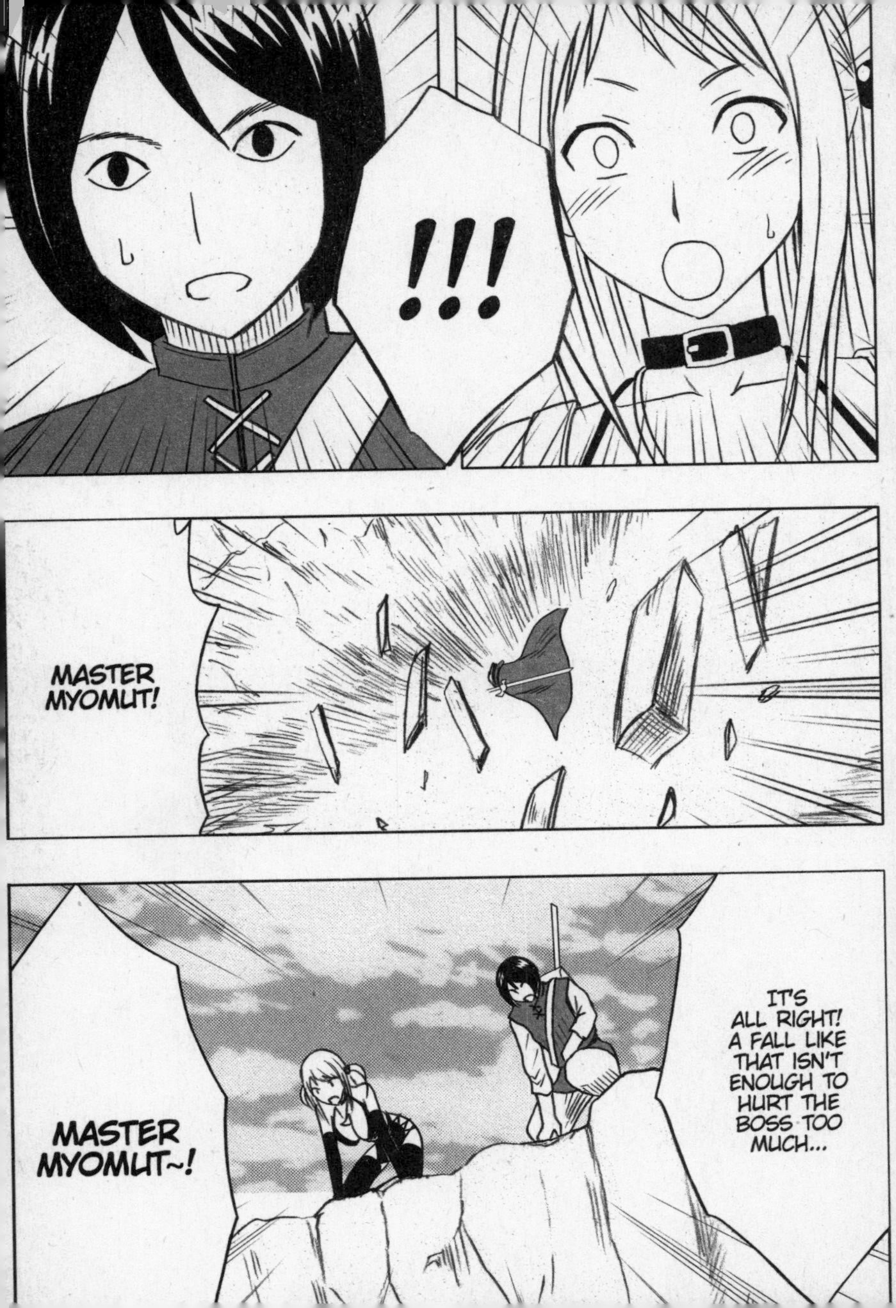
!!!
MASTER MYOMUT!
IT'S ALL RIGHT! A FALL LIKE THAT ISN'T ENOUGH TO HURT THE BOSS TOO MUCH...
MASTER MYOMUT~!

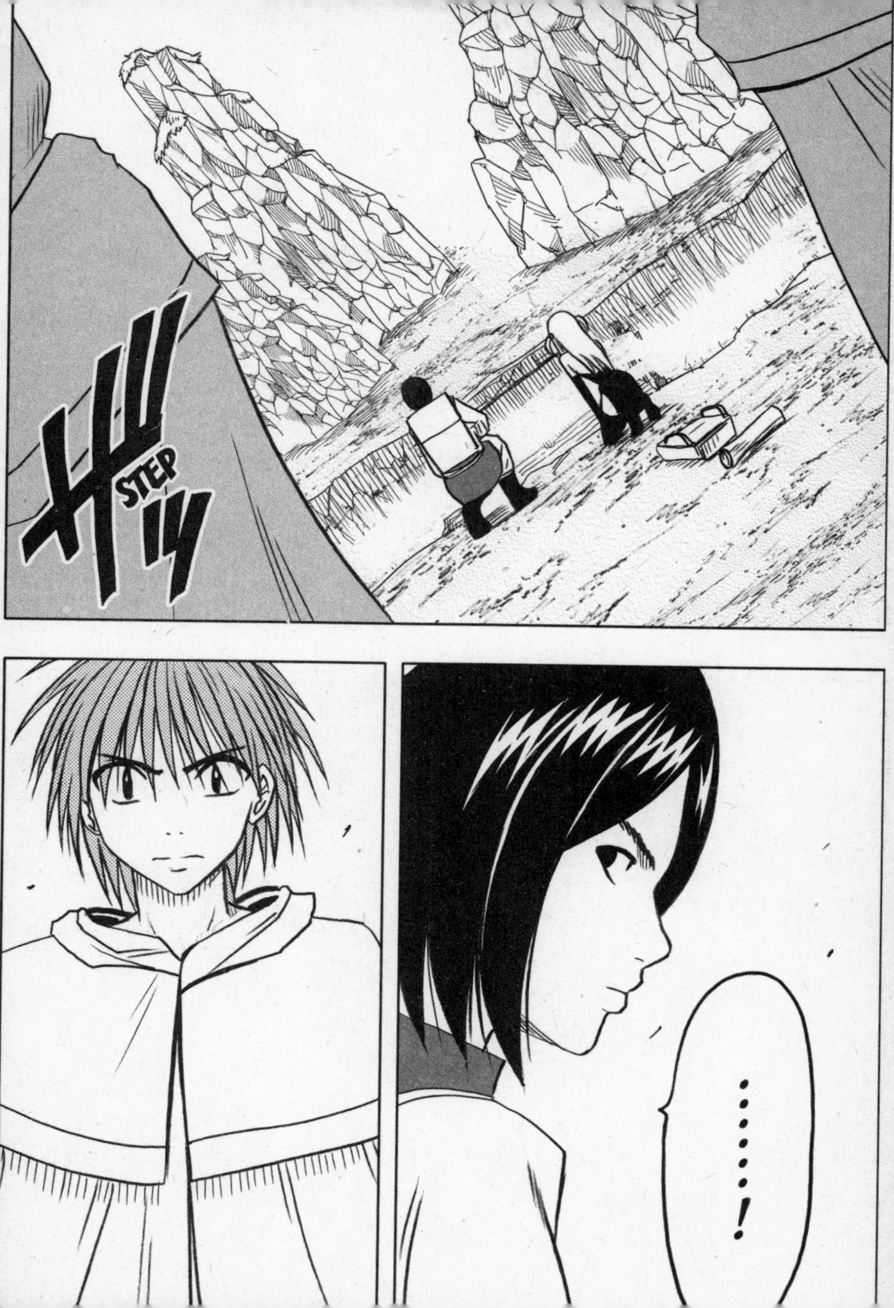
ザッ
STEP
......!

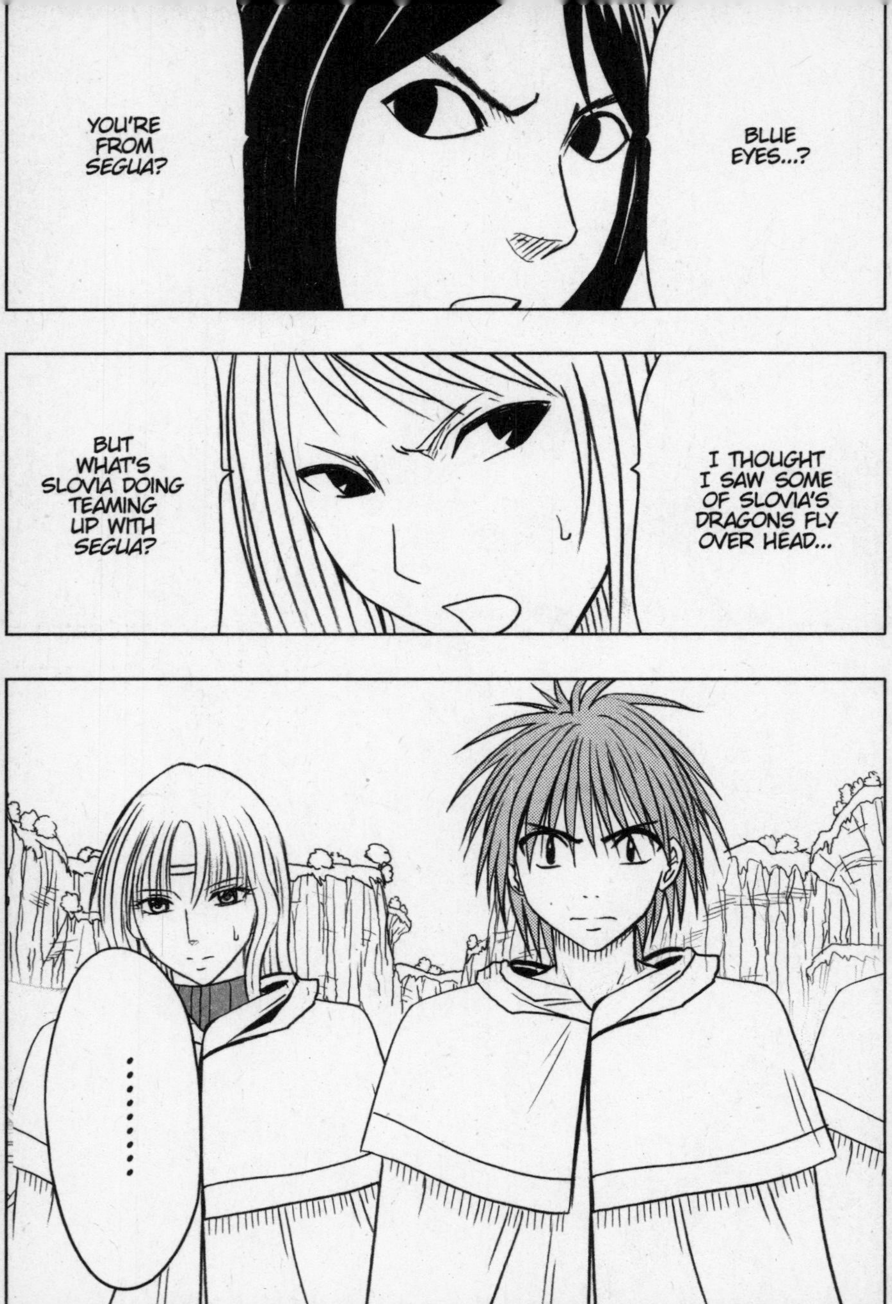
BLUE EYES...?
YOU'RE FROM SEGUA?
I THOUGHT I SAW SOME OF SLOVIA'S DRAGONS FLY OVER HEAD...
BUT WHAT'S SLOVIA DOING TEAMING UP WITH SEGUA?
....

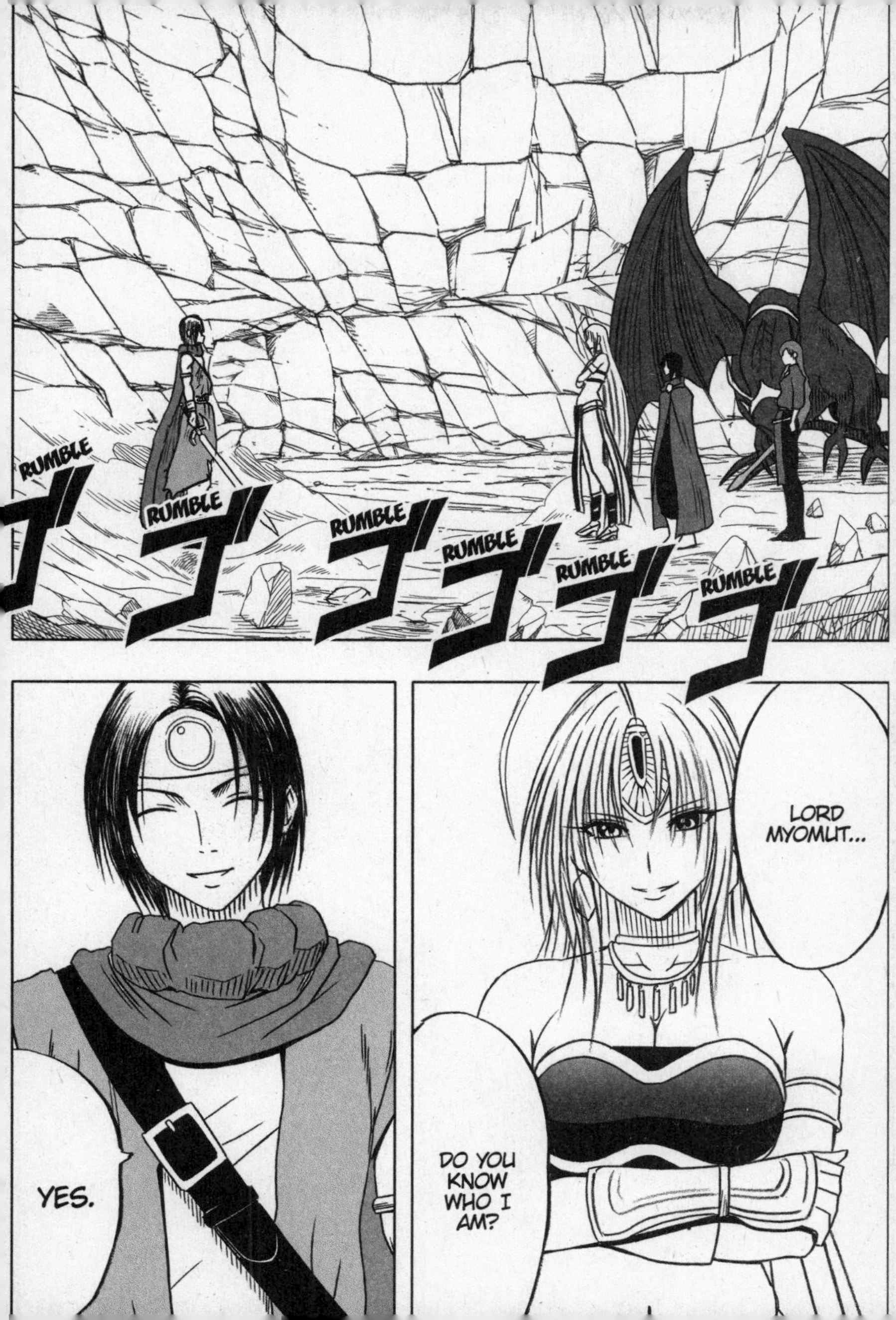
RUMBLE
RUMBLE
RUMBLE
RUMBLE
RUMBLE
RUMBLE
LORD MYOMUT...
DO YOU KNOW WHO I AM?
YES.

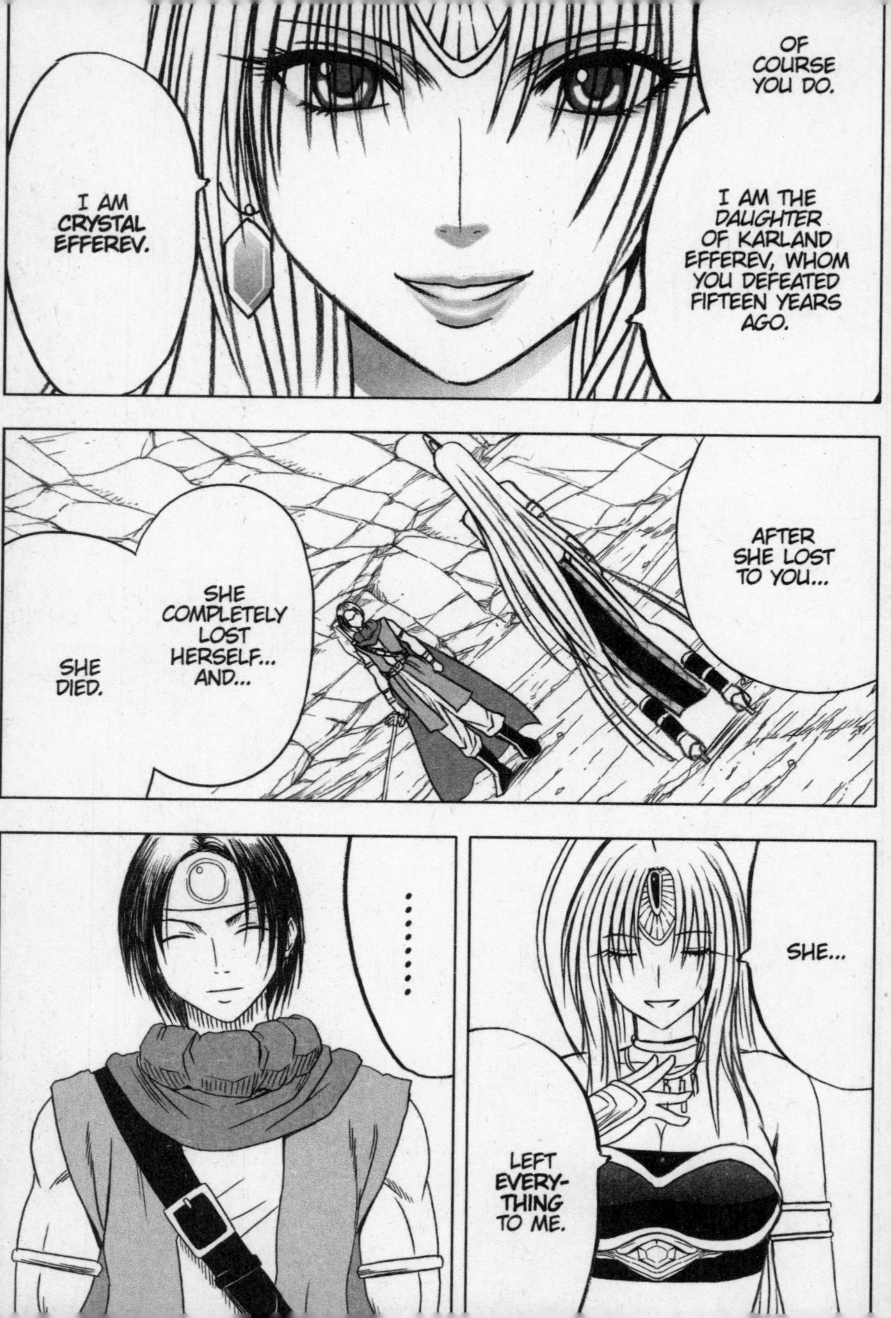
OF COURSE YOU DO.
I AM CRYSTAL EFFEREV.
I AM THE DAUGHTER OF KARLAND EFFEREV, WHOM YOU DEFEATED FIFTEEN YEARS AGO.
AFTER SHE LOST TO YOU...
SHE COMPLETELY LOST HERSELF... AND...
SHE DIED.
SHE...
LEFT EVERYTHING TO ME.
......

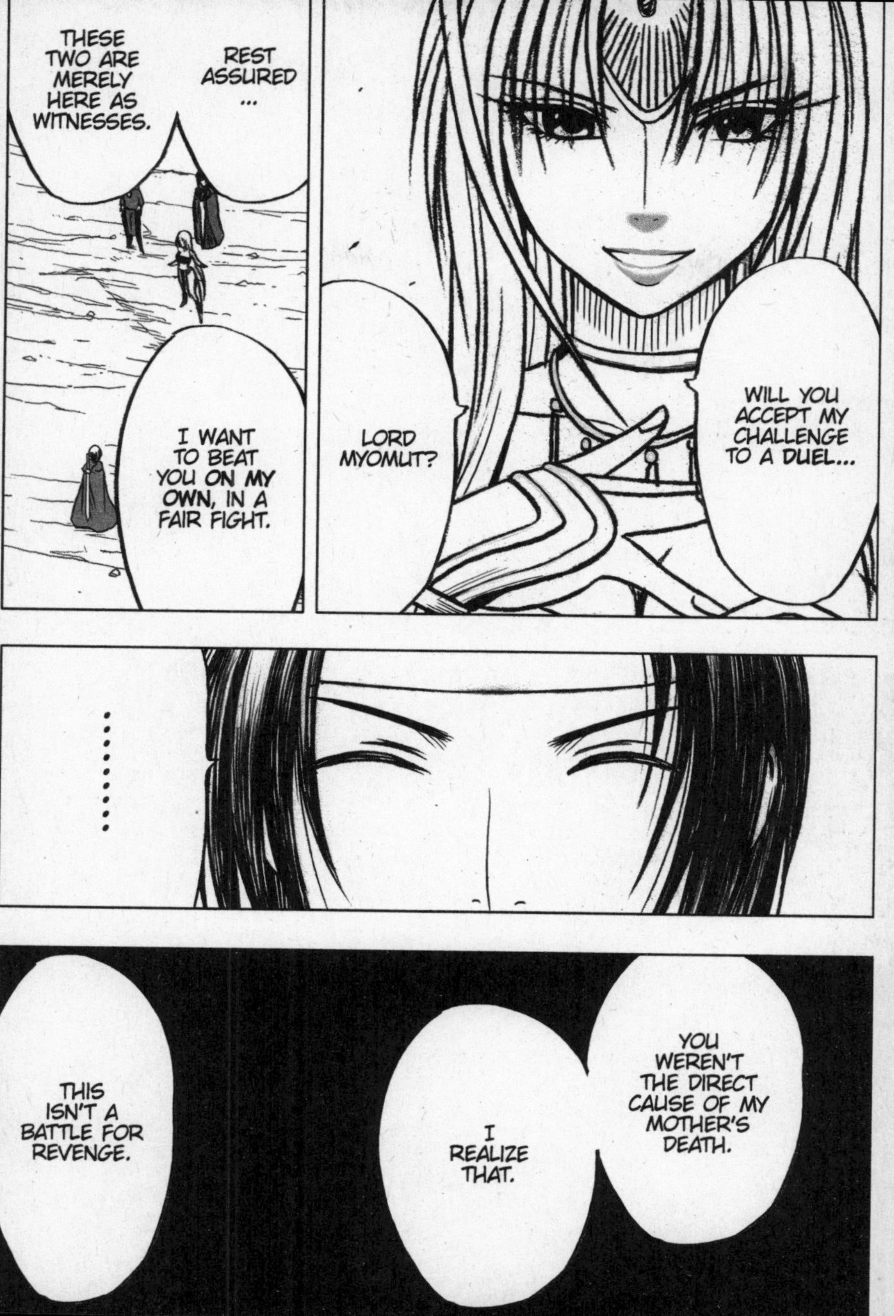
WILL YOU ACCEPT MY CHALLENGE TO A DUEL...
LORD MYOMUT?
REST ASSURED ...
THESE TWO ARE MERELY HERE AS WITNESSES.
I WANT TO BEAT YOU ON MY OWN, IN A FAIR FIGHT.
....
YOU WEREN'T THE DIRECT CAUSE OF MY MOTHER'S DEATH.
I REALIZE THAT.
THIS ISN'T A BATTLE FOR REVENGE.

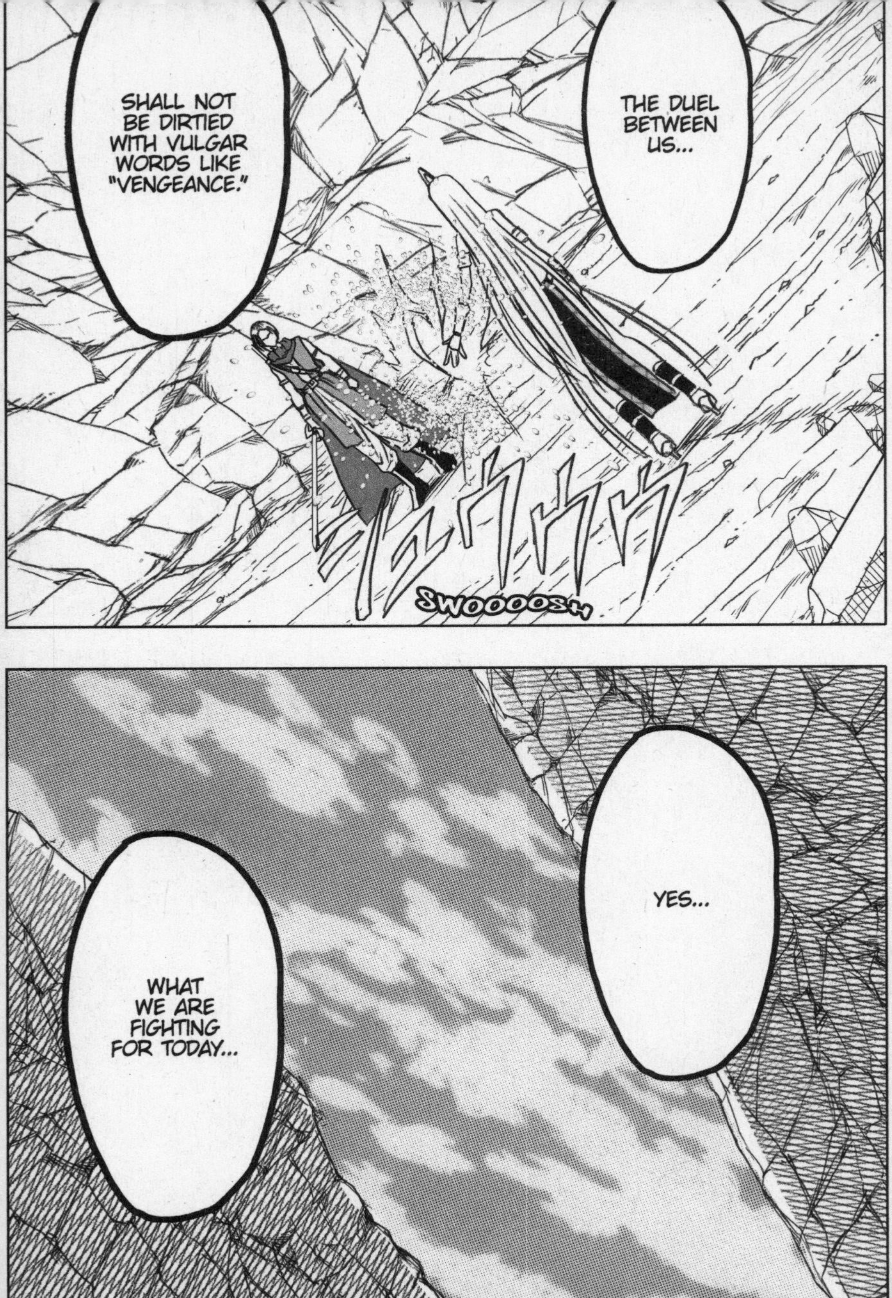
THE DUEL BETWEEN US...
SHALL NOT BE DIRTIED WITH VULGAR WORDS LIKE "VENGEANCE."
SWOOOOSH
YES...
WHAT WE ARE FIGHTING FOR TODAY...

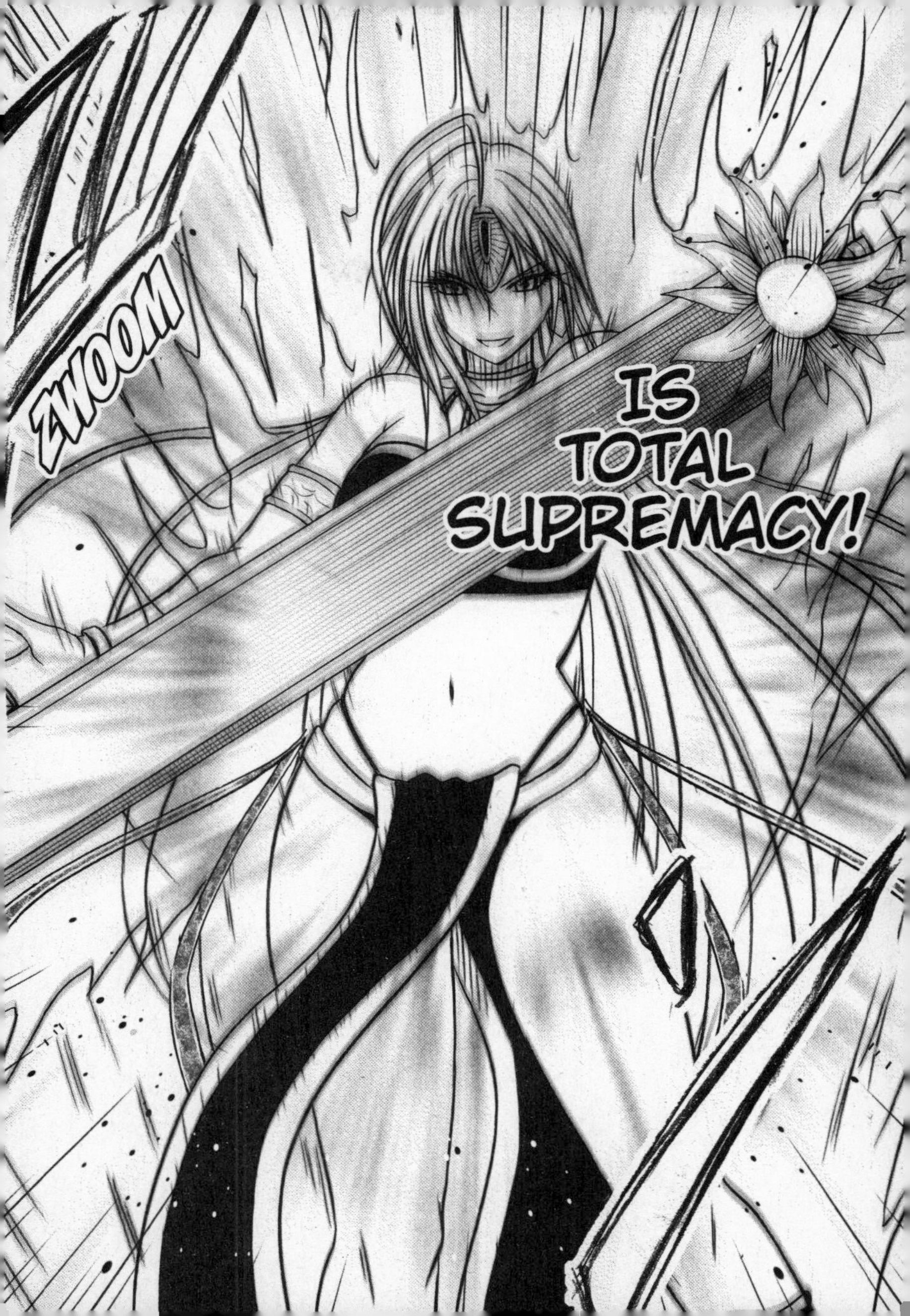
ZWOOM
IS TOTAL SUPREMACY!

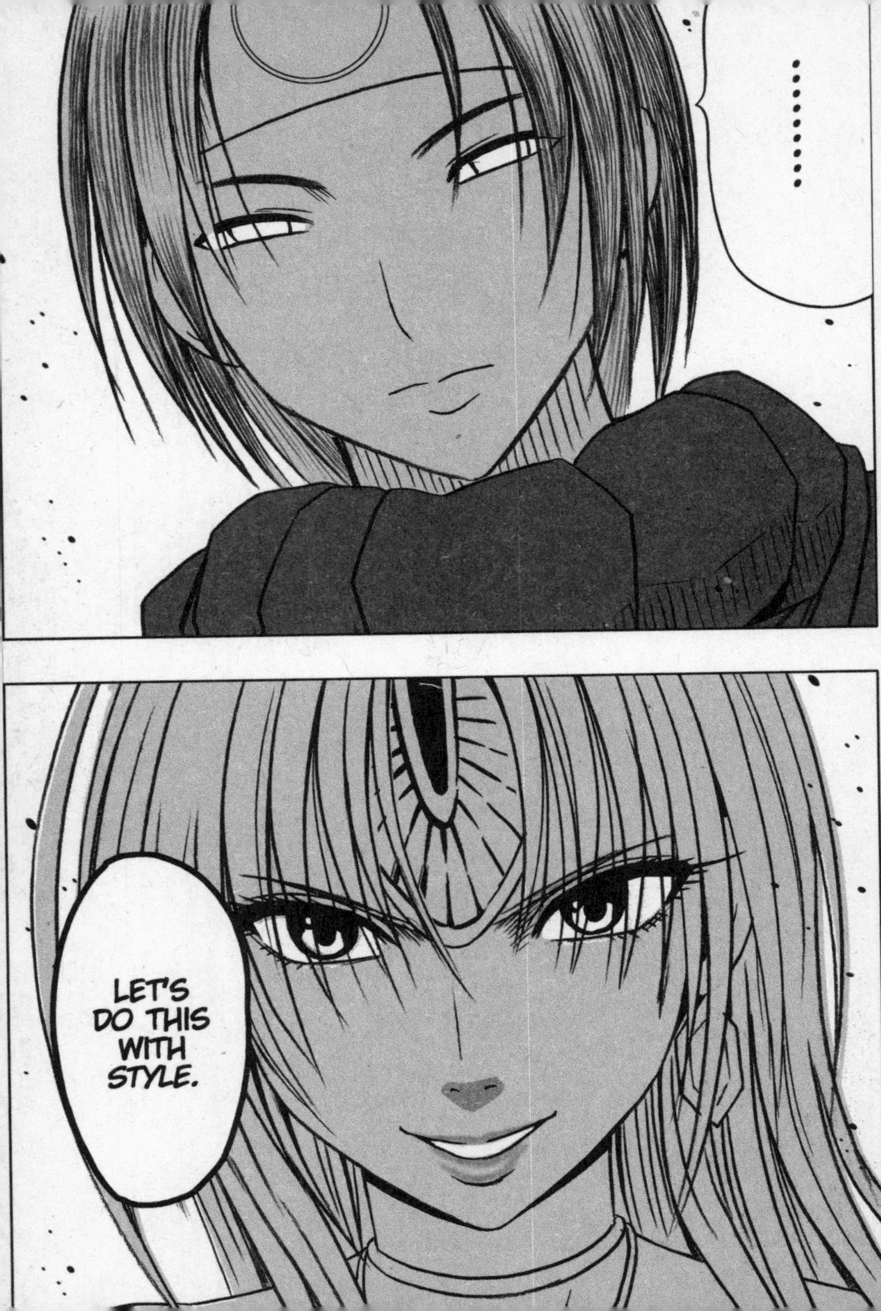
......
LET'S DO THIS WITH STYLE.

Part 2

CHAPTER 26

WARCRY

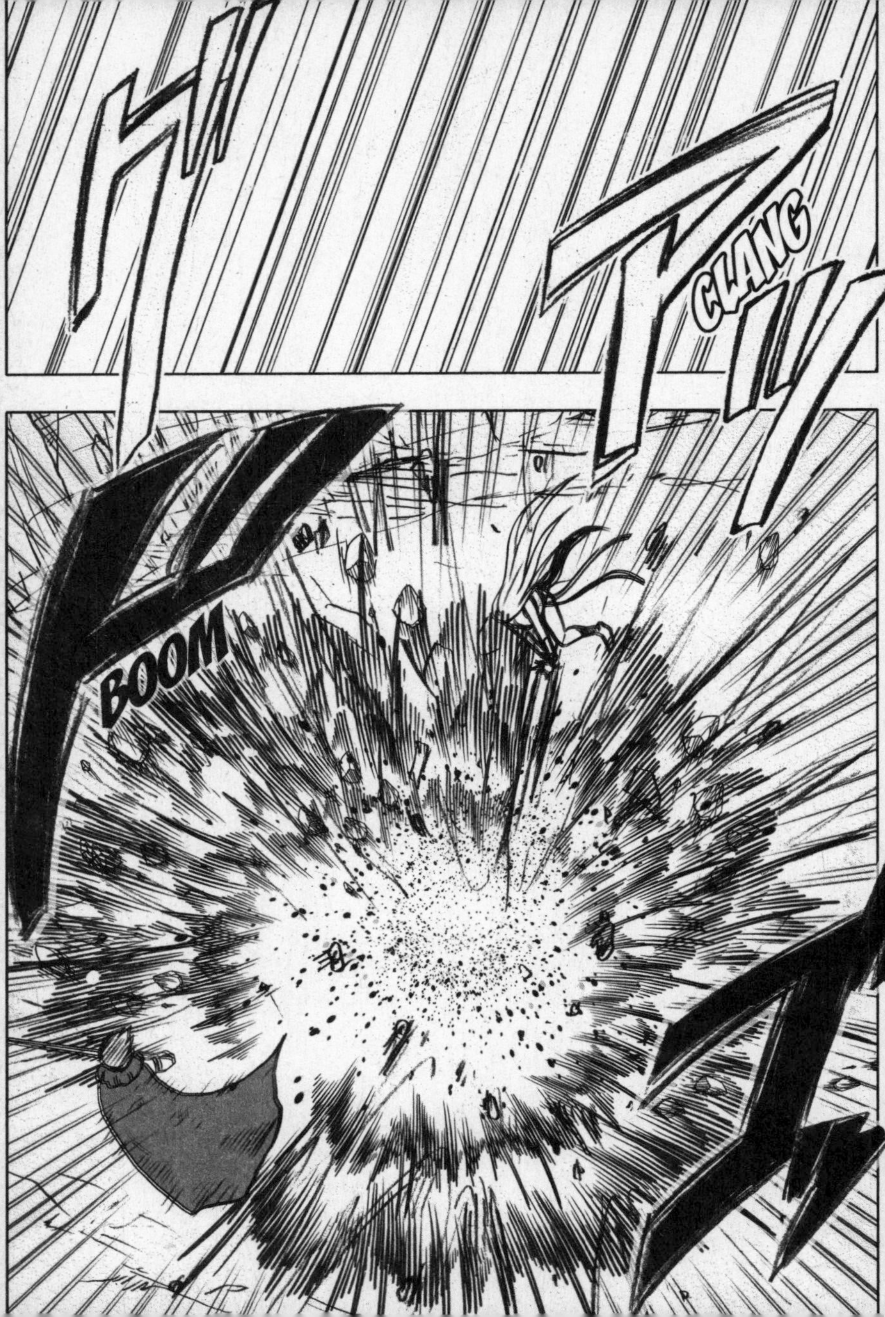
CLANG
BOOM

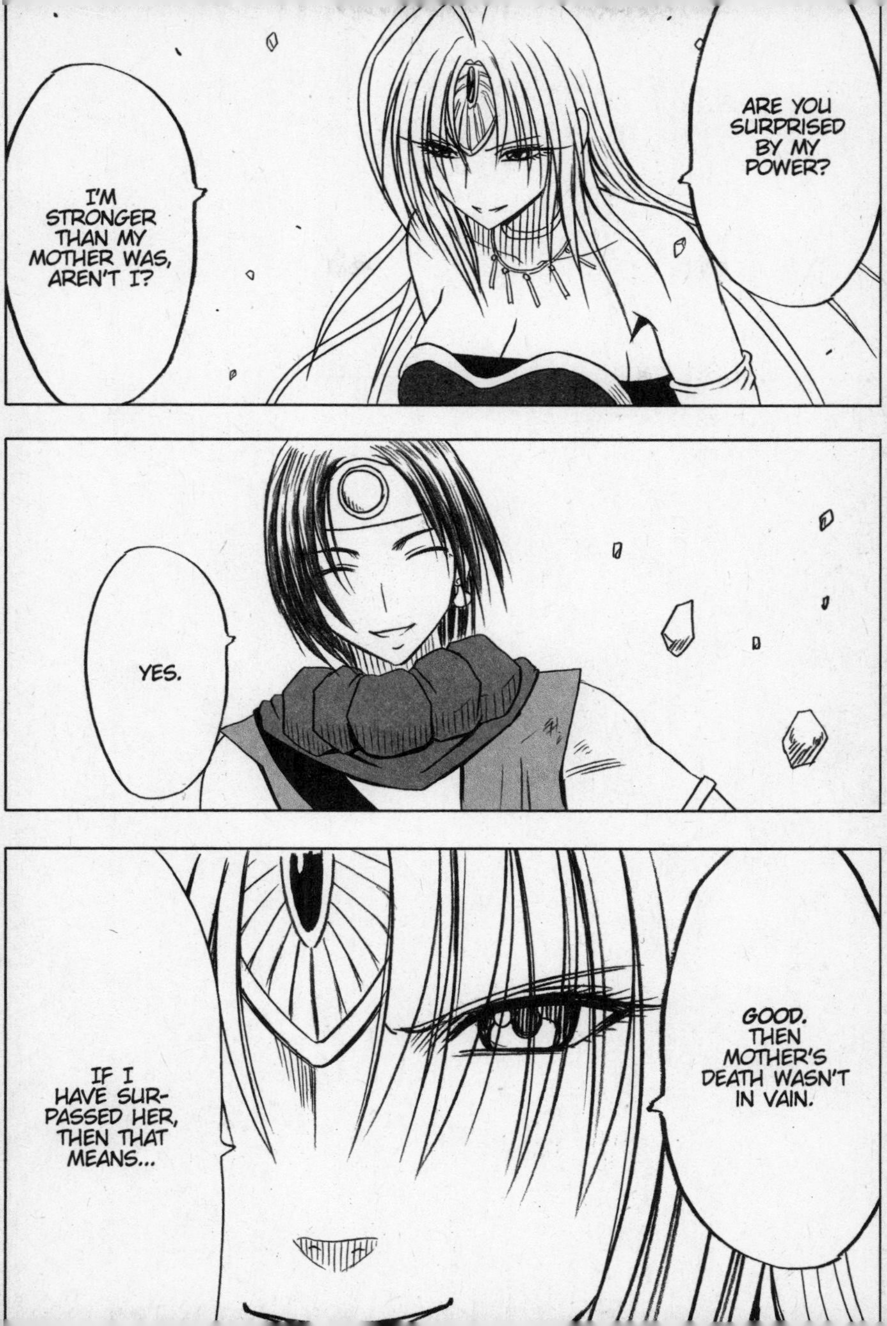
ARE YOU SURPRISED BY MY POWER?
I'M STRONGER THAN MY MOTHER WAS, AREN'T I?
YES.
GOOD. THEN MOTHER'S DEATH WASN'T IN VAIN.
IF I HAVE SURPASSED HER, THEN THAT MEANS...

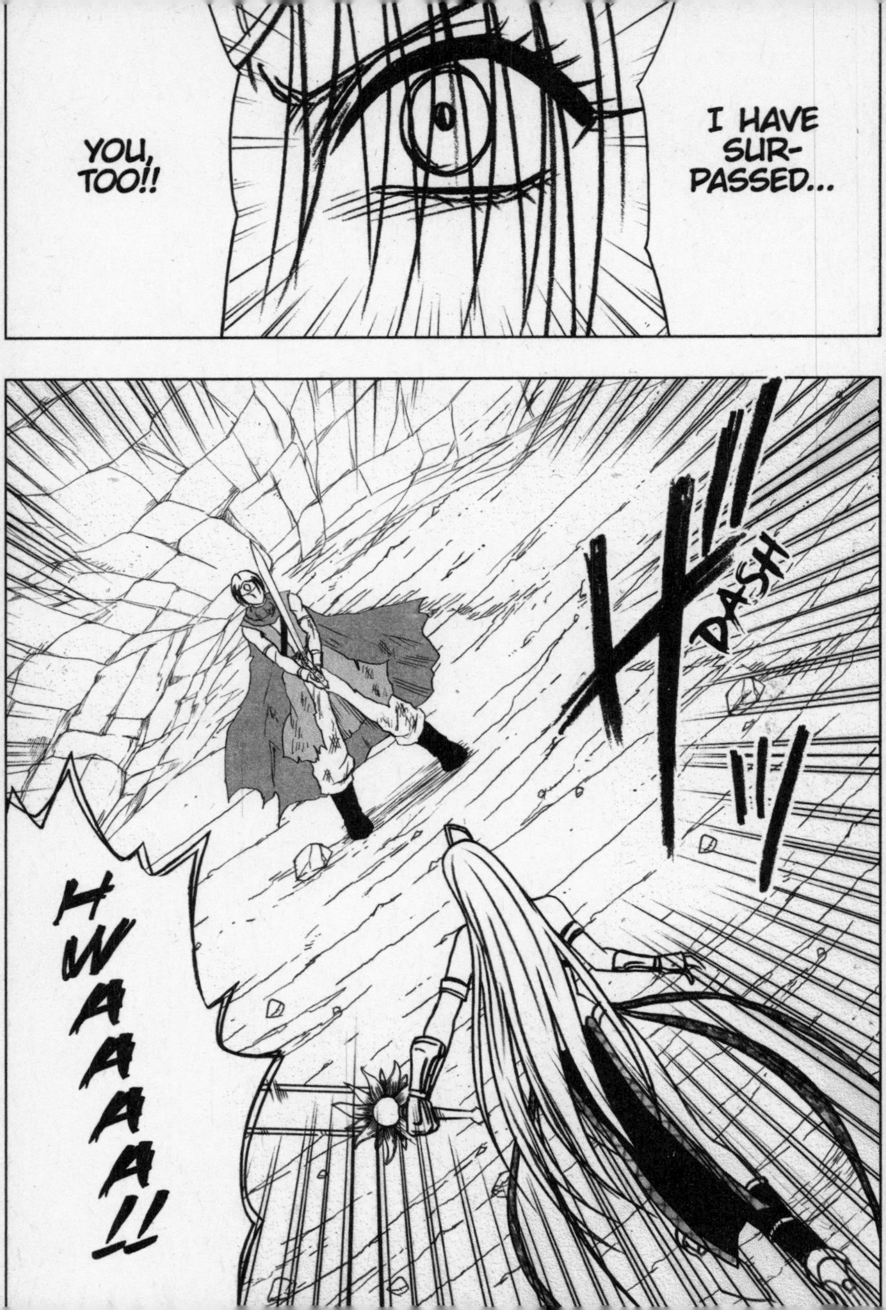
I HAVE SUR-PASSED...
YOU, TOO!!
DASH
HWAAAA!!

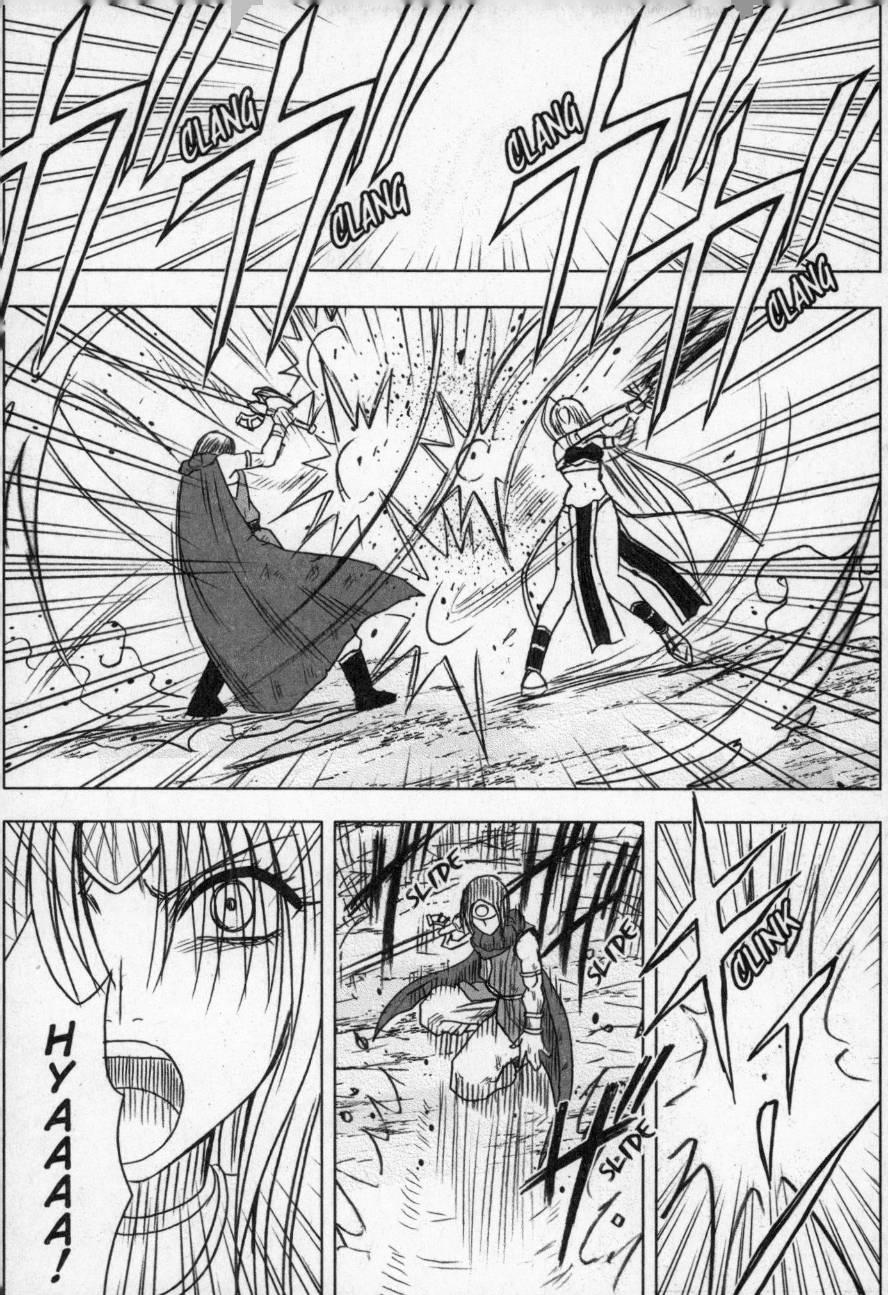
CLANG
CLANG
CLANG
CLANG
CLINK
SLIDE
SLIDE
SLIDE
HYAAAAA!

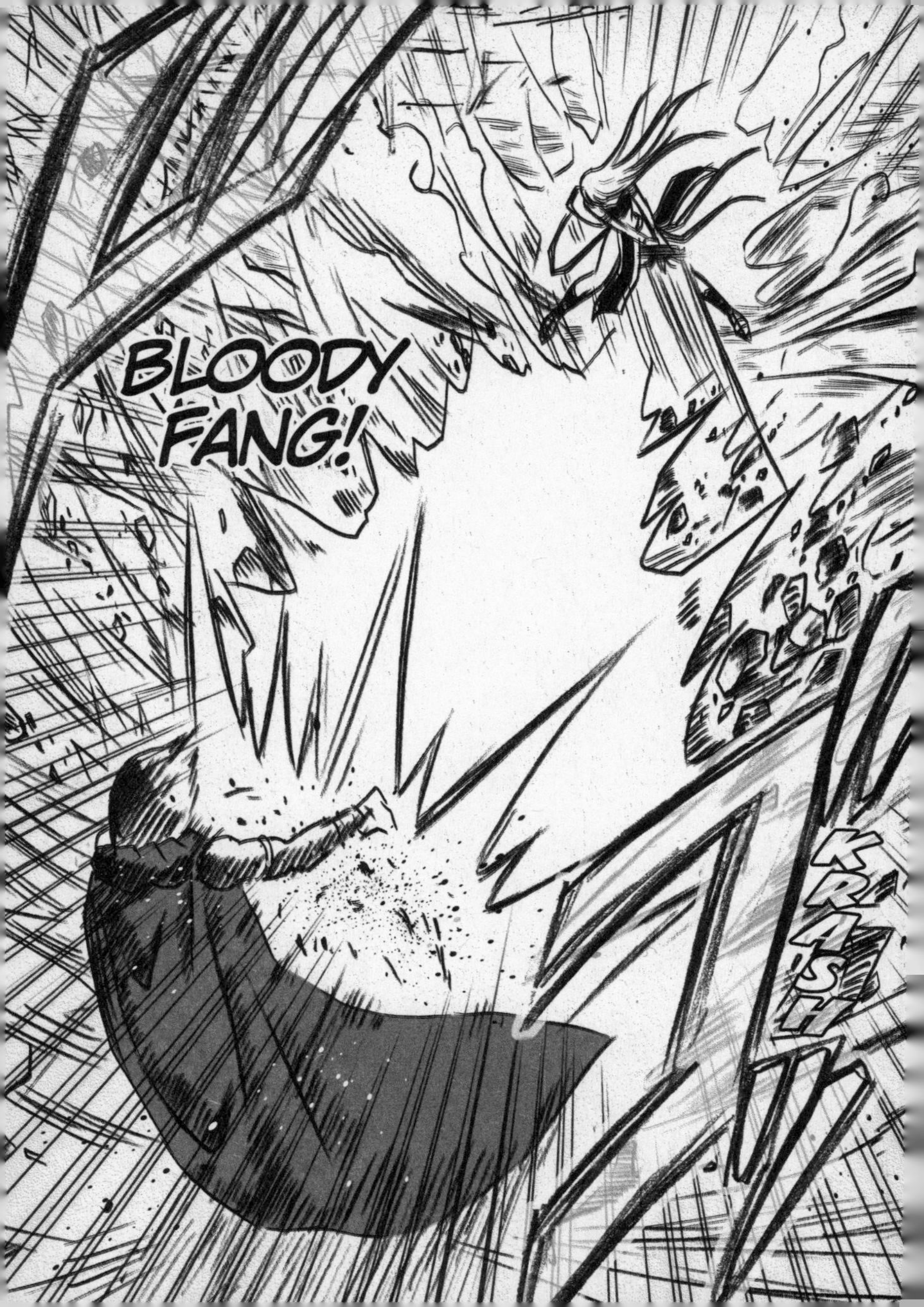
BLOODY FANG!
KRASH

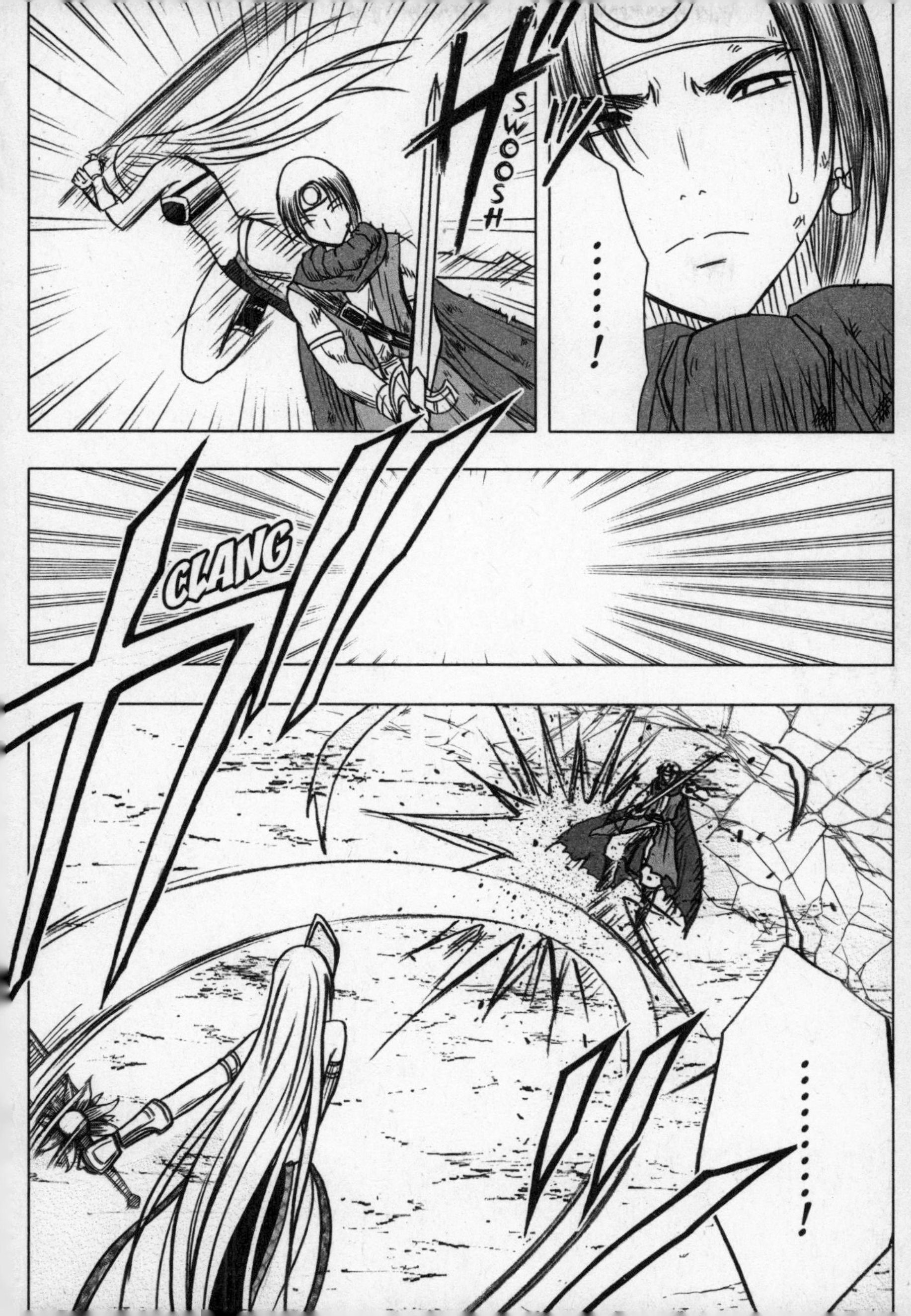
......!
SWOOSH
CLANG
.........!

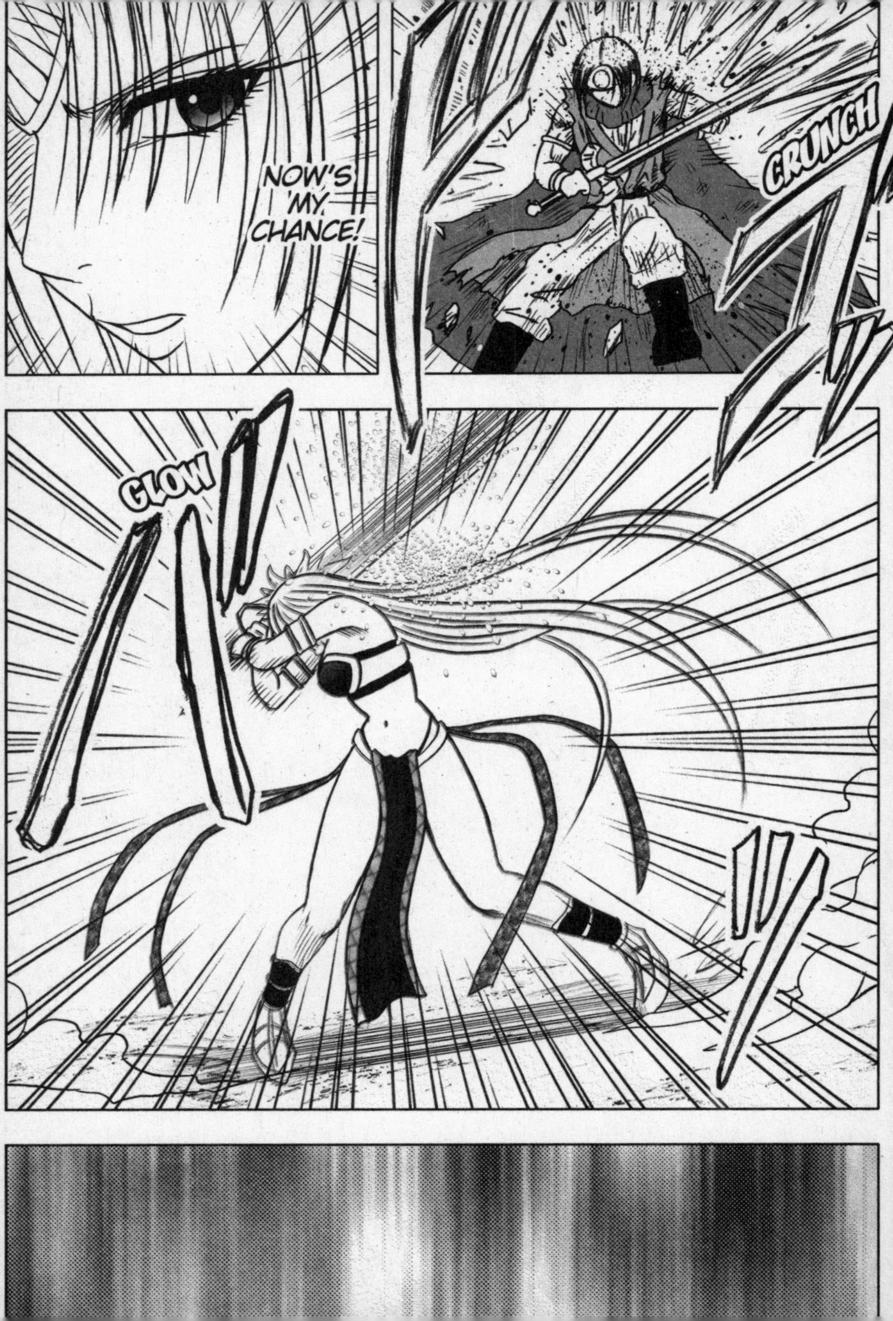
CRUNCH
NOW'S MY CHANCE!
GLOW

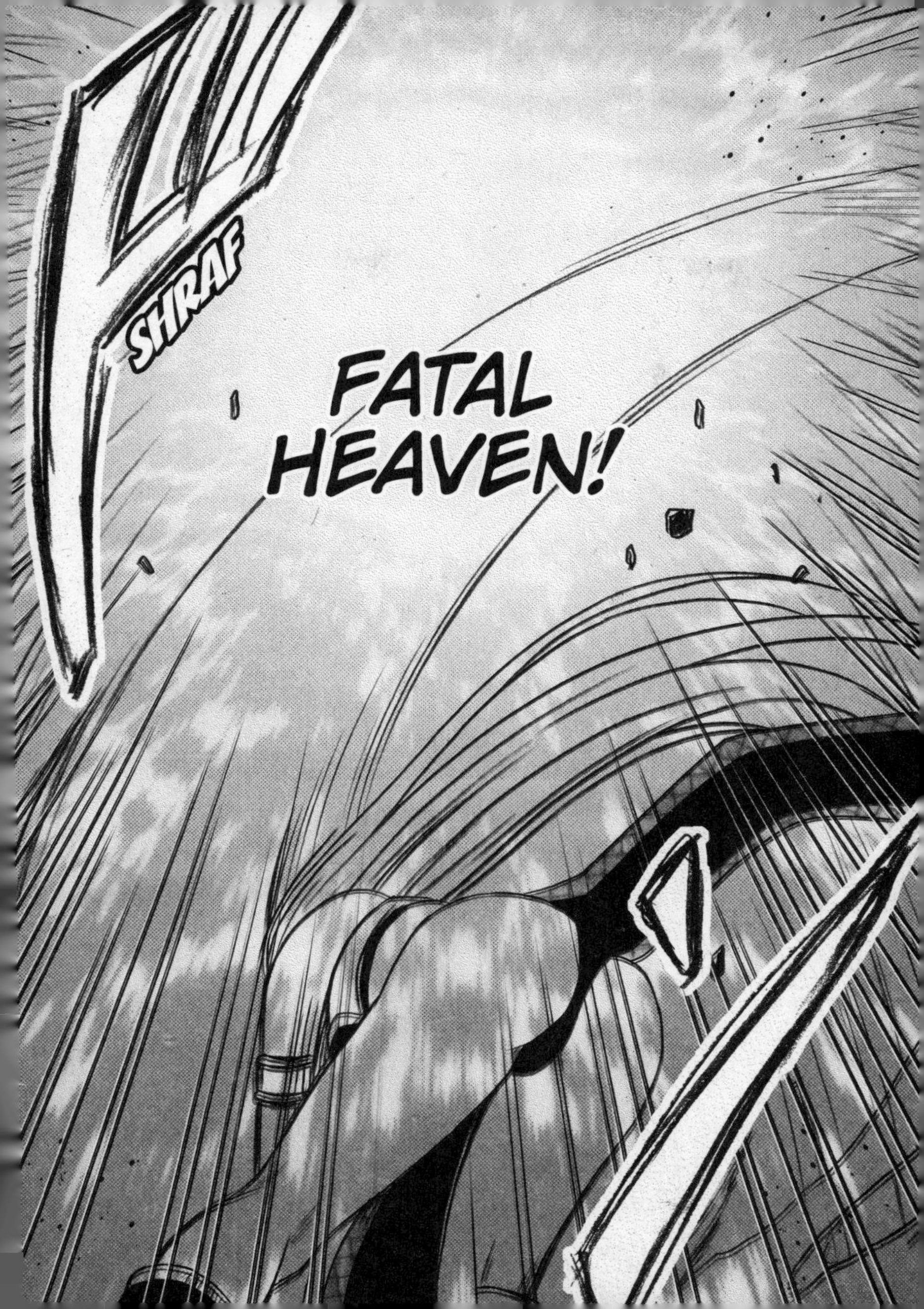
SHRAF
FATAL HEAVEN!

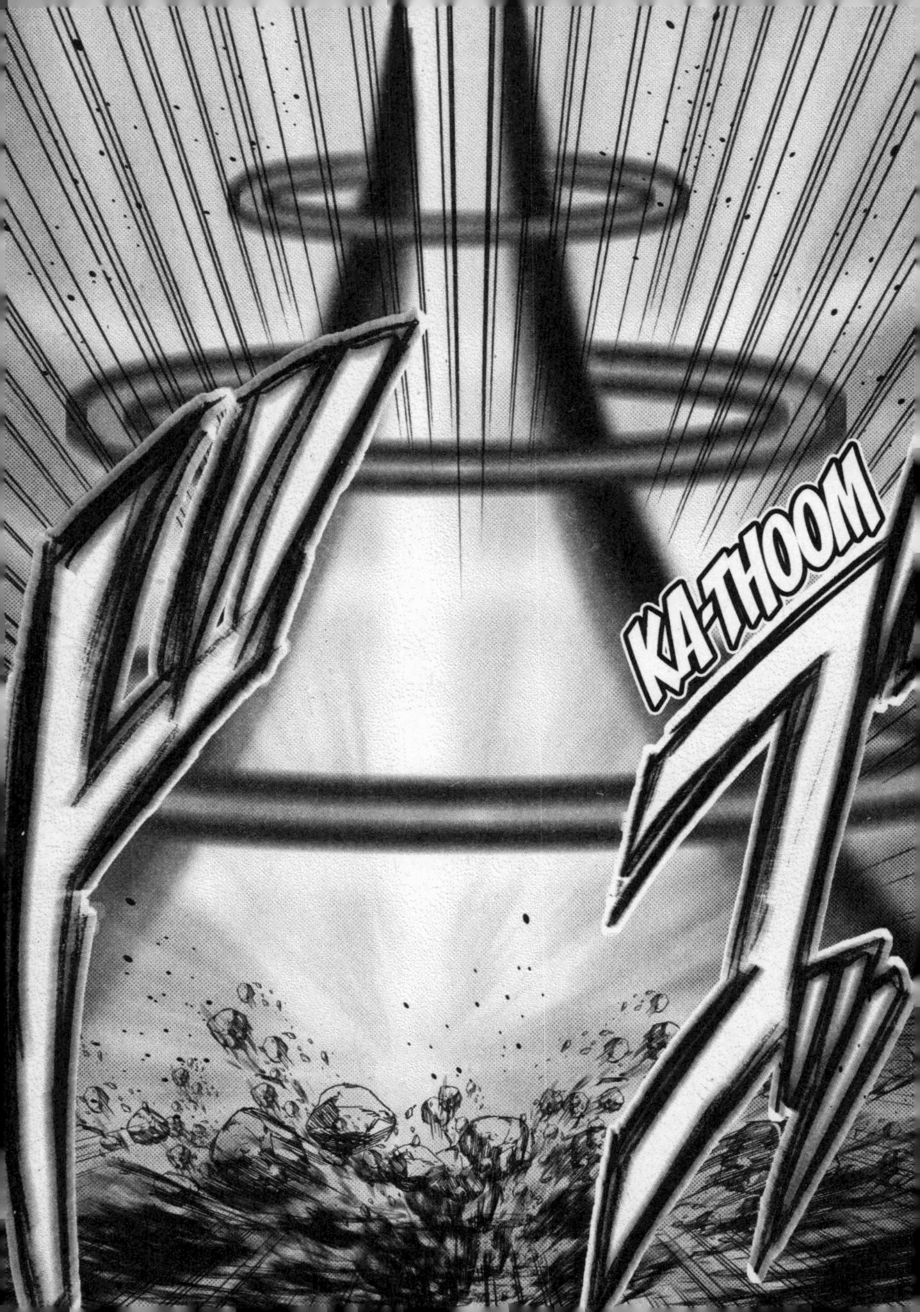
KA-THOOM

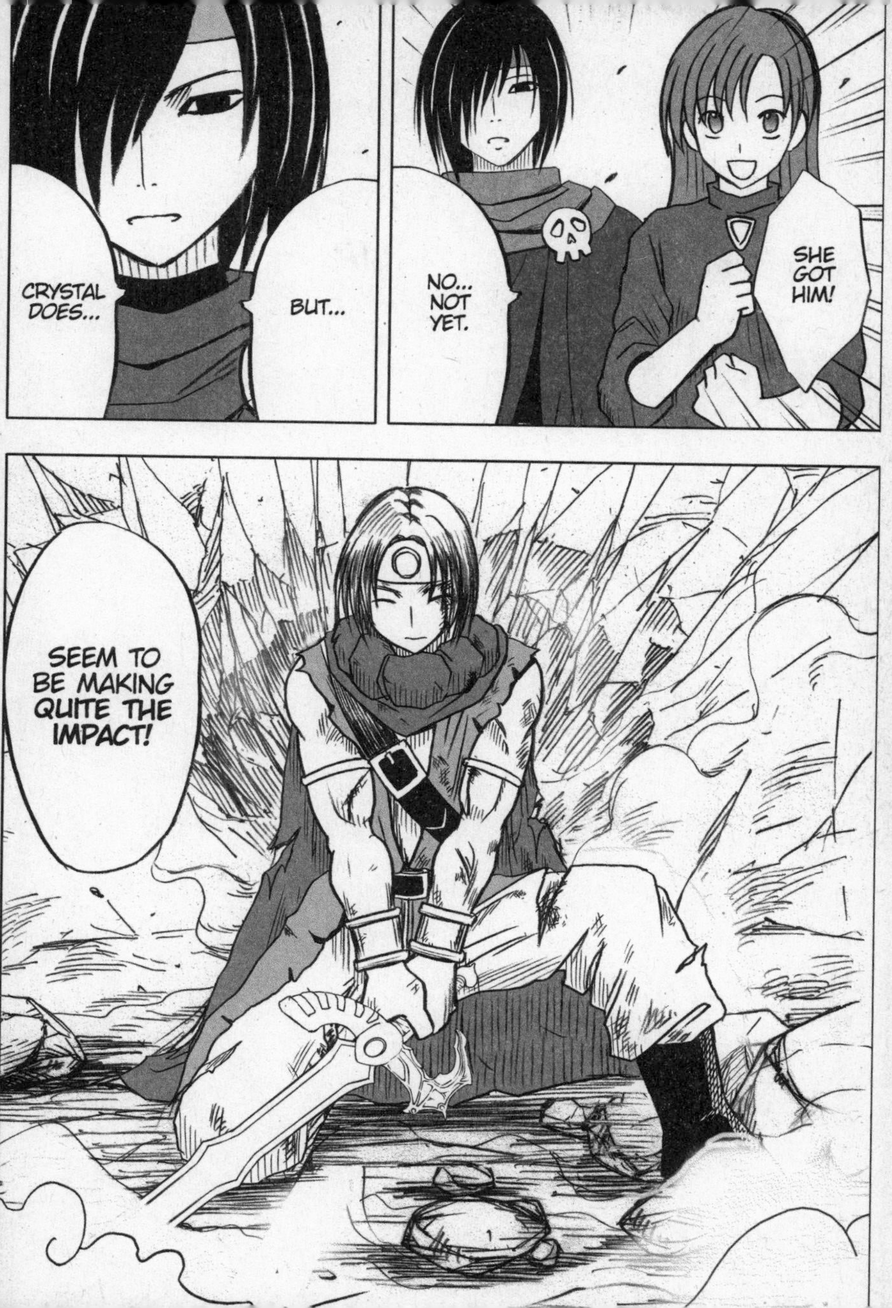
SHE GOT HIM!
NO... NOT YET.
BUT...
CRYSTAL DOES...
SEEM TO BE MAKING QUITE THE IMPACT!

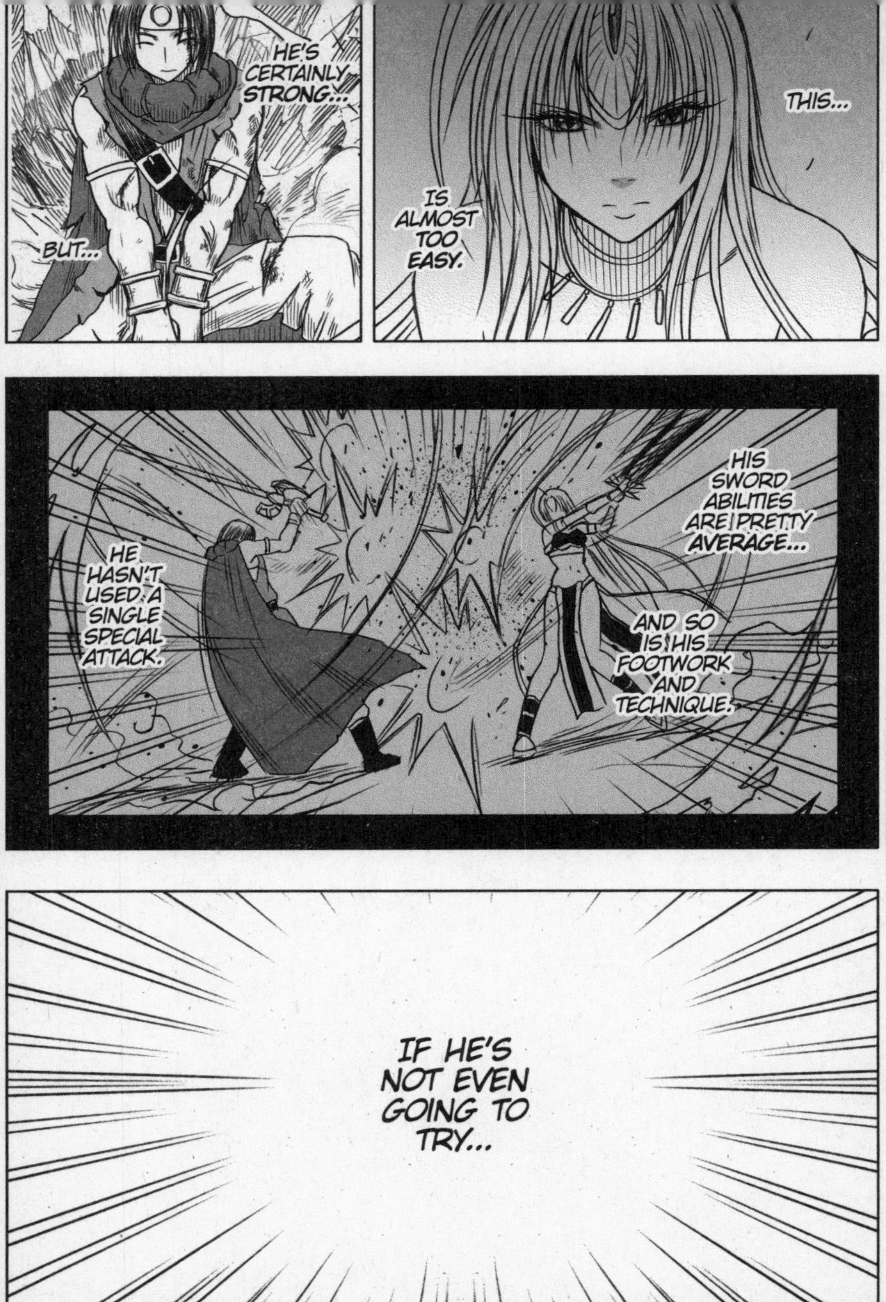
THIS...
IS ALMOST TOO EASY.
HE'S CERTAINLY STRONG...
BUT...
HIS SWORD ABILITIES ARE PRETTY AVERAGE...
AND SO IS HIS FOOTWORK AND TECHNIQUE.
HE HASN'T USED A SINGLE SPECIAL ATTACK.
IF HE'S NOT EVEN GOING TO TRY...

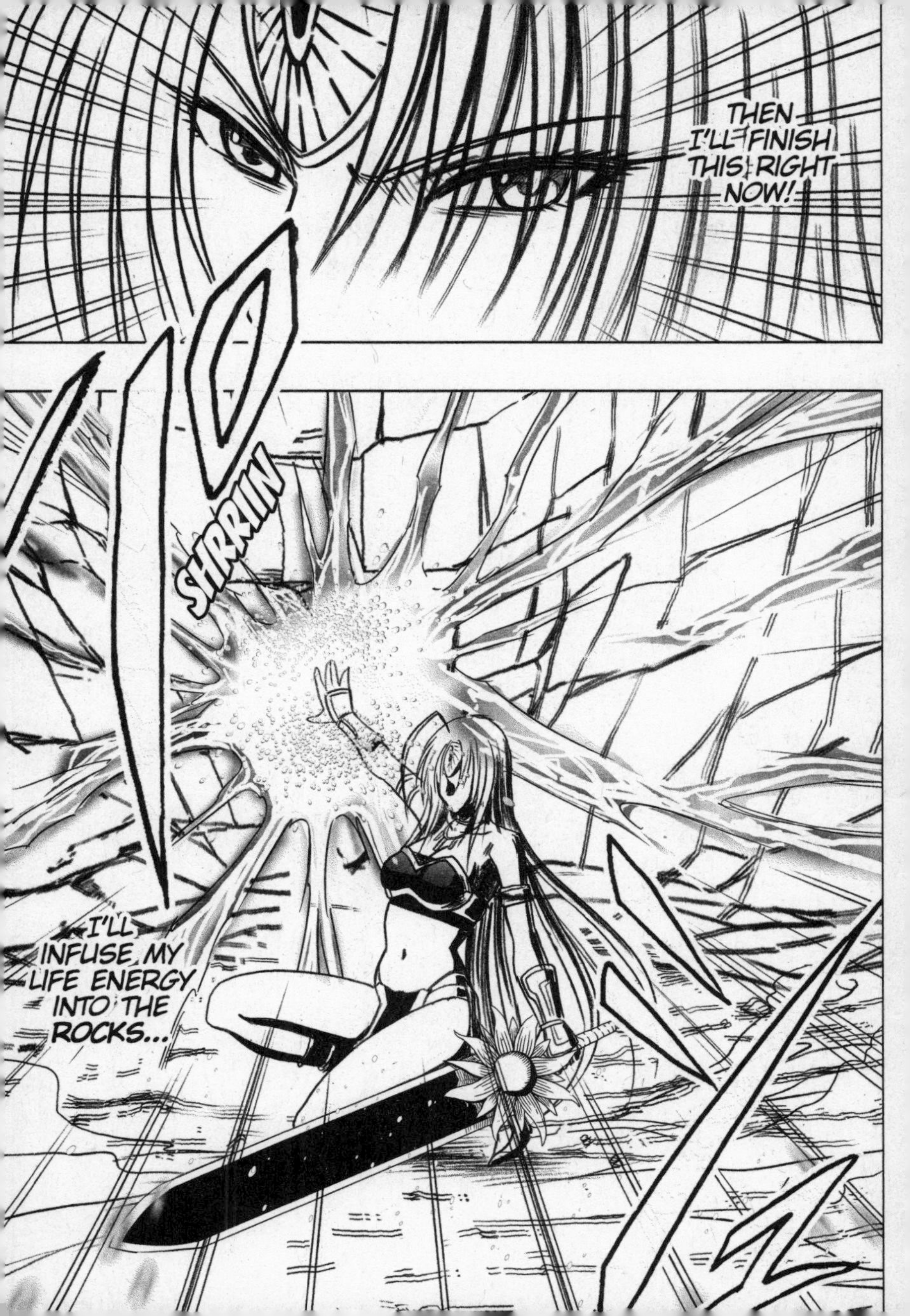
THEN I'LL FINISH THIS RIGHT NOW!
SHRIIN
I'LL INFUSE MY LIFE ENERGY INTO THE ROCKS...

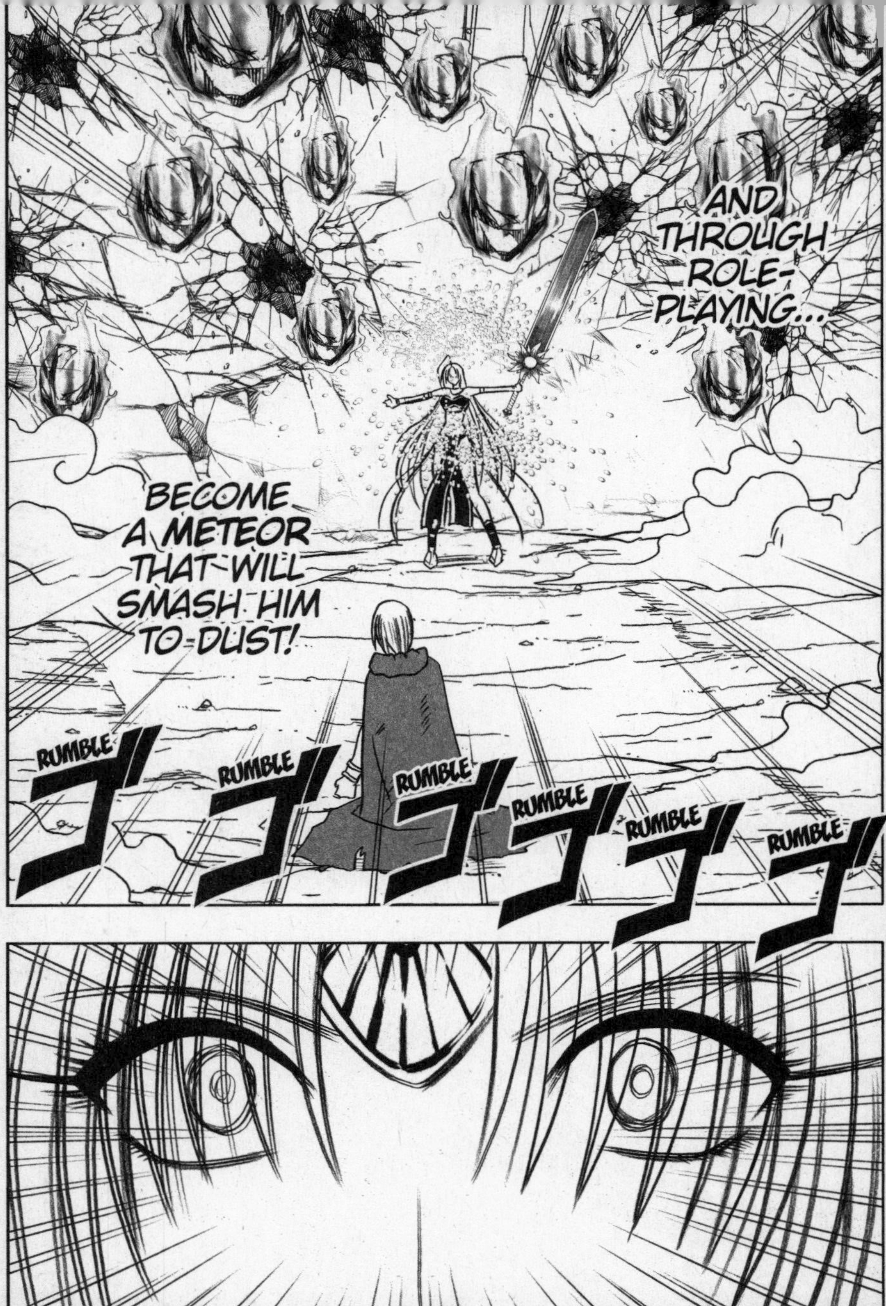
AND THROUGH ROLE-PLAYING...
BECOME A METEOR THAT WILL SMASH HIM TO DUST!
RUMBLE RUMBLE RUMBLE RUMBLE RUMBLE RUMBLE
ゴゴゴゴゴゴ

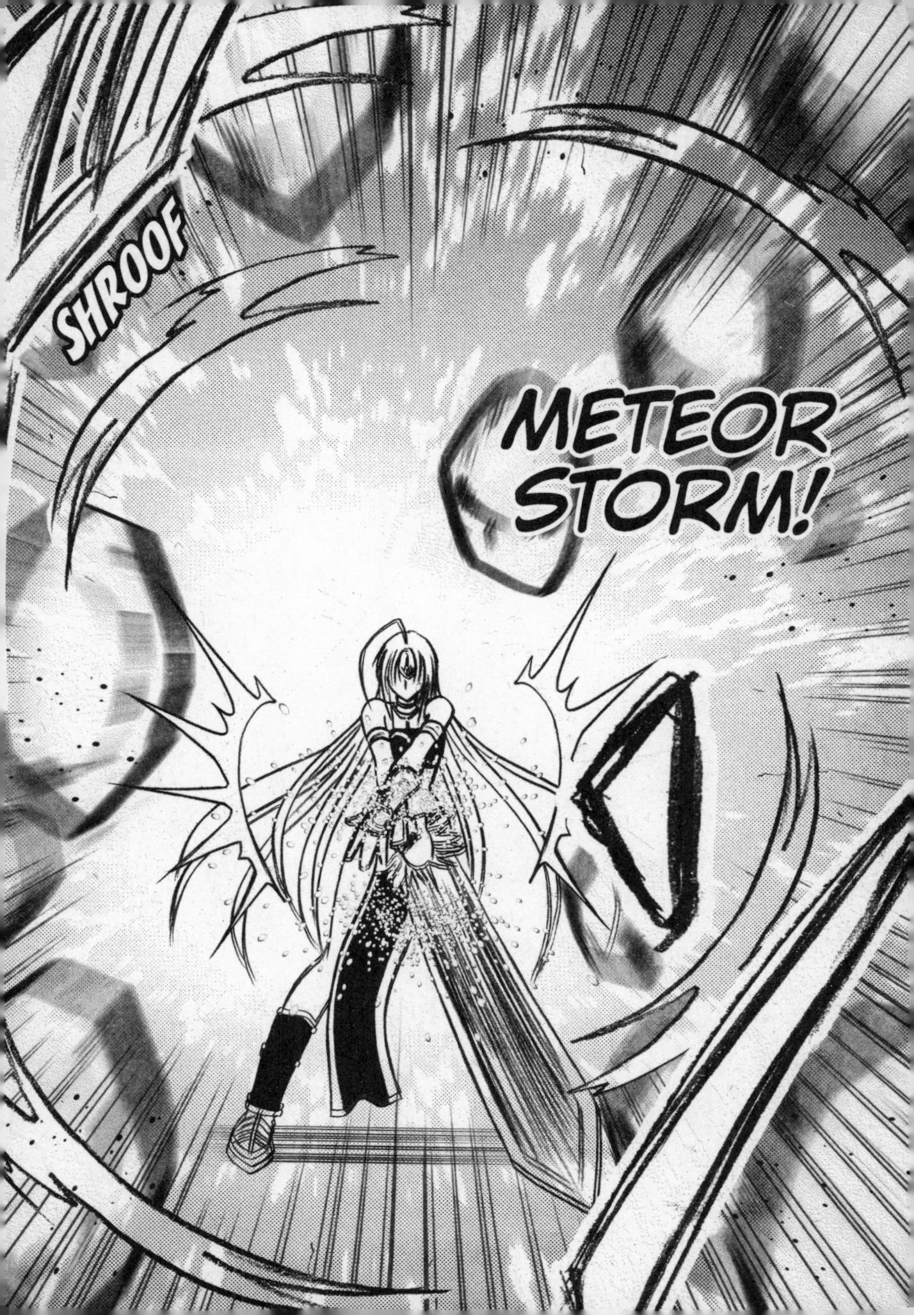
METEOR STORM!
SHROOF

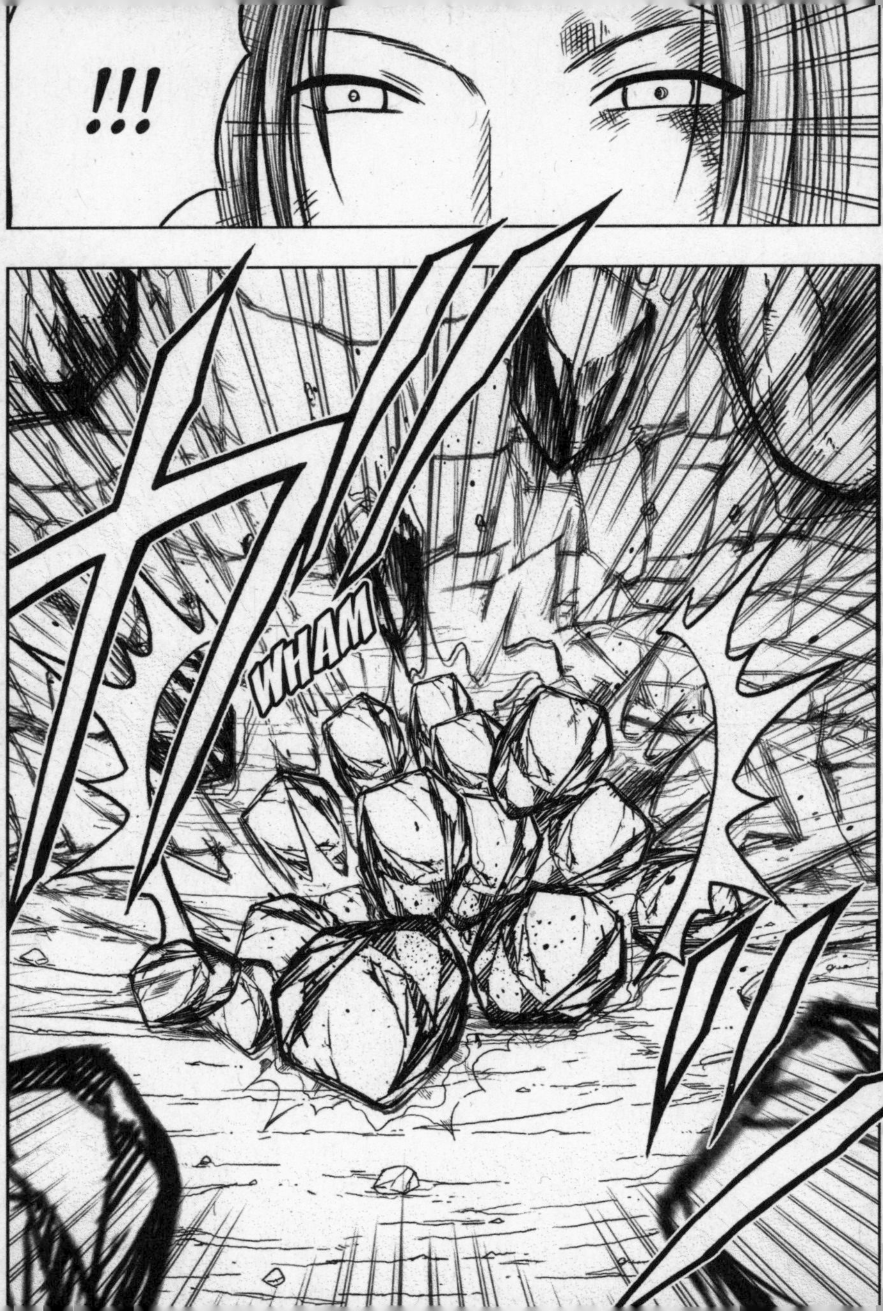
!!!
WHAM

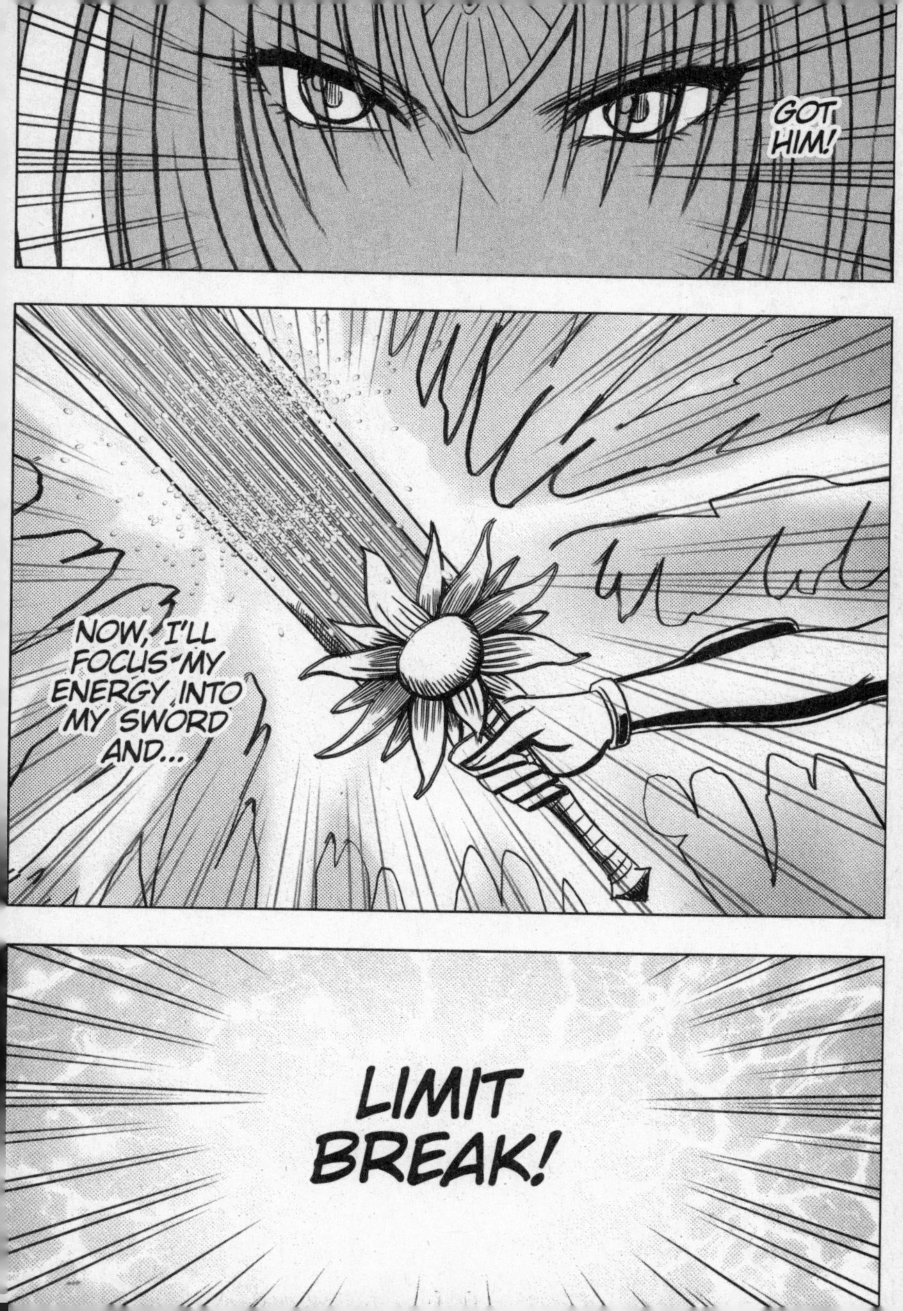
GOT HIM!
NOW, I'LL FOCUS MY ENERGY INTO MY SWORD AND...
LIMIT BREAK!

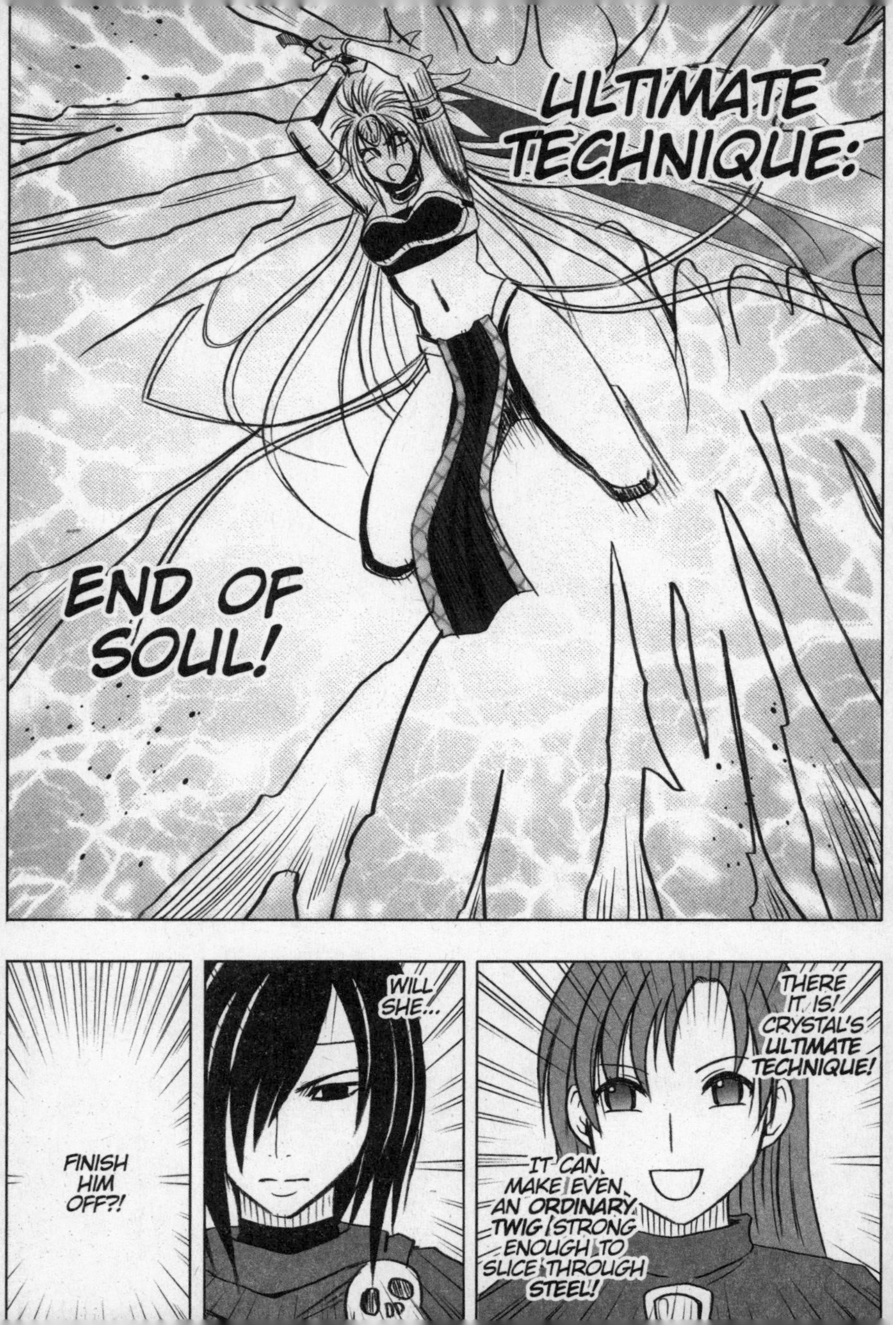
ULTIMATE TECHNIQUE:
END OF SOUL!
THERE IT IS! CRYSTAL'S ULTIMATE TECHNIQUE!
IT CAN MAKE EVEN AN ORDINARY TWIG STRONG ENOUGH TO SLICE THROUGH STEEL!
WILL SHE...
FINISH HIM OFF?!

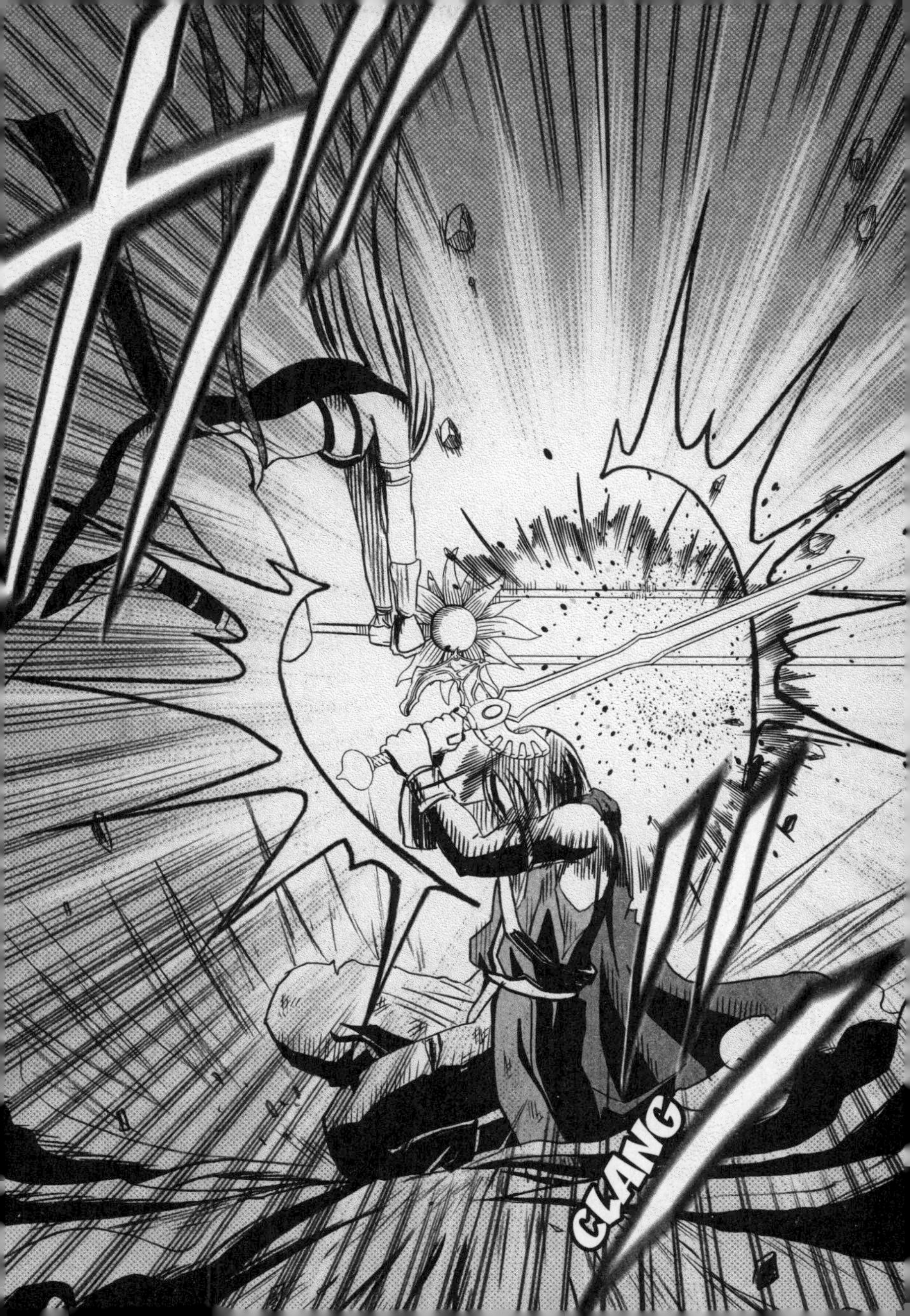
CLANG

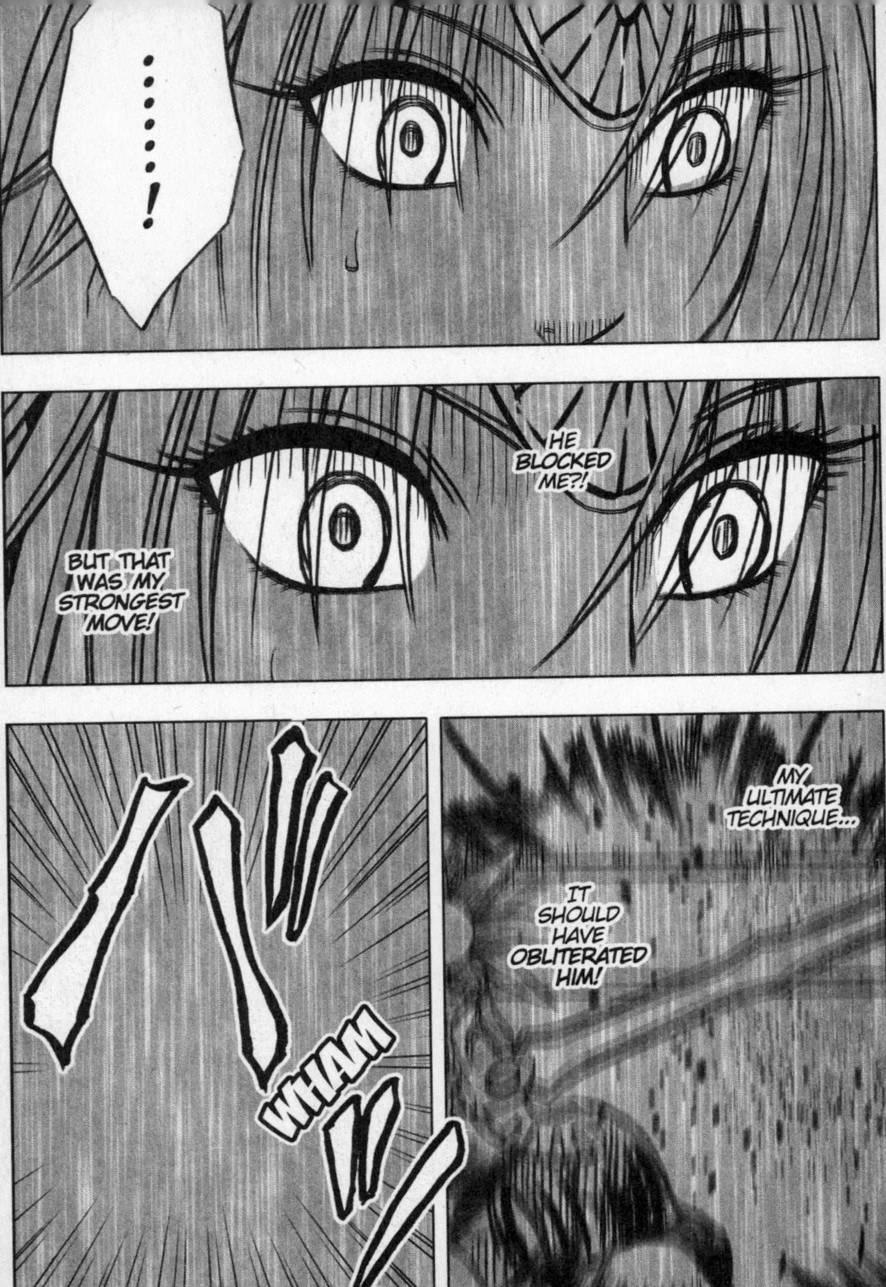
......!
HE BLOCKED ME?!
BUT THAT WAS MY STRONGEST MOVE!
MY ULTIMATE TECHNIQUE...
IT SHOULD HAVE OBLITERATED HIM!
WHAM

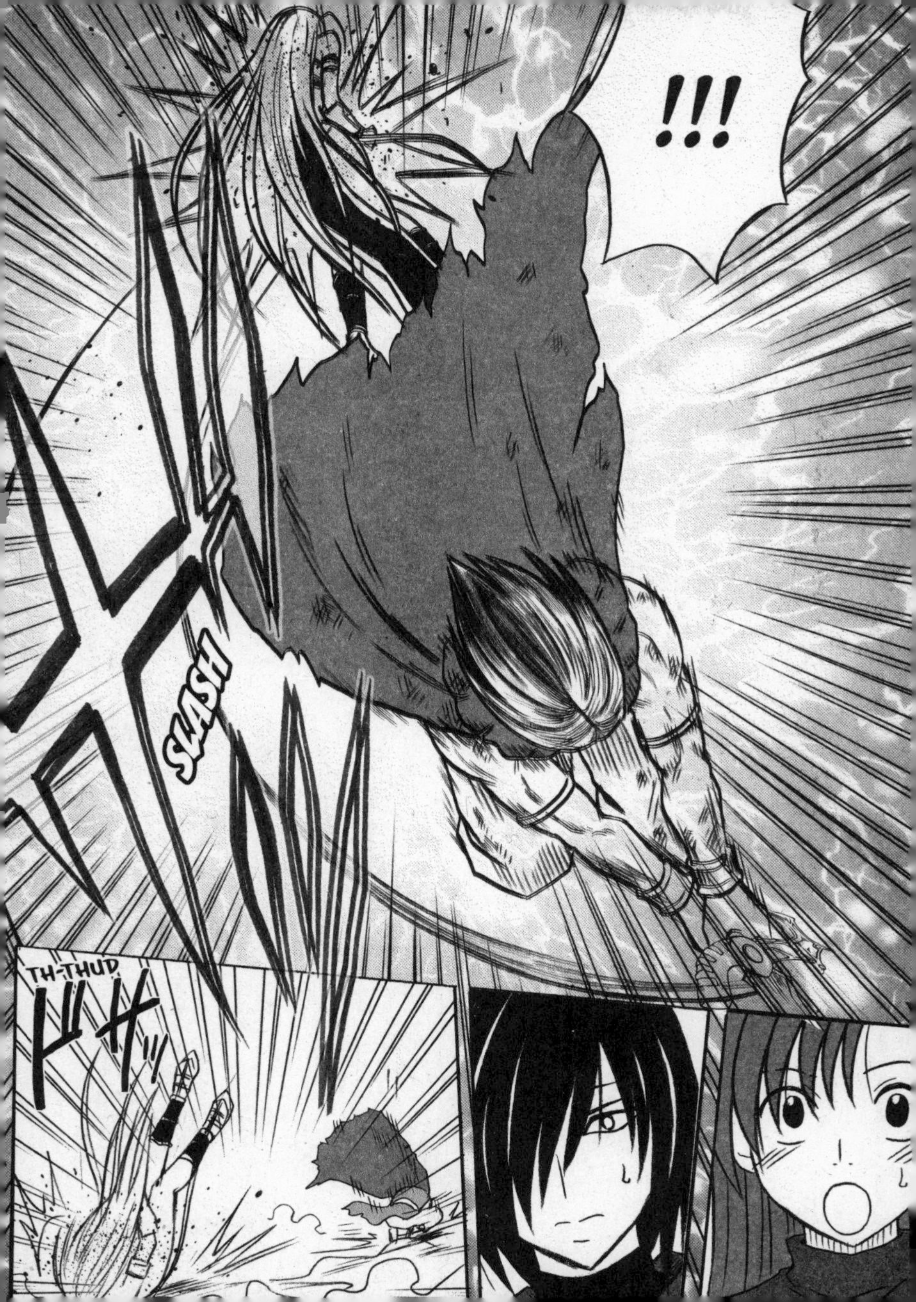
!!!
SLASH
TH-THUD

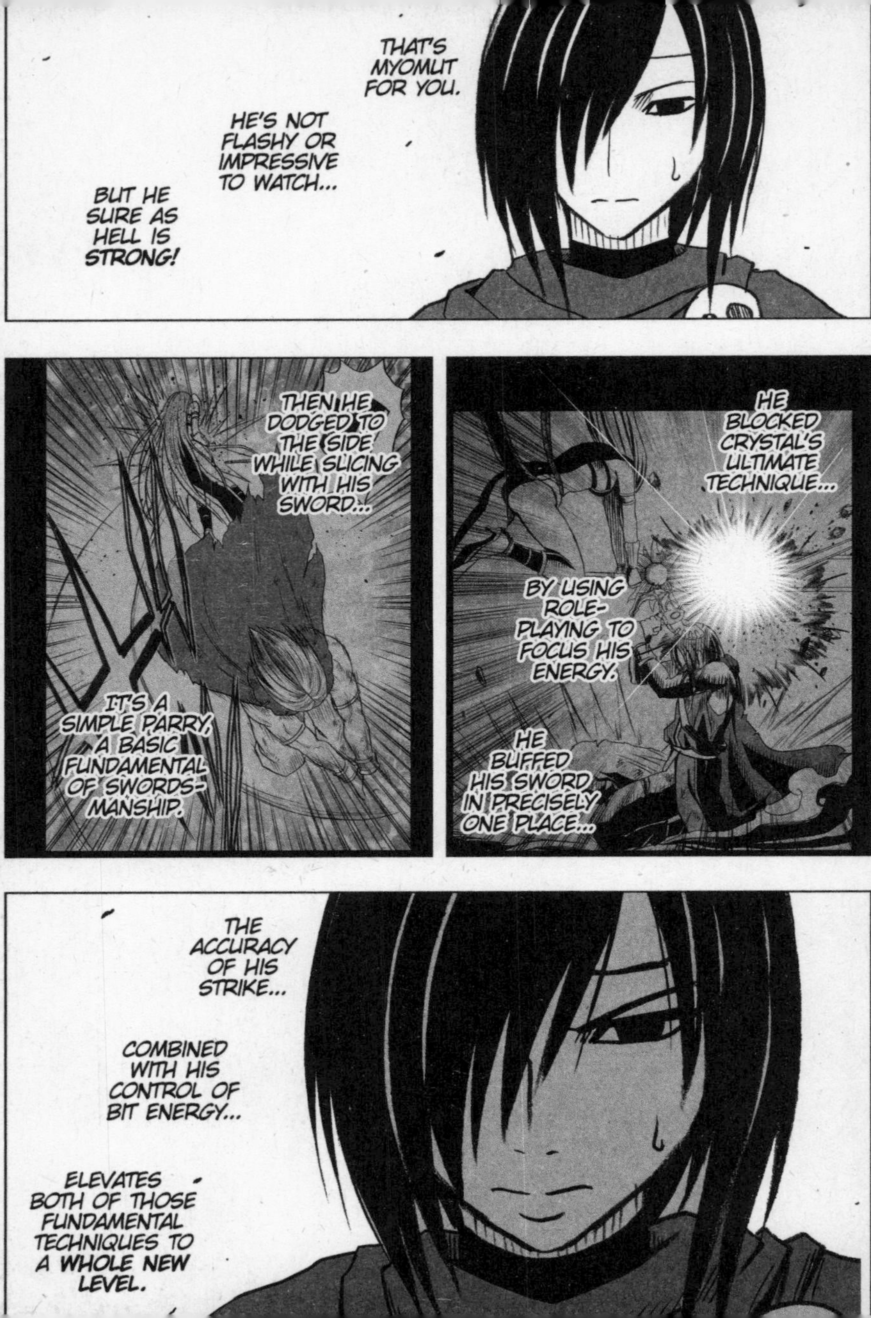
THAT'S MYOMUT FOR YOU.
HE'S NOT FLASHY OR IMPRESSIVE TO WATCH...
BUT HE SURE AS HELL IS STRONG!
HE BLOCKED CRYSTAL'S ULTIMATE TECHNIQUE...
BY USING ROLE-PLAYING TO FOCUS HIS ENERGY.
HE BUFFED HIS SWORD IN PRECISELY ONE PLACE...
THEN HE DODGED TO THE SIDE WHILE SLICING WITH HIS SWORD...
IT'S A SIMPLE PARRY, A BASIC FUNDAMENTAL OF SWORDS-MANSHIP.
THE ACCURACY OF HIS STRIKE...
COMBINED WITH HIS CONTROL OF BIT ENERGY...
ELEVATES BOTH OF THOSE FUNDAMENTAL TECHNIQUES TO A WHOLE NEW LEVEL.

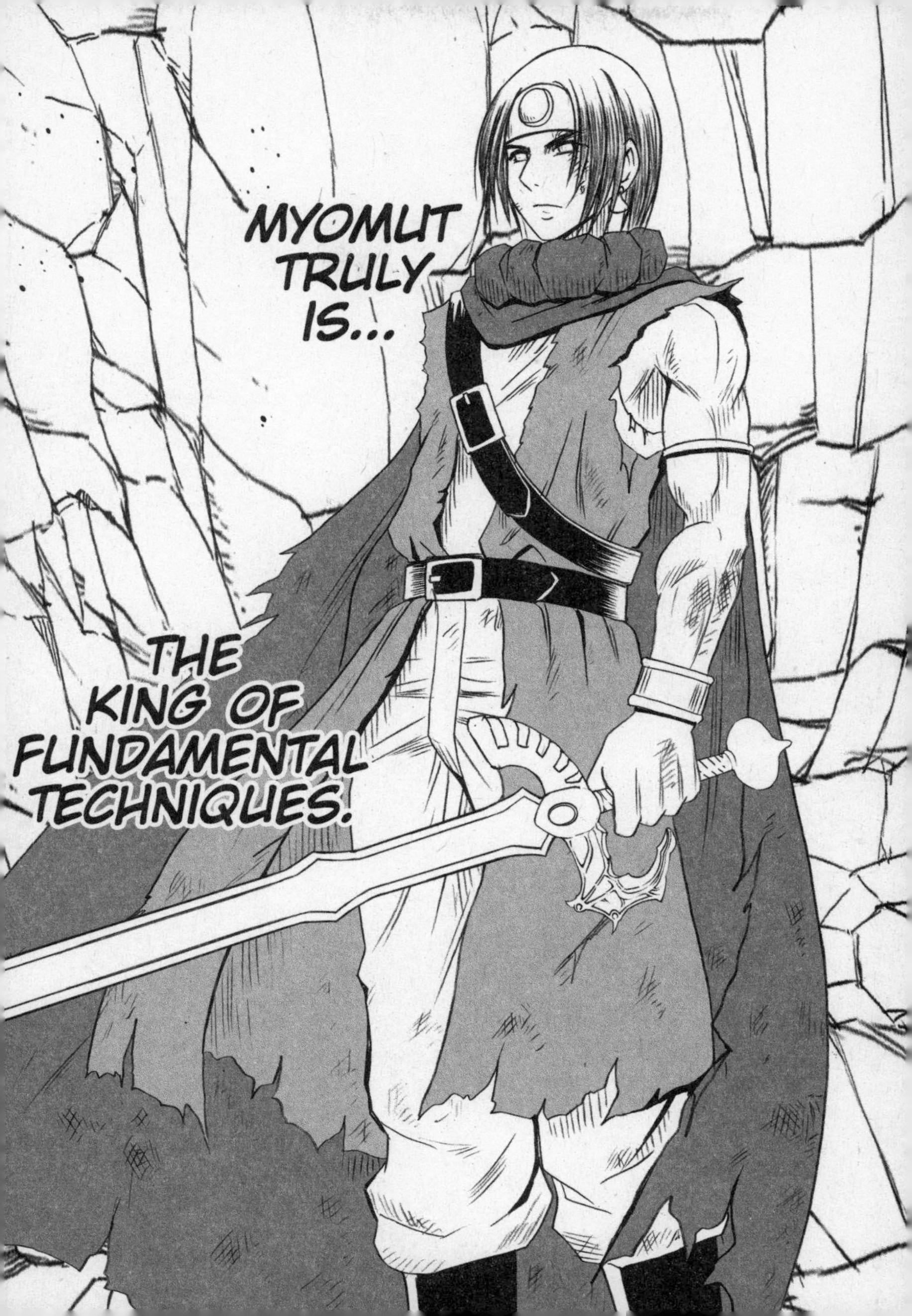
MYOMUT TRULY IS...
THE KING OF FUNDAMENTAL TECHNIQUES.

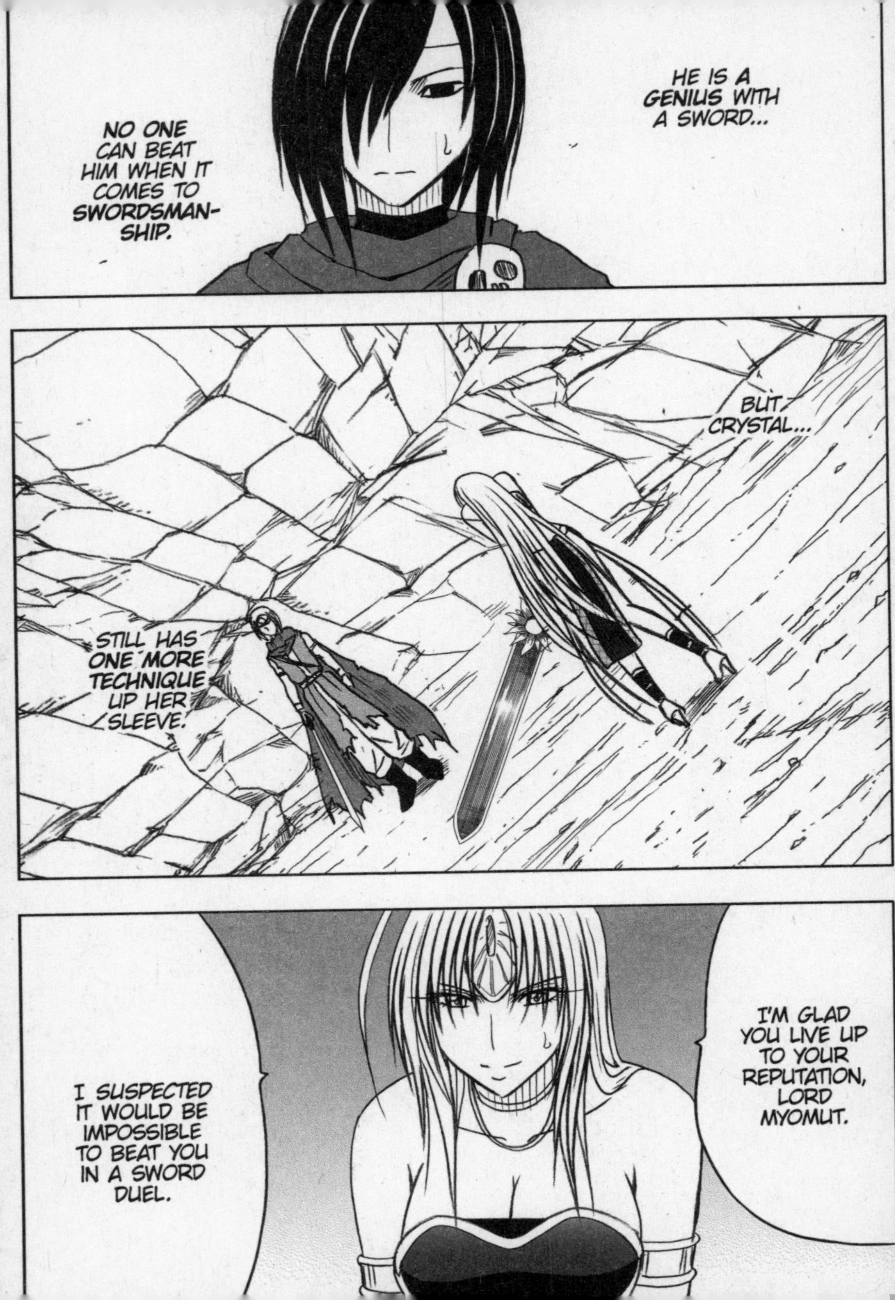
HE IS A GENIUS WITH A SWORD...
NO ONE CAN BEAT HIM WHEN IT COMES TO SWORDSMAN-SHIP.
BUT CRYSTAL...
STILL HAS ONE MORE TECHNIQUE UP HER SLEEVE.
I'M GLAD YOU LIVE UP TO YOUR REPUTATION, LORD MYOMUT.
I SUSPECTED IT WOULD BE IMPOSSIBLE TO BEAT YOU IN A SWORD DUEL.

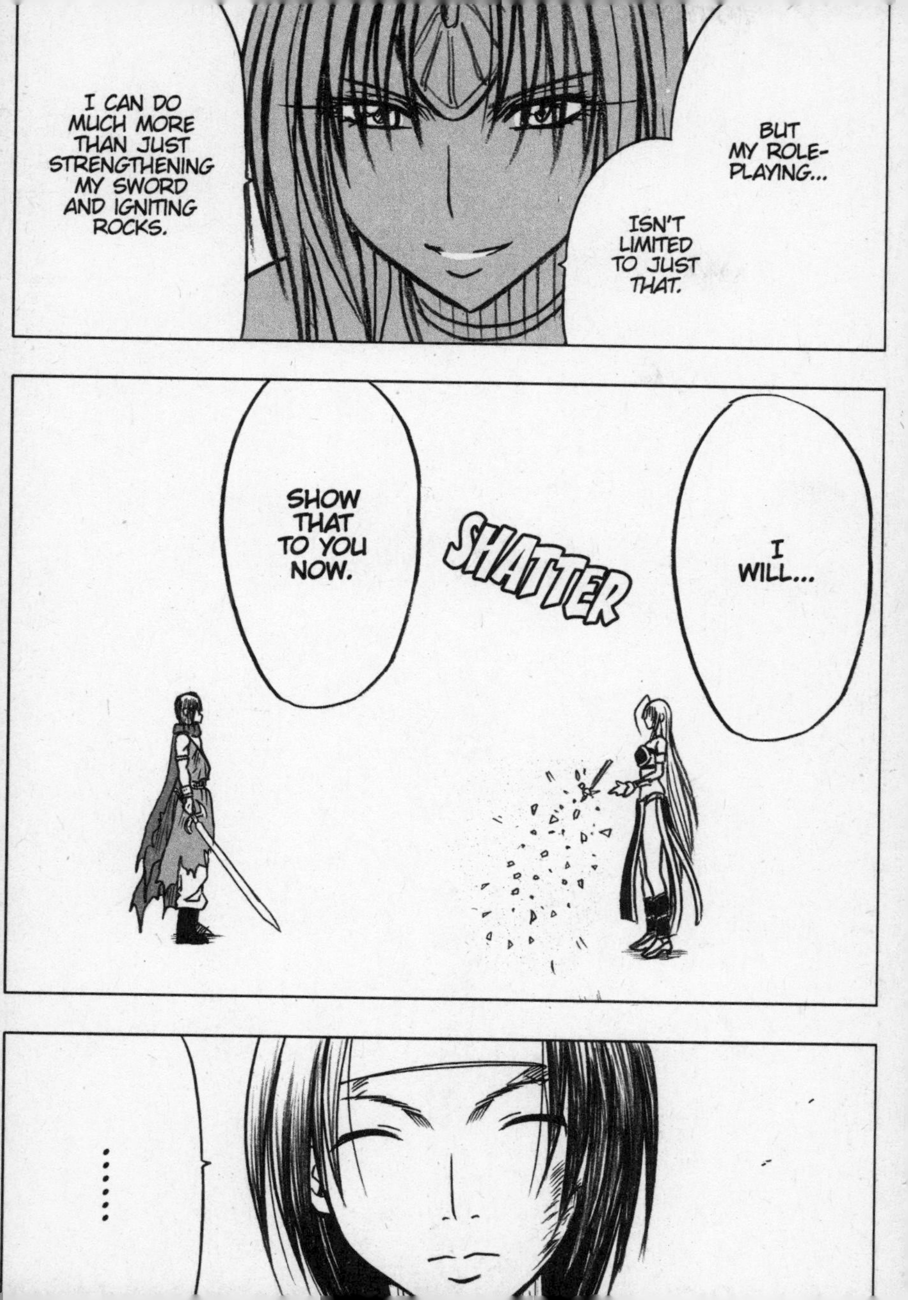
BUT MY ROLE-PLAYING...
ISN'T LIMITED TO JUST THAT.
I CAN DO MUCH MORE THAN JUST STRENGTHENING MY SWORD AND IGNITING ROCKS.
I WILL...
SHATTER
SHOW THAT TO YOU NOW.
......

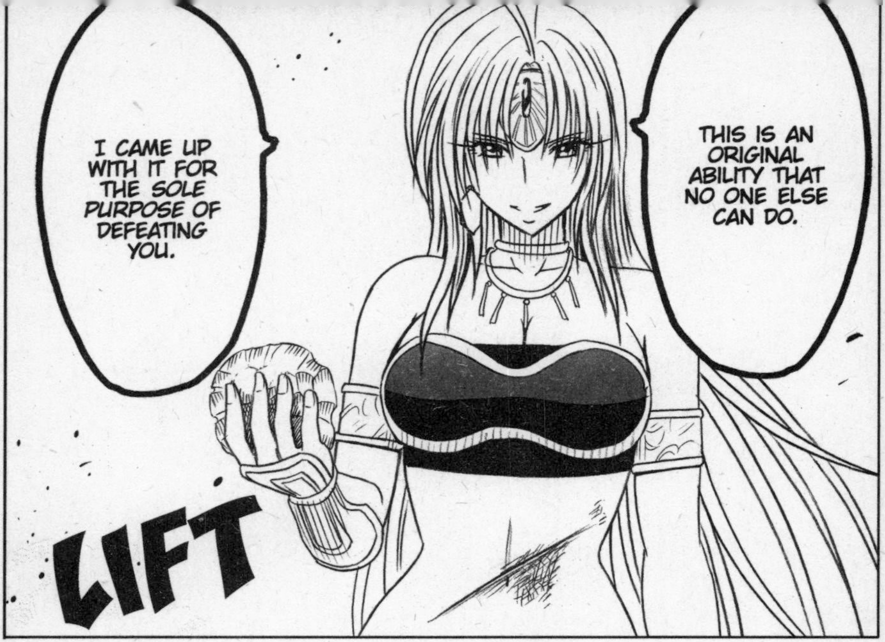
THIS IS AN ORIGINAL ABILITY THAT NO ONE ELSE CAN DO.
I CAME UP WITH IT FOR THE SOLE PURPOSE OF DEFEATING YOU.
LIFT

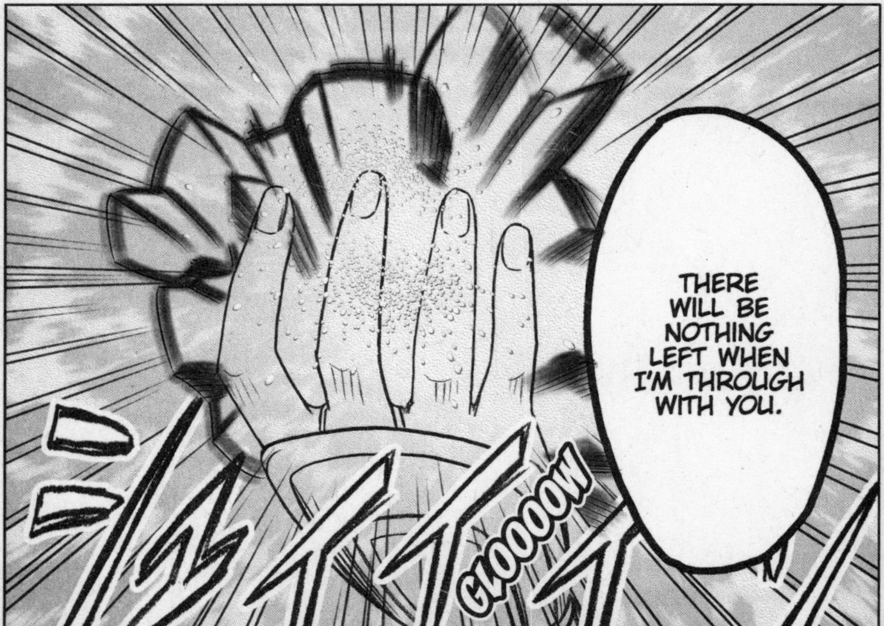
THERE WILL BE NOTHING LEFT WHEN I'M THROUGH WITH YOU.
GLOOOOW

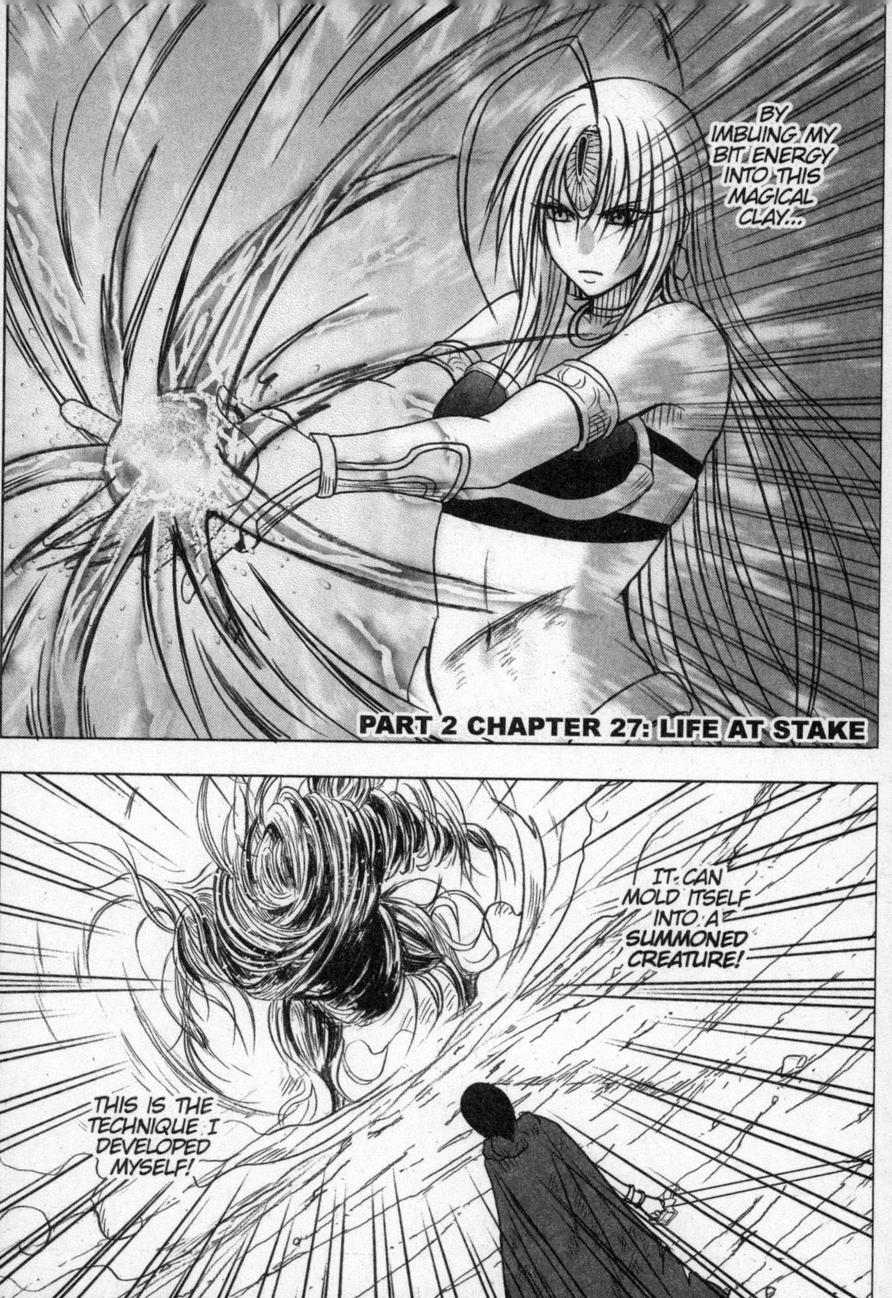
BY IMBUING MY BIT ENERGY INTO THIS MAGICAL CLAY...
PART 2 CHAPTER 27: LIFE AT STAKE
IT CAN MOLD ITSELF INTO A SUMMONED CREATURE!
THIS IS THE TECHNIQUE I DEVELOPED MYSELF!

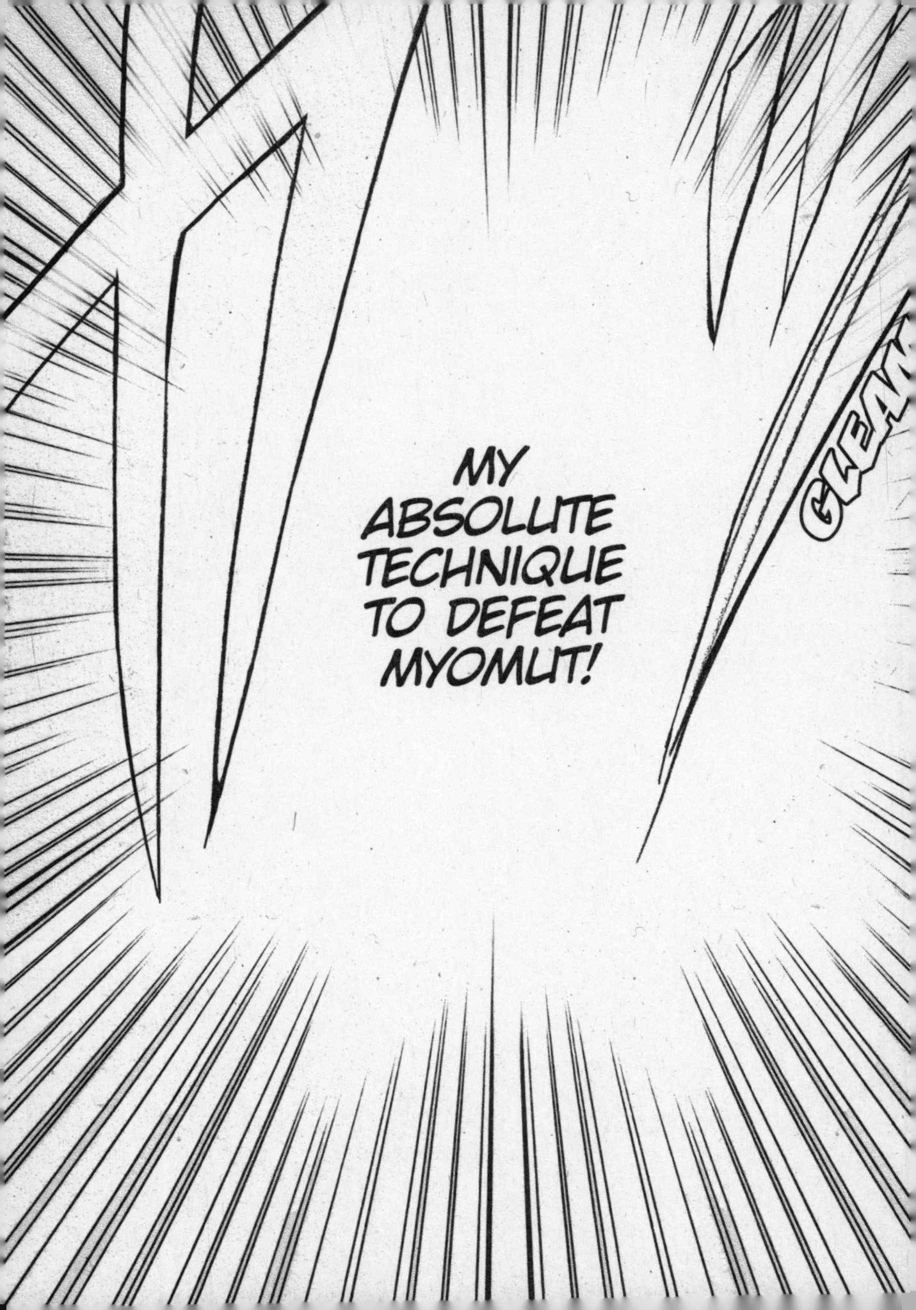
MY ABSOLUTE TECHNIQUE TO DEFEAT MYOMUT!
GLEAM

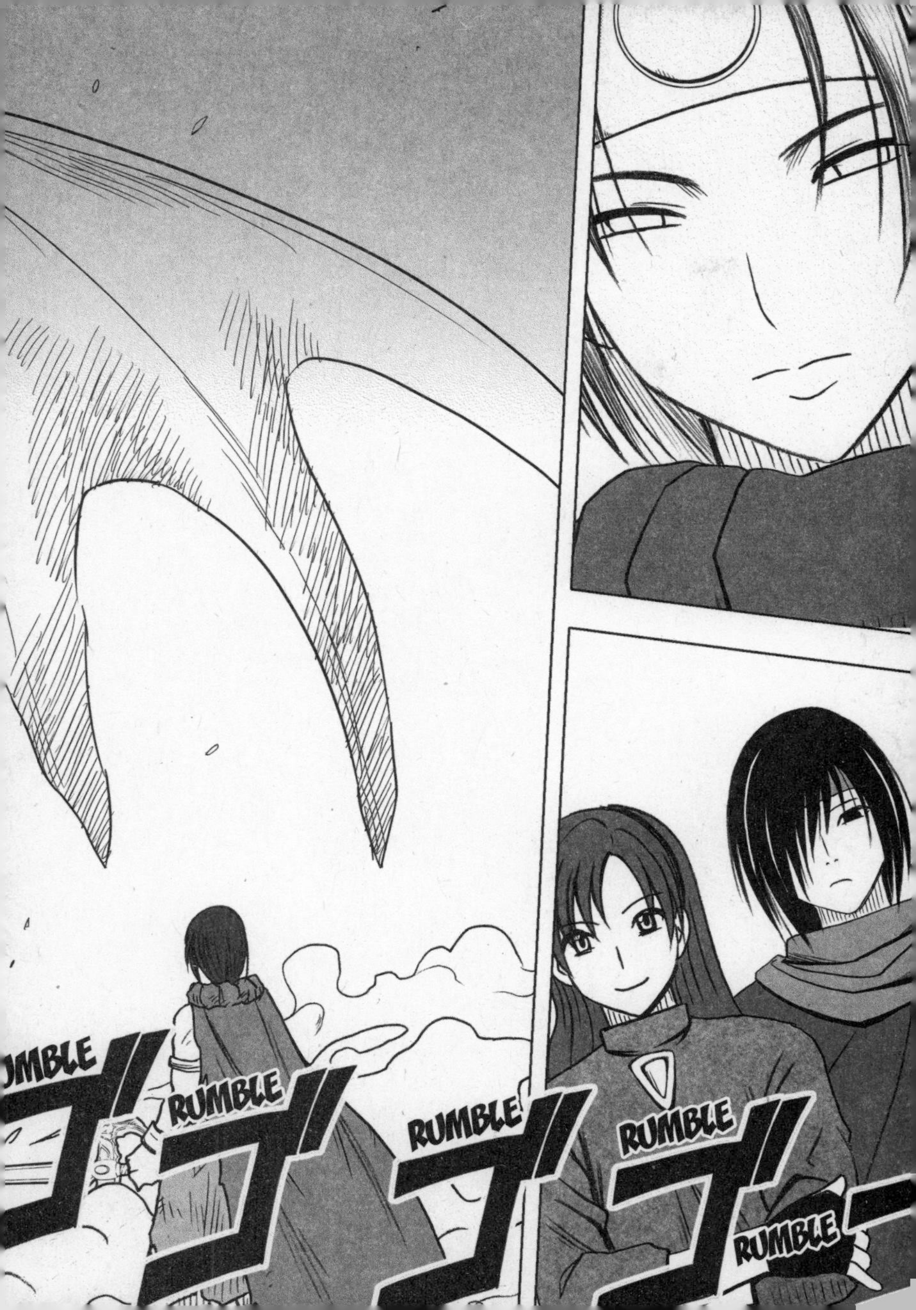
RUMBLE
RUMBLE
RUMBLE
RUMBLE
UMBLE

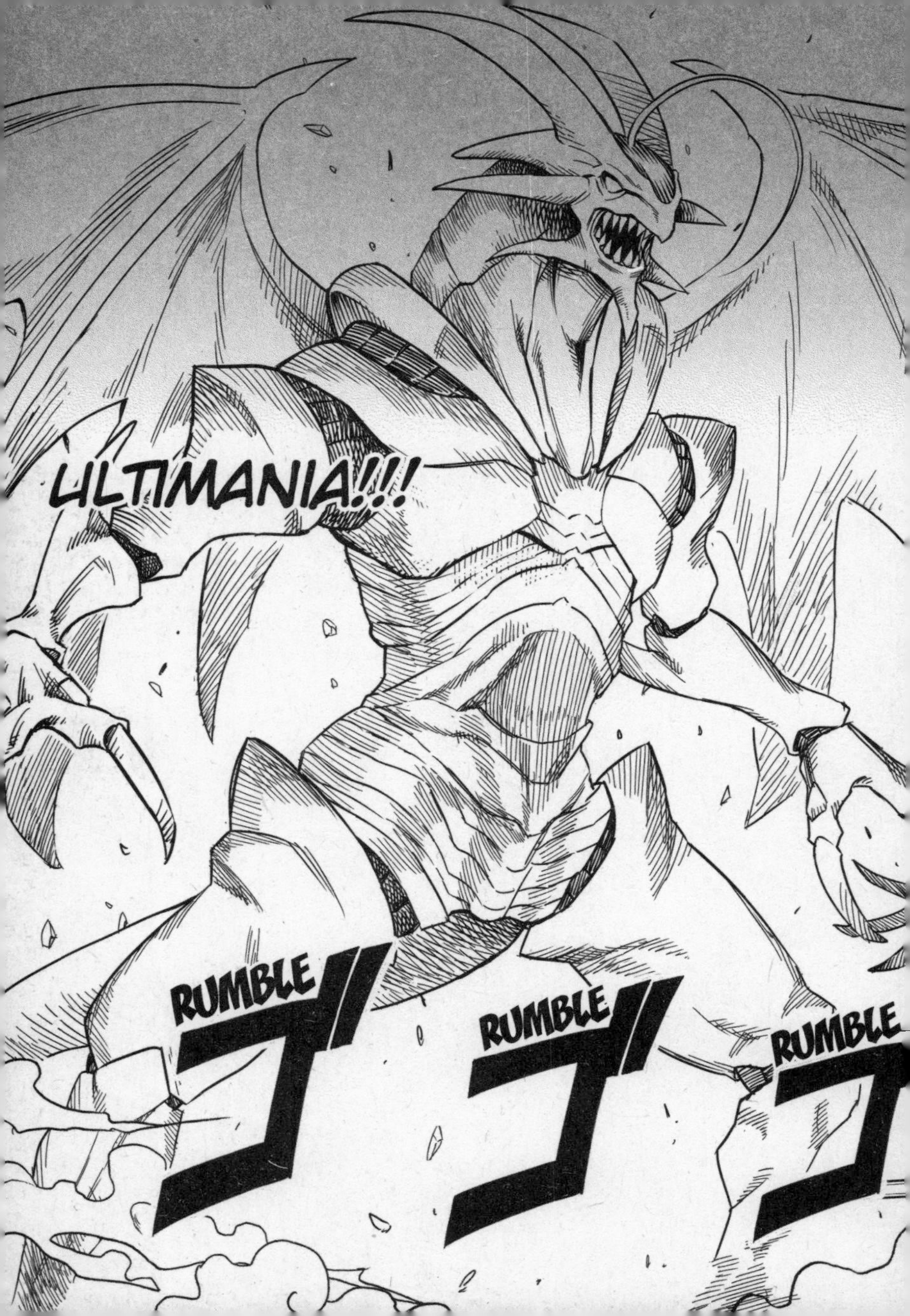
ULTIMANIA!!!
RUMBLE
ゴ
RUMBLE
ゴ
RUMBLE
ゴ

Part 2

CHAPTER 27

LIFE
AT
STAKE

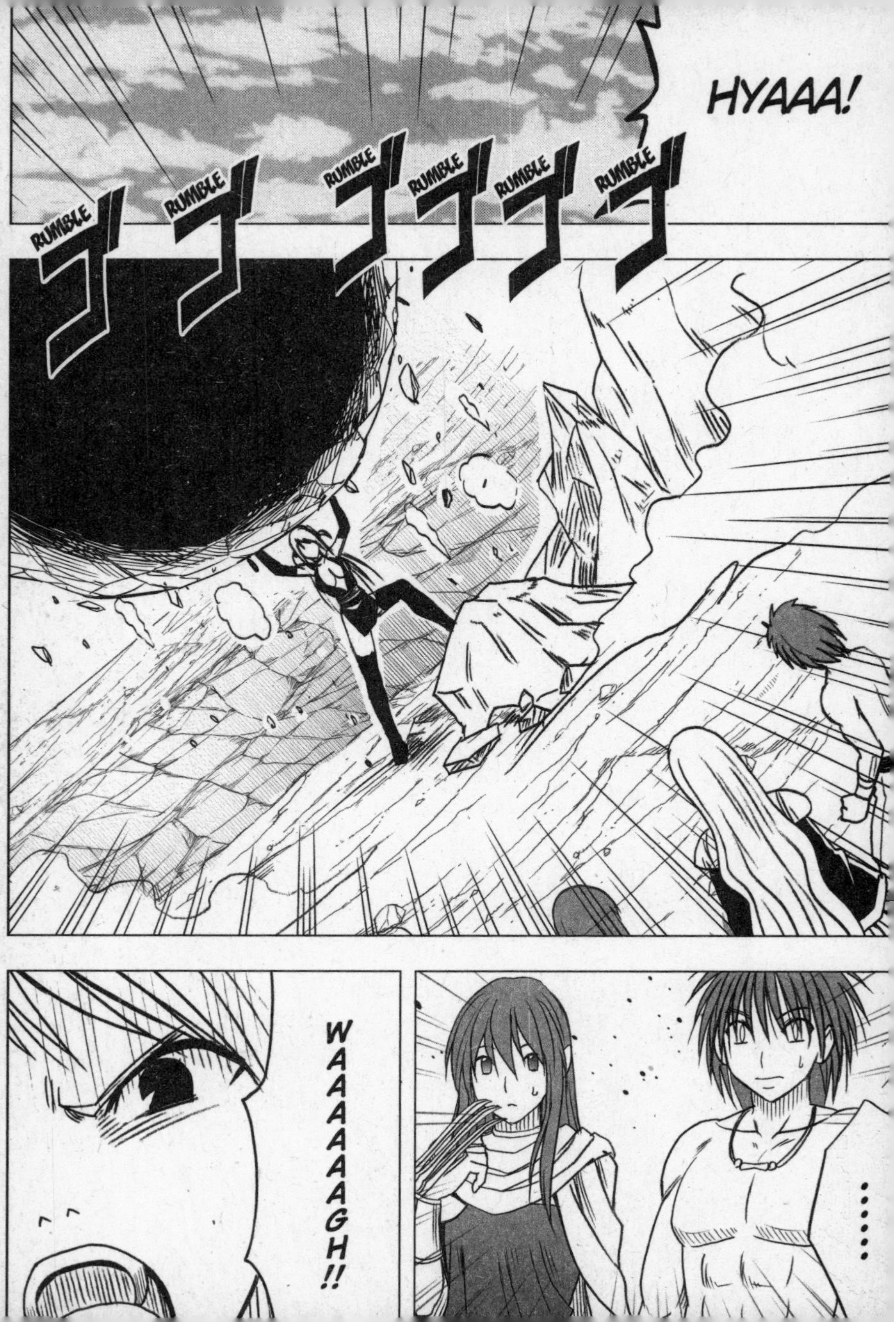
HYAAA!
RUMBLE
RUMBLE
RUMBLE
RUMBLE
RUMBLE
RUMBLE
......
WAAAAAAGH!!

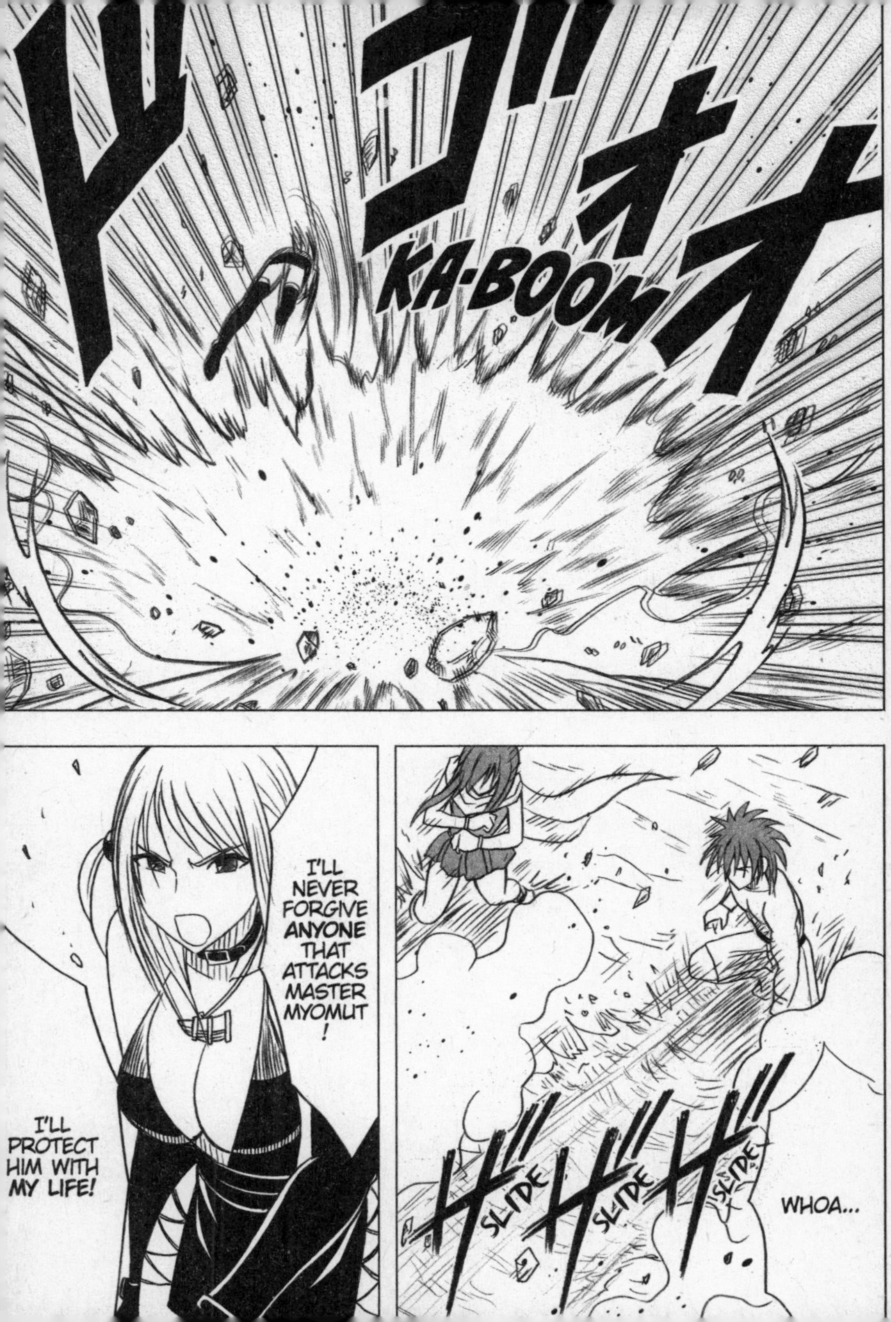
KA-BOOM
WHOA...
SLIDE
SLIDE
SLIDE
I'LL NEVER FORGIVE ANYONE THAT ATTACKS MASTER MYOMUT!
I'LL PROTECT HIM WITH MY LIFE!

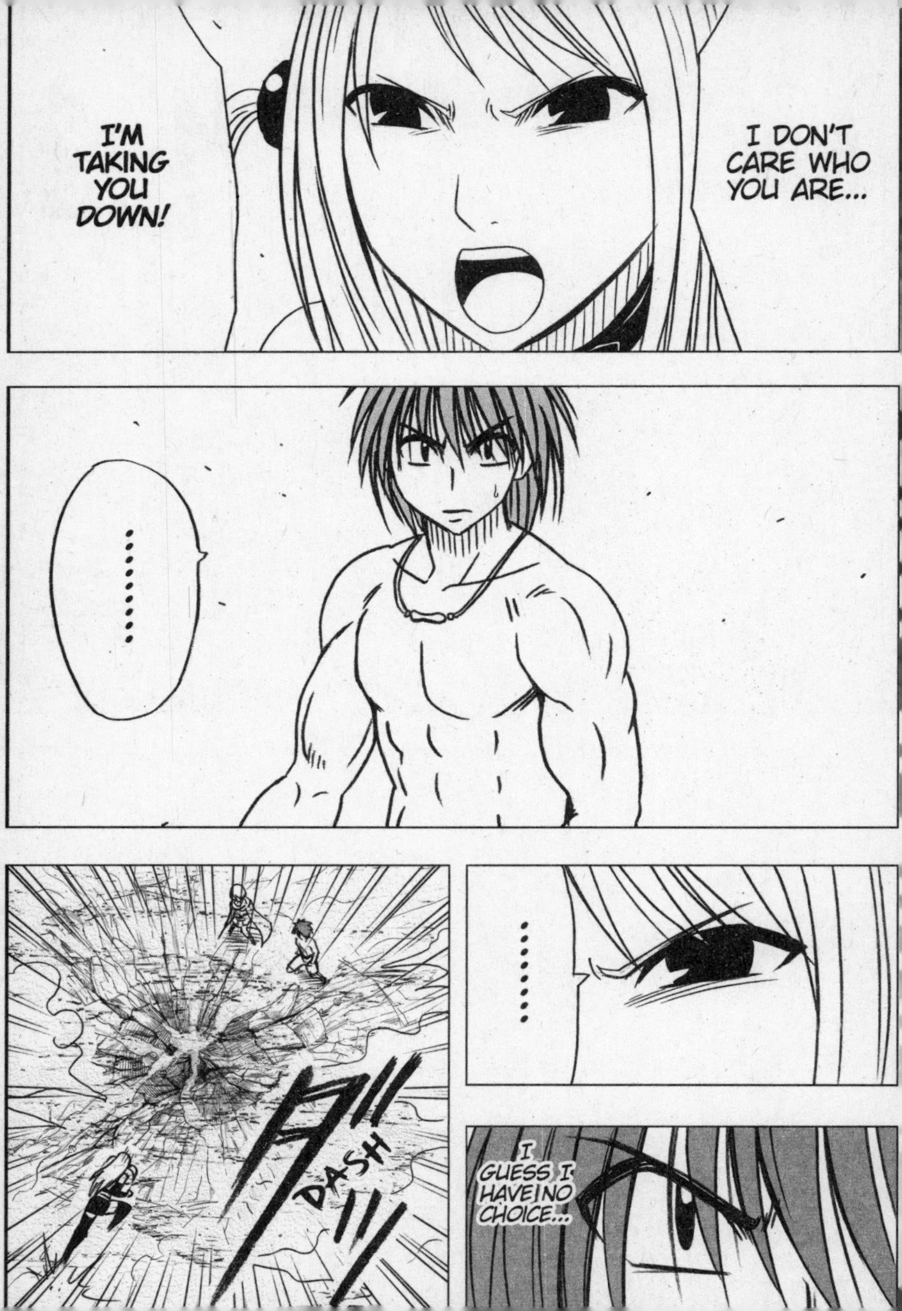
I DON'T CARE WHO YOU ARE...
I'M TAKING YOU DOWN!
......
......
I GUESS I HAVE NO CHOICE...
DASH

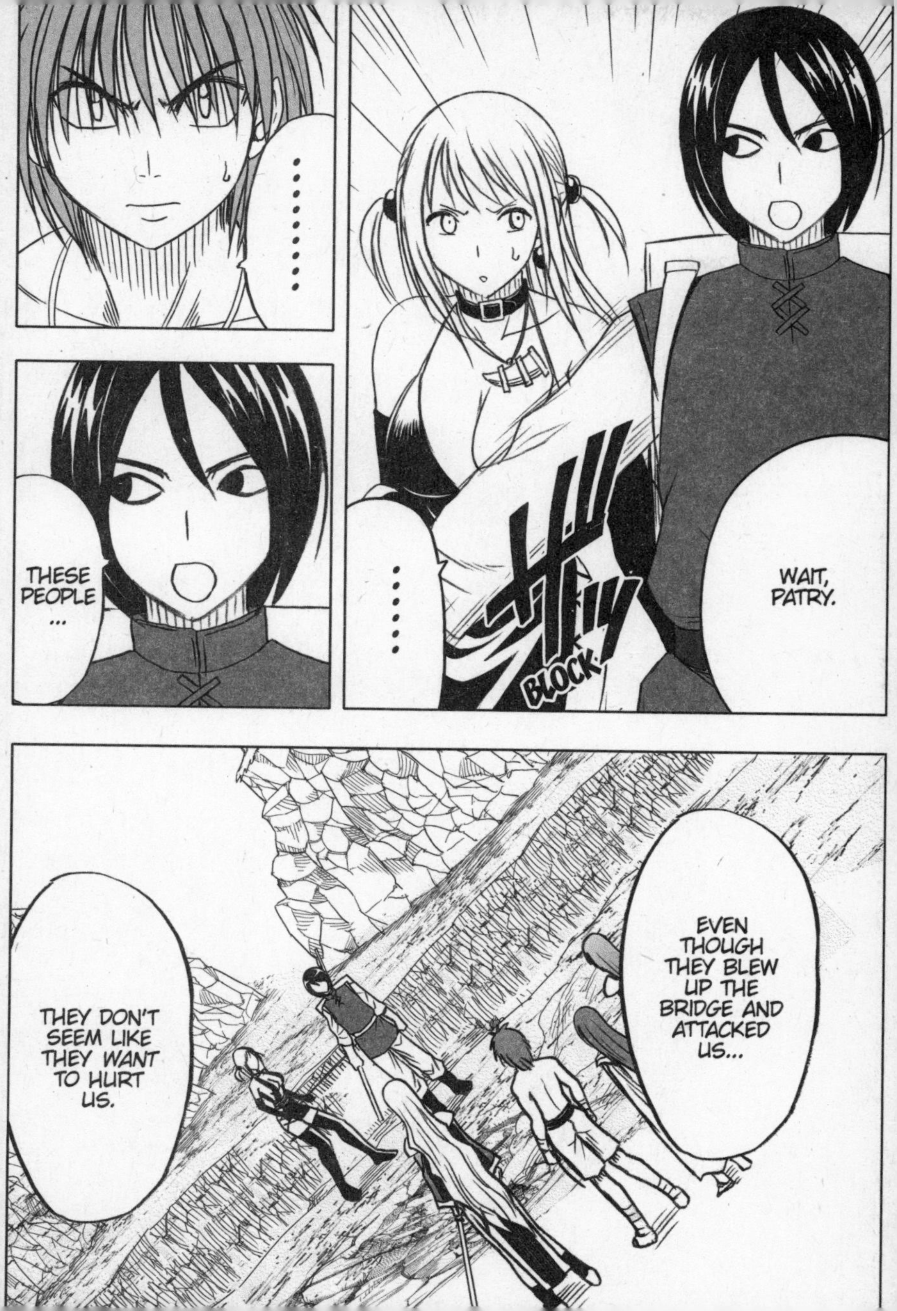
WAIT, PATRY.
......
BLOCK
......
THESE PEOPLE ...
EVEN THOUGH THEY BLEW UP THE BRIDGE AND ATTACKED US...
THEY DON'T SEEM LIKE THEY WANT TO HURT US.

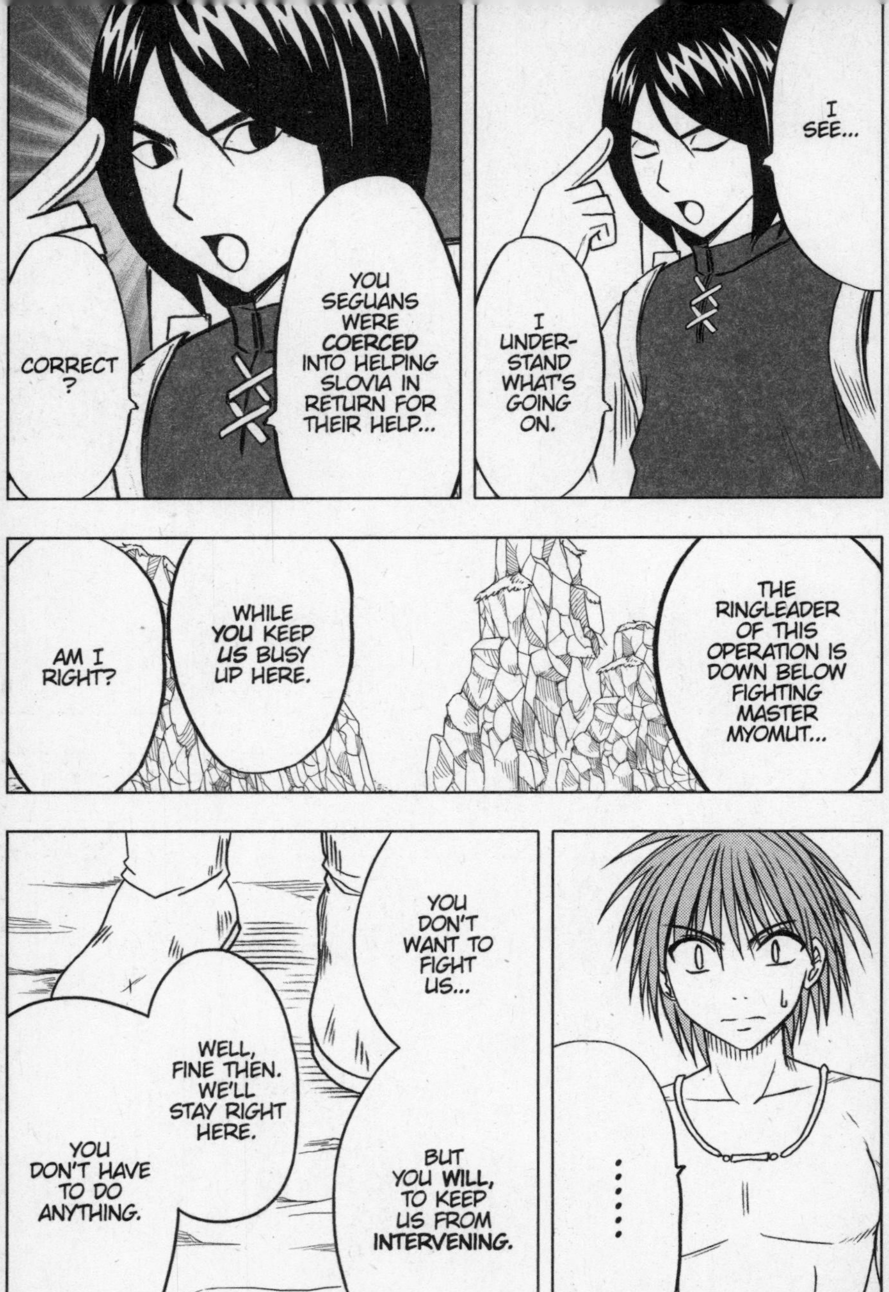
I SEE...
I UNDERSTAND WHAT'S GOING ON.
YOU SEGUANS WERE COERCED INTO HELPING SLOVIA IN RETURN FOR THEIR HELP...
CORRECT?
THE RINGLEADER OF THIS OPERATION IS DOWN BELOW FIGHTING MASTER MYOMUT...
WHILE YOU KEEP US BUSY UP HERE.
AM I RIGHT?
......
YOU DON'T WANT TO FIGHT US...
BUT YOU WILL, TO KEEP US FROM INTERVENING.
WELL, FINE THEN. WE'LL STAY RIGHT HERE.
YOU DON'T HAVE TO DO ANYTHING.

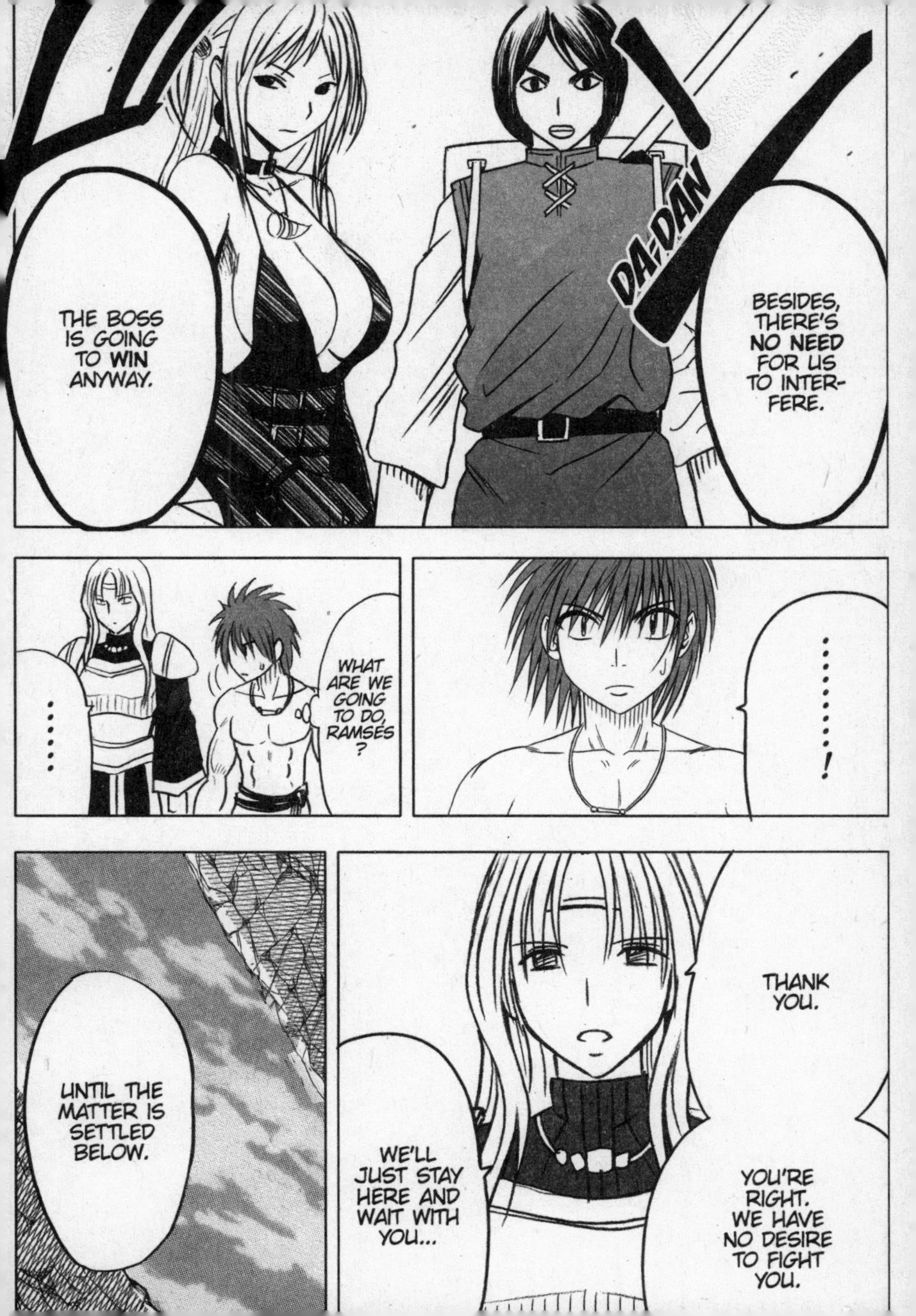
BESIDES, THERE'S NO NEED FOR US TO INTERFERE.
DA-DAN
THE BOSS IS GOING TO WIN ANYWAY.
........!
WHAT ARE WE GOING TO DO, RAMSES?
......
THANK YOU.
YOU'RE RIGHT. WE HAVE NO DESIRE TO FIGHT YOU.
WE'LL JUST STAY HERE AND WAIT WITH YOU...
UNTIL THE MATTER IS SETTLED BELOW.

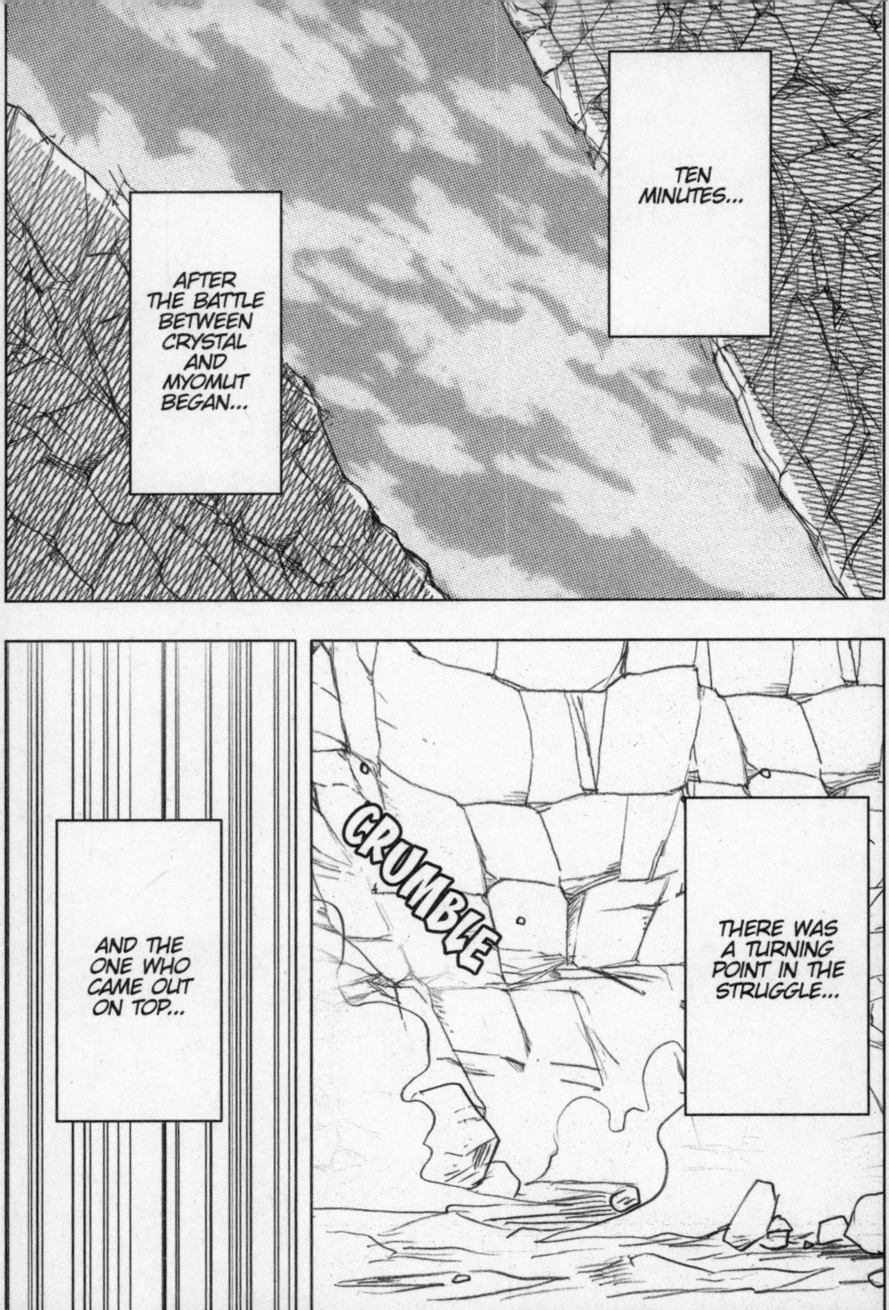
TEN MINUTES...
AFTER THE BATTLE BETWEEN CRYSTAL AND MYOMUT BEGAN...
THERE WAS A TURNING POINT IN THE STRUGGLE...
CRUMBLE
AND THE ONE WHO CAME OUT ON TOP...

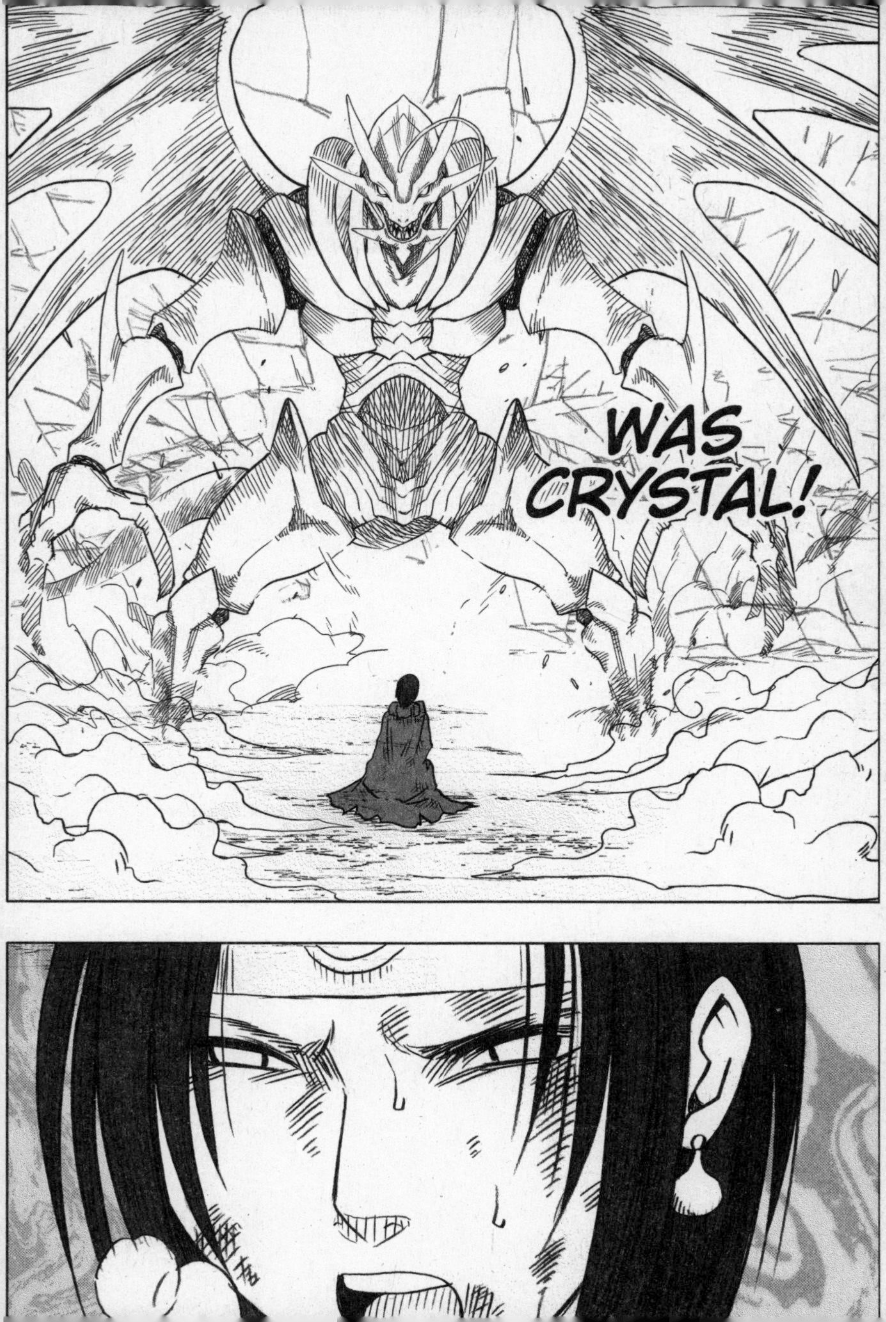
WAS CRYSTAL!

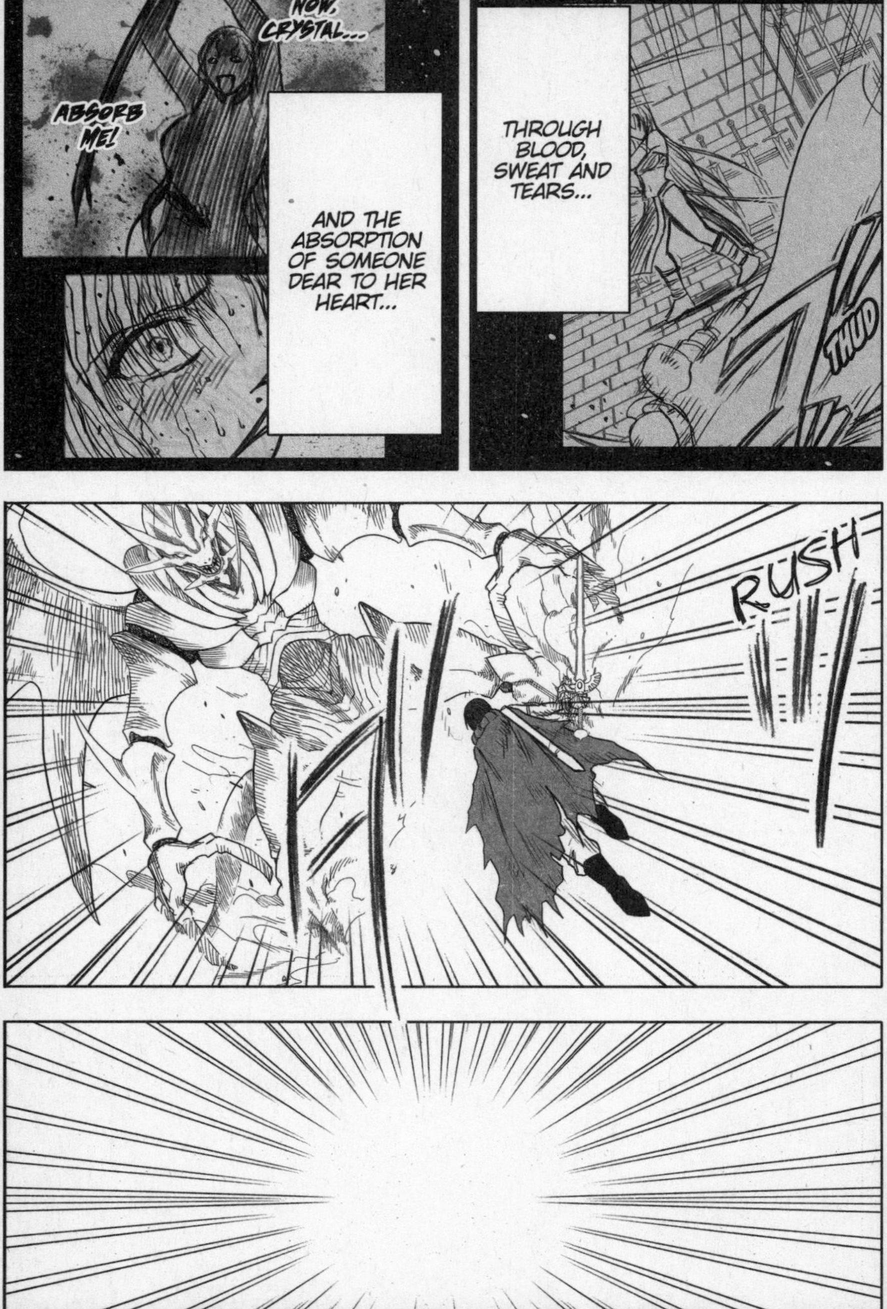
THROUGH BLOOD, SWEAT AND TEARS...
THUD
NOW, CRYSTAL...
ABSORB ME!
AND THE ABSORPTION OF SOMEONE DEAR TO HER HEART...
RUSH

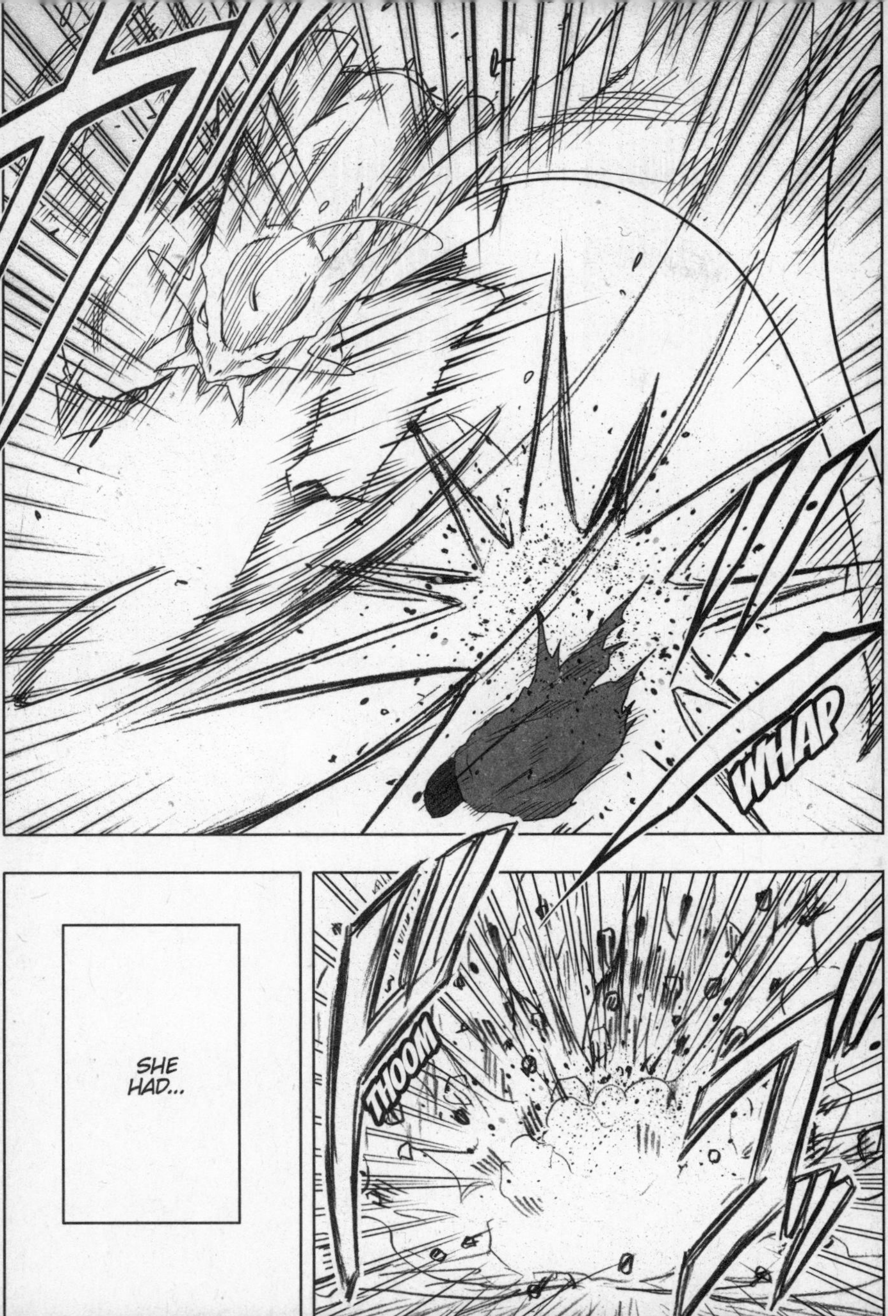
WHAP
THOOM
SHE HAD...

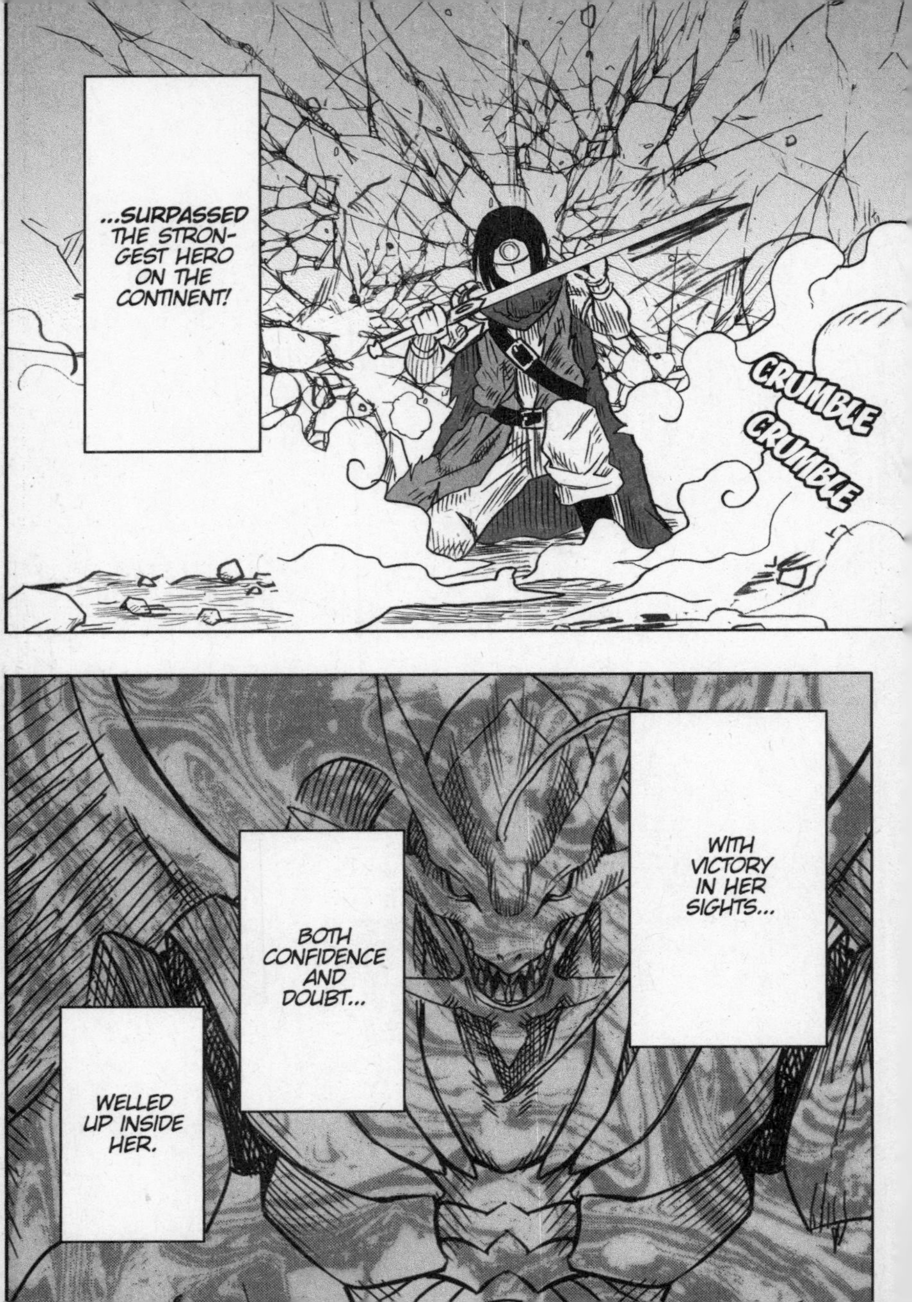

CRUMBLE CRUMBLE
...SURPASSED THE STRONGEST HERO ON THE CONTINENT!
WITH VICTORY IN HER SIGHTS...
BOTH CONFIDENCE AND DOUBT...
WELLED UP INSIDE HER.

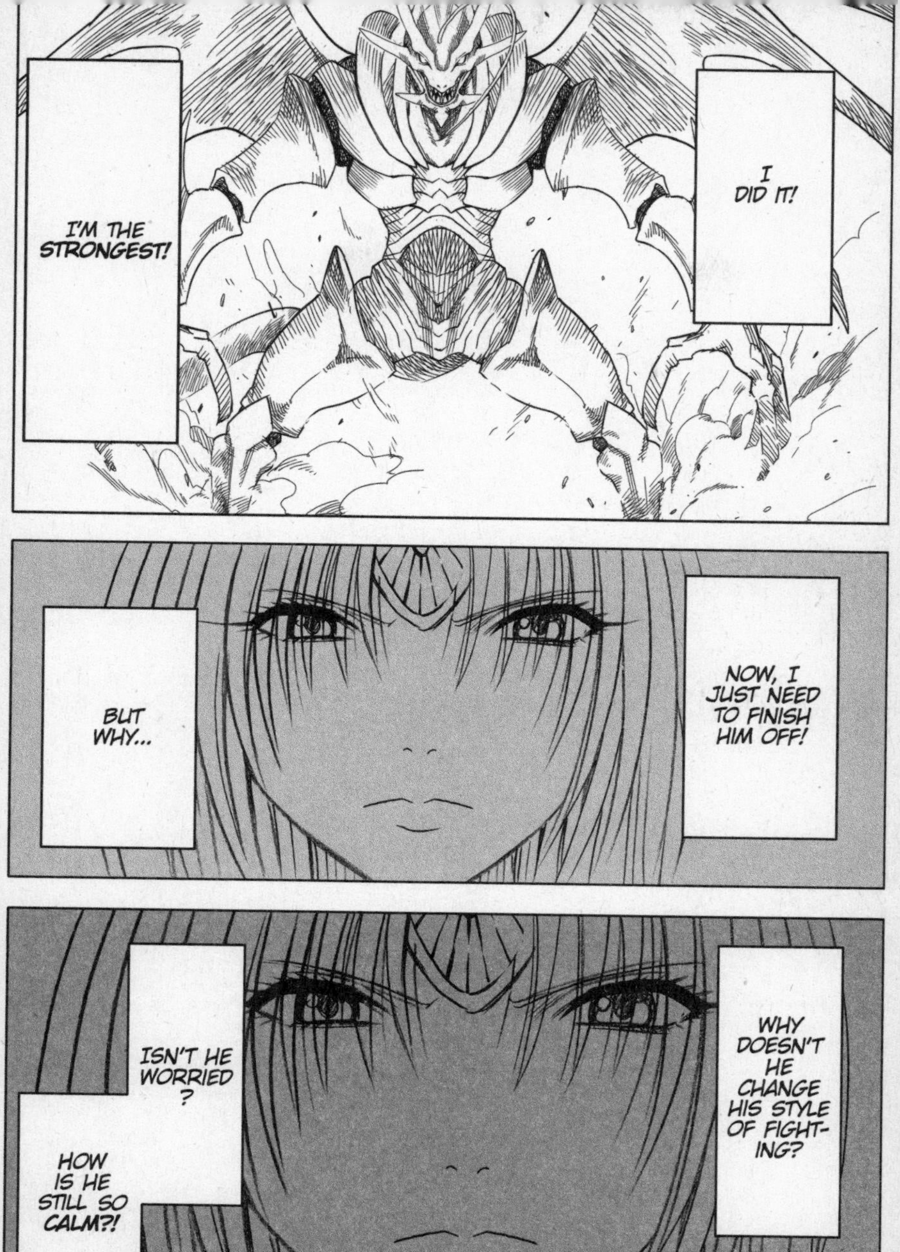
I DID IT!
I'M THE STRONGEST!
NOW, I JUST NEED TO FINISH HIM OFF!
BUT WHY...
WHY DOESN'T HE CHANGE HIS STYLE OF FIGHTING?
ISN'T HE WORRIED?
HOW IS HE STILL SO CALM?!

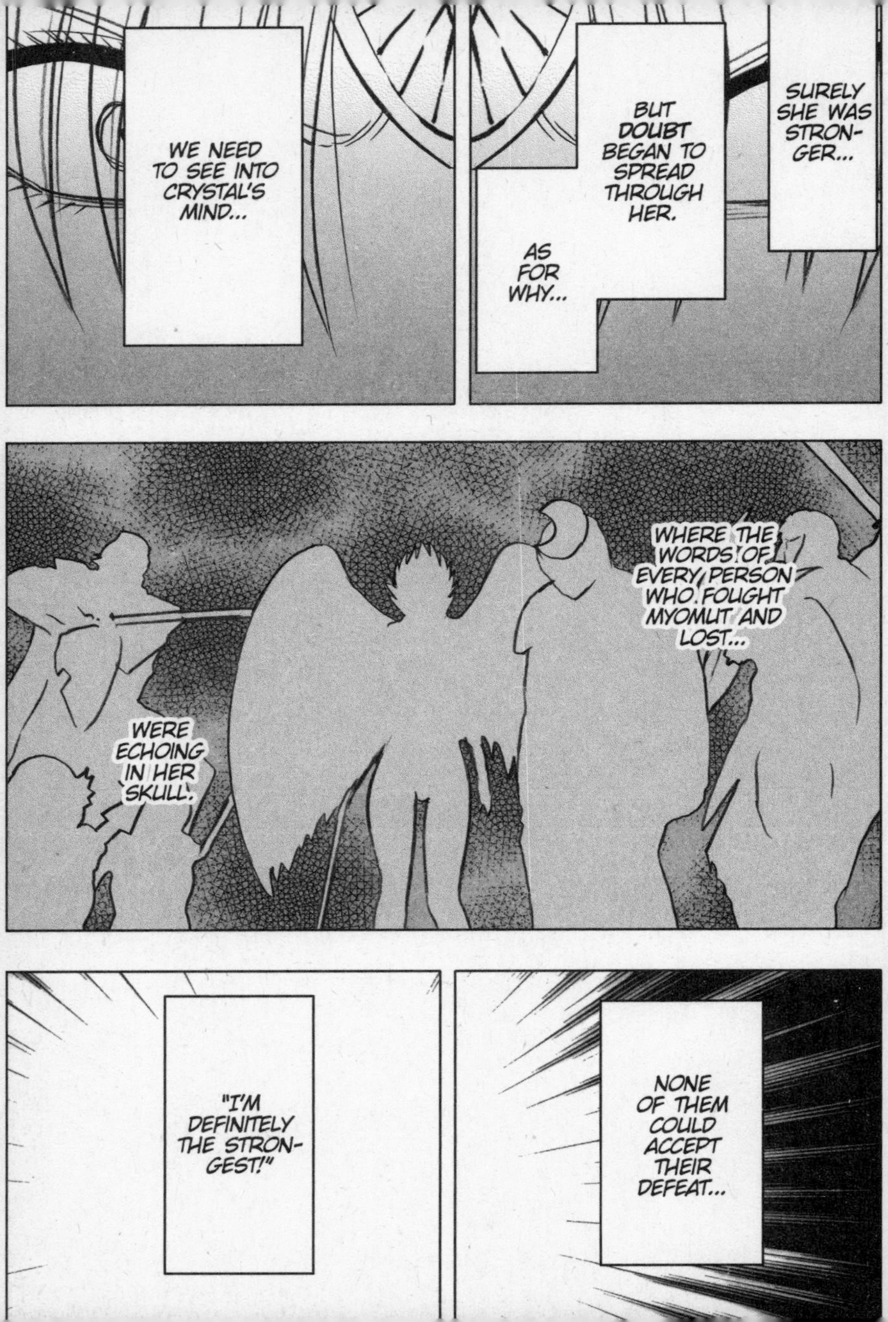
SURELY SHE WAS STRONGER...
BUT DOUBT BEGAN TO SPREAD THROUGH HER.
AS FOR WHY...
WE NEED TO SEE INTO CRYSTAL'S MIND...
WHERE THE WORDS OF EVERY PERSON WHO FOUGHT MYOMUT AND LOST...
WERE ECHOING IN HER SKULL.
NONE OF THEM COULD ACCEPT THEIR DEFEAT...
"I'M DEFINITELY THE STRONGEST!"

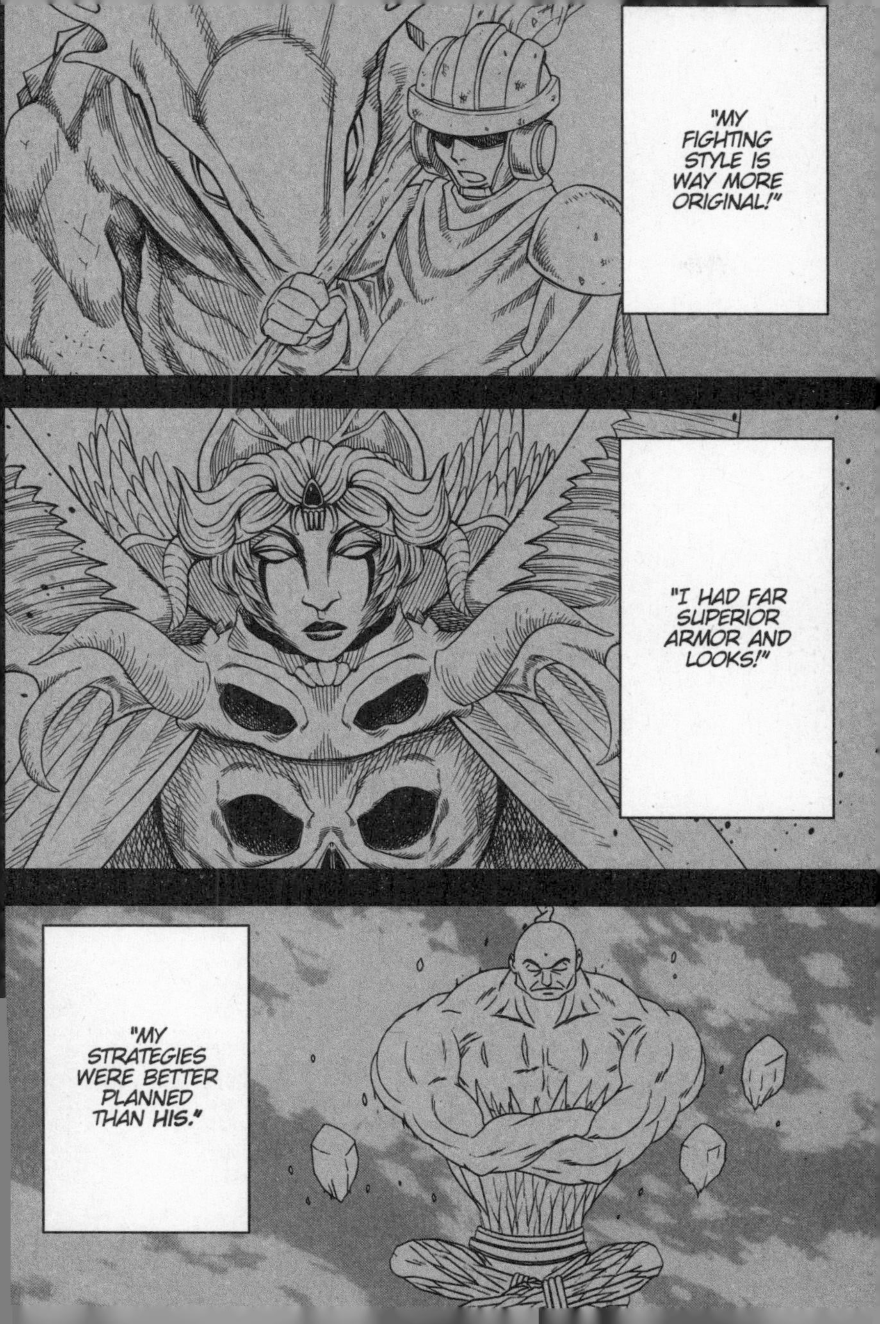
"MY FIGHTING STYLE IS WAY MORE ORIGINAL!"
"I HAD FAR SUPERIOR ARMOR AND LOOKS!"
"MY STRATEGIES WERE BETTER PLANNED THAN HIS."

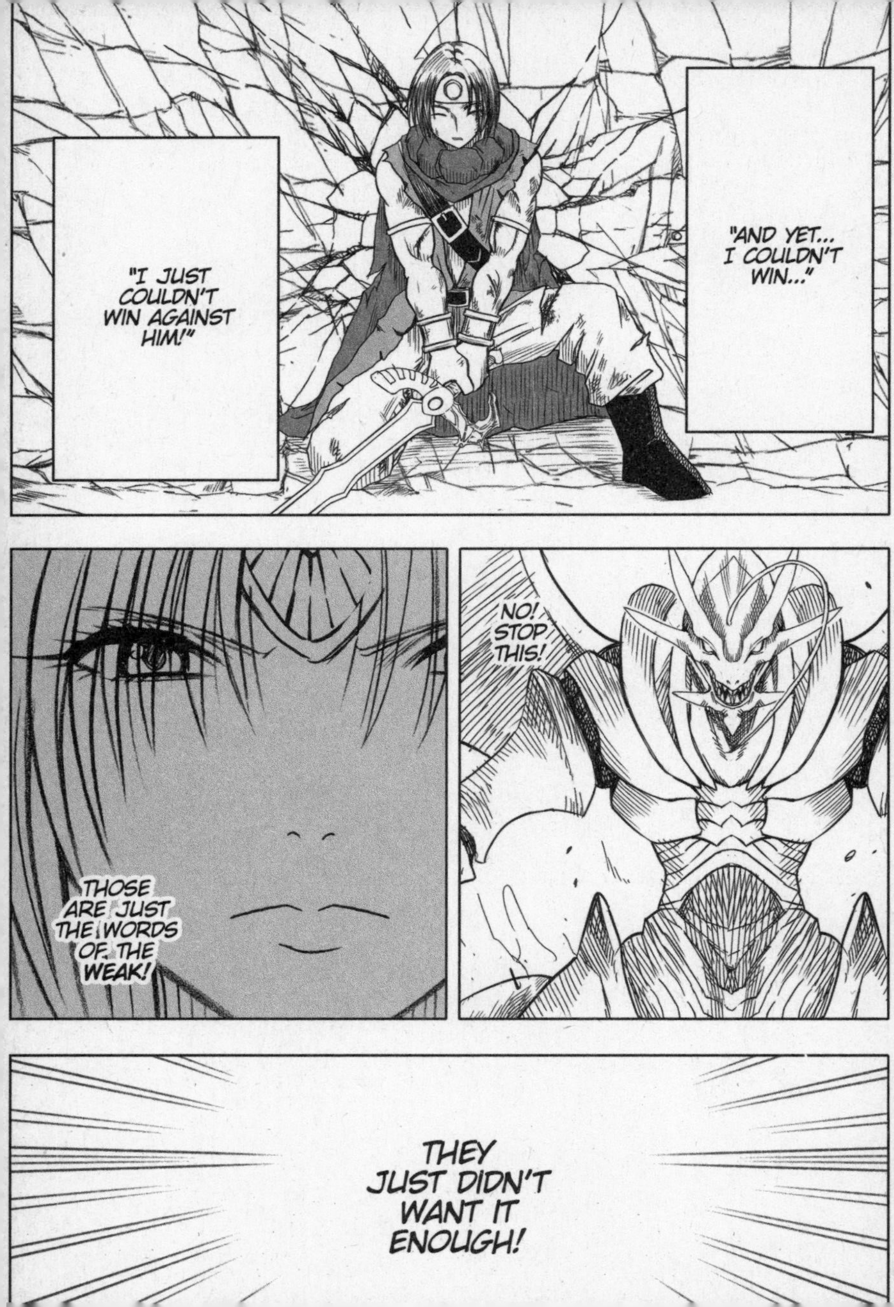
"AND YET... I COULDN'T WIN..."
"I JUST COULDN'T WIN AGAINST HIM!"
NO! STOP THIS!
THOSE ARE JUST THE WORDS OF THE WEAK!
THEY JUST DIDN'T WANT IT ENOUGH!

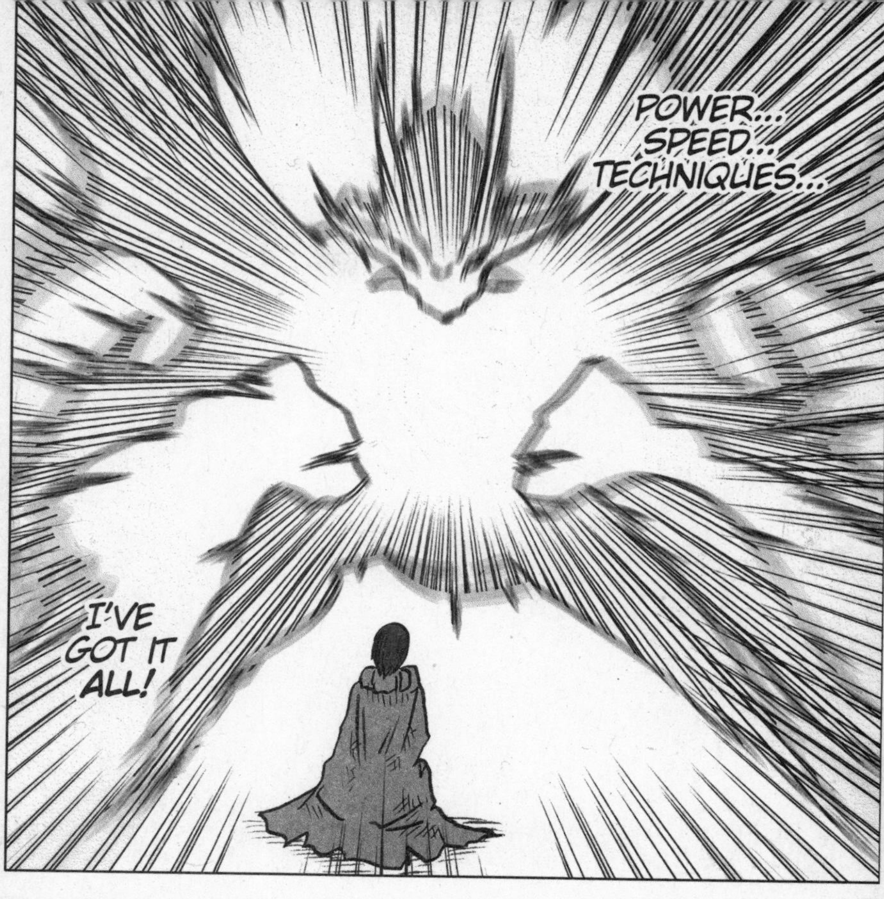
POWER... SPEED... TECHNIQUES...
I'VE GOT IT ALL!
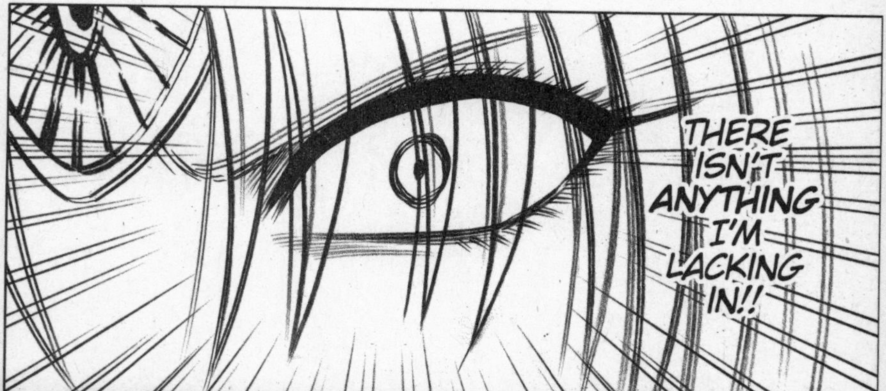
THERE ISN'T ANYTHING I'M LACKING IN!!

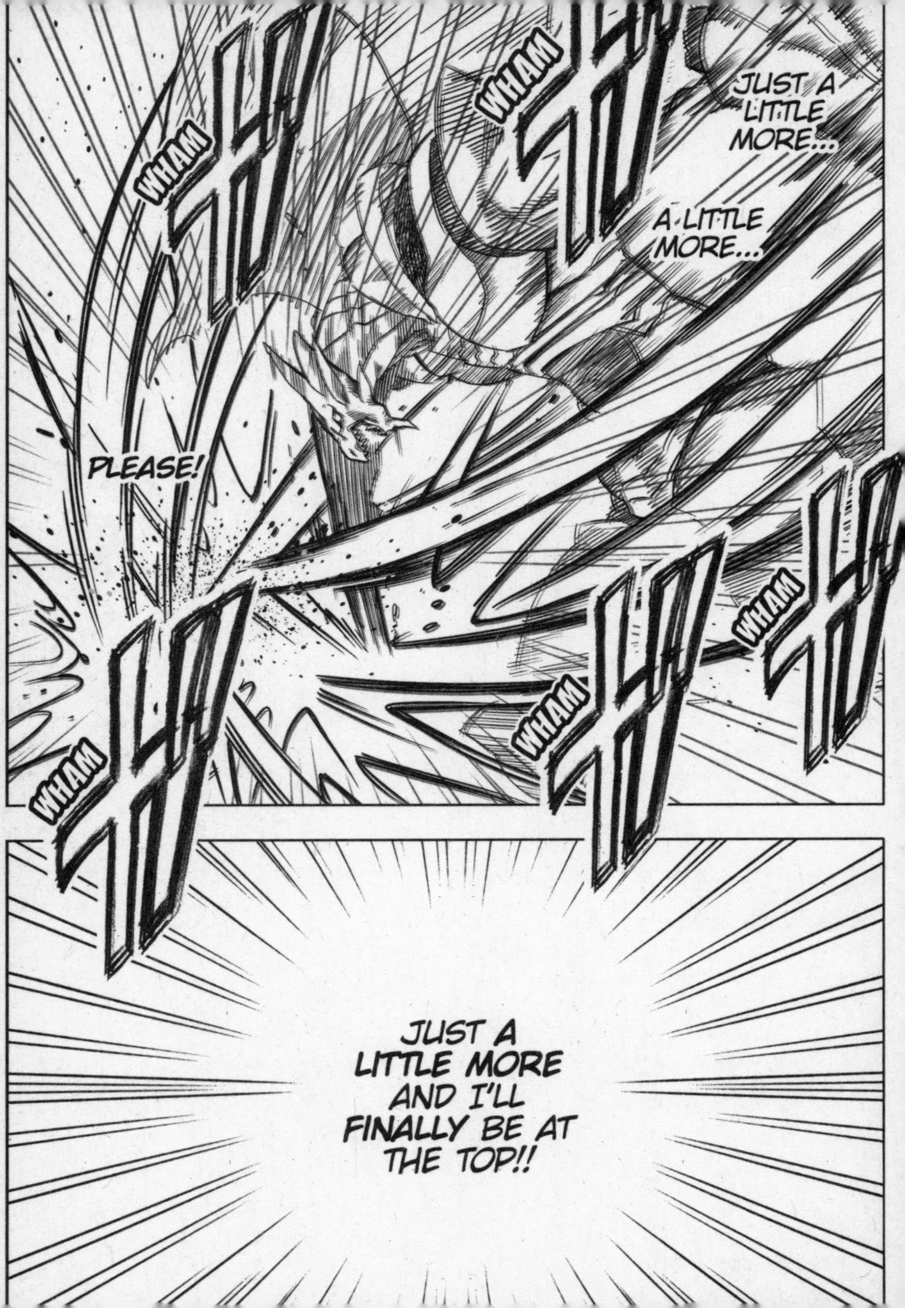
JUST A LITTLE MORE...
WHAM
A LITTLE MORE...
WHAM
PLEASE!
WHAM
WHAM
WHAM
JUST A LITTLE MORE AND I'LL FINALLY BE AT THE TOP!!

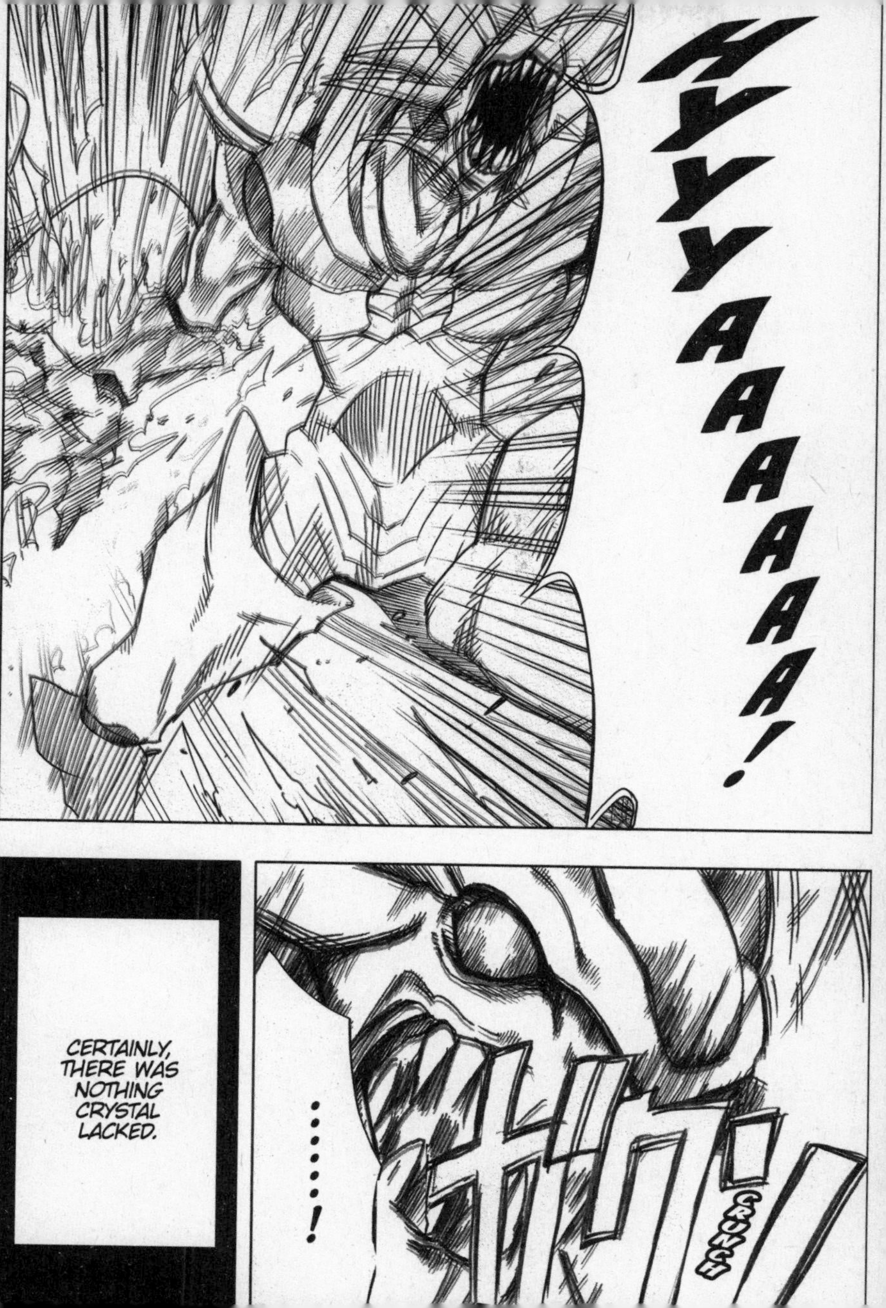

HYYAAAAAA!
......!
CRUNCH
CERTAINLY, THERE WAS NOTHING CRYSTAL LACKED.

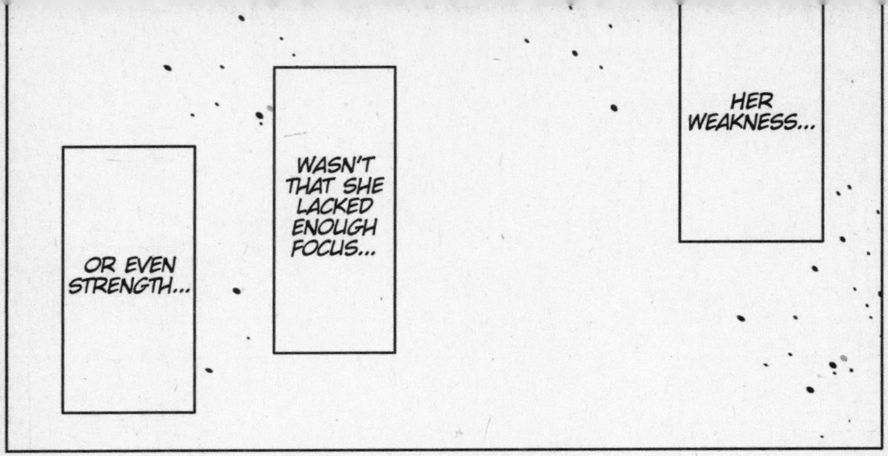
HER WEAKNESS...
WASN'T THAT SHE LACKED ENOUGH FOCUS...
OR EVEN STRENGTH...
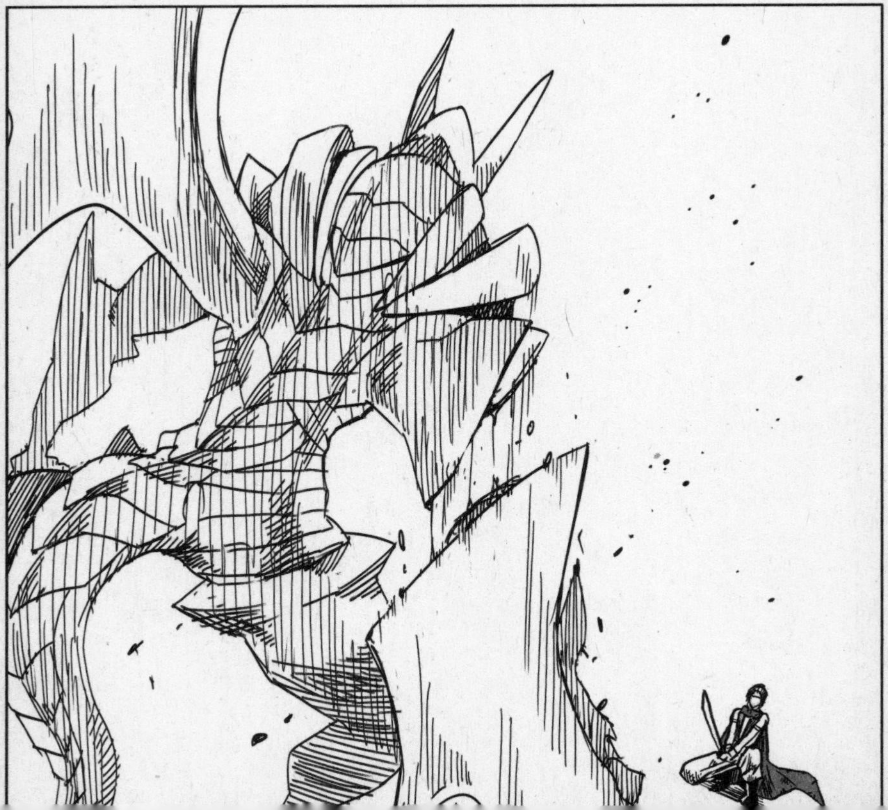

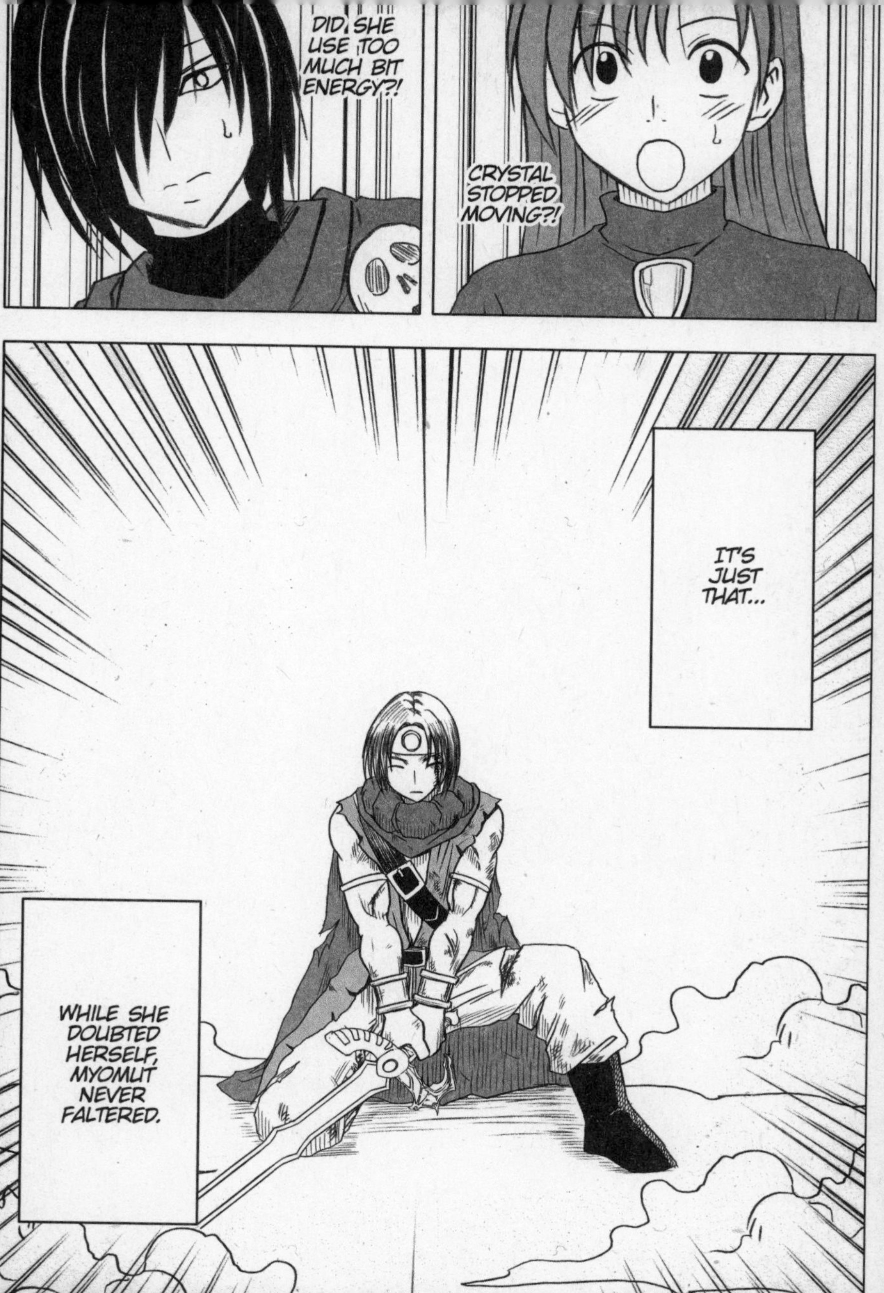
CRYSTAL STOPPED MOVING?!
DID SHE USE TOO MUCH BIT ENERGY?!
IT'S JUST THAT...
WHILE SHE DOUBTED HERSELF, MYOMUT NEVER FALTERED.

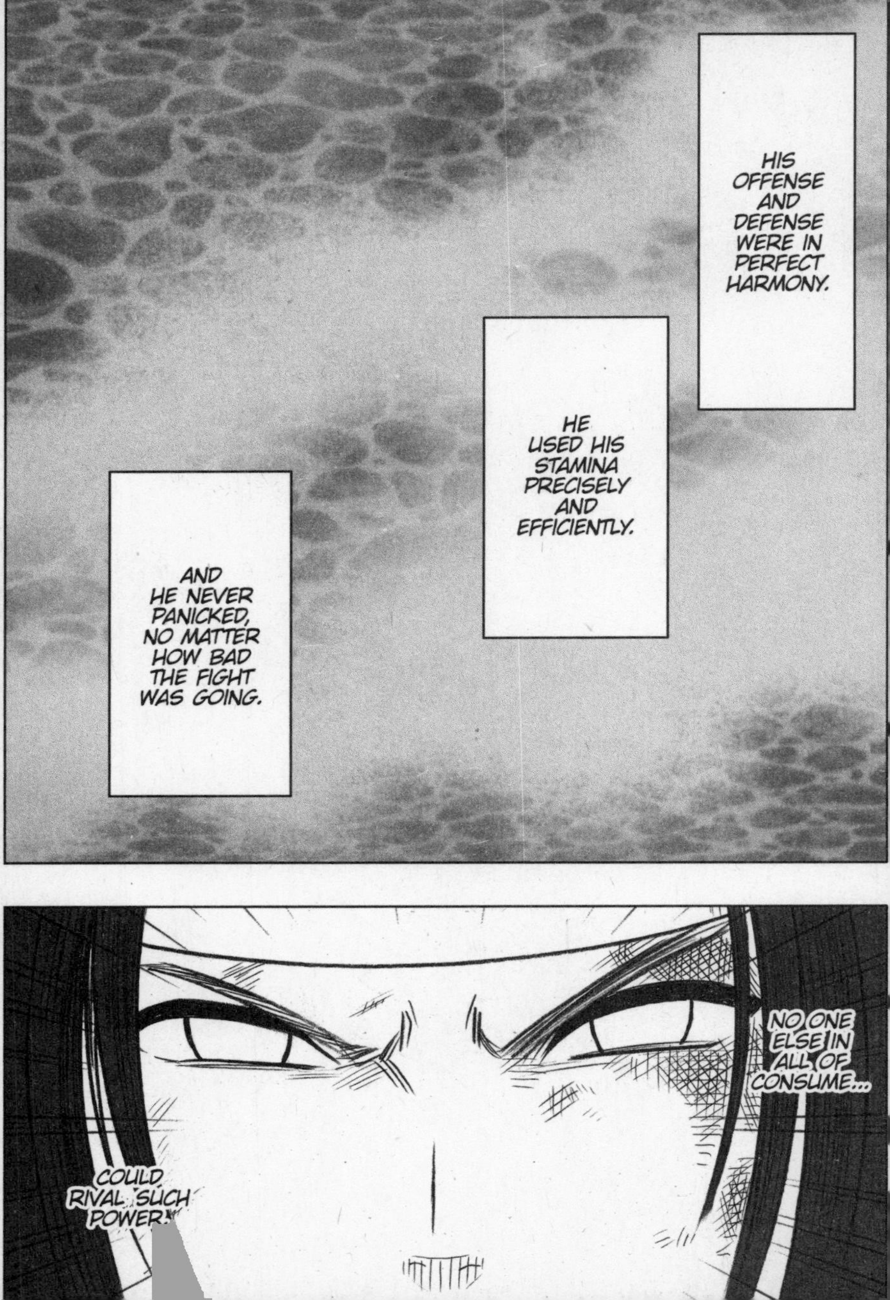
HIS OFFENSE AND DEFENSE WERE IN PERFECT HARMONY.
HE USED HIS STAMINA PRECISELY AND EFFICIENTLY.
AND HE NEVER PANICKED, NO MATTER HOW BAD THE FIGHT WAS GOING.
NO ONE ELSE IN ALL OF CONSUME...
COULD RIVAL SUCH POWER.

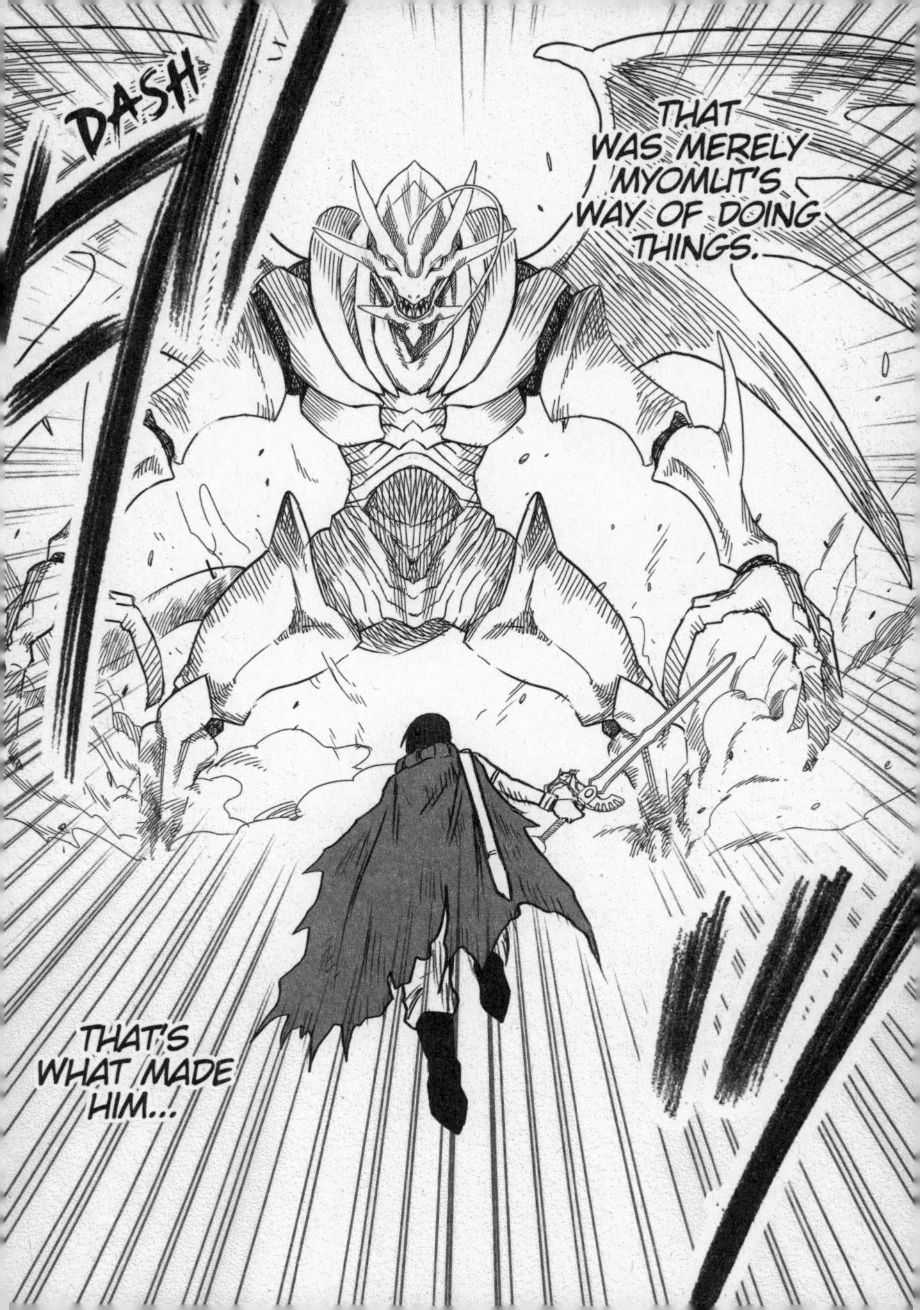
THAT WAS MERELY MYOMUT'S WAY OF DOING THINGS.
DASH
THAT'S WHAT MADE HIM...

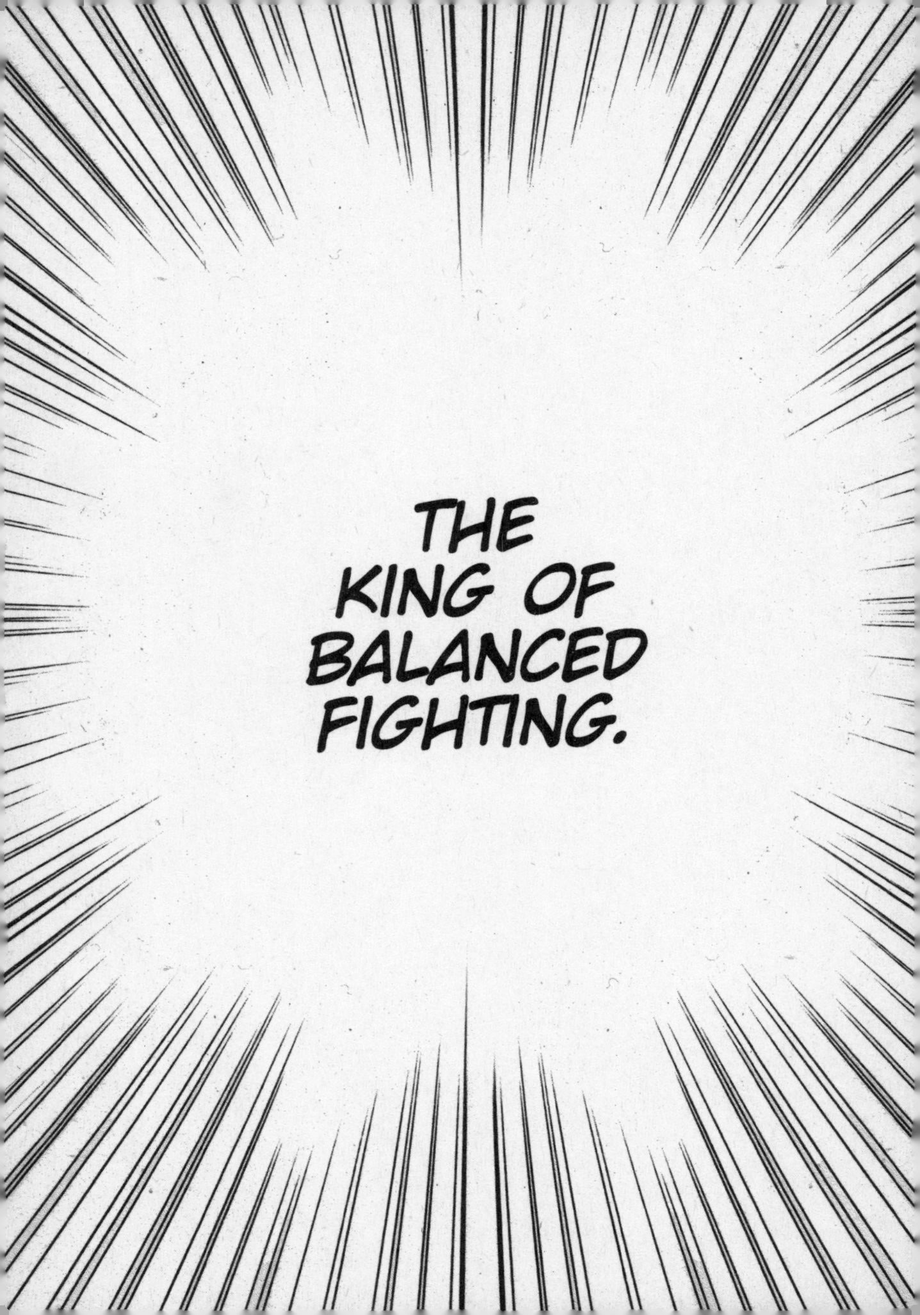
THE KING OF BALANCED FIGHTING.

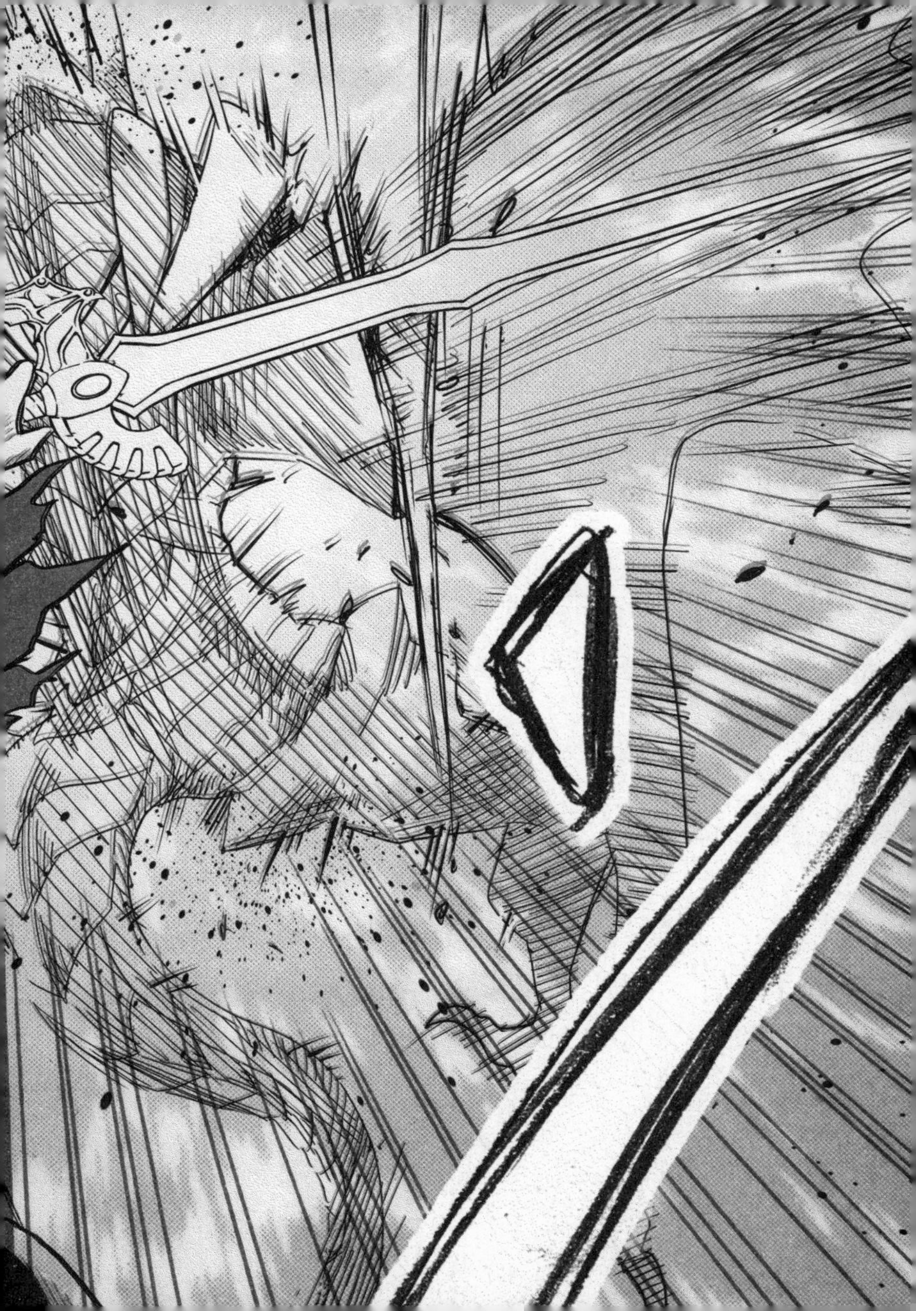

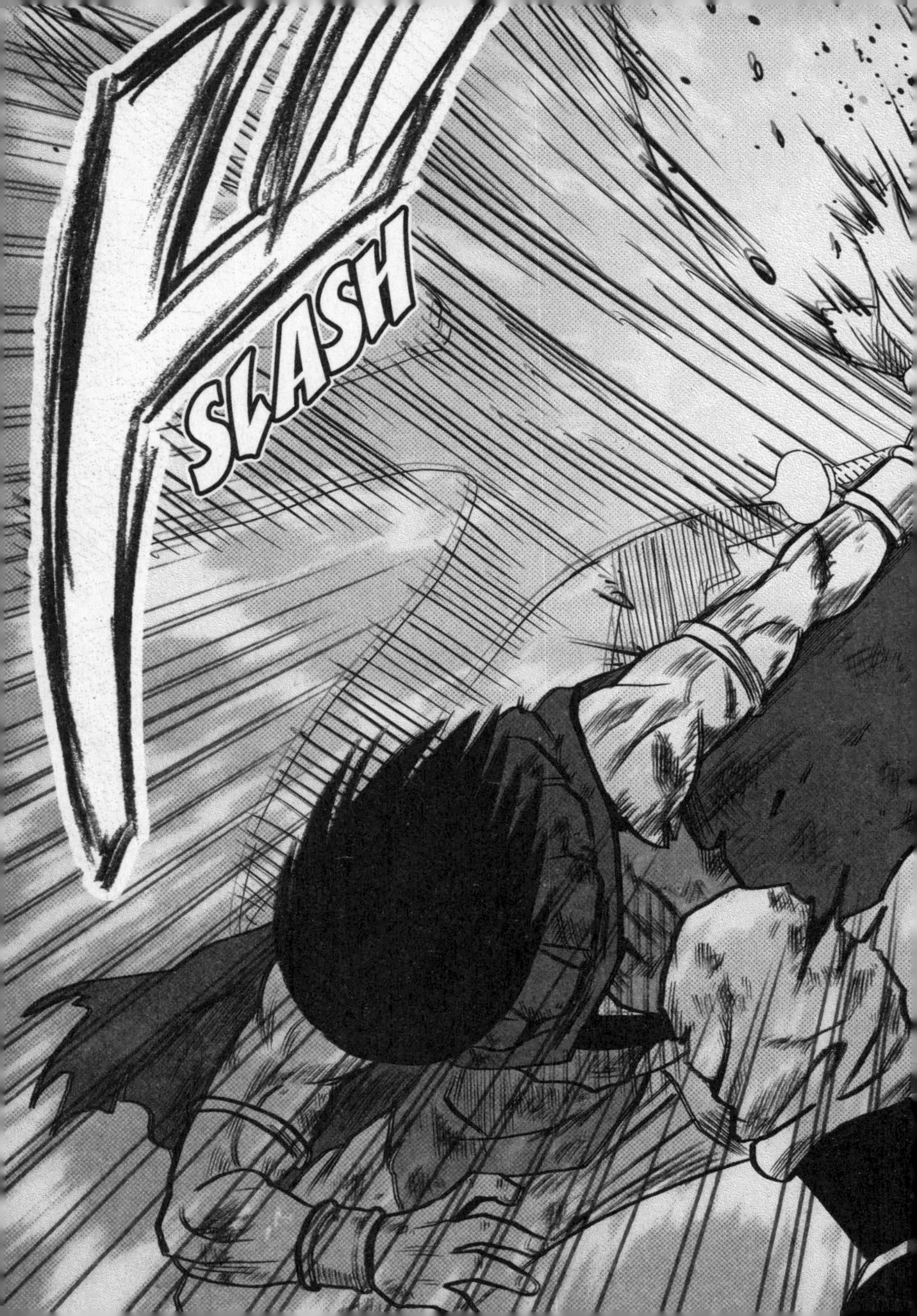
SLASH

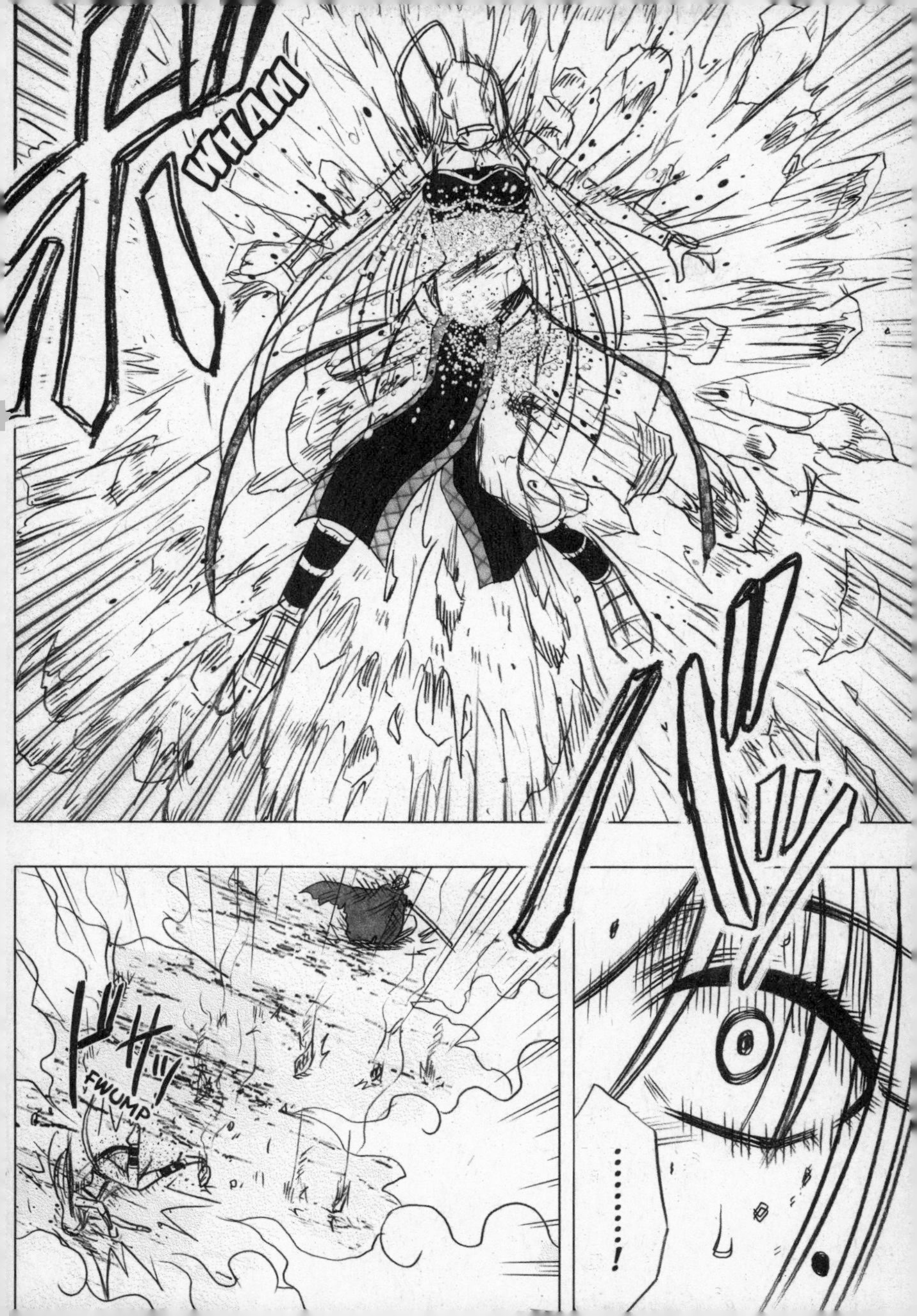
WHAM
......!
FWUMP

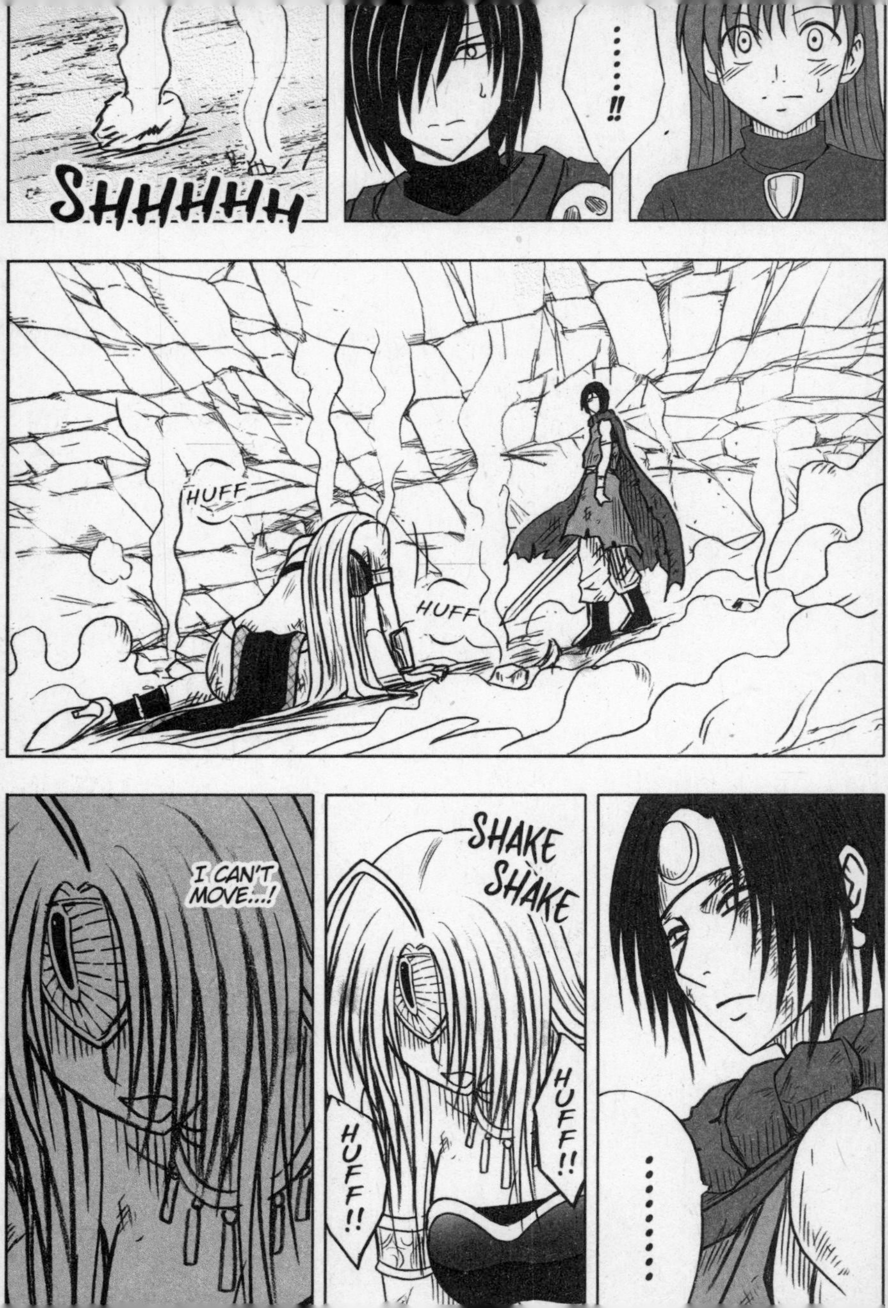
......!!
SHHHHH
HUFF
HUFF
......
SHAKE SHAKE
HUFF!!
HUFF!!
I CAN'T MOVE...!

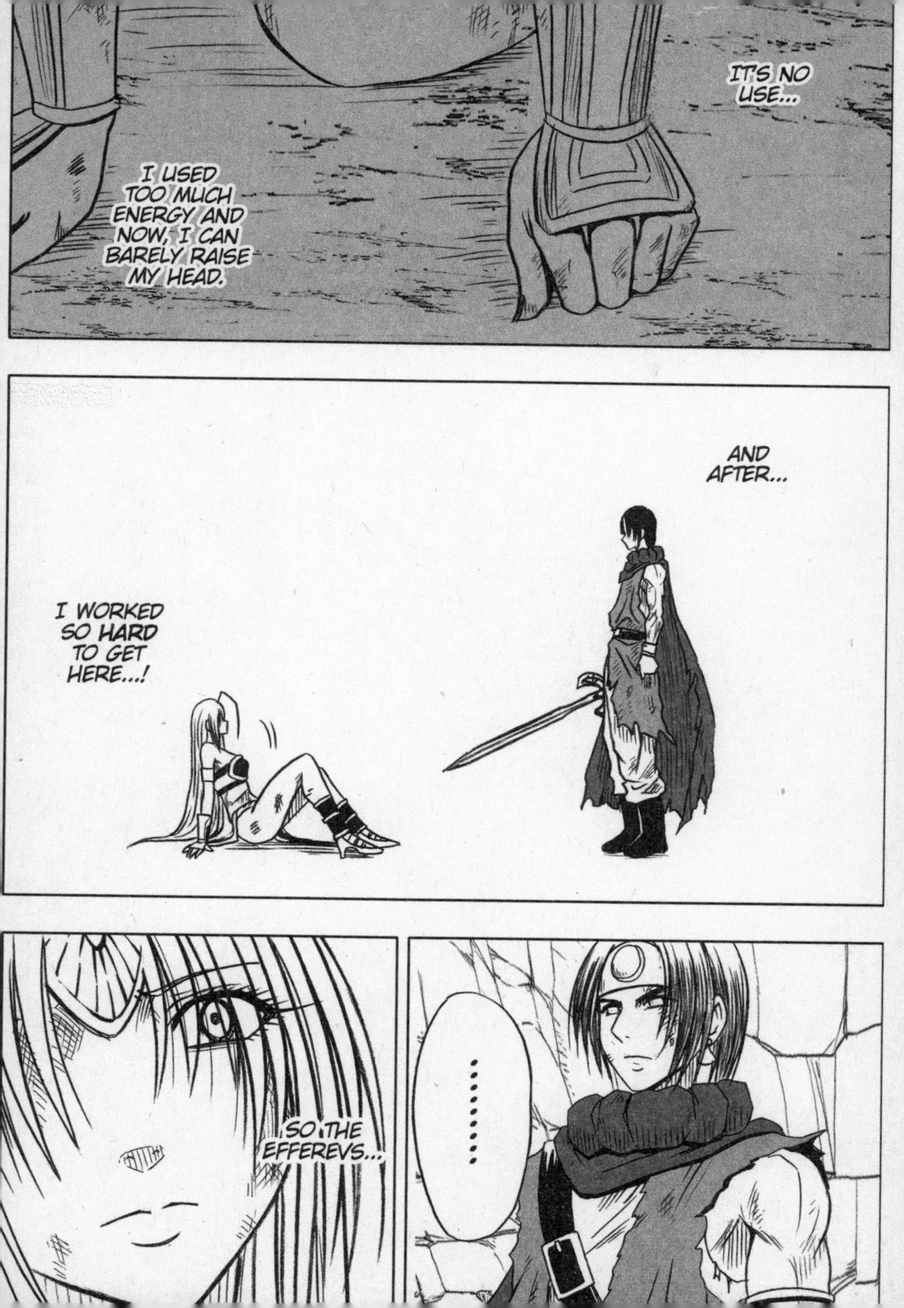

IT'S NO USE...
I USED TOO MUCH ENERGY AND NOW, I CAN BARELY RAISE MY HEAD.
AND AFTER...
I WORKED SO HARD TO GET HERE...!
......
SO THE EFFEREVS...

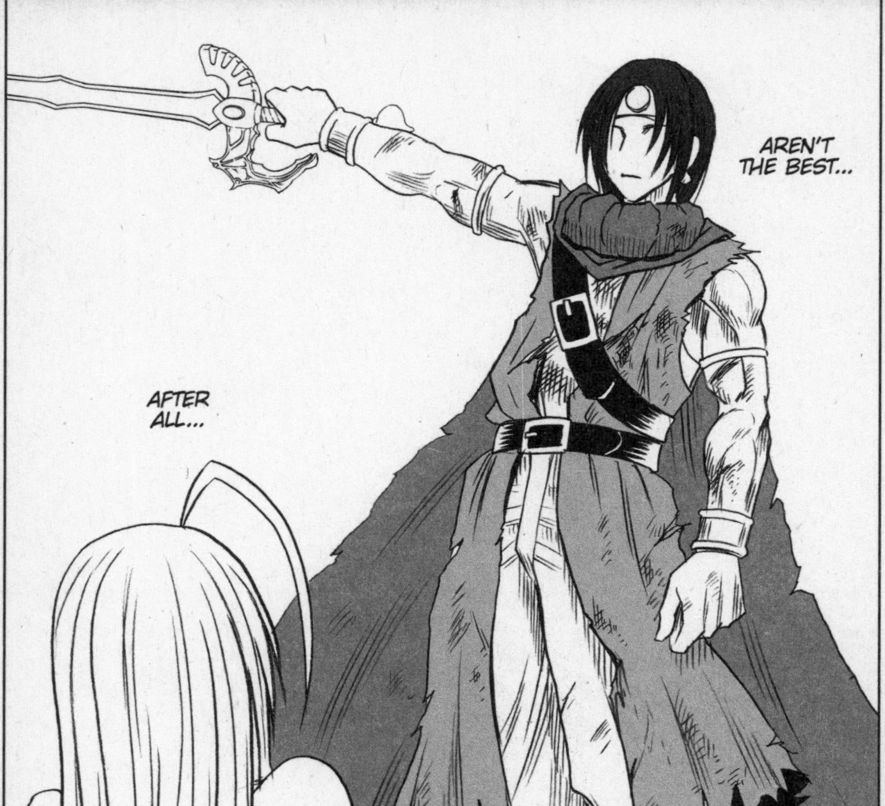
AREN'T THE BEST...
AFTER ALL...
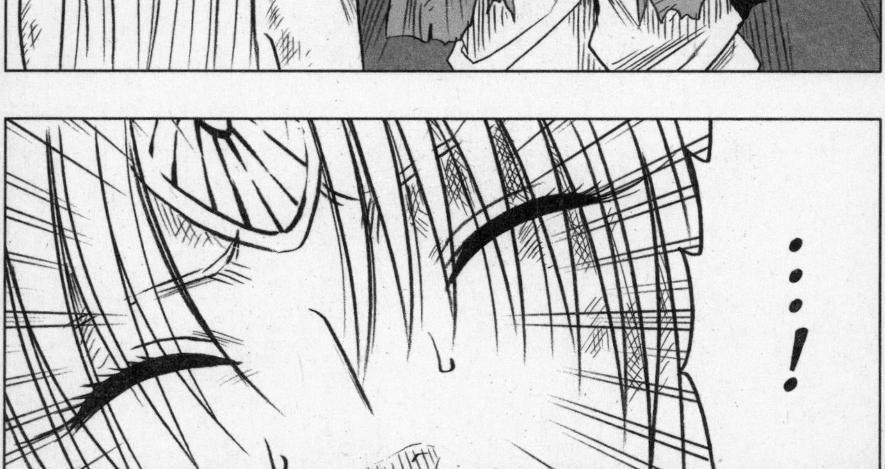
...!

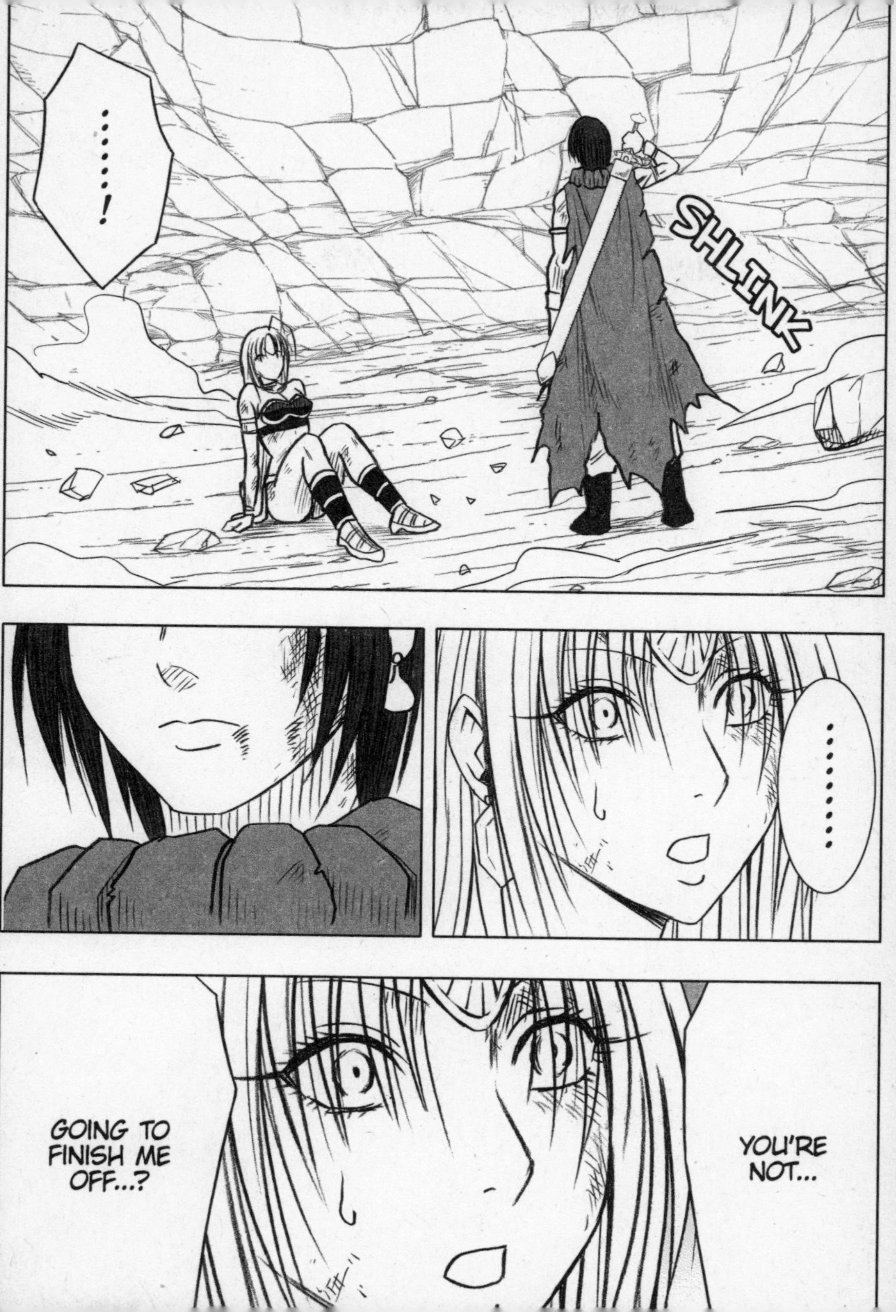
SHLINK
......!
....
YOU'RE NOT...
GOING TO FINISH ME OFF...?

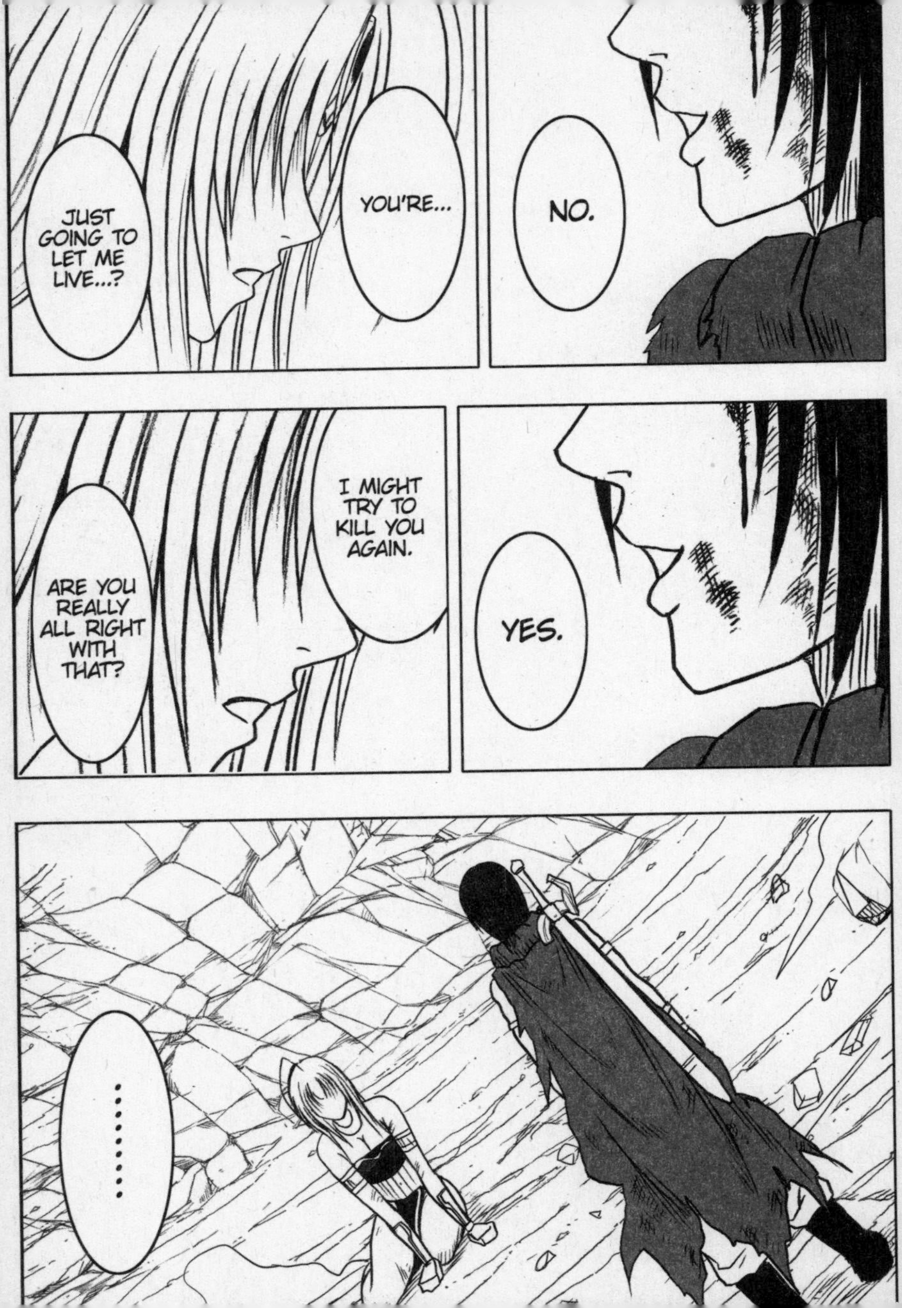
NO.
YOU'RE...
JUST GOING TO LET ME LIVE...?
YES.
I MIGHT TRY TO KILL YOU AGAIN.
ARE YOU REALLY ALL RIGHT WITH THAT?
....

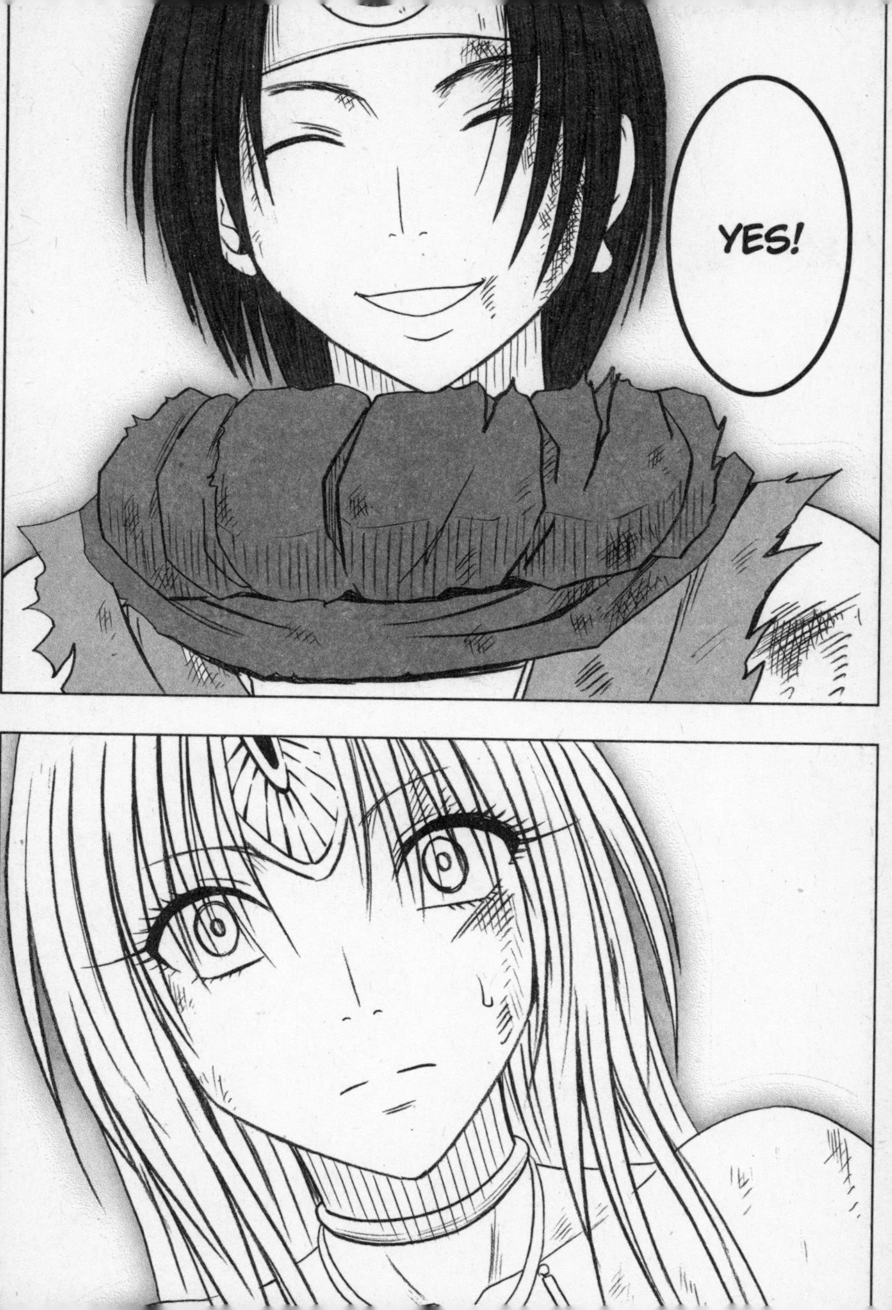
YES!

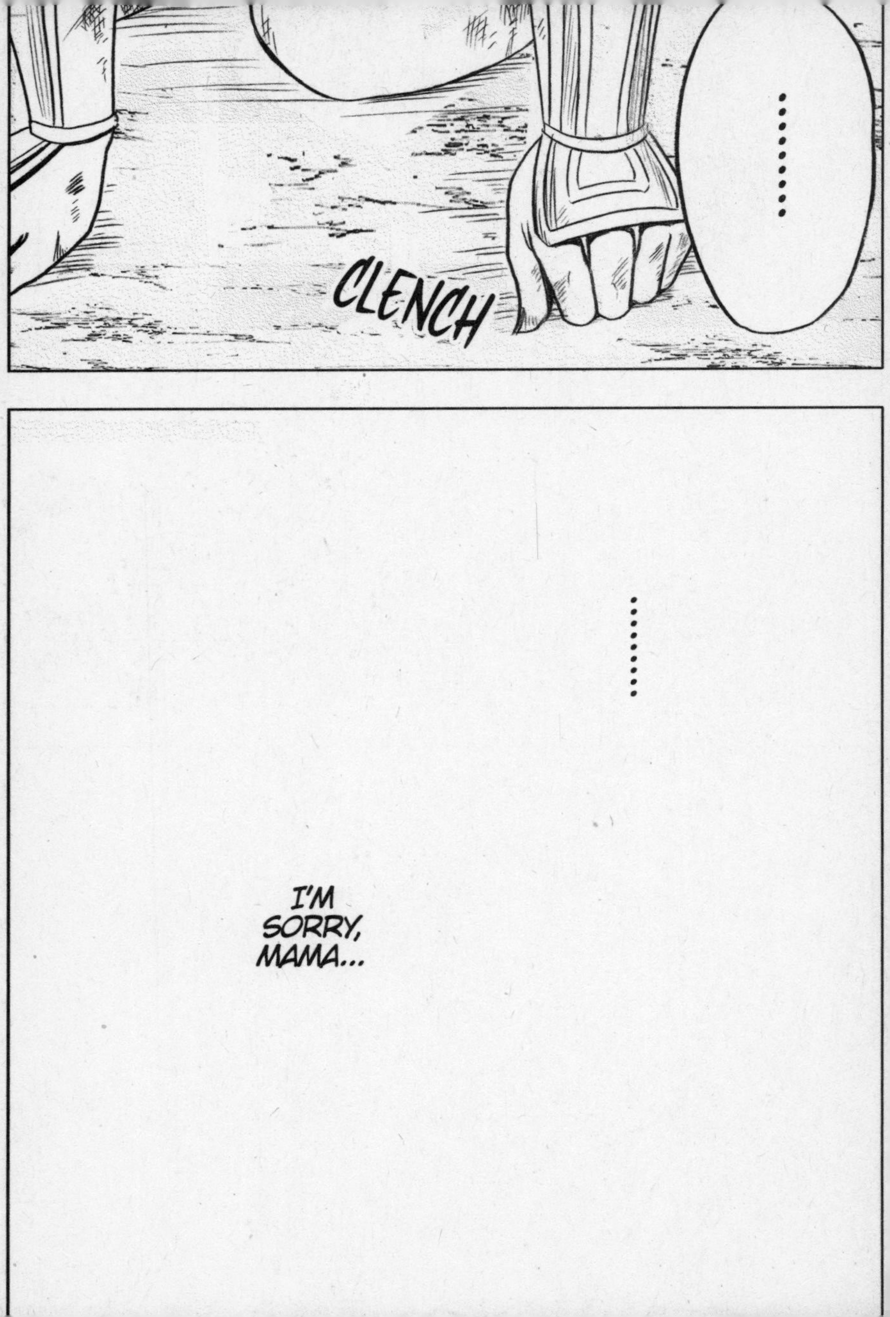
......
CLENCH
......
I'M SORRY, MAMA...

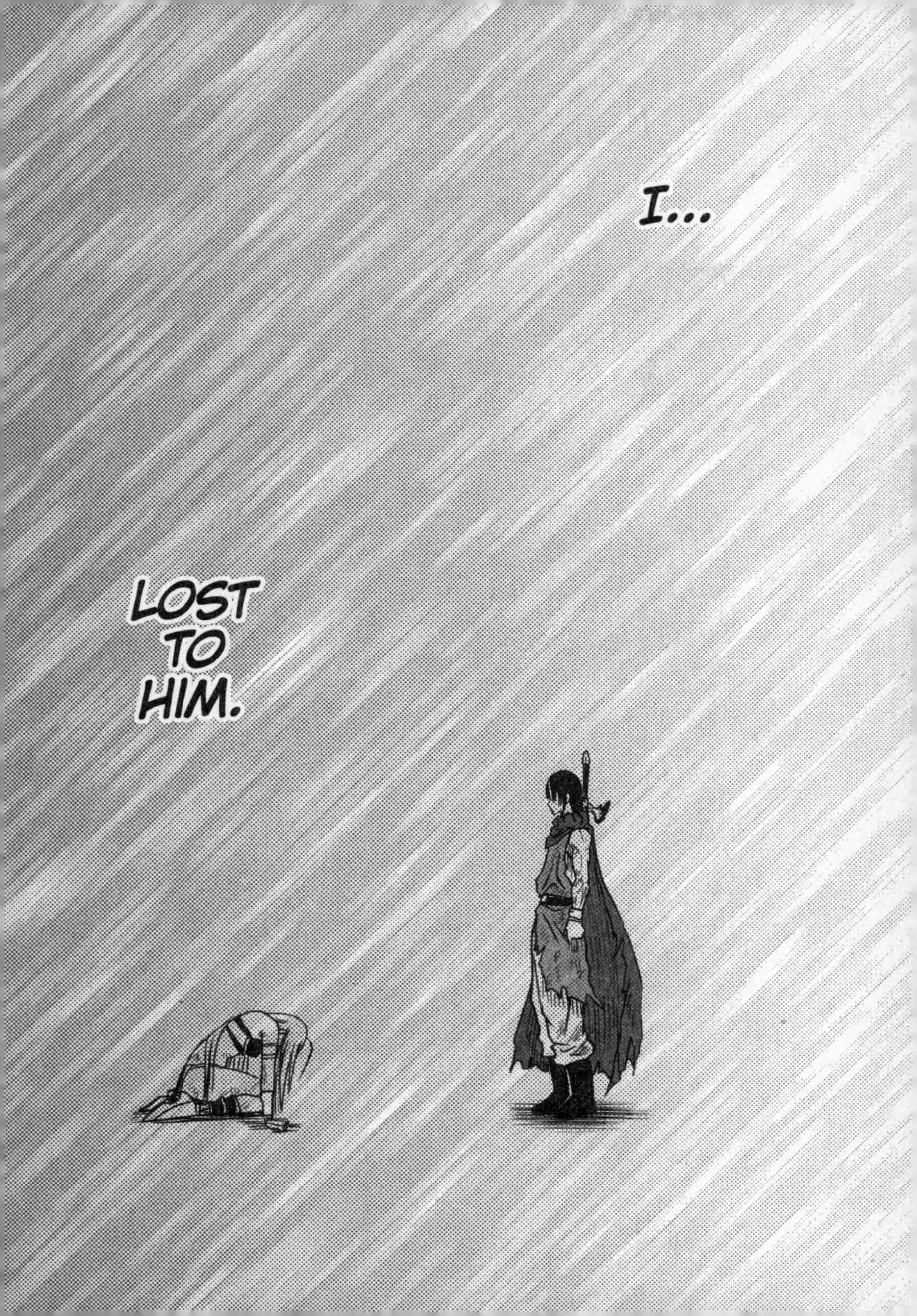
I...
LOST TO HIM.

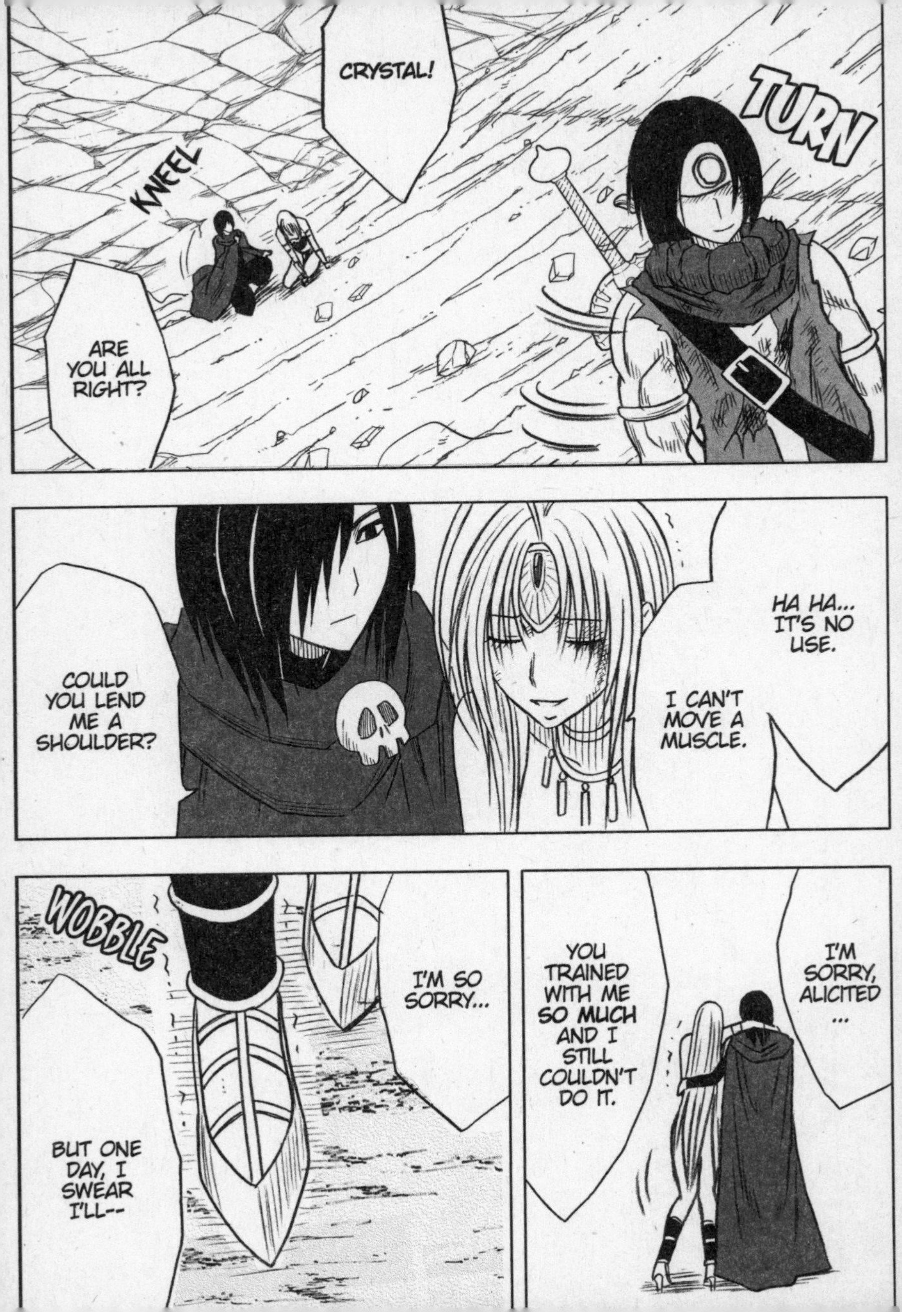
TURN
CRYSTAL!
KNEEL
ARE YOU ALL RIGHT?
HA HA... IT'S NO USE.
I CAN'T MOVE A MUSCLE.
COULD YOU LEND ME A SHOULDER?
I'M SORRY, ALICITED ...
YOU TRAINED WITH ME SO MUCH AND I STILL COULDN'T DO IT.
WOBBLE
I'M SO SORRY...
BUT ONE DAY, I SWEAR I'LL--

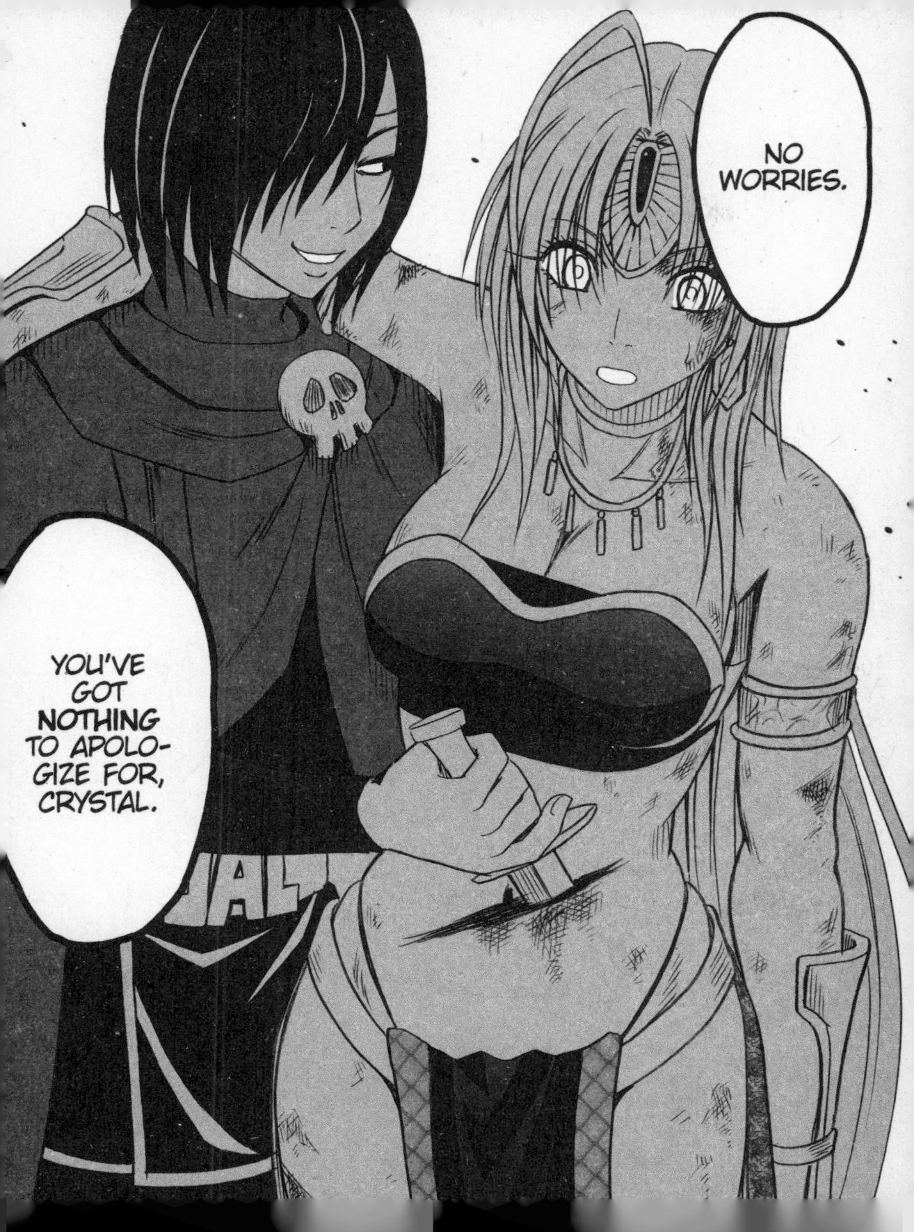
NO WORRIES.
YOU'VE GOT NOTHING TO APOLO-GIZE FOR, CRYSTAL.

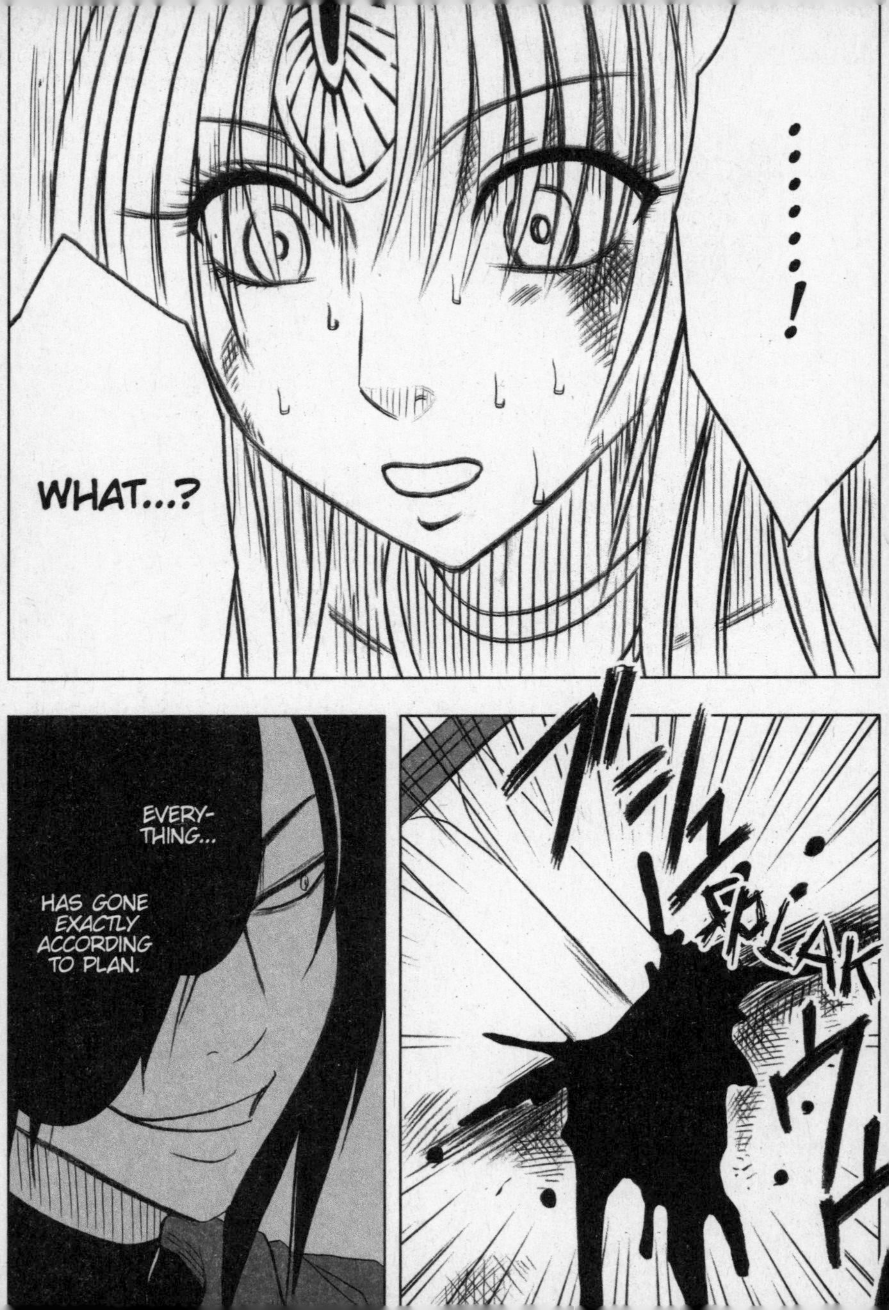
......!
WHAT...?
SPLAK
EVERY-THING...
HAS GONE EXACTLY ACCORDING TO PLAN.

Perusing Video Game History

ON THE EDGE OF THE BLUE WORLD

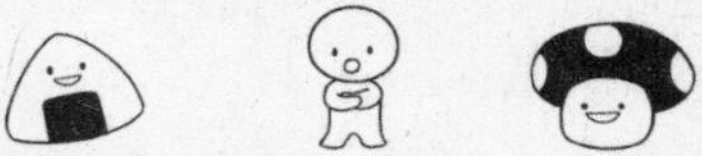

Dr. Onigiri Mr. Why Prof. Mushroom

Today's Topic

THE TWO BIG RPGS (Part 3)

Mr. Why: Oh. My. God. The manga really left things off at quite the cliffhanger, didn't it?! Anyway, we were talking about SquareSoft's *Final Fantasy* series and how high quality it was. Is there anything else that makes it stand out?

Dr. Onigiri: Well, in *Final Fantasy*, the big game changer was how the combat is done. Especially with the limit attacks.

Prof. Mushroom: Indeed. The visuals for the big limit attacks really struck a chord.

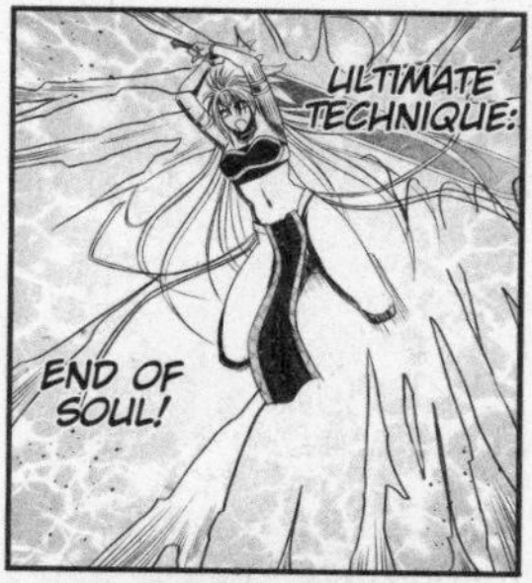
ULTIMATE TECHNIQUE:
END OF SOUL!

Crystal's ultimate technique. Not only is it incredibly strong, but it looks pretty damn cool!

Dr. Onigiri: Indeed. You could use the spell "Meteo" in *Final Fantasy IV* (renamed "Meteor" in the rereleases) to call down a barrage of meteors on your foes for massive damage. In *Final Fantasy VII* there was Tifa's powerhouse Limit Break, "Final Heaven." Then in *Final Fantasy VIII,* you had Squall's ultimate finishing move, "Lion Heart," which was a sword technique that went just a little overboard at times--it could strike a single opponent seventeen times!

Prof. Mushroom: And of course, with *Final Fantasy,* you have the summons.

Mr. Why: Summons?!

Dr. Onigiri: You could call dragons and other summoned creatures onto the battlefield to attack. It was a whole lot of fun and just seeing them come out and fighting for you was such an awesome sight. It really solidified *Final Fantasy* as the ultimate RPG.

Mr. Why: All right, all right... But what about the other big RPG, *Dragon Quest?*

Dr. Onigiri: Well, *Dragon Quest* didn't really have anything that made it stand out at all.

Mr. Why: What?! Then it should have lost to *Final Fantasy* and other RPGs like it, right?!

Prof. Mushroom: You'd think so. *Dragon Quest* didn't really have anything really special about it, to the point where it was often called the hyper-normal RPG.

Dr. Onigiri: Some Japanese gamers said that *Final Fantasy* was too flashy, that it forgot the essence of what made a good RPG. That's why *Dragon Quest* is considered to be the top, despite how well-loved the *Final Fantasy* series is.

Mr. Why: I see...

To Be Continued...

"MY FIGHTING STYLE IS WAY MORE ORIGINAL!"

"I HAD FAR SUPERIOR ARMOR AND LOOKS!"

These opponents may have had an edge over Myomut, but they just couldn't beat him in the end.

I...

LOST TO HIM

Myomut won this time, but the battle between the two big RPGs will rage on.

Dr. Onigiri: All the game makers were well aware of that, and they tried to make RPGs that could knock *Dragon Quest* off its pedestal.

Mr. Why: For example?

Dr. Onigiri: In 1994, *Samsara Naga* was released for the Famicom/NES. In it you raised dragons, a very original element for RPGs at the time. *Jaseiken Necromancer*, released in 1988 on the PC Engine, tried to attack *Dragon Quest's* position with some really nice graphics. *Lufia* (known as *Estpolis Denki* in Japan), released in 1993 for the Super Famicom/Super Nintendo, was a large-scale project with a series planned right from the start.

Prof. Mushroom: But none of them could bump *Dragon Quest* off its throne.

Mr. Why: Why?

Dr. Onigiri: Well, we can speculate on the reasons (like the character designs being from Akira Toriyama of *Dragon Ball* fame), but *Dragon Quest* was simply the most fun of all the RPGs out there at the time.

Prof. Mushroom: It never stood out in terms of graphics, story, or battle mechanics. It never changed the way it presented itself-- it just kept on with its pure and simple, tried and true RPG system. Its game balance never weakened. Its familiar gameplay gave the users a sense of stability. It was an RPG that looked so easy to copy, but no one could quite get it. That's why the *Dragon Quest* series is largely considered the King of RPGs-- in Japan, at least.

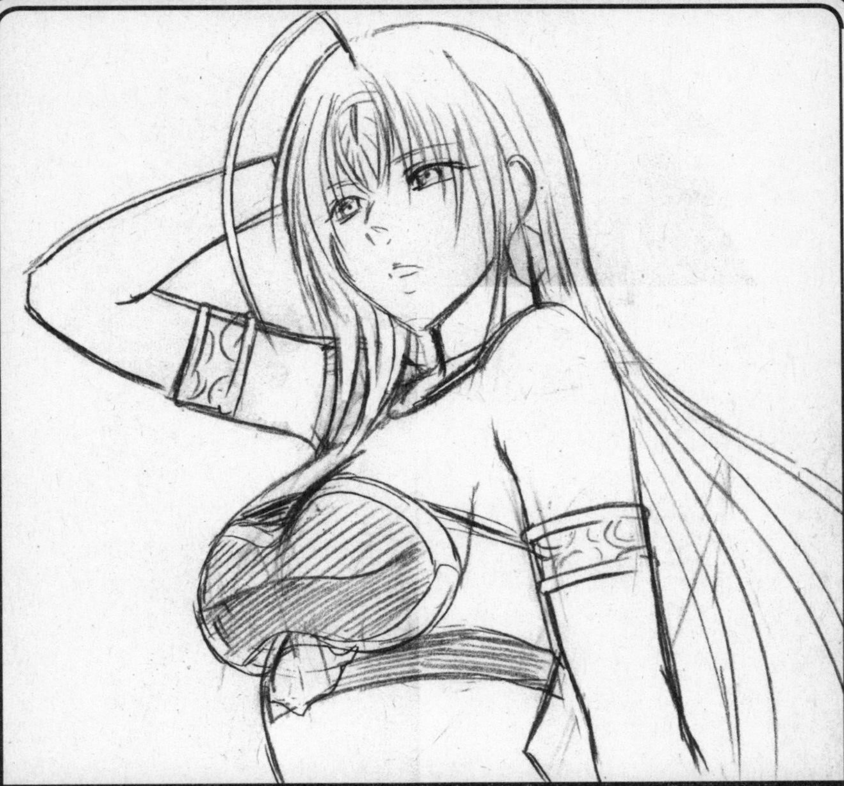

Q: What happened to Queen Karland's body?

A: It was quickly cleaned up and disposed of by a trusted servant. Queen Karland had arranged it all beforehand.

Q: Wasn't there a political crisis after the Queen's death?

A: The Senate took care of all the political matters for Crystal until she was old enough to take the throne.

Q: What happened to Crystal's father?

A: He was absorbed by Karland. That is one of the reasons that Karland was so obsessed with becoming the best at everything.

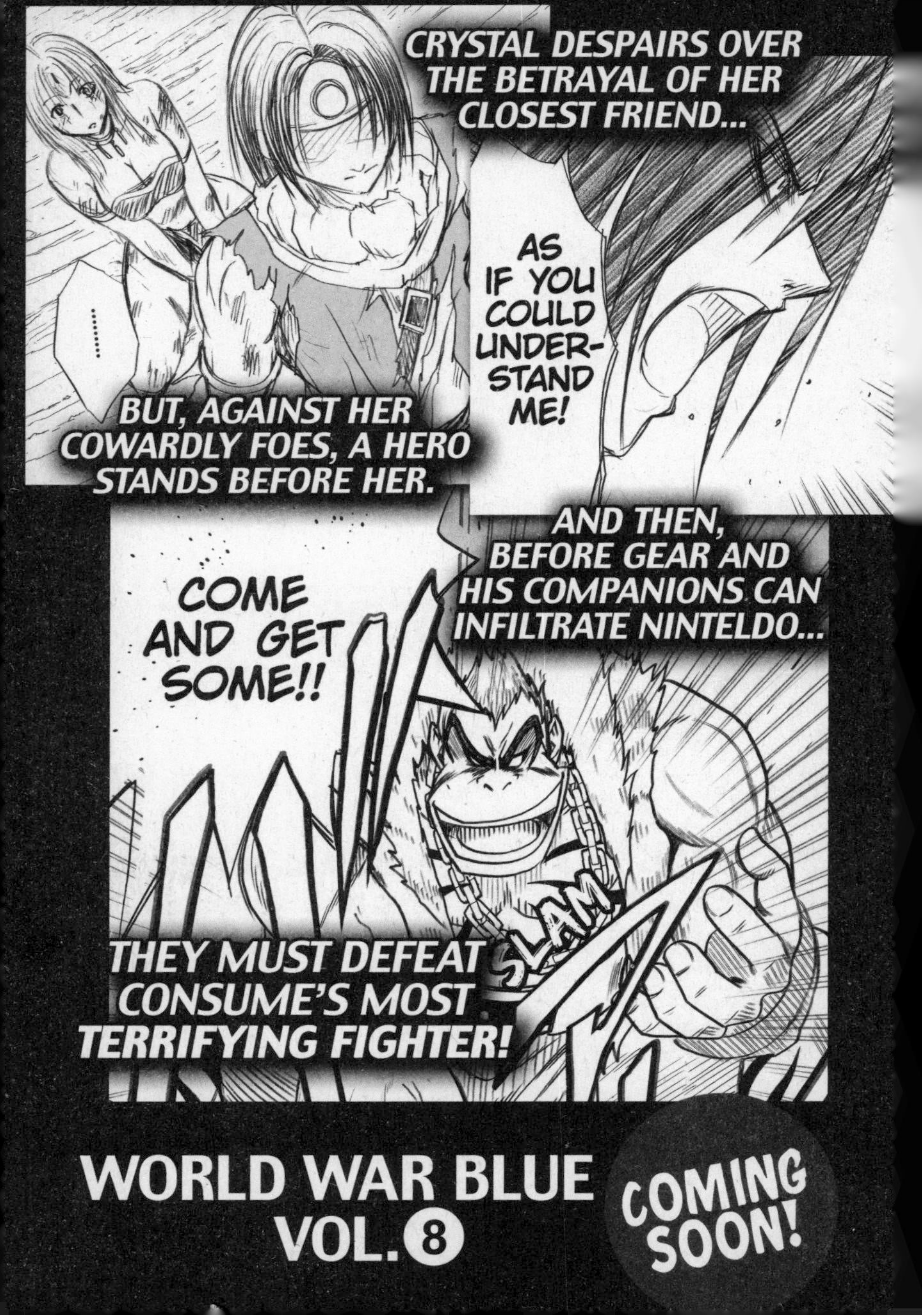
CRYSTAL DESPAIRS OVER THE BETRAYAL OF HER CLOSEST FRIEND...
AS IF YOU COULD UNDER-STAND ME!
......
BUT, AGAINST HER COWARDLY FOES, A HERO STANDS BEFORE HER.
AND THEN, BEFORE GEAR AND HIS COMPANIONS CAN INFILTRATE NINTELDO...
COME AND GET SOME!!
SLAM
THEY MUST DEFEAT CONSUME'S MOST TERRIFYING FIGHTER!

WORLD WAR BLUE
VOL. 8

COMING SOON!

SEVEN SEAS ENTERTAINMENT PRESENTS

KL APR 2017
LU APR 2015

WORLD WAR BLUE

art by **CRIMSON** / story by **ANASTASIA SHESTAKOVA**   **VOLUME 7**

TRANSLATION
Wesley Bridges

ADAPTATION
Shannon Fay

LETTERING AND LAYOUT
Laura Scoville

LOGO DESIGN
Courtney Williams

COVER DESIGN
Nicky Lim

PROOFREADER
Patrick King
Janet Houck

MANAGING EDITOR
Adam Arnold

PUBLISHER
Jason DeAngelis

AOI SEKAI NO CHUSINDE KANZENBAN VOL. 7
© 2011 ANASTASIA SHESTAKOVA / © 2011 CRIMSON
This edition originally published in Japan in 2011 by
MICROMAGAZINE PUBLISHING CO., Tokyo. English translation rights
arranged with MICROMAGAZINE PUBLISHING CO., Tokyo through
TOHAN CORPORATION, Tokyo.

Seven Seas books may be purchased in bulk for educational, business, or
promotional use. For information on bulk purchases, please contact Macmillan
Corporate & Premium Sales Department at 1-800-221-7945 (ext 5442)
or write specialmarkets@macmillan.com.

Seven Seas and the Seven Seas logo are trademarks of
Seven Seas Entertainment, LLC. All rights reserved.

ISBN: 978-1-626920-66-8

Printed in Canada

First Printing: September 2014

10 9 8 7 6 5 4 3 2 1

FOLLOW US ONLINE: *www.*

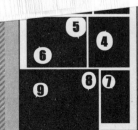

READING DIRECTIONS

This book reads from *right to left*, Japanese style.
If this is your first time reading manga, you start
reading from the top right panel on each page and
take it from there. If you get lost, just follow the
numbered diagram here. It may seem backwards at
first, but you'll get the hang of it! Have fun!!